Teaching Today

A Practical Guide

Teaching Today

A Practical Guide

Geoffrey Petty

Stanley Thornes (Publishers) Limited

First published in 1993 by:

Stanley Thornes (Publishers) Ltd
Ellenborough House
Wellington Street
CHELTENHAM
GL50 1YW
United Kingdom

96 97 98 99 00 / 10 9 8 7 6 5 4

A catalogue record for this book is available from the British Library.

ISBN 0 7487 1697 1

Setting and layout by Richard Slessor
Camera copy by Graphic Communications

Printed and bound in Great Britain by
Redwood Books, Trowbridge, Wiltshire

Contents

Introduction

This book aims to be a straight-forward and practical 'how to teach' book. It is intended for those teaching in either schools or colleges, as well as those teaching or training in industry, commerce or the public services. In fact, it is written for *anyone* who wants to know how to go about helping people to learn.

Part I explores the emotional and practical learning needs which all learners have. Part 2 gives advice on the use of the most common teaching methods or learning strategies, and analyses their strengths and weaknesses. Part 3 looks at how to make and use learning aids. Part 4 shows you how to go about planning lessons and courses, how to measure their effectiveness, and how to improve them. This is *not* an academic text book; learning theory is referred to only where it helps teachers make everyday decisions.

For the most part, I have avoided issues concerned with the organisation and structure of the National Curriculum, National Vocational Qualifications, or any other curriculum matter. Rather than attempt to nail these jellies to the wall, I have tried to deal with the practical skills, the techniques, and the emotional awareness and sensitivities that teachers require, whatever and wherever they teach.

For some years now I have both taught an 'ordinary timetable' and trained teachers. So, whilst developing my ideas and writing this book, I have had my nose rubbed daily in the chalky reality of learning and teaching. If my ideas don't work – well, my students are the first to make this clear. I hope you will be able to learn from both my successes and my failures, and so take George Bernard Shaw's advice: 'Only a fool learns from experience, a wise man learns from the experience of others.'

I am impatient with jargon, so throughout the book I have used the word 'teacher' to mean any of the following: 'teacher', 'lecturer', 'trainer', 'instructor' or 'facilitator'. Similarly, I have used the words 'student' and 'learner' interchangeably, in places where I could also have written 'pupil', 'trainee', 'course participant', or 'candidate'.

The mistakes and omissions are mine (and I hope you will tell me about them), but I would like to thank John Parsons, Graham Davies, Jenny Kimberlee and Jan Mallam for reading the manuscript and making helpful suggestions; and Sean Hughes for his suggestions on, and illustrations for, the chapter on creativity. Most of all I would like to thank Liz Singh for her unshakeable faith and patient help in preparing this book, and for her cartoons and drawings.

Geoffrey Petty, 1993

The learner's practical and emotional needs

1 How do we learn?

Learning and memory

What was the weather like on March 4th 1981? You knew once! Psychologists are still not sure how we remember and why we forget, but they believe the process of remembering involves information passing from our short term memory into our long term memory. Information may only be stored in the short term memory for as little as a few seconds. The long term memory can store information for a life-time, but nearly all of what passes through our brain is promptly forgotten.

The short term memory (STM)

An unfortunate man who has lost his short term memory, as a result of a head injury in a car accident, can still tell his doctor in great detail what he did in the war. But when asked where he has put his coffee, he asks: 'What coffee?' The accident has damaged his short term memory (STM).

Our STM stores what we are thinking at the time, along with information that has come from our eyes, ears etc. After storing and processing this information for a few seconds, the STM promptly forgets nearly all of it. For example, if someone read out five telephone numbers one after the other, you might be able to remember the last one, but the earlier numbers would probably have been forgotten. *The content of the short term memory is short lived, and is easily displaced by new information.* That last sentence has important implications for the way teachers should plan their lessons; you might like to think what these implications are. (They will be summarised later in the chapter.)

Sometimes, of course, the contents of the STM are passed on to the long term memory (LTM). The contents of the LTM are structured. If you try to remember how to do long division, you are not swamped by irrelevant memories concerning other skills you were learning at the time. The LTM is like a super-efficient filing cabinet with information filed for future access. In order to pass into the long term memory, information must first be processed and structured in the short term memory so that it 'makes sense' to the student. The process of structuring new information takes time; but it is time well spent, because students find it almost impossible to remember something that they do not properly understand.

> **Thick wall it tea of myrrh seize knots trained**
>
> Spend a few moments trying to remember the above group of words before reading on. I will test you later to find out how well you have done!

If a student is given new information too quickly, he or she will not have time to process it properly in the short term memory, so the information will not be retained. Experimenters tried halving their normal speech rate to students with learning difficulties, and found that the students' retention was doubled (Riding and Shove, 1974).

This vital process of structuring or giving meaning to new information is demanding as well as time-consuming, so we must try to give our students as much help as we can. Learning activities that involve students in *using* the new ideas will aid clarification.

This search for structure also explains why many learners appreciate being given summaries and well-organised notes.

> Suppose you were given five newspaper articles about wine-making in Germany, and you were asked to learn this information for a test. How would you go about studying them? Most people would write notes breaking the information down into main headings, e.g. wine varieties, vine varieties, growing methods, etc. We feel a need to organise and structure what we want to understand and remember.

The long term memory (LTM)

Once the STM has 'made sense' of the information, it is then passed into the long term memory (LTM) where, unless it is subsequently used or recalled in some other way, it is again eventually forgotten! I remember finding my university lecture notes in the attic ten years after graduation. If they had not been written in my own handwriting I would not have believed I had written them! I had not used this knowledge, so my brain appears to have judged it of no use, and thrown it out of my LTM.

What we call 'forgetting' is the brain's built-in technique for ensuring that it is not cluttered up with useless knowledge. Its aim is to remember nothing but useful information. Unfortunately, however, it tends to consider a fact or idea 'useful' in the long term *only if it comes across it regularly*.

Forgetting and remembering, then, are not under direct conscious control; they are automatic. There is only one way to ensure that something is remembered – repetition. As teachers we must make sure that any knowledge we want our students to remember is recalled and used frequently.

There are exceptions to this rule; sometimes a one-off experience will be remembered for a lifetime – for example, an event with great emotional significance. But as far as teaching is concerned, we are at the mercy of the brain's automatic mechanisms, and repetition is vital.

The 'learning curve' is shown below; perhaps it would be better to call it the 'forgetting curve'! It shows us that, immediately after initial learning of a simple idea or after a review of that learning, our recall is 100%. Then we begin to forget what we have learned. However, each recall fixes that learning more firmly in the long term memory. As a result, it takes progressively longer for the learning to be forgotten after each recall.

As a result of this forgetting mechanism, we only remember ideas:

    a. that have been recalled frequently; or
    b. that we have heard recently.

Watson, the father of the behaviourist school of psychology developed by Skinner, said that remembering depended on 'frequency and recency'.

Our knowledge about short and long term memories suggests the following advice for teachers, which is dealt with in more detail in later chapters:

- **Don't cover new material too quickly**.
  If you tend to speak quickly, try to slow down. Also, leave a silence after an important sentence, so as to leave time for it to 'sink in'.
- **Students need activities which encourage them to process new material.**
  Activities that make students use – and hence develop a personal restructuring of – the ideas you are trying to teach them will often make students learn more efficiently than passive activities such as listening.
- **For information to be stored in the LTM it must be used and recalled often.**
  A teacher cannot expect to teach an idea in September and, without referring to it again, have the students remember it in June.

In 1989 a man approached the staff of a railway station, saying he didn't know his name or address and had no idea why he had made a train journey. He had entirely lost his long term memory. His wife recognised him on television and rang the station to arrange to collect him. It was discovered that he had suffered a blow to his head earlier in the day. Luckily his LTM re-established itself as he recovered. The long and the short term memory really do exist separately.

Learning is an active process

Most non-teachers believe that teaching is telling students something, and learning occurs if students remember it.

The truth is a good deal more complicated than this. Students don't just remember what their teacher has told them; they make up their own personal version of the knowledge they have been given. For example, suppose you have recently read a novel and someone asks you to recount it. You will not tell the story in the same words as the author. In fact, the author may even disagree with your version of the story.

You have forgotten the author's words, and what you have remembered is not his exact story, but your own version of it. The same goes for students making sense of what you teach them. They forget your words, and they make up their own version of what you have told them.

We are usually unaware of this restructuring process, until it goes wrong. Ann (aged 6) asked why there were regional accents, and was told that people who grew up in different places learned to talk differently. She thought for a minute, and then asked, 'Does that mean that Julie *[who lived next door to her]* speaks differently from me?'

Young children are a wonderful mine for the 'misunderstandings' which demonstrate that learning is active. My daughter once complained of diarrhoea, but said she had not been to the toilet. I was alarmed until I discovered she had ear ache ('dire ear'). Such misunderstandings are as delightful as they are common, because they show children actively trying to make sense of their world.

But we never grow out of this way of learning. Exam howlers show the same creative hypothesis-making:

'A common disease in cereal crops is wheat germ.'
The student was never told by his teacher that wheat germ was a cereal disease! He heard a jumble of information about cereals, and then tried to 'make sense' of it. The very phrase 'make sense' alerts us to the fact that learning is a creative process, not a passive one.

Name a food suitable for pickling. - **'A branston.'**
Again the student was never told that a branston was a fruit used for pickling. She simply 'made up' that piece of knowledge. Nearly all our knowledge is created in much the same way, but usually more successfully! That is, all our knowledge is in the form of personal versions of what we have been taught.

More creative hypothesis-making from exam candidates:

'Worms hold themselves together by the suction power of their little legs.'
'Some bacteria are used as food e.g. marshmallows and ice creams.'
How do mammals keep warm in cold weather? 'They wear cardigans.'
'There are not many cases of tape worm in the Third World because there is not much food for them there.'

Anyone who doubts that learning is active need only talk to a five year old about their conception of science, God, work, or any other 'adult' topic. If the youngster trusts you enough to answer your questions, you will be well rewarded; the child will be full of ideas on these topics, many of them insightful, others comically off beam. These five year old 'students' are learning by making up what seem to them to be sensible ideas, and only changing them when they are proved wrong. (This is the same method used by scientists in developing their theories; they call it hypothesis and refutation. Indeed, it is probably the process underlying all learning.)

Successful learning, then, happens by a process of personal hypothesis-making. How can your students be helped to develop their own meanings for the ideas you present? They need to be able to think over, discuss, and use the ideas in order to restructure them into personal meanings. They need to 'own' the ideas they are working with.

Psychologists believe that learning involves making 'cognitive models' – hypotheses which model reality, rather as the mental map you have of your home town models reality. And just as our mental map has errors and omissions, so does our learning. Your students will learn best if they *use* the ideas, skills and knowledge you try to teach them. They will learn best by doing, not listening.

We learn best by doing

I am told, and I forget. I see, and I remember. I do, and I understand.

The saying above is a Chinese proverb which is over 2,000 years old. It is true for both practical and intellectual skills. However, it is often forgotten in the race to cover the syllabus in as little time as possible.

I remember a colleague telling me that since his father had died, his mother never went out in her car for fear of getting a puncture. So he decided to teach his mother how to change the wheel on her Mini. He demonstrated to her how this was done, and then asked her to try it by herself. 'Oh no,' she said, 'it's too cold and windy to try that now.' He didn't insist. Three weeks later she had a puncture. Full of confidence, she prepared to fit the new wheel, but found that she couldn't remember how to get the hub cap off! As she said later: 'If I had got cold and grazed my knuckles removing a hub cap, I would have remembered how to get it off without any difficulty.'

We learn by doing better than by watching or listening.

This statement may seem a platitude, yet most teachers spend over 60% of their time *talking* to their students. In the next two chapters we will see that while learners do need explanations, they also need corrected practice in the skills and knowledge being learned, and this is a much more time-consuming activity.

Rewards and motivation

Behaviourist psychologists have studied learning in animals by teaching them simple tasks. Thorndike (1874 – 1949) caged hungry cats in 'puzzle boxes' within sight of food; the cats learned to pull a string, or operate a lever, to escape from the box and take the food. Skinner (born 1904) taught pigeons, dogs, rats, and other animals using a 'Skinner box'; in this there was a lever which, when pressed, delivered food to the animal. Similar techniques were used by experimenters to teach rats to find their way through mazes.

In each case, the animals were taught by rewarding them with food when they did well; much the same method is used to train pets or circus animals. Some of the findings apply well to human learning, though they hardly tell the whole story. Here is a simplified summary of behaviourist research findings which are of particular interest to the teacher:

- ■ ***Learners require some reward or 'reinforcement' for learning.***
  If one puts a recently fed cat in a puzzle box it will go to sleep. Only
  hungry cats will learn how to escape. Human learners are also motivated by

an expected reward of some kind (such as praise or a satisfied curiosity); learning will not take place without it. Nobody learns for nothing!

- **Reinforcement should follow the desired behaviour as soon as possible.**
  If a rat pushes a lever and food drops immediately into its cage, then it learns quickly. If reinforcement is delayed, learning takes longer. A similar effect is seen in human learning. A student whose work is usually marked immediately is more motivated than one who expects to wait weeks for reinforcement in the form of praise, or knowledge of how they have done.

- **Learning proceeds step by step rather than happening all at once, and is strengthened by repeated success.**
  Cats naturally take time to escape from their puzzle boxes, but the time taken steadily diminishes with practice. Similarly human learning takes time, and past successes provide motivation for present learning. If a learner is never successful in your lessons, he or she will soon give up.

- **We remember what we have experienced** frequently *and* recently.
  If you teach something in September, and never refer to it again, it will soon be forgotten.

Sadly, much teaching in our schools and colleges violates the behaviourists' findings. Weaker students in some classes are set work that is so difficult for them that they never experience genuine success. Partly as a result some students rarely, or never, get praise or encouragement. Work may not be marked promptly, and knowledge and skills are often taught and then not referred to again for months. As a result, many learners simply give up.

Learning is a complex process, and the behaviourists only give us part of the story. We will look at other approaches to learning in Chapters 24 (on 'discovery and guided discovery') and 27 (on 'learning from experience').

Emotional needs of learners

Humanist psychologists suggest that learning is easiest, most meaningful and most effective when it takes place in a non-threatening situation.

Learners should not be motivated by fear of failure, but by a desire to succeed. In *How Children Fail* (1964), John Holt claimed the school system could destroy the minds and emotions of young children. In a blistering attack, he accused schools of inducing fear in pupils, and of humiliating, ridiculing and devaluing them. Humanist psychologists believe that fear of failure and rejection produces mal-adjustment. Either learners play it safe and withdraw, feeling crushed and lacking in self-confidence as a result; or they hit out in retaliation, becoming disruptive. Either way, pupils are damaged and learning is poor.

Removing threats is particularly important where learning involves changes in personal perception.

Most teachers have found their own learning to be a reasonably straight-forward process. Though you may well have found *some* learning difficult, you must have been a very successful learner in other areas to have gained the qualifications or skills required to become a teacher. For many people, though, learning is a process filled with pain, anxiety and frustration. 40% of school pupils leave school without a GCSE of any grade. It is estimated that between 7% and 10% of people are functionally illiterate – that is, they are unable to read newspapers and road signs or to fill in forms. Learning may have been easy for you, but it is not easy for everyone.

Untaught learning

If a teacher tells students that one must always wash one's hands before handling food, but doesn't actually do so, then students learn that this hand washing is not important. Studies show that what we as teachers *do* is overwhelmingly more influential than what we say. Setting an example in this way is called 'modelling'. What do you need to model in your teaching: enthusiasm? thoroughness? patience? neat presentation? safe practices? Whatever you decide, remember that 'Do what I say, not what I do' simply doesn't work as a teaching strategy.

We also teach unconsciously by our behaviour towards our students. A teacher who talks to, smiles at, encourages and helps students of Asian and European origin equally, is teaching the students to respect everyone regardless of their origins.

That list of words

Can you remember the list of words that you were asked to remember on page 2? Is it possible to remember what you can't make sense of? The word list: 'thick, wall, it, tea, of, myrrh, seize, knots, trained' is phonetically almost identical to 'The quality of mercy is not strained.' You would have found the latter much easier to remember – because it makes sense. On the whole we don't remember words, we remember meanings; and these meanings we must make ourselves.

You will find much more on how people learn in other chapters of this book, especially in the next two chapters, and also Chapters 21 (on learning for remembering), 24 (on discovery and guided discovery), 27 (on learning from experience) and 38 (on assessment).

In some very large experiments, genuinely vitamin-deficient learners were given vitamin supplements. There was a 20-30 point increase in the non-verbal reasoning IQ of 45% of those studied; verbal intelligence was not affected. Whether vitamin deficiency affects the structure of the brain or simply the learners' ability to concentrate is not known.

Summary and checklist

Learning is not the same as remembering; it is an active 'meaning-making' process. Only information that has been structured and organised by the student can pass into the long term memory. This organisation process is helped by *doing* rather than listening.

Information will only stay in the LTM if it is re-used or recalled often. 'Frequency and recency' govern our ability to recall what we have learned.

Motivation is crucial for learning; it is provided in part by repeated success, and by prompt reinforcement for this success. Learning is more effective if it is motivated by a desire to succeed rather than a fear of failure.

We teach unconsciously by setting an example.

☑ *Checklist*

- ☐ Do your students spend most of their time learning by doing?
- ☐ What new student activities could you try in the near future?
- ☐ Do all your students get some measure of success in their learning?
- ☐ Does this success get quickly reinforced?
- ☐ Do your students reuse previous learning?
- ☐ Do you use old learning to help new learning?
- ☐ Have you decided what you as a teacher must model?

2 Learning practical and intellectual skills

You have been learning all your life. You know what makes you learn, and as a result, you know more than you realise about what makes others learn. The problem is that this knowledge is intuitive and unstructured. We need to uncover this unconscious knowledge of how we best learn, so that we can use it to discover how we should best teach.

To examine how we like to learn, we will carry out what scientists call a 'thought experiment'. You will be surprised how much it shows you about what makes us learn.

Desert assignment

Imagine you must travel entirely alone, in a Land-Rover, from A to B on the map. This involves travelling for hundreds of miles across the Sahara Desert. In order to survive this journey you need to be taught two skills, and it is a matter of life or death that you have learned them effectively.

1. You must be able to dismantle, clean and then reassemble a carburettor.
Driving across the desert means that sand blowing into your engine may eventually get into the carburettor. This causes the engine to die. Unless you are able to put this right, you will be stranded in the desert with a limited supply of water, and your fate is certain death!

2. You must be able to navigate by the stars.
No compass will be provided; so you will need to be able to determine your position and your direction of travel from the stars alone. Star charts and other necessary equipment will of course be provided. Should you get lost, you will run out of fuel and water, and your fate – yes, again it is certain death!

The learning in each case is *skill learning*. Skill learning often requires and includes 'understanding', but goes further than that: when a skill is learned you should be able to *do* something. You should, for example, be able to understand navigation by the stars; but you should also be able to do it. Skill 1 is *practical*, skill 2 is *intellectual*.

You will be relieved to hear that you are to be taught these two vital skills before your journey! In each case you can choose how you are to learn these skills, and no expense is to be spared. However, remember that it is a matter of life or death that the skills are, without any doubt, properly learned.

What learning experiences would you need, to be sure you had learned these skills; and in what order would you prefer to have these learning experiences? You are at liberty to choose any learning experiences you like. Here are a few examples for you to choose from.

Reading:	students are set relevant reading.
Test:	a test may be simple or realistic, marked by the teacher.
Class practical or exercise:	the students practise under supervision.
Note-taking:	notes or handouts are given to provide a permanent record.
Demonstration:	students watch a teacher show them how it should be done.
Explanation:	student listens to an explanation given by the teacher.
Discussion:	the class discusses informally.
Question and answer:	the class can ask questions of the teacher.
Watching a video:	students watch a relevant topic.
Summarising:	students are given a summary of the most important points.
Investigation:	students are asked to research a topic for themselves.
Role-play:	students take part in a realistic simulation.

You may choose any other learning experiences you like; the chapter headings (see the contents list at the beginning of the book) will give you more ideas.

Sit down with a pencil and paper, and try to decide what learning experiences you would choose, and in what order, for each of the two skills. Do this before reading further. (Start with the carburettor.)

It is very noticeable that most people choose very similar learning experiences to acquire these skills, which suggests that there are certain patterns in the way we like to learn. Below is an example of a typical suggestion for methods to learn the carburettor skill:

To learn how to clean a carburettor:

a. **Explanation** of the function of the carburettor, where it can be found in the engine, how it works, etc. – with plenty of **visual aids and handouts** specific to the carburettor on *our* vehicle.

b. **Demonstration** of the removal, dismantling, cleaning, and reassembly of the carburettor, including **notes** containing hints, warnings and tips.

c. **Class practice** i.e. students do **b.** above themselves, under supervision.

d. A realistic **field practice test** in a desert, unsupervised, but assessed by the teacher (and with emergency support, please!)

There is an explanation, so that the students understand what they will be doing; and a demonstration, so that they are shown 'doing-detail' – that is, what to do, and how to do it properly. Everyone feels the need to practise the skill themselves, and most people take for granted that their performance will be checked by the teacher. We all tend to forget, so we want a handout or a manual or notes or some other 'aide-mémoire'; and to clear up any queries, we need an opportunity to ask questions at some time or at all times during the lessons. Lastly, no one would stake their lives on their carburettor-cleaning skills unless these skills had been realistically tested or 'evaluated', and found to be adequate.

Most skills learning falls into this pattern, which is summarised by the mnemonic EDUCARE? (*Educare*, meaning 'to lead out', is the Latin root of the word 'educate'.)

Learning a skill requires that the following needs be met:

E   **Explanation:** the students need to understand why the skill is carried out in the way it is, along with any important background information.

D   **Doing-detail:** the students must discover precisely what they are expected to do, and how it should be done. This is the 'doing-detail' which students often best learn by being 'shown how', e.g. via a demonstration or case study. These provide models of good practice to copy or adapt, and are useful precisely because they provide 'doing-detail'.

U   **Use:** the students must use – that is, practise – the skill.

C   **Check and correct:** students' practice must of course be checked and corrected by the students themselves, and usually by the teacher.

A   **Aide-mémoire:** the students need some reminder or other – for example, notes, handout, book, tape etc.

R   **Review** and re-use of earlier work is required to ensure that old learning is not forgotten.

E   **Evaluation:** learning must be tested under realistic conditions, if the learner and the teacher are to be confident of the learning.

?   Learners always require an opportunity to ask **questions**.

The 'use' and 'check and correct' needs are cyclic, and must continue until the skill is mastered. In our thought experiment we imagined a short series of lessons, so review may not have occurred to you, though you may have thought of including a summary. When teaching covers an appreciable length of time, it is very important to revise or reuse old learning, or earlier work will be forgotten.

It is very important to understand that the EDUCARE? elements are all learning experiences, **not** teaching methods. For example, the *explanation* can be provided in a multitude of ways. It could of course be provided by 'teacher talk', but just as effectively by the student: through reading, watching a video, carrying out an experiment, discovering for themselves etc. What matters is that, at some time or other, the student does come across an explanation of why the activity is done in the way it is. How the explanation is obtained is not important – even if they read it on the back of a crisp packet they find on the floor of a bus, they still get the explanation, after all! The same goes for the other elements: the mode of delivery is irrelevant, but *having each need met* is vital.

The needs may be combined; for example, it is often effective for students to get their explanation and the 'doing-detail' at the same time. 'Use' and 'check and correct' are also sometimes experienced concurrently. However, *successful learning requires that all the needs are met*. Other aspects of learning a practical skill are considered in the 'Teacher's toolkit' section of this book (pages 105-264).

Of course the learner also has physiological, emotional, and motivational needs; the EDUCARE? mnemonic only deals with what could loosely be called *cognitive* needs. What we have discovered is the learning experiences a motivated student requires in order to learn a practical skill effectively and confidently.

However, whether one is learning a practical skill, an intellectual skill, or even a language skill, one will nearly always need the EDUCARE? elements if successful learning is to take place. To test this, let's look at the following list of learning experiences, suggested by some trainee teachers, for learning the navigation skill. Compare them with your own.

To learn how to navigate with the stars

a. **Lecture**. Introductory talk on the sky at night, recognising constellations etc., star charts, what they are and how they are used.
b. **Demo** of how to find your position with a star chart, and how to find north etc.
c. Some easy **class exercises** using the charts but in the classroom if possible, followed by a **question and answer session**.
d. **Notes** given out, along with a **description of where people went wrong** in their class exercises.
e. A realistic **class practical**; for example, at the Planetarium or actually at night, preferably in the desert so that the sky looks the same, but with help in case we make a mistake.
f. Series of **tests** that are realistic but more difficult, set and assessed by the teacher.

Look through the navigation skills list and see if you can make out the EDUCARE? elements. Do this before reading further.

Skills and abilities commonly taught

We will see in the chapter on 'aims and objectives' that most learning enables the learner to *do something* that they were unable to do before. It develops skills and abilities. Here are some examples of skills or abilities that are commonly taught in schools and colleges:

The ability to:

- distinguish between conduction, convection and radiation.
- answer exam-style questions on soil fertility.
- type a business letter in the accepted manner.
- add fractions.
- blow-dry hair.
- recall the most important dates in the reign of Henry V.
- recall an outline of how a radio works.
- fill in a form correctly.
- use the French verb *avoir* correctly in sentences.
- make a hotel reservation in Spanish.
- use a wood drill correctly.
- diagnose a fault in a colour TV.

We learn skills and abilities like these by *corrected practice*, so learners have the needs described in the EDUCARE? mnemonic.

When teaching a physical skill it is important not to teach too much at once. A complex task is best broken into a chain of steps, each of which is learned separately. These steps should next be practised slowly and accurately until the required speed is attained. Then the steps can be chained together to make up the complex task. For example, a music teacher might teach a student to play a complex four-bar passage in this way, perhaps one bar at a time.

The EDUCARE? mnemonic can be used to devise learning activities, to check a lesson plan for important omissions, or to help with troubleshooting when learning has not taken place. The next chapter looks at the mnemonic in more detail, and on page 24 you will find a summary of *this* chapter as well as the next.

3 The learner's needs

In the previous chapter I used a simple 'thought experiment' to show that when learning any skill or ability, physical or intellectual, the learner has certain learning needs. These needs I have called: explanation, 'doing-detail', use, check and correct, aide-mémoire, review, evaluation, and questions (or queries) – they can be remembered by the mnemonic EDUCARE?. They are present in any learning that requires corrected practice. Let's look in detail at each of the learner's needs in turn, to see why each of them is so vital to the effective learning of a skill or ability.

Explanation

Would you be content if you were shown how to navigate without ever being told *why* you should navigate in this way? Would you be content to follow a procedure for cleaning the carburettor, without having the least knowledge of how the device worked, and why you should clean some parts and leave others untouched? We tend to feel very uneasy when carrying out a procedure we do not understand. We need an 'explanation'. The explanation should include relevant background information: for example, what a carburettor does, why it sometimes needs cleaning, etc.

You might expect that any teacher would see the need for an adequate explanation, but some teachers eliminate the explanation by teaching a routine. This may occur in the teaching of almost any kind of skill, from filleting a fish to solving quadratic equations. The students are given a list of things to do, and told in what order they must carry them out, without any explanation of *why* each step is necessary, why it is done as it is, or what exactly is achieved by each step.

Routines teach without understanding, and are soon forgotten; they leave learners unable to cope with the unexpected, or a situation where something goes wrong. Such learners will lack confidence even when they have learned correctly. Learning without understanding is shallow learning indeed – but it is attempted more often than you might realise. There is, for example, a widespread myth that *training* does not require understanding.

Some teachers leave out the explanation because they think it is 'obvious'. However, what is obvious to the teacher is rarely obvious to all the students. Take a look at the average computer manual! Does it *explain*, or does it just *tell* the student what to do as a sequence of orders? Computer manuals need not give the learner every detail about the electronics, but they do need to include simple explanations such as: 'Now press the return key; this tells the computer that you have finished entering the name.' It is not surprising that people find many computer manuals baffling, when they are told to carry out instructions that they do not understand. We always find knowledge without understanding uncomfortable, and may lack confidence as a result.

Only students who understand what they are doing, in terms of previous knowledge and experience, will be able to go on learning and developing after your teaching input ends.

If some teachers omit the explanation, others believe this is *all* they need provide. A university-style lecture on its own cannot teach a skill or ability; this requires corrected practice, and fulfillment of the other needs represented in the mnemonic EDUCARE?

Remember that, as we saw in Chapter 2, explanations are a learner's need, not a teaching method. It is not necessary for the *teacher* to do the explaining, if the students get the explanation in some other way – for example, by reading or by discovering for themselves. (See Chapters 11 and 12 for more detail.)

'Doing-detail' - what we learn from being shown how

Why do learners feel a need for a demonstration when they are learning a skill? It is because they want to know, preferably in concrete terms:

- what they are expected to do;
- how they can best do it;
- how they can tell when they have used the skill or ability correctly;

and perhaps:

- when and where it is appropriate to make use of their skill.

In short, they need 'doing-detail': a concrete definition of their learning task. This can be provided in many ways, but most learners prefer a concrete example of good practice to copy or to adapt. For example, it is almost impossible to imagine being taught how to strip down a carburettor without being *shown* how to do it at some stage. Discovering 'doing-detail' is vital in any skill learning; it can be done in many ways. Some examples:

By demonstration:
- demonstrating how to wire a three-pin plug.
- demonstrating how to solve quadratic equations 'on the board', before expecting students to do it for themselves.
- demonstrating how to pronounce a word in a foreign language.

By case study:
- A teacher in retail training might ask students to watch a video of a salesman dealing with a difficult customer.
- A teacher of accounting might give students examples of bad practice, asking them to deduce *good* practice from these.

By exemplar:
- A teacher of computer programming might show students a correctly constructed program, and discuss this with them to provide 'doing-detail' on program structure. Later, the students could be asked to find the faults in bad programs.
- A history teacher wishing to teach essay-writing skills might show students examples of good and bad essays, and discuss these with the class.
- A law teacher may demonstrate the skill of recognising libel and slander by describing a scenario and then arguing aloud to the class whether or not it involves libel, slander or neither.
  (Examples containing deliberate mistakes can also provide 'doing-detail'.)

By being told how:
- A teacher may give an ordered list of instructions, e.g. for how to change an air filter (but 'telling someone how' usually only works if students already have substantial relevant experience).

By discovery:
- Students of welding can discover for themselves how best to weld mild steel, by trying different methods and, with their teacher's help, evaluating their results.

Learning by imitation is one of the main forms of learning in and out of the classroom, because it is an excellent way of obtaining 'doing-detail'. Sometimes the learners need little or no extra guidance – one example might be learning how to poach an egg. At other times, it is not *immediately* clear what can be learned from other people's good practice. For example, students may need the teacher's help if they are to learn general rules of composition or colour use from a painting; or how to write a report, from an exemplar.

Unfortunately many teachers, especially of academic subjects, miss 'doing-detail' out of their teaching. As a result, learners are left to discover for themselves – or from each other – what is expected of them. Here are just a few examples:

- A maths teacher says, 'These equations are solved by squaring both sides and then rearranging to make the unknown the subject of the equation.' without 'doing one on the board' – that is, without showing how it is done.

- An inexperienced geography teacher expects his students to answer complex map interpretation questions, never having shown (in contrast to *told*) his students how these questions are best approached.

- A computer teacher says, 'Using the file menu, you can change the printer options to suit your purposes.' without gathering the students around a computer screen and demonstrating how this is done.

> If you are usually teaching physical skills rather than intellectual skills, you may invariably give 'doing-detail' by means of a demonstration. If this is so, you might like to remember the D element in the mnemonic as 'demonstration' rather than as 'doing-detail'.

Students will find 'doing-detail' useful even if it only confirms their expectations. It gives them confidence that they have understood, and that they really are doing the right thing when they do it for themselves.

Sometimes, when teaching a simple skill, or a skill very like one taught earlier, the 'doing-detail' has already been provided and need not be repeated. For example, a teacher may decide to teach how to poach haddock without demonstrating, if the class has already been taught to poach cod. But beware: most novice teachers overestimate their students, so play safe! When a teacher explains how to find the unknown angle in a triangle by using the fact that the angles add up to 180°, this may as well be demonstrated, even though it only involves simple addition and subtraction; the demonstration gives the students confidence that they have understood, and is more likely to be remembered. (See Chapter 13 for more detail.)

Using the skill

Would you feel able to strip down, clean and reassemble a carburettor, or read a star chart and make deductions, if you had never practised?

Whether we are learning to solve quadratic equations in a mathematics class, or to deal with difficult customers in a retail shop – indeed, whatever skill we are learning – we need *practice*. Most students rightly value practice very highly as a method of learning. Unfortunately many teachers do not rate it so highly as a method of teaching!

I remember a student chemistry teacher who was teaching a class how to tackle questions involving chemical formulae. He explained well and demonstrated the solution of some problems on the blackboard; and the students copied these into their notes. But he seemed to regard student practice as just a luxury. He told me, 'I would love to give them a chance to practise doing some questions themselves, but there just isn't time.' There was time, however, for an hour and a half of explanation and demonstration of how to tackle such problems!

I wonder how he would have felt if there wasn't time for him to practise cleaning his carburettor, because the teacher had spent so long demonstrating how to do it?

We very rarely have as much time as we would like, to teach what our students must learn. But this does not mean that we should alter the proportion of total time spent on each of the individual EDUCARE? elements. How *should* we divide the time between these activities? It will of course depend on the circumstances, but student practice will frequently be the single most time-consuming activity, often by a very wide margin.

In a later chapter on aims and objectives, we will see that even academic teaching involves teaching learners how to *do* something (if only answering exam-style questions). This of course needs practice. See Chapter 14 for more detail.

Check and correct

You probably don't need the carburettor or navigation learning examples to convince you that it is important for the teacher to check a skill as it is practised. The ideal is that every student's work should be checked a number of times every lesson, and corrected with extra explanation and demonstration where necessary. A major aim is to prevent the student from repeating incorrect methods, and thereby learning those rather than the correct version. The check shows the student what needs correcting.

The overall intention is to give students an ability to check and correct their own work. When this occurs, the skill has been learned. Whenever possible, the 'checking and correcting' should be carried out by the learners themselves; indeed, self-checking is a vital skill possessed by all able learners, and is very much to be fostered and encouraged. The more responsibility learners take for their own correcting, the better.

However, some caution is needed. Though self-checks can save a teacher considerable time, high-order skills do need also to be checked by the teacher; and in any case, only rarely can students independently check their own (or each other's) work in the *early* stages of a new area of activity.

In most situations learners should *correct* themselves, even if they can't check themselves. This aids learning more than marking the work down, or having it corrected by the teacher. There are times where it would be too time-consuming, but in general, getting students to correct their own work is an old-fashioned but very effective approach that teachers are now rediscovering. When I have marked a set of questions completed by my science students, I expect them to redo the questions they got wrong, and bring them to me to confirm they can now do them correctly.

The 'check and correct' phase also provides vital feedback for the teacher. Is learning taking place? Am I teaching too quickly? Are they doing it properly? The importance of this feedback cannot be over-stressed.

19

The 'use' and 'check and correct' phases together form a repeatable feedback cycle which must continue until mastery of the learning has been achieved.

Students should have their work checked and corrected as quickly as possible after its completion, and ideally while it is being done. Wherever possible this phase should be continuous, student-led, and teacher-supervised; but this ideal is often difficult to achieve in practice. (See Chapter 14 for more detail.)

Aide-mémoire

If you were about to set off to find your way through the Sahara, you would almost certainly want to take a book, notes or some other reminder to make sure you could deal with a mental block, or some other unexpected event. Your students too will need a record of what they are supposed to know .

Notes compensate for the fallibility of human memory, but they also have other functions. They can summarise a learning session, and indicate the key points students are expected to understand and remember. (See Chapter 29 for more detail on this.)

Review or revision

Skills and abilities, especially simple ones like the ability to recall information, are soon forgotten. Much teaching ignores this obvious fact; many teachers seem to follow a 'teach it in September and forget it till June' strategy.

Learning needs to be reinforced by recall and practice, not left to be revised right at the end of the course. This important aspect of teaching is considered in more depth in Chapter 21, 'Learning for remembering'.

Evaluation

It is one thing for learners to be capable of a skill or ability when the teacher and other learners are available to help, but can they do it by themselves in realistic conditions? Going through learning experiences does not guarantee learning. There is only one way to be sure, and that is to evaluate the learning, which in this context means 'assess', 'test' or 'examine'.

Suppose you were in a class of students who were being taught to navigate by the stars. What would you need, to give yourself confidence that you were sufficiently competent in navigation to let your life depend on your skills? After your pro-gramme of lessons you would want a realistic practical test of your skill You would want to navigate from one place to another without help from the teacher, and you would want this performance evaluated by the teacher. If you managed on your own, and your teacher was happy with your performance, that would give you confidence in your learning.

If this evaluation takes place during a course, then remedial action can be taken where learning is not up to standard. This is a crucial aspect of the teaching process. Tests to evaluate learning can be structured in any number of ways; in very sensitive areas the students may not even know that their learning is being tested. A teacher of adult literacy may just give the student an unfamiliar piece of text to read, and evaluate the student's reading of it. A woodwork teacher may, after teaching the use of the plane, ask the students to make something and evaluate the planing on this.

Evaluation can be done surreptitiously, and it can be done with flags and trumpets; but it must *be* done, otherwise the teacher will not know if learning is taking place. Novice teachers are nearly always surprised by the results of evaluation; it is not easy to guess who is learning and who is not.

There is more on evaluation and how it helps learning in Chapters 38 and 39.

? Queries: the student's need to ask questions

The last element in the EDUCARE? mnemonic is the question mark. When one is learning, one may want to ask questions at any stage during the learning process. It is important to realise that some students are too shy to ask questions in front of their classmates; the teacher needs to give such students the opportunity to ask questions in a one-to-one situation. This opportunity is often best provided during the 'use' phase of the learning process, where the teacher usually moves amongst the students, checking and answering individual queries.

Can you imagine being taught to clean a carburettor without being able to ask questions? One of the major difficulties for students studying on their own, for example on correspondence courses or in 'open learning', is that this questioning facility is absent much of the time. It is very frustrating to become 'stuck' and have no-one there to help, or to be too frightened to ask for help.

Putting the elements together

If you feel sure that your lesson outlines for learning to clean carburettors and navigate by the stars are satisfactory, it is very likely that each of the EDUCARE? elements will be present in every lesson. They may not be in any specific order, and some may be combined in one activity, but they will all be there.

Shortage of time may mean reduced time for each need represented in the EDUCARE? mnemonic. But a need should never be missed out entirely, unless you are *sure* it has already been met. If a carpenter has to make a table in a hurry, he will still not miss off one of the legs!

Making use of the EDUCARE? pattern

Learning can be said to fall into three broad categories or 'domains'. These domains were first suggested by B.S. Bloom and are now widely accepted; we look at them in more detail in Part 4. The three domains are:

The cognitive domain: learning intellectual or thinking skills, e.g. how to add fractions; how to write a report; acquiring knowledge – that is, learning how to recall specific facts.

The psychomotor domain: learning practical skills, e.g. learning how to use a wood chisel, or how to do a somersault.

The affective domain: developing values, feelings, and attitudes, e.g. learning to value people who are elderly; or learning positive attitudes towards a particular subject.

The EDUCARE? mnemonic can be used to help choose activities to aid learning. We have already seen some examples of its use, in psychomotor and cognitive learning, in the previous chapter. Let us now see how the mnemonic can guide the choice of activities in further areas of learning. (This is considered in more detail in Part 4, along with the learner's needs for affective learning.)

Learning facts

Learning facts involves acquiring the simple skill of recall, which is achieved through corrected practice focussing on *recall itself*. Examples in this category might include students learning the main features and characteristics of terrace farming, or an account of the reign of Elizabeth I.

Explanation: students must understand what they are learning; this makes the learning meaningful and easier to remember.

'Doing-detail': students need to know exactly what they should be able to do – in this case, exactly what facts they need to be able to recall, and in what detail. It is not always obvious to all students what the main points are. Students (or the teacher) can devise summary notes, mnemonics, mind maps etc. Asking questions the students should be able to answer, giving pretests, and providing self-check tests all help to define exactly what students should be able to recall (they also help to meet the next two needs).

Use: it is not enough repeatedly to read the notes; the skill of recall must be *practised*. Verbal and written question and answer, quizzes and tests provide this, and also cater for the next EDUCARE? phase.

Check and correct: this is best done by the learner, or by friends and family. Short self-marked recall tests give students a chance to check their own recall.

Aide-mémoire: the need for this is self-evident.

Review: the ability to recall fades with time unless it is reused.

Evaluation: eventually a recall test can be used to evaluate the learning.

?: the question mark reminds us of the learner's need to be able to ask questions.

Many poor learners (and poor teachers!) are unaware that factual learning requires the corrected practice of recall. Be careful, however, not to confuse learning facts with the development of higher-order skills. For example, a law lecturer teaching students about slander and libel is not just teaching the definitions of these words, or the ability to recall the relevant case histories. The students will also need to look at a hypothetical legal case and decide whether there is libel, slander, both, or neither, explaining why. This is a higher-order skill, which itself needs corrected practice.

Learning an intellectual skill

Let's see how the mnemonic could be used to help in the teaching of an intellectual skill – examples might be the ability to solve quadratic equations, write a précis, or answer examination-style questions on a given topic. Choose any one of those three examples, and imagine yourself teaching it.

How would you start? Perhaps by demonstrating how to 'do one' on the board, explaining the process at the same time by thinking out loud. This provides some 'doing-detail', and the explanation. You may then ask the class to 'do one' collectively. Where necessary you can elicit it by question and answer, and provide any other help required, gradually writing the class's solution on the board as they decide upon it.

Students can then examine examplar solutions in order to find 'deliberate mistakes', or to discover good practice. It is particularly useful to see a worked exemplar solution for a task one has just attempted oneself. If the task is complex, learners can draw up a checklist of criteria for success. All this provides 'doing-detail'. The students are discovering exactly what they are expected to be able to do, and how to do it.

Once the skill is clear, the learners must of course 'do one' by themselves, and this work must be checked and corrected. The 'check and correct' phase will probably involve you, but students can also check their own or each other's work. Ideally the correction itself should be done by the student. The need for an aide-mémoire, and for review, evaluation and the need to be able to ask queries, is self-explanatory.

The suggestions on the last few pages are not meant to be in any way prescriptive. There is an infinity of ways of teaching or learning any intellectual or physical skill; but whatever methods are used, the learner's needs must be met if learning is to be successful.

It may be possible to master completely the learning of intellectual skills which are narrow and specific, such as the ability to solve simple simultaneous equations. However, more general developmental skills such as the ability to communicate in writing can never be *fully* learned; improvement is always possible, and the skill can always be used in a novel area. The breadth, the depth, and the transferability of such learning is more or less infinite. However, this learning still involves corrected practice, and the mnemonic still reminds us of the learner's needs. In such learning the 'use' and 'check and correct' phases are cyclic, and indefinite; and the other needs of the learner remain, as we will see in the section of this book which deals with choosing activities and lesson planning.

Summary

Students must know what they are expected to be able to do, and how it is best done ('doing-detail'); they must know why it is best done that way, along with relevant background information (explanation). They must have had the opportunity to practice (use); and have had that practice checked and corrected. Our fallible memory means that learners need an aide-mémoire, and an opportunity to review previous learning. They need to have their learning evaluated, and they need to be able to ask questions.

Each of these needs can be met by a multitude of learning experiences or teaching methods. They can be provided together or separately, and in many different orders. (There is much more detail on this and related matters later in this book – in Parts 2 and 4 especially.)

Exercises

Have a look at the two lesson summaries on the following page. They were both done by trainee teachers before they were taught how to plan a lesson. Look for the learner's needs in the EDUCARE? mnemonic, and see if you can identify which ones are missing. Don't worry if you don't understand the content of the lessons; you should still be able to criticise the learning activities that the teachers have chosen. If you can, replan the lessons. Look very carefully at the objective of each lesson before you start. The objective states the skill or ability that the students should learn in the lesson. It is this skill that requires the explanation, 'doing-detail', corrected practice etc. These lesson outlines are far from satisfactory; how would you improve them?

Objective: *To teach students to choose indoor plants suitable for various environments in their own home.*

a   Environmental factors that affect plants: humidity, temperature, light etc.

b   Ferns, and other plants that don't mind dark and cold conditions.

c   Plants that need a high humidity.

d   Plants that don't mind direct sunlight.

Objective: *To teach students to be able to read a simple weather map, and interpret it well enough to predict likely changes in the weather.*

a   Description of the symbols used on the map. How temperatures and wind direction are shown on the map.

b   Description of high and low pressure regions and isobars.

c   Description of how to recognise cold and warm fronts.

d   Direction of movements of cold and warm fronts, and high and low pressure regions.

e   I will show how to predict weather changes over 24 hours on a selection of maps from recent newspapers.

4 Teaching is a two-way process

Here is a game to play. Two people sit back to back. The 'teacher' has a diagram of a structure which is to be drawn by the 'student'. The teacher tells the student how to draw the structure (without showing the student the diagram); however, one-way communication only is allowed. The teacher cannot look at the student's drawing, and the student cannot ask questions or even acknowledge any comment from the teacher.

This apparently simple task turns out to be extraordinarily difficult to complete successfully, and anyone watching is soon in fits of laughter. It is not long before the student misinterprets at least one of the teacher's instructions, and as a result later instructions are often impossible to carry out. The student becomes paralysed by indecision, and by the relentless flow of apparently nonsensical instruction.

The reaction of those playing the game is interesting. The 'teacher' may feel an overwhelming desire to check that instructions are being carried out properly. The 'student' is desperate to ask questions to clarify the instructions, or is itching to tell the 'teacher' to slow down.

It is evident from the game that the process of learning is doomed to failure unless

- the student can question the teacher to resolve ambiguities or clarify difficulties.
- the teacher is given some feedback about the student's understanding.

If teaching were a one-way process, we would learn perfectly satisfactorily from books and videos, and teachers would just be an unnecessary irritation.

The student communicating directly with the teacher, and the teacher checking the student's work, are both examples of 'feedback' for the teacher. Without this feedback the teacher cannot know whether or not learning has taken place.

Learning is a hidden mental process over which the teacher has no *direct* control. Learners develop a personal understanding of the material studied, and the abilities to be acquired. This learning is an approximation; it will usually be incomplete and inaccurate in the first instance. During the teaching/learning process the learners improve by correcting misconceptions and adding to their understanding, thus achieving a closer and closer approximation to the ideal learning outcome. This process requires corrected practice, but it is not enough for the teacher to correct the student's work – learners must correct their own understanding. Learning is a private problem-solving process, the student's problem being to create a personal understanding of the skills and knowledge to be learned.

Communication blocks

Achieving the two-way flow of communication which learning requires is no easy matter. In practice a number of barriers present themselves, preventing or inhibiting effective communication. Which barriers to learning are experienced will depend on the teaching situation, but some of the more common are considered below.

Level of work is inappropriate

It is crucial for motivation that the level of work is such that each student feels they have accomplished something of value in your lesson, and get recognition for these accomplishments. Clearly this can only be achieved if the level of work is matched to the ability and previous attainment of each student, and if the speed of teaching matches the speed of learning. Easy to say, but not so easy to do!

Ask experienced teachers to guide you and, if at all possible, watch an experienced teacher working with the group you will teach, or a similar group. Look at the previous work of your potential students.

Jargon

It goes without saying that teachers should not use unexplained jargon, but again, this is not as easy as it sounds. For a nurse, 'path lab' does not seem like jargon; it is an expression she uses many times a day. The same is true of 'menu' for a computer user, and 'evaluate' for a maths teacher. Teachers must become aware of the special vocabulary they use, and explain it as they use it. Write such words or expressions on the board. Ideally, the first five or six uses of a new word or expression should be accompanied with an explanation. After this introductory period you can ask the occasional question to confirm that students understand the meaning of previously taught jargon: 'What happens in a path lab, Julie?'

Everybody knows what 'menu' means in its usual sense, but a computer user has a special meaning for the word. The words 'power' and 'energy' also have special, very specific meanings for a scientist. This is sometimes called 'hidden jargon'. Is there any in your subject area? If so, jot all the jargon down and teach it. (If there is a lot of jargon you could even produce a glossary.)

Vocabulary and use of language

Teachers usually have a larger vocabulary than their students. A little informal research I carried out recently showed that above-average 17-year-old students with grade A to C in GCSE English did not understand the following words (among others):

facilitate, assign, rapport, define, analyse, spurious, unison, align, postpone, abrasion, credentials, divulge, deduce, effigy, euphemism, flagrant, futile, heathen

The students were asked to give a sentence in which these words were used correctly, *or* explain their meaning. The great majority were unable even to attempt either task for the words given above.

Similarly, teachers may tend to use more complex grammar than their students. Keep your language simple; don't try to impress with over-formal English – it may alienate students instead. Say 'go', not 'procede'; 'shows', not 'indicates'.

Are you worried about your accent? Given time, your students will soon get used to it; but try to speak particularly slowly and clearly at first if your accent is strong.

Environmental factors

Is the teaching situation distracting or noisy? Is it the last lesson on Friday afternoon? You may need to consider such factors in your preparation and lesson planning. Students who are tired, hungry, or thirsty will find learning difficult.

Specific learning difficulties (e.g. dyslexia)

Autopsies of people who had suffered with dyslexia have shown that they have extra connections between the right and the left side of their brain. Dyslexic students have trouble with reading and writing, often jumbling the order of letters in a word. Dyslexia is not fully understood, the effects are very variable, and it requires special training to assess whether or not a particular person suffers from the condition. Dyslexia does not seem to be connected with particular intelligence levels.

Fear of failure and low student expectations

Imagine you are:

> A school pupil who hates maths, just starting with a new maths teacher.
> A woman returning to education, after seventeen years bringing up children.
> An adult who hated school, undergoing retraining to update computing skills.
> A fifty-year-old manager of a retail store, being sent to management classes by her new area manager.

How do you feel about your first few classes?

Not having experienced success in maths before, the school pupil will be expecting failure with his or her new teacher. The 'woman returner' will be afraid that she has forgotten how to learn. The adult who hated school will be expecting not to enjoy his new classes. The manager will be feeling resentful that she has been asked to go to classes, and will not be expecting to learn anything new.

In one way or another many students expect their lessons to be unproductive, and as a result they have a negative or fearful approach to their classes. Such students may also lack motivation.

The cure for such difficulties is first to understand your students. What are their anxieties? What are their motives for attending your classes? Get to know your students by talking with them as a group or one to one; talk with individuals in private if necessary. Ask them questions about their motives, fears and anxieties; only by knowing their problems will you be able to find solutions. Developing a rapport with your students, and discovering how to motivate them, is considered in the next few chapters.

'Unapproachable' teacher

We have seen in this chapter that 'students asking questions' is a vital part of the learning process; but students, especially shy ones, will not ask questions of an over-formal or forbidding teacher. How does a teacher become 'approachable'? This is not just a matter of personality and dedication; there are a number of techniques and skills that can help, as you will find in Chapters 7 and 8. Chapter 12 deals with the art of explaining.

During the first few sessions with a new class, try to discover what the learners' attitudes and expectations are. Ask each learner to jot down on paper what they hope to get out of their classes, and what they are most anxious about. Make the last question anonymous if you like. (In adult education, you could also ask why they enrolled on your course.)

You will find the replies most helpful in planning the course; the other students will also be interested in the answers.

Learners are of mixed ability (achieving 'differentiation' of work)

By 'mixed ability' I mean that the experience, aptitude, attainment or ability of a class is so mixed that any attempt to set common learning experiences or a common pace throughout the work would be ineffective. If the differences are very marked, do not try to teach such a class as one group for more than a few minutes. Set individual work, e.g. worksheet- or textbook-based activities, so that students are working at their own rate. Make the first few tasks easy enough for the weaker learners, and make the last few tasks demanding enough for the more able. A good mix of mastery and developmental objectives will make this easier, as will become clear in Chapter 33 on 'Aims and objectives'.

Try to choose adaptable, open tasks rather than fixed, closed tasks. For example, 'Write a letter to an imaginary French pen pal about your favourite TV programme.' is adaptable and open, and so would suit the able and moderately able equally. 'Translate the following passage...' is fixed and closed, so would not. Similarly, 'Find out what you can about why capitals are often sited on rivers.' is open, while 'Are the following capitals on rivers? London, Paris...' is not.

You may wish to split the class into groups based on the ability/attainment of the students. For example, a teacher running an evening class in Greek may divide the class into beginners, improvers and advanced. Separate activities appropriate to the particular group can then be set for each of these different groups. (See Chapter 17 on groups.) You may also wish to negotiate activities with individuals or with ability groups. Carefully monitor the appropriateness of the work you set for each ability group.

☑ Checklist

- ☐ What barriers to communication do you expect to experience in your teaching?
- ☐ What jargon will you need to explain?
- ☐ Do you frequently see the work of your students to discover the extent of their learning?
- ☐ Are any of your students too shy to approach you with difficulties?
- ☐ Have you asked your students what they expect to find most difficult about learning what you are teaching?

If your class is of 'mixed ability':

- ☐ Do you avoid too much class teaching – e.g. avoid 'chalk and talk'?
- ☐ Are some of the learning activities easy enough for successful completion by the least accomplished/knowledgeable learners?
- ☐ Are some of the learning activities demanding enough for the most accomplished/ knowledgeable learners?
- ☐ Is a large enough proportion of the tasks you set open and adaptable to the learners' abilities?
- ☐ Do you make enough use of group work?
- ☐ Do you make enough use of 'individualised learning'? (That is, learners working at their own pace through a series of graded tasks.)
- ☐ Have you arranged for students of different abilities to work on different tasks?
- ☐ Do all students achieve some success and get some reinforcement?
- ☐ Finally – and crucially – do you make use of mastery and developmental objectives? (See Chapter 33.)

5 Motivation

You are a fly on the wall of a class of students in a further education college. They are on a course preparing them for nurse training. A teacher has just explained to the class that each student is to search in a pile of books to discover the symptoms, incubation periods, and typical recovery times for six common childhood diseases. Katrina makes a dash for the pile of books, eager to find the best one to take back to her desk. Rachel remains seated, and slowly turns her head to stare out of the window.

Motivation is regarded by experienced and inexperienced teachers alike as a pre-requisite for effective learning, and the greatest challenge that many teachers face is to make their students *want* to learn. If students do not want to learn, their learning efficiency will be so low that they may learn virtually nothing. If you know how to motivate students, you can hugely increase their learning rate.

Sandra teaches mathematics in a comprehensive school; she tells the following story, but it is such a common experience that you may well have heard a story very like it yourself. Sandra spent years trying to teach elementary arithmetic to Terry, a slow learning pupil. She claimed very little success, and the boy left school without even a minimum qualification in mathematics. Two years later Sandra came across Terry scoring for a darts team in a pub. They were playing '501' which involved Terry doing calculations such as $501 - (17 + 11 + [2 \times 19])$ in his head. Terry had no difficulty with this; he could complete such a calculation accurately in seconds. Sandra could barely keep up with him.

She asked him how he had learned to do in his head, in two years, what he was unable to learn how to do on paper in five years. He replied that if he had not been able to score, he would not have been allowed in the darts team; he loved playing darts, 'so I had to learn it, didn't I?'

How can we make a student *want* to learn? Let's start by looking at the most common reasons that students have for wanting to learn.

The reasons for wanting to learn

1 *What I am learning is useful to me.*
   Some students want to be able to swim like their friends, or to be able to speak French on holiday, or to be able to do their own car maintenance; but we have to

recognise the fact that most school and college learning has little everyday application for most learners.

2 *The qualification for which I am studying is useful to me.*
Some students want qualifications for a career, or for progression to another course or college. This is a long term aim for some students, but it is not the main day-to-day short term motivator even for the relatively few students who know 'what they want to do'.

3 *I find I usually make a success of my learning, and this success increases my self-esteem.*
This is the main motivator for most students (even the not very motivated ones). We all have our self-esteem raised by learning successfully; it gives us a sense of achievement. This is why students are sometimes competitive about their learning, showing at least as much interest in their fellow students' marks as their own. They enjoy challenges for a similar reason – it's fun to succeed. Do *you* remain motivated in the face of persistent failure?

When you set a student a task you provide them with a target. Consider the following cycle:

target ⇨ success ⇨ reinforcement ⇨ new target ⇨ [etc.]

The faster this cycle acts, the more motivating it becomes. The addictive nature of video and computer games is thought to be due to the immediacy of the success and reinforcement they provide. If players learned their score (and which planes they had 'shot down') a week after the game, then they would not be so popular! Yet students often wait weeks for marked work. Can you make the reinforcement that students get from success more immediate?

4 *I will get the acceptance of my teacher, and/or my peers, if I learn effectively.*
This is also linked with self-esteem. Even if a student does not enjoy learning, he or she will often try to 'keep up' with the rest of the class for the sake of being accepted by the teacher, and/or by other class and family members. Few people enjoy being the class dunce. However, some students gain credence from their peers by *rejecting* learning and the values associated with it.

5 *I expect the consequences of not learning will be unpleasant (and fairly immediate).*
'If I fail next week's test, Mr Jones will be furious and I'll have to do extra work.' 'My mother will kill me if I get a bad report.'

6 *What I am learning is interesting and appeals to my curiosity.*
Learning can satisfy the natural curiosity we feel about many subjects, and even appeal to our sense of wonder about the world.

7 *I find that the learning activities are fun.*

Even if we have no great interest in the subject of our studies, we can enjoy the activities the teacher has prepared. They may be novel, lighthearted, fun, or involve us in self-expression or creativity.

> In October 1992 a Canadian prisoner smashed up his cell, because he wanted to finish a three-month cookery course but was about to be released. He was sentenced to two more years and finished the course!

Motivators can be long or short term. In my list above No. 1 and No. 2 are long term, while the others are usually short term. On the whole the short term motivators are more powerful, especially for younger learners. An adult is happy to plant an oak tree, but 16 year olds get impatient waiting for mustard and cress!

Increasing motivation

Let us examine the seven motivators in turn, to find ways of increasing our student's desire to learn. The first was:

1 *What I am learning is useful to me.*

Most teachers do not teach a subject which their students see as being of direct use to them. However, if you are teaching bricklaying to someone who wants to build a garden wall, or astronomy to someone dying to use their new astronomical telescope, your motivation problems will simply evaporate. We need, then, to try to make connections to their interests.

'What's the point?'

2 *The qualification for which I am studying is useful to me.*

It is generally recognised that schools in areas of high unemployment have a great deal of trouble motivating their pupils. Young people often do not see the point of working for qualifications that they believe will be of no use to them when they leave school. Without a long term goal for their studies, students become demotivated.

To avoid this demotivating effect, which can occur in most learning situations, it is important that teachers underline the purposes of learning what they are teaching. Preferably these purposes should be both long term and short term. For example, consider students studying surveying on a building course. They should understand the **long term point** that it is not just surveyors who need to understand surveying; that everyone in the building trade should be able to understand a surveyor's plans. Students also need to be clear about the long term advantages of the qualifications for which they are studying, in terms of career opportunities etc.

The surveyor students should also be told of the **short term point** of, for example, studying gradients. They need to be told that you will never understand drainage systems without understanding gradients; and that there is a test on gradients in two weeks, there is always a question in the final exam on gradients, and so on. It may be very clear to the *teacher* why gradients are being taught, but the importance of the topic must also be made clear to the students.

A long term motivator can become a strong short term motivator if course work forms part of the assessment for a course. Students will work much harder on a project if the mark contributes to their final grade.

To be convinced of the purpose of learning, students must look at the world outside their college or school. Work-experience, trips, visits and visitors can all help to make learning seem relevant and purposeful. Students need frequent reminders of the short term and the long term point of studying what you are offering them. You need to 'sell' what you are teaching.

The carrot

3 *I find I usually make a success of my learning, and this success increases my self-esteem.*

This motivator is the most powerful. It is dominant even when the other motivators are involved. It is the engine that drives the learning process. But it can work both ways.

It's 'human nature' to enjoy doing something you are good at — and *not* to enjoy something you are bad at. If someone produces five wonderful meals the first few times they try, they believe in their ability, they find cookery fun, and before you know it they are trying more and more advanced recipes. Their self-belief gives them the persistence and determination that success requires, and will give them the confidence to shrug off the occasional failure. Nothing succeeds like success.

By contrast, someone whose first attempts at cooking have involved burnt saucepans and consistently inedible meals will tend to avoid cooking if at all possible. Should starvation drive them to the kitchen, they will open the recipe book with trepidation. And expecting failure, they will usually find it: their lack of persistence, effort and determination will ensure that they will be easily defeated by minor difficulties. In the end they simply say, 'I can't cook'.

In the same way, if a student completed the work in your last lesson satisfactorily, and was given some praise or recognition for this, success will make him or her approach your next lesson more positively. If they are usually successful in their learning, they will develop a positive belief in their ability to learn in your classes. Beliefs are permissions which switch on our capabilities. They have a way of making themselves true. There is a saying: 'Whether you believe you *can* or you *can't* do something – *you're right!*'

The vicious and the virtuous circle

Success breeds success, by a virtuous circle, as shown in the diagram below. As a result, the effects of success and reinforcement are much greater than many teachers realise.

The learning engine

This is the engine that drives all learning. Even if the other motivators are working flat out, failure to get this engine going will mean that the learner is going nowhere. However, engines can work in reverse, producing a vicious circle:

Many students will fall into this vicious circle due to an absence of praise or other reinforcement. Few of us would persist in the face of consistent failure. Praise or reinforcement earned by success is the engine that drives the learning process. The lesson for teachers is:

- Make sure students know exactly what they are expected to do and how to do it, and that help is available when they need it.

- Some tasks must be straight-forward, and quickly achievable with sufficient corrected practice so that *all students* experience success in them. Other tasks can stretch the more able.

- Give lots of praise and other forms of recognition for any success in learning, and give this regularly for routine success, e.g. for finishing a task more or less successfully. This reinforcement should come as quickly as possible after the completion of the activity.

The above three points are crucial to motivation in most teaching situations. They need very careful consideration indeed. Beware the trap of feeling satisfied if you provide success for *most* of your students; success should be routine for all of your students, or some will lose the self-belief that makes learning possible. Those who learn are those who believe in themselves. Those who believe in themselves are those who experience success.

But can weak students experience success and reinforcement? *Yes!* We will see how this can be achieved in the next chapter, and in chapter 32. The chances of success are increased greatly if at least some of the learning tasks are specific, and carefully defined so that the learner and the teacher know when they are met. And the tasks need to be designed in such a way that corrected practice leads to success, and reinforcement, for all students. For much routine learning, success is a matter of time and effort, not ability.

Your students must see the tasks you set as being both achievable and substantial. This is a difficult balance to strike, and varies from individual to individual. You must think carefully about the standards you set. Students will not value reinforcement or gain a sense of self-belief by completing tasks they see as trivial. Nor will they learn from them.

Most novice teachers set tasks that are too difficult. Try to observe the students you will teach, look at their work and talk to their regular teachers. Remember, it is the students' perceptions of the difficulty of the tasks which count – not yours.

Often it is worthwhile to set personal targets for your students, which must of course be reinforced when they are met. For example, if a student's essays are rather short, you might discuss with them how this might be improved – then set a personal target to make the next essay, say, at least two sides long. When personal targets are achieved there should be plenty of recognition and praise. Targets help to make students involved and responsible for their own learning.

> 'The ultimate goal of the educational system is to shift to the individual the burden of pursuing his own education.' – *J.W. Gardener in Self Renewal, 1963*

You may remember that pupils in the 'bottom' form at school were not keen on doing school work, whilst students in the top form were on the whole harder-working – and even did their homework! Students who have been successful at learning in the past are always the most motivated students. Imagine a message permanently tattooed on the forehead of your students: 'Please give me regular success and reinforcement'!

Working for the teacher

4 I will get the acceptance of my teacher, and/or my peers, if I learn effectively.

Michael Argyle in *The Psychology of Interpersonal Behaviour* points out that 'some students may be motivated by a need to be approved by the teacher.' This is more likely to occur if the lecturer has a good relationship with the student; we will look at this further in Chapters 7 and 8.

Students also want approval from their peers, or at least enjoy being successful in measuring themselves against their peers. This is why competitions or challenges can often produce strong motivation in a class of students, even in fairly trivial games. Competition does need to be treated with care, however, or the gain in motivation and self-esteem of the 'winners' may be more than offset by the drop in motivation and self-esteem of the losers.

Another problem with competitiveness is that some students delight in pointing out errors made by their peers, often ridiculing each other without mercy. This can be a measure of their own anxiety about being unsuccessful in learning, and perhaps for this reason it is more characteristic of poor learners than of effective ones. Teachers must not allow this behaviour to develop, as it produces a negative self-image in the criticised students. We need to develop a 'can do' attitude to learning in our students. It goes without saying that a teacher should never ridicule, even in fun, a student or a student's work.

The stick

*5 I expect the consequences of **not** learning will be unpleasant (and fairly immediate).*

When I was at school I hated learning French vocabulary, but not as much as I feared Miss Browning. I was fully aware of what she would do to me if I failed to learn this week's ten words – so I learned them!

I have already mentioned how important checks and tests are in ensuring that learning really has taken place; however, they are also very important as motivators. I am not, of course, suggesting that you should terrify your students into learning by threat, but do not underestimate the motivating effect of an anticipated test. Even if all the students claim they have not revised for it (which is unlikely to be true), the very fact that you test regularly will encourage them to try to learn in your lessons. Failing a test can motivate, but only if learners believe in their own ability to succeed eventually. Persistent failure is a huge demotivator.

Deadlines are good motivators, but you must be consistent in your management of them.

Increasing student interest

I will deal with how to use the sixth and seventh motivators together.

6 What I am learning is interesting and appeals to my curiosity.
7 I find that the learning activities are fun.

It is an obvious enough point that students will be motivated if learning is interesting, appeals to their curiosity, or is fun. But *how* do we make learning like this? Some teachers seem to have a natural talent for making learning enjoyable, but most of us have to learn.

Some years ago I paid a visit to a trainee teacher on teaching practice. I spoke first to the teacher who normally took the class; he said they were a 'difficult' class of 16-year-old students who were studying basic numeracy. Apparently they found this work boring and were poorly motivated.

Some ways of increasing student interest

- Show interest yourself – be enthusiastic.
- Show the relevance of what you are teaching to the real world. Bring in real objects, show videos of applications, go on visits, have visitors etc.
- Make use of student creativity and self-expression.
- Make sure students are active.
- Change the students' activity regularly.
- Make use of surprises and novel activities.
- Use group competitions and challenges.
- Give puzzles or teasers and then explain them later.
- Make the learning directly relevant to the students' lives.
- Give the subject human interest.

I came into the classroom after the class had started, and made my way to the back. None of the students paid me much attention; they were working furiously from handouts. Every now and then a student would finish his work, rush over to a class-mate to compare answers, and then rush back to his desk. The student teacher was besieged by requests for help from students who were genuinely impatient to succeed in their sums. I looked at the student teacher's lesson plan. At the top was the title for the lesson: 'Percentages'. These students had been taught percentages every year since their first year at school. By rights they ought to have been bored to tears in this lesson.

What was it that motivated the students so much? It was not, as I had first suspected, a challenge or a competition – it was student relevance. The trainee teacher had used data she had collected on football league results, to prepare a handout on 'analysis of team performance'. This was thinly disguised practice on percentages. Each student worked out, in terms of percentages, how often their favourite team won, drew, or lost; how often they scored one, two and three goals; and so on. They were fascinated by what they were doing, and enjoyed comparing their figures with those of their classmates. The basic principle is simple here: students, like most people, find something more interesting if it relates directly to their own lives or to their own enthusiasms. The idea is to aim for **student relevance** in preparing work for them.

The USA has 25 million adults classified as functionally illiterate - defined as being unable to decipher a road sign - and 20 per cent of its 12-year-olds cannot find their country on a map. Failure to learn is often due to a teacher's failure to motivate.

Try to get into the habit of thinking in terms of student relevance. Give examples that relate to the student's own experiences. Don't ask, 'Why does dilation of the blood vessels cause reddening?' Ask, 'Why does your face redden after heavy exercise, or when you are embarrassed?' If you are a science teacher teaching power, don't just do an experiment to measure the power output of an electric motor; get the students to measure their own power output by running up stairs or doing press-ups. If you are teaching geology, talk about the geology of the locality; ask students where they have found fossils, or quarries. If you are teaching about muscles and tendons, talk about the sports injuries of the students themselves and of famous sportsmen and women. If something on the TV last night related to what you are teaching, ask students if they saw it – get them to talk about it. Try and make what you are teaching relate to the students' own lives. This is not always easy, but when you are successful, it will be very well rewarded.

Human interest

An important but subtle method for making a topic more interesting is to attack it from the 'human interest' angle. Newspaper editors and TV producers know this, and teachers need to remember it too.

Any general principle, academic idea etc. will be made more interesting if seen from the point of view of the individuals it affects. Suppose a TV producer was going to do a programme on the symptoms and treatment of mental disease. An amateur producer might attack this topic by asking psychiatrists, doctors and nurses to explain the subject matter directly. If you were teaching the same topic you might do that too. But a professional producer is trained to attack the topic from the human interest angle. They would find a 'typical' patient for each disease or condition, and would interview them on screen to discover their case history, treatment etc.

The trick is to see the phenomenon *in terms of its impact on individuals.* Compare quality newspapers with the tabloid newspapers, compare academic and popular non-fiction. The professionals in the media know the power of human interest. But teachers are professional communicators too. 'Ah,' I hear you say, 'but it's not possible to teach my subject from the human interest angle. I teach physics, catering, law, or typing...'

But a law teacher who intends covering the procedure of arrest, trial and punishment is not obliged to teach it only from a general point of view. Human interest is provided when the students see a topic from *one* person's point of view, rather than in generalities. So why not pick on one person, perhaps a famous person recently caught speeding, and follow their arrest, trial and punishment through the newspapers, introducing the general principles through this particular example?

If you teach catering, you can tell stories about mistakes and disasters you personally have made, or heard of others making (students love these!), using them to underline the principles you are teaching. If you are teaching hygiene, cut out newspaper articles on food poisoning, get a video of an environmental health officer relating bad practice that he has discovered...

The limits of the use of human interest are not the subject, but your imagination. Keep an eye on the newspapers, collect anecdotes, try to see your subject from the point of view of the people who practise it – or who are affected or described by it.

The puzzle

Another media trick used to create interest is the puzzle. It plays on our curiosity. News magazine programmes use this technique: 'Later in the programme we meet the business man who is going to work on roller skates.' Intrigued, you watch the programme to the end, only to find out that the business man is redesigning roller skates rather than travelling to work on them. (The best puzzles, though, *don't* have a 'let down' as a solution!)

The puzzle is the classic thriller writer's technique for maintaining reader interest. Present a paradox at the beginning of a chapter and don't give the answer until the end of the chapter, by which time we have been given another paradox; and so on. (Why was the nice quiet vicar's daughter riding her bicycle at midnight with a revolver in her saddle bag? I must read on...)

How can puzzles be used in your teaching? This depends very much on your creativity, and your ability to steal other people's ideas. Here are a couple of examples of the puzzle as a motivator that I have heard in classrooms recently.

'Last week this glycerine weighed 104 g, but now it weighs more: 143 g. Where has the extra mass come from? That's what we are going to find out this lesson. We will also discover why Eskimos' toffees never stick together.'

'Shakespeare wanted to convey that Romeo's love for Juliet was as deep as it could be. So, how does he portray Romeo before he meets Juliet? Does he represent him

---

How would you teach the following topics, making them interesting by the use of human interest, student relevance, curiosity etc.? The answer to the first is in a box at the end of the chapter.
- a. How to fill out forms.
- b. The idea that the correct fuse (5A or 13A) should be fitted in the three pin plug of an appliance to help to protect us from electric shock.
- c. The paper work involved with the process of admission, monitoring and discharge of patients in a surgical ward.
- d. The principle that the simpler a company logo, the more impact it has and the more easily it tends to be remembered.
- e. At least one topic from your own teaching subject.

---

as unhappy with another lover, or unhappy because he has no lover at all? No, Shakespeare is far too clever for that! Let's see what he does by reading Act I.'

Anything that surprises, puzzles, teases the intellect, or arouses curiosity will help to motivate your students. Have a look at the box at the bottom of page 42.

Maslow's hierarchy of needs

Maslow, a humanist psychologist, suggested that there are universal needs which every human being strives to satisfy. Almost all human activity can be seen in terms of these needs. His list was:

Maslow gives the needs a hierarchical order. Those at the *bottom* of the list are of greatest importance. A need towards the top of the list would only be of importance to someone if the needs lower down were already satisfied. For example, a researcher observing a gang noticed that one of its members, who was a very good bowler, deliberately lowered the standard of his game when he played cricket with his gang. He didn't want to humiliate his friends by getting them all out first ball. His need for belonging was greater than his need to boost his self-esteem.

Maslow's list of needs underlines the importance of peer and teacher approval (belonging needs), making a success of learning (esteem needs), and creative and personal development (self-actualization). These are the student's crucially important 'go buttons', which the teacher must be able to press.

Some teachers think motivation is an end in itself, but it benefits learning because it increases attention to the learning task, mental effort, and perseverance in the face of difficulty. If a classroom is noisy and distracting, students may find it difficult to achieve attention, effort and perseverence despite being motivated.

Giving your students the responsibility for learning

Humanist psychologists such as Carl Rogers place great emphasis on the idea that learning is not something done to students, but something students do to themselves. Many students, especially poor learners, nevertheless seem genuinely to believe that in order to learn, all they need do is attend classes and carry out the activities more or less willingly. They expect learning will follow automatically. This 'passive learner' approach is dangerous, and much modern educational thinking has gone into trying to remedy it.

How can we make our learners into 'active learners'? This is not a straight-forward question, and teachers differ in how they answer it. You must decide for yourself how you will encourage your students to realise that they must teach themselves with your help (not sit back and expect to pick it up by osmosis!) It is often worth talking one-to-one with demotivated students to diagnose the reason for their lack of effort, and encourage them to take the responsibility to put this right.

Active learning can be encouraged by:

- discussing the nature of learning with your students.
- devising activities where students check and correct their own or each other's work.
- setting at least some topics for students to teach themselves from books etc.
- using the discovery method and encouraging active experimentation.
- encouraging students to make use of the experiential learning cycle (Chapter 27).

But most importantly, you yourself need to have the correct attitude and approach. You must see yourself as a learning facilitator or learning manager, and encourage students to take responsibility for their own learning.

Taking responsibility for learning is equally important in the motivation of adult learners. They must be encouraged to decide and negotiate for their own learning needs, set their own targets, and monitor and assess their own learning. All this shows respect for the learner, and develops self-belief and autonomy rather than dependency.

Demotivators

Earlier in the chapter it was pointed out that some factors tend to demotivate students. Emotional factors such as depression or anxiety due to previous failure can demotivate. So can environmental and physiological factors such as cold, noise, hunger etc. It is also possible to be *too* motivated! If students are anxious about examinations, for example, they can overwork and tire themselves, or become so anxious that their efficiency falls.

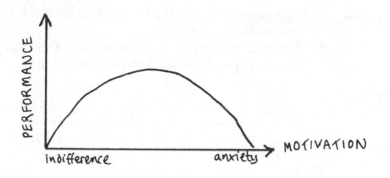

☑ Motivation check list

Here is a checklist of factors which increase motivation. There is some overlap between them, but they summarise the ideas mentioned in this chapter. You can use it during lesson planning or as an aid to trouble shooting. Students will come to your class with some motivation; how you manage in terms of the factors mentioned below will decide whether you increase or decrease this initial motivation. Try to get as many of these factors working as possible.

Success: ☐ Is the work you set at the right level and speed for all your students?

☐ Does *every* student have a programme of work to suit their ability, and their previous learning and experience?

☐ If a student's work is not up to standard, are they asked to rework it until they are successful?

Purpose: ☐ Do the students understand the personal advantage they will gain from studying what you are teaching?

☐ Do students appreciate the relevance of what they are studying to the world of work?

☐ Do you actively 'sell' your subject, and the topics you cover within it?

Enjoyment:
- ☐ Are your lessons varied?
- ☐ Do your lessons involve plenty of student activity?
- ☐ Are the student activities you use often fun, e.g. discussion, groupwork, games, competitions, challenges etc.?
- ☐ Do you make use of student relevance and human interest?
- ☐ Is there an opportunity for students to show creativity, or self-expression – for example, in problem-solving or design activities?
- ☐ Are you enthusiastic in your teaching?
- ☐ Do you have a good rapport with your students?

Reinforcement:
- ☐ Do your students get frequent reinforcement e.g. marks, comments, praise etc.?
- ☐ Does your reinforcement or recognition of success come as quickly as possible after the student has completed the work?

Targets:
- ☐ Are the standards you set seen as worth achieving by your students, as well as being achievable by them?
- ☐ Do you test regularly, and set well-managed deadlines for students' work?
- ☐ Are the consequences of *not* learning unpleasant enough to motivate?
- ☐ Do you set personal targets for learners, and praise them when they are met?
- ☐ Do you encourage students to take responsibility for their own learning?
- ☐ Can you encourage your more mature learners to negotiate their own learning needs, set their own targets, and monitor and assess their own learning?

The first letters of **s**uccess, **p**urpose, **e**njoyment, **r**einforcement and **t**argets spell 'SPERT'. If you will excuse the spelling, these factors make your learners 'spert' on to greater achievement!

Exercises: putting the theory into practice

The advice in this chapter expects a great deal of the teacher. It is often hard to motivate students in practice. Indeed, the consistently negative experience of education which some young people suffer gives many teachers an impossible brief. However, much can be done to galvanise the majority. Look at the following teaching situations, and try to formulate a strategy to increase the motivation of the students concerned. Go through the SPERT factors for each case.

1. 'Simon is quite a bright student who picks up the work reasonably quickly, but he never hands in homework on time, and never concentrates in class. My guess is that his parents have made him come to college because he can't find a job.'

2. 'A Youth Training class of British Telecom trainees come to my college for "off the job training". I take them for "Communication", and I have been told to improve their basic writing skills which are on the whole of a very poor standard. They all say they'll never get a job with BT at the end of their year, so what's the point my bothering?'

3. 'I teach "keep fit" in an Adult Education College. Most of the people who come have shown improvement over the weeks but Joan, 65 years old, seems to think that she is too old to make any progress. I often wonder why she bothers to come, quite frankly. I admit it would take time, but she is perfectly capable of improving her suppleness and her stamina, both of which she complains about.'

4. 'I teach people basic computer skills, at their place of work mainly. The main problem I have is with older people, who come to the classes with the idea that computers are impossible to understand for anybody over the age of fifty. The depressing thing is that it turns out to be a self-fulfilling prophecy – they don't really try, so they end up being nowhere near as good as the younger people I teach. Then they say, "I told you so!"'

Possible answers for Question (a) on page 42

i.   Choosing a student in the class who needs to fill out a form – for example, a motorcycle insurance form – and talking over the completion of this form with the class. *(Human interest)*

ii. Each student could fill out a form that is of direct use or interest to him or her, e.g. application for a provisional driving licence, or an exam application form. A dating agency form would also be of interest to most students. *(Student relevance)*

iii. To encourage curiosity, the teacher could hand out incorrectly filled out forms with non-obvious errors, and ask the students whether they can see the errors made. *(Paradox or puzzle)*

6 Praise and criticism

Let's try another thought experiment. A teacher training tutor, an experienced teacher, is going to observe every one of your next thirty lessons. Suppose you have just taught one of the first lessons to be observed, and you are packing away your things as the last student leaves the room. It is only the third or fourth lesson you have ever taught, so naturally you are relieved it is over and anxious to hear how you did. Assuming you have no reason to distrust the tutor's judgment, what would be the effect of the following responses on your confidence, motivation, and work rate?

a. The tutor walks straight out of the classroom, saying nothing.
b. The tutor praises you effusively, even praising aspects of the lesson that you knew did not go well.
c. The tutor gives you a detailed analysis of each mistake you made, telling you how to put it right and implying that you should try to improve your performance.
d. The tutor praises some aspects of your lesson, but criticises other aspects, and finishes off by saying that on the whole you had made a good effort and that your lessons were improving.
e. You get a mixture of praise and criticism, as in d., but overall the tutor implies that the lesson was rather mediocre.

If every one of your next lessons was received in the same way – that is, each got response a., or each got response b., etc. – how would you feel after 30 lessons? Nearly everyone feels quite strongly that they would be most motivated, and learn fastest, with a response similar in style to d. above. It is encouraging in that it recognises success, but outlines ways of achieving a higher standard in the future.

It is most unlikely that the students in your classes will differ from you in their emotional reactions to praise and criticism. They will hate being ignored; they will be encouraged by praise; and as long as their successes are recognised and praised, they will probably find any reasonable constructive criticism challenging rather than demotivating.

It is worth mentioning that even a weak student can be praised for his or her minor successes or improvements. If a weak student persistently gets reaction a. or c. they will eventually give up. So would you or I! In the previous chapter on motivation I mentioned the 'learning engine', which makes it clear that unless the learner experiences success followed by some form of reinforcement, learning will not take place.

If praise, self-praise, or any other form of reinforcement is to be awarded, the learner must be at least partly successful in the tasks the teacher has set. Your opportunity to praise or reinforce learning will be maximised if you:

- **Set attainable goals:** at least some of the learning tasks you set should be attainable by every student in a matter of hours or less, given sufficient time or corrected practice. This requires that the tasks be well defined, specific, and not highly dependent on previous learning. Lower order skills like recall, and some simple intellectual skills, are suitable – e.g. learning to recall three advantages of terrace farming, or science students learning how to carry out routine calculations by correct substitution into a formula.

  If students are exclusively assessed on their essay writing or report writing skills, then success will elude a substantial majority. Such skills take time to develop, are highly dependent on previous learning, and involve high-order cognitive skills. (There is more on mastery and developmental objectives in Part 4.)

- **Break tasks down:** difficult or protracted tasks should be broken down into manageable steps, which are practised and rewarded separately. Only when success is achieved on one step is the next step attempted.

- **Give learning time:** time should be given for students to practice until mastery of the learning is achieved. Retests and resubmissions should be accepted so that the learners are eventually successful, even if they 'fail' at first.

- **Praise partial success:** you should look for something to praise in every piece of work; you will often find *something* right if you look carefully!
- **Praise effort,** progress, and the achievement of simple tasks as well as conspicuous attainment (rather than aptitude or flair).

How should we praise and criticise?

You can't teach without criticising, but most people find criticism unpleasant. How can teachers sweeten the pill? Experienced teachers can criticise a student's work almost without the student realising it. Read the examples below, and see if you can see how the teacher does it.

1. *'That's great, the graph is much better now. Use a pencil, though, then you can rub out any mistakes. All the points look correctly plotted – well done!'*

   Compare the above with: *'Don't use a pen to do graphs'.*

2. *'Keep it in the future tense, Sheila – can you see where you slipped into the past tense? Yes, that's it. I like your opening sentence.'*

   Compare with: *'Don't mix your tenses up.'*

To summarise:

- Criticism should be **constructive**. That is, it should point out what is wrong, and explain how to put it right. This leads students to view criticism as advice. Say 'Keep both hands on the plane.', rather than 'That's not how I told you to do it.'

- Criticism should also be **positive** rather than negative:
  'Come on, Paul, get started.', and not 'Stop fooling about.'
  'Use a pencil.', rather than 'Don't use a pen.'

- If possible, mix criticism with praise, finishing up with the praise.

All this will help your students accept criticism gracefully and work positively towards improvement. It will also create a positive atmosphere in your classes – nobody likes a nagger.

Try not to give a really low mark or criticise a student's performance severely; instead, give the student a chance to try again. For example, ask the student to repeat or improve the work until they can earn a reasonable mark.

Wright and Nuthall in 1970 examined 28 variables they thought might be related to a teacher's effectiveness. One of the few they found to be important was that successful teachers are more likely to praise students who answer questions.

Praise is greatly strengthened by eye contact, especially if this is sustained and accompanied with a smile. Absence of praise makes for a very formal and impersonal lesson, but novice teachers will not be used to giving a great deal of praise, so some effort is required especially in the early stages.

> Some teachers suggest that unless you teach English you should correct grammar, punctuation etc. in pencil rather than in red pen. The red pen should be reserved for subject content.

Praise is only one form of what behaviourist psychologists call 'positive reinforcement'; Skinner defined this as 'responding to the student's success rather than his failures'. There are many ways of encouraging a student's efforts to learn, as the box below shows.

Reinforcement should come as soon as possible, and should be experienced by every student.

Forms of positive reinforcement

Extrinsic (from outside the learner)

The teacher:
    listening with interest to a student
    accepting an idea from a student
    using a student's work as an exemplar
    showing interest in the student's work
    spending time with the learner
    laughing at learners' jokes
    showing high regard for the learner
    giving grades and marks
    writing comments on written work
    giving smiles, eye contact, thumbs up sign etc.
    ticking in the margin in response to a good point made in an essay
    exhibiting work
    giving a special privilege
Praise from peers, parents and others
Passing a test or exam
Something useful to take away from the lesson

Intrinsic (from within the learner)

Feeling of satisfaction on completion
Ticking off competences or a task list
'I can do it! – I got it right!'
Achieving personal objectives
Meeting criteria which the learner can evaluate

Mastery learning techniques are excellent for reinforcing learning; they are dealt with in Chapter 38, on assessment. Some students will see *public* praise as a slur on their anti-establishment image. However, I have yet to meet a student who will not accept praise on a one-to-one basis! Both reinforcement and criticism can be given informally by non-verbal means: for example with facial expression, through tone of voice, by ignoring, by gestures and so on.

> 'God himself does not presume to judge a man till the end of his days. Why then should you or I?' – *Ben Jonson*

The effect of self-praise and self-criticism is much greater than most teachers recognise. This self-praise is sometimes called 'intrinsic praise', and many theorists believe that it is a most important motivator. It is the glow of satisfaction we get when we feel we have done a job well: 'I've made a widget and it WORKS!' 'I can do FRACTIONS!'

Though, for many students, self-praise may not have as much credibility as praise from a teacher, it comes *much* more often, so its effect is very strong. Even so, most students need to have their self-praise 'legitimised' by reasonably frequent praise from the teacher.

There is also self-criticism. Most students recognise when their work is poor, or when their work rate is low; they need only compare their performance with other students, or with what they know they could produce if they tried. It is demotivating and frustrating for many students not to learn as effectively as they might.

> From some written work by a 14-year-old boy: 'When I get a piece of work back and I think it is good, and I get a bad mark, I feel like frotling the teacher.'

When you praise, remember that it is often helpful to point out exactly what you are praising and why. For example 'Good accent, you are making the **r** sound right in the back of your throat.' is better than 'Good accent.', and *much* better than just 'Good.', which could mean simply 'Good grammar.' If you make clear what you are praising and why, both the student being praised and (more importantly) the other students in the group will know how it should be done. Reinforcement is a useful way of fleshing out 'doing-detail'.

> President Lincoln wrote a damning letter to General Meade, criticising him severely for his failure to win a battle in the American Civil War. Lincoln's view was that many men had lost their lives because of Meade's mistake – certainly more than adequate justification for writing the letter.
>
> And how did the General respond to the letter? He *didn't*, for it was never sent; it was found in President Lincoln's papers after his death. As Dale Carnegie writes in *How to Win Friends and Influence People*, Lincoln had learned that severe criticism was almost never productive.

When should we praise or criticise?

One of the commonest faults when teachers are learning is that they don't praise enough. I've seen hundreds in their first few hours of teaching, and I've never seen one praise too much. Suppose you start in September with a class of 20 students, whom you see once a week for an hour, and you use praise once per lesson. At best some students will have to wait till June for their turn! If you want every student to get a little praise every lesson, then on average you must praise at least once every two minutes. During student practice, some teachers can praise more than once a minute. This seems very odd until you get used to it.

It is common for written comments on students' work to be almost exclusively critical. Your students' mistakes may leap from the page, but don't let their successes be taken for granted.

> Research consistently shows that even experienced teachers think they praise *much* more than they actually do; and that increasing the rates of reinforcement dramatically improves the atmosphere and work rate in their classes.

Perhaps you doubt whether you can find enough praiseworthy work to make it possible to praise as frequently as I am suggesting? Don't be afraid to praise ordinary things. If a student satisfactorily does what you asked her to do, it may not be cause for fanfares, flags and rejoicing; but it *is* cause for praise. There is a lot to be said for a simple recognition of everyday effort. 'You've finished the worksheet – well done.' If you reserve praise for conspicuous merit some students will never get any, and they will soon be tail-spinning into the vicious circle I described earlier.

> 'Never underestimate the pleasure, satisfaction and educational value which pupils get from satisfactorily completing an action *however simple*.'
> – *Michael Marland in* **The Craft of the Classroom** *(his italics)*

As behaviourists have shown, the more frequent and immediate the praise the greater is its motivating effect. I have seen reluctant learners transformed by the following simple strategy. Suppose the class must complete ten questions from a worksheet. Don't ask them to complete the ten, and then hand them in. Ask them to complete the first three and present these to you for immediate marking; then set the next three; and so on. You will be surprised what a difference this makes, even with 16-year-olds.

Attainment and effort

Some students achieve a great deal without trying, others achieve very little despite Herculean efforts. Attainment should of course be recorded and acknowledged, but it is effort to achieve that should be rewarded. If you only praise achievement, you will discourage weak students and make the able lazy.

Do weak students deserve praise?

But do weak students deserve praise? The answer is an emphatic YES! Indeed, it is the weaker students who need and deserve it most; they have to battle with work they find difficult and daunting, without the advantage of natural flair or ability, and this struggle rarely brings the rewards of work well done. Also, they must suffer the indignity of watching capable students overtake them with little effort. If some of our students are attempting to scale Everest without oxygen or crampons, the least we can do is to nod politely in their direction from time to time!

If you come across weak or demotivated students who appear to have given up, try putting them on an intensive praise and reinforcement diet. At least twice a lesson, find something to praise in their work or attitude.

There is, however, a danger in reserving reinforcement *exclusively* for effort. A weak student may then get excellent marks and comments throughout the course, only to fail at the end! Learners nearly always need to know how they are doing by external standards too, not solely by comparison with their own previous work.

Many teachers are so blinded by attainment that they find it difficult to set high standards for the very able, or help the weaker students achieve a minimum standard. In the box at the top of the next page you will see alternative marks and comments for the same pieces of work. What would be their effect on the learners?

Is it possible to praise too readily? Yes, it is – and then your praise becomes devalued. Reserve praise for genuine (if ordinary) achievements and attempts; and with all but the most demotivated, mix praise with some constructive criticism. Some say that adult learners don't need praise and encouragement. Think back to the thought experiment at the beginning of this chapter, and I think you will realise this is a myth. Apparently over-confident learners, whose behaviour is often due to

---

On a history essay

B+ Excellent work as usual!

or B+ Excellent essay, but you didn't get beyond the
text book. Please make more use of the library!

On chemistry homework

3/10 Not up to standard.

or Please see me. I will explain how to
make this work satisfactory.

---

lack of confidence, also need praise. Learning is a difficult process, and we all need
encouragement.

> 'I began by thinking I was marking my students, but then I realized I was marking my teaching.' – *A student teacher*

Students who lack confidence, feel demotivated or alienated, or are very sensitive
need much more praise (and perhaps less criticism) than others. Occasionally praise
may not work with such students. It does not work by magic – it is the emotional
response to the praise that produces its effect. This only occurs if learners respect
the teacher's opinion, believe the teacher is being honest in his or her praise, and
ascribe at least some value themselves to the work being praised. If a student
appears not to respond to praise, keep trying; it may take time. It is useful, too, to
consider the SPERT motivation factors.

Ideally, then, during every learning session there should be lots of praise and some
constructive criticism for every student in your teaching group. This is expecting a
great deal, and not just because of shortage of time. Take snotty detestable little
Darren, who smells of grease or worse, and who regularly emits sacrilegious
expletives about how boring your classes are. When he finally stops his habit of
kicking Sandra while staring vacantly out of the window, and actually puts pen to
paper, you must step up to him and offer smiling encouragement. You will not be
alone in finding this difficult. But if you can't do it, Darren will never improve;
indeed, he will probably get worse, making your life even more difficult.

If you can encourage people like Darren, students of all kinds will come to respect
you, and you will enjoy good relationships with your classes. You will also become
a more effective teacher. But first you must get used to being pleasant and

encouraging to people you fear or dislike. Strangely, if you manage this you may soon find Darren is less fearsome and detestable than you thought. He may start to respect you, start to do more work, and spend less time 'playing you up'.

The main arguments I've heard against the use of praise are that students rarely deserve it; that it makes them complacent; and that the world is competitive and achievement-orientated, so students may as well get used to it now. But I argue that learners who try to improve deserve encouragement; that if it is mixed with constructive criticism, complacency will not arise; and that if achievement is required in the 'real world', praise, encouragement and reinforcement is the only way to get it. (Most management consultants would agree!)

Perhaps the strongest evidence in favour of praise and encouragement, or 'reinforcement', comes from behaviourist psychology. Put simply, reinforcement (that is, responding to students' successes rather than their failures) has been proved beyond doubt to be more effective than any alternative stratagem – be it criticism, punishment, fear, competition or ignoring. Reinforcement is not an educational fad, it is unanimously accepted as crucial to success by educationists and psychologists of all persuasions.

Reinforcement helps to maximise your students' rate of learning, it improves your relationships with them enormously, it minimises disruption, and in the long run it makes your teaching easier, more rewarding and much more effective. So why do so many teachers make little use of it? Perhaps because:

- It is very difficult, in practice, adequately to reinforce all students and criticise them constructively – especially the weakest and the most able.

- It is particularly difficult to muster the emotional generosity to reinforce learners who are demotivated or disruptive; yet these need reinforcement most, and will cause you the most difficulty if they don't get the reinforcement.

- Few teachers are aware how little they praise.

It may be difficult to use reinforcement, and it takes concerted practice to increase your reinforcement rate. But in the long run it is much harder *not* to do so. Remember the 'thought experiment' I mentioned at the beginning of this chapter. Readers of this book are in all probability motivated adults; if *you* would give up without encouragement, won't your students do the same?

Summary and checklist

Think out a strategy for your use of praise; to some extent the strategy will depend on your teaching situation. Adults learning to read may need more praise than those training to be airline pilots. Work out in advance how you will feed back reinforcement and criticism to students. Will you decide to use margin ticks for every creditable statement in an essay? Will you use grades or percentages to signal attainment, and comments to recognise effort and improvement? If there is no written work in your subject, will you talk to students about how they are doing, or provide feedback in some other way? Whatever you decide, remember: improvement is achieved in stages by a combination of the acceptance of the student's abilities and attainment to date; frequent praise and encouragement in recognition of their efforts to improve; and the judicious use of constructive criticism.

☑ *Checklist for the use of reinforcement and criticism*

Criticism

☐ Do you accept the student's standard, however high or low, and set about improving it in stages, by reinforcement and encouragement?

☐ Is your criticism constructive, and do you mix it with praise?

☐ Do you allow resubmission of unsatisfactory work?

Praise

☐ Do you set *each student* achievable goals?

☐ Do you always acknowledge positively a correct answer given to a verbal question?

☐ Do you *look* for something positive to say on every piece of work?

☐ Are you able to praise effort, progress and the completion of routine tasks?

☐ Does every student get some reinforcement and some constructive criticism?

Targets

☐ Do you set the most able students the highest targets?

☐ Are your students kept informed of how their attainment compares with the needs of the course?

☐ Do you break tasks down into manageable steps, and reward their achievement?

Exercises

1. Ask a colleague to observe one of your lessons, and to count the number of times you reinforce a student. Also, to count the number of students who receive no reinforcement.

2. If all the students in a group are having trouble with something, many teachers would blame the group. Others would blame their own teaching. What do you think?

3. What are the relative values of ticks, marks, and comments on written work?

4. What are your feelings about having your own work marked? Do you remember your feelings about marking at school?

7 The teacher-learner relationship and equal opportunities

First impressions

When you go for an interview, you put on your best clothes. Employers are affected by first impressions, but so are you as a teacher. Social psychologists believe that when we meet someone for the first time, we select information from what we perceive, and process it in an attempt to develop a rapid characterisation of that person. We do this because we want to know how to behave towards the person, and how we can expect them to behave towards us. It would of course be fairer to suspend judgment, but few of us manage this in practice.

'Here are the test marks. All those with neat handwriting and new blazers: A. Everyone else: B. Except, scruffy, gum-chewing personal stereo-users: fail.'

Individuals differ in the information they use to form this initial characterisation. Typically, impressions are obtained from factors such as dress, hairstyle, facial expressions, posture, gestures, age, ethnic origins, gender, as well as what the person says, or how they say it. Teachers may also be affected by the student's handwriting, friendship group, previous attainment, reputation and so on.

Once these characterisations are formed, they are used to make judgments about the thoughts, feelings, attitudes, goals and traits of the person concerned. The table on the next page shows a teacher's initial characterisations of two students, Samantha and Kevin, both in the same class.

NAME	Teacher notices:	Teacher's personality theory' leads him/her to surmise:
Samantha	She is quiet, polite, well-dressed, attractive, and middle class.	She will be interested in study, intelligent, hard-working and pleasant.
Kevin	He is large, ungainly, unfashionably dressed, communicative, strong rural accent, loud voice.	He's 'thick', uninterested in study; working class; likely to become a farm labourer; could be a trouble maker.

These initial characterisations will of course influence the teacher's behaviour towards Kevin and Samantha.

> 'It is perception not reality which is crucial in determining behaviour.'
> – *Carl Rogers*

First impressions stick

The problem with our first impressions or 'initial characterisations' is that they are resistant to change: rationalisations preserve them from contradictory evidence. For example, Samantha in the table above has been seen as a committed student. Suppose she starts to smile in a lesson. The teacher might then think, 'She's enjoying my lesson. I knew she would be a good student.' If, however, *Kevin* starts to smile the teacher is likely to think, 'What mischief is he up to?' The same evidence is used to draw opposite conclusions, each confirming the initial characterisation.

If Samantha turns in a poor piece of work – well, 'She must be tired.' If Kevin hands in a good piece – 'Who did he copy?' If Samantha is short-tempered: 'Poor thing, she must be upset about something.' If Kevin is polite and pleasant: 'Why is he trying to butter me up?' I exaggerate for effect, but it is dangerous to believe one is above such rationalisations; I am certainly aware of having fallen prey to them.

> Darwin concluded that he needed to keep a notebook and pencil with him at all times, as he found that he remembered evidence in favour of his theories, but quickly forgot evidence against them! We too tend to have selective memories about our students' work and behaviour.

60

Both students will become aware of the teacher's appraisal of them. Samantha will get eye contact, smiles, and friendliness – and Kevin will notice their absence. This in turn will affect the students' behaviour; they are both likely to behave more like the teacher's characterisations of them.

Stereotyping

We all have prejudices and stereotypes. Here are some of mine, though I probably have others I am not aware of. Students with good handwriting and neat presentation are conscientious, while those without are slapdash. Outgoing, communicative students are interested in my lessons; those who are quiet and reserved are not.

Stereotyping is the tendency to attribute, to an individual, traits that we assume are characteristics of the *group* to which we believe they belong. This of course tends to blind the perceiver to the differences between the members of a group. We all have stereotypes; but we rarely see them for what they are, because they are sometimes partially true, and as a result they fall easy prey to our rationalisations and our selective memory. Research shows that teachers, like the rest of the population, have their stereotypes: 'Students of Afro-Caribbean origin are not academically ambitious.', 'Girls are no good at science.', and so on. If we are honest, many people have stereotypes based on class, gender, ethnic origin, age, or special need. I am not alone in my handwriting stereotype either; research shows that well-presented written work gets disproportionately high marks compared to untidy written work.

The self-fulfilling prophecy

Likes, dislikes, prejudices and stereotyping would matter less if it were not for the effect of the teacher's expectations on a student's learning. Rosenthal and Jacobson, in a celebrated book *Pygmalion in the Classroom* (1968), describe research in which they deliberately gave teachers false expectations of their pupils. They tested school pupils, and pretended to their teachers that they were able to identify pupils whose attainment was about to improve substantially. In reality, the names of the 'improvers' which were passed on to their teachers were chosen at random.

When the researchers returned a year later, objective tests showed that those reported as 'improvers' had indeed improved! The authors showed that the IQ of the 'improvers' had increased significantly in comparison with the IQs of 'non-improvers'. Thus the prophecy, despite having no basis in fact, was 'self-fulfilling'.

Rosenthal and Jacobson claimed, then, that a teacher's expectations affected the student's performance in the direction of that expectation. In other words, if a teacher thinks a student is 'good', they get better – and conversely, if the teacher thinks the student is 'bad', they get worse. Other researchers have shown the self-fulfilling prophecy at work in almost every conceivable teaching situation, from nursery teaching to the teaching of adult professionals.

Can a low expectation be fulfilled? Indeed it can. Research shows that slow learners are given less time and less help when answering questions; they get less praise and more criticism, less teacher time overall and a less friendly approach, e.g. they are smiled at less often. Less work is demanded of them, and their test papers are marked more severely.

This self-fulfilling prophecy is not inevitable. A good teacher will need to make sure that low expectations of a poor student are not conveyed to that student. If they succeed in this, then the process will not occur.

> 'If men define situations as real, they are real in their consequences.'
> – W.I Thomas

The self-fulfilling prophecy places a heavy responsibility on the teacher. It is not easy to share our time, encouragement, smiles and jokes equally. You may not feel like encouraging an ungrateful morose individual with a funny hairstyle! Teachers of adults may find it difficult to give reinforcement to a student who thinks he 'knows it all'. Yet we have a professional duty to do our best by every student. Everybody needs a sense of dignity, purpose, and self-worth. If you can help to provide this for your students you will get the best out of them. If you don't provide it, you may get the worst.

As with stereotypes and prejudices, it is important for teachers to be aware of their likes and dislikes. *What characteristics do you like in your students?* Score these from 1 to 5; a 3 means you are indifferent.

	Like very much	↔		Dislike very much
	1	2	3	4	5

politeness
interest in your lessons
clear handwriting and neat presentation
very fashionable clothes and hairstyle
attractiveness and friendliness
jolly, outgoing personality
quietness and reservedness
good personal hygiene
a know-it-all student
poor English (second-language speaker)
students of the opposite sex
students of your own sex
students from a very different culture to your own
students from a very different class to your own

People like people who are similar to themselves – those who share their basic values and assumptions. Teachers are no exception; they like students who are hardworking, attentive, neat, polite and good-looking! Whatever your likes and dislikes, you should not show them unless there is a sound educational, ethical, vocational or safety reason for doing so. You may, for example, have sound reasons for requiring a student to improve the presentation of his or her work, but this does not give you reason to react towards that student with unreasonable dislike or irritation. Beware any fives or ones in your scores in the questionnaire above.

Working towards equal opportunities in the classroom

All students must feel that they are positively and equally valued and accepted, and that their efforts to learn are recognised, and judged without bias. It is not enough that they are tolerated. They must feel that they, and the groups to which they belong (e.g. ethnic, gender, social-class or attainment groups) are fully and equally accepted and valued by you, and by the establishment in which you work. Translated into studentese, this reads: 'Teachers should be fair, with no teachers' pets, and no pet hates.'

Few teachers intend to give *un*equal opportunities, yet most do. For example, research has consistently shown that female students get less classroom attention than males, have less access to computers or other specialist equipment, and are marked down if they are very able; and that the offending teachers are unaware of such unequal treatment. Research has also continued to show that Afro-Caribbeans, Asians, other ethnic minority students, and learners with special needs also get an unfair deal in the classroom from most teachers. So do students who are shy, working class, less able, or disruptive.

Why is this? Few teachers are deliberately prejudiced; most of the discrimination is unintentional. For example, most of us behave most positively towards students who are able, pleasant or hardworking. This is understandable, but not professional. Parents who pay their fair share of taxes expect a fair share of educational effort to be spent on their offspring. After all, refuse-collectors empty *everyone's* bin, not just those of pleasant, good-looking, hardworking, intelligent white males! I, at least, have reason to be grateful for their fair-mindedness, and students deserve the same fairness from me – though I hesitate to claim success every time.

Many teachers assume that if they set the same learning activities for the whole class, and give help to anyone who asks for it, they will deliver equal opportunities. This is not the case. Shy students need more help than they ask for, and the vociferous less. Every student deserves his or her fair share of your effort, but because students have different needs you will find you must treat them differently.

Monitor carefully how and to whom you ask questions, use eye contact and smiling, crack jokes, give emotional support and so on. It would be very surprising if you find you naturally behave in the same way towards everyone. I am aware, for example, that I tend to joke more with males; I give more eye-contact and emotional support to females, especially the ones I like; and I tend to be more serious-minded in my support for students who are disabled. Also, I tend to give less attention to shy students than they need. But my awareness of these tendencies to discriminate at least helps me to compensate for them.

I try not to read the name of the student before I mark his or her work. (Research shows that female students tend to have good work marked down, and poor work marked up. Some universities ensure all marking is 'blind' by giving students code numbers to put on their work.) I also try to vary assessment methods so that no group is unfairly disadvantaged – for example, those with English as a second language.

The reasons for trying to achieve equal opportunities are essentially ethical and professional; we want all our learners to benefit from our teaching. But there are also legal and economic reasons: our economy will not thrive if barriers to opportunity prevent us from making the best of our human resources.

Gender

Research shows that many teachers have different expectations of males and females; that males generally receive more teacher attention; and that males dominate in the use of equipment in science, design, technology and computer studies. Also, males and females leave school or college with different skills and different expectations of their future lives, females setting their sights lower than males. It is well known, too, that females are under-represented (especially post-16) in maths, physical sciences and technology. How can teachers help to prevent these barriers to opportunity developing?

Of course, one should be careful with careers advice; it is unlawful to give guidance on gender or racial grounds. But also:

- Avoid characterising your subject as a 'male' or 'female' one. Try to portray these gender assumptions as old-fashioned.
- Make a point of researching and mentioning the role of women and men in your subject area. Mention positive 'role models'.
- Avoid assumptions about traditional roles. For example, if one of your assignments mentions a fictional factory inspector by name, why not make the inspector female? If one of your class must operate a video or move a table, don't assume the helper will be male.
- Ensure that your wording in handouts and assignments is not sexist.

Non-sexist writing for the teacher

Increasing numbers of women are irritated and offended by sexist language, so it is a matter of common courtesy to avoid it (even if you personally find this a trial). First, avoid obviously sexist assumptions in your material:

Not: 'The ancient Egyptians allowed women considerable control over property.'
But: 'Women in ancient Egypt had considerable control over property.'

Not: 'The prairie farmer was concerned about the price of his wheat.'
But: 'Prairie farmers were concerned about the price of wheat.'

Try, at appropriate moments, to work positive role models into your writing:

Question 2: A bus driver has a reaction time of 0.2 seconds and is travelling at 50 km/hr. How far will she move before beginning to brake?

The Further Education Unit (FEU) and many other authorities suggest that 'man' should now only be applied to males. If women are included, use 'people' or 'person(s)'. Here are some expressions which could be held to contain sexist assumptions, along with alternatives:

man in the street	average citizen
to man the office	to staff the office
man-made	synthetic
craftsman	craft worker etc.

Avoiding the pronoun problem

Avoid using 'he' to mean 'he or she'. This is easier than it sounds; take, as an example, the phrases:
'The student can then identify _his_ learning needs if _he_ wishes.'
'A surveyor should always be insured, as _he_ is vulnerable to legal claims.'

One can of course use 'he or she', 'he/she', 'she/he', 's/he', and also 'his or her' or 'her or his'; but if, like me, you feel these are often clumsy, try one of the following:

> **Use plurals:**
> 'Student*s* can then identify *their* learning needs if *they* wish.'
> 'Surveyor*s* should always be insured , as *they* are vulnerable to legal claims.'
>
> **Address directly with 'you' or 'one':**
> 'One can then address learning needs if one wishes.'
> 'As a surveyor, you should be insured, as you are vulnerable to legal claims.'
>
> **Rewrite to avoid gender altogether:**
> 'Learning needs can then be addressed if this is desirable.'
> 'A surveyor is vulnerable to legal claims, and so requires insurance.'

Use 'woman' rather than 'girl' or 'lady'; avoid reference to 'the fair sex' – and of course any flirtatious behaviour, which offends many women deeply.

Ethnicity

It is said that when Margaret Thatcher was visiting an inner city school, she had a conversation with a young working class white boy in which he complained of insufficient pocket money. Mrs Thatcher thought he could offer to earn money at home, and suggested: 'Why not offer to clean the family silver?' We all need to be fully aware of our cultural, ethnic and class-based assumptions. If we did but know it, we all share Mrs Thatcher's difficulties in this respect. It is easy to forget (or even not to know) that some of our learners may live in homes where it is improper for women's legs or upper arms to be seen uncovered, and where alcohol or meat consumption are considered sacrilegious. (See also the box on page 69.)

Many teachers believe that we should attempt to acknowledge in our teaching the contributions made by every culture. Arabs developed our number system, the Chinese invented the suspension bridge, and Africans developed writing and the first cities; but you would hardly know this from the ethnocentric curriculum delivered in most schools and colleges. Perhaps it is not only Government ministers who suffer from ethnocentrism.

Third world agricultural methods, Asian music and cookery, Caribbean and Chinese poetry, and African art enliven the curricula in many schools and colleges. Can you do anything to make the teaching of your subject **multicultural**? This is even more important in schools and colleges which do not have a cultural mix. Teachers are important role models; through multicultural education they can teach their students to value cultures different from their own. The Swann Report (1985) regarded unintentional racism as the main cause for the considerable under-performance of students from ethnic minorities, and was strongly in favour of multiculturalism.

Anti-racist education seeks to challenge racist assumptions. For example, a science teacher may mention that 'races' are genetically almost identical, and that there are no differences in innate intelligence between races. Can you integrate anti-racist aspects into your teaching?

Can you imagine trying to learn a conceptually difficult subject in your second language? Many teachers mistake **language difficulties** for more fundamental learning difficulties. If you have people in your classes for whom English is their second language, try to make your English particularly clear, and encourage peer-tutoring in the first language.

Special needs

Students who use wheelchairs, whose hearing or sight is impaired, or who tend to learn very slowly, are all examples of students with special needs. Students with really acute learning difficulties spend most of their time in special care, but of course the others mix in with everyone else.

> It has been shown that dyslexia is caused by too many connections between the two hemispheres in the brain; it affects 4% of the population. It causes confusion over the order and the identification of letters and numbers, and hence affects reading and writing. Sufferers include Michael Heseltine and our plumber.

Special provision needs to be made for such students. Is wheelchair access sufficient? Students who are hearing-impaired should sit near the front, and you should not turn your back when speaking to them or to the class as a whole. Will a sight-impaired student need handouts in extra-large lettering? Will a dyslexic student need extra tutorial help or extra time in exams? You won't have to deal with these problems by yourself; wherever you teach, there will be someone with specialist knowledge to help you – seek their advice.

Others whose opportunities are at risk

Do you ensure that all your students get a fair share of your efforts, smiles, and good humour, whatever their ethnicity, sex, or class, and no matter how shy or self-confident, attractive or unpleasant, cooperative or disruptive, weak or able they may be? This is a high expectation; if you believe you could meet it without considerable effort you have underestimated the problem. But you have taken the King's Shilling in becoming a teacher, and you must do your best, for two reasons: because it is equitable, and because if you value all your learners, they will value your teaching. If particular students are not valued by their school or college, then those students may protect their self-esteem by rejecting the school or college, and the values for which it stands.

Modelling equal opportunities

Many teachers believe that all members of the profession should model the fair-mindedness of equal opportunities to their students. You will have considerable influence on students who respect and admire you; if you come across books, videos or other material that are discriminatory or patronising, it is important to refer to this – to do otherwise is to condone them. Except in extreme cases, this may be more effective than avoiding such material altogether.

When dealing with student prejudice, factual rather than emotional responses are most effective. 'That's a sexist remark.' or 'Some people would find that joke offensive.' or 'That remark suggests that you regard homosexuals with scorn.' – responses of that kind are much better than 'How dare you make such a remark in one of my classes!'

How should one deal with discriminatory behaviour in the class? Suppose, for example, female students are not taking part in a discussion. Don't assume weakness and protect or help; such patronising behaviour reinforces the dependence one should be trying to remove. Rather, try to raise awareness of what is happening and leave the women to assert their own independence. Again, a straight-forward factual approach is often best: 'I notice that no women have spoken yet.' is usually enough to get a response from a female student soon after.

☑ Checklist

Ethnic origin

☐ Do you behave in your usual way to students of ethnic minorities: smiles, help etc.?
☐ Do you spend roughly equal time and effort with such students?
☐ Are you tempted to ridicule dress, speech or language?
☐ Do you allow other students to do so?
☐ Does your curriculum material mention Asians, Afro-Caribbeans, etc.?
☐ Does your material make use of contributions from other cultures?
☐ Do your assignments include Asian names, including women, in high-status jobs?
☐ Are your assessment and course materials difficult for people with English as a second language?

Gender

☐ Do you have different expectations of male and female students?
☐ Do males receive more teacher attention and questions?
☐ Do males dominate in the use of equipment in science, design and technology and computer studies?
☐ Do you encourage both sexes to take your subject seriously as a career?

☐ Do you use sex-stereotyped material without comment?

☐ Do you give moral support to the minority gender on your courses?

☐ Does your subject allow you to explore the issue of sexism?

☐ Do you deal with students on your course who are sexist?

☐ Do you respond differently to particular kinds of behaviour, depending on whether it comes from boys or girls, e.g. lack of interest in your subject, rowdiness, bad handwriting?

Special needs

☐ Do students with dyslexia get extra time in assessments?

☐ Are your assessment and course materials approachable for people with reading difficulties?

Others whose opportunities are at risk

☐ Do you make a special effort to help shy students?

Further reading

Brophy, J.E. and Good, T.L., *Looking in Classrooms.*

Some important religious laws and customs

Adherence to laws and customs varies, but in general:

HINDUS
Believe in many gods which are all part of one God. They have a caste system, and believe in reincarnation and *karma*, a moral law whereby evil deeds will result in accident, failure or misfortune.
Traditions and prohibitions: No Hindu may eat beef, as the cow is sacred. Higher castes have stricter diets – many are vegetarian (as also are Buddhists).

JEWS
Their religion is Judaism, from which Christianity and Islam are in a sense descended. They believe in one God, and regard the Old (but of course not the New) Testament as scripture.
Traditions and prohibitions: Meals have great religious significance. Only ritually clean (*kosher*) meat may be eaten. Pig meat is not *kosher*. Cooking utensils must be specially cared for.

MUSLIMS
Believe in one God, *Allah*, and study the teaching of the Prophet Mohammed. Jesus is accepted as a prophet. Islam lays down detailed laws covering every aspect of life: moral, legal, economic and religious.
Traditions and prohibitions: Only ritually clean (*halal*) meat may be eaten; the avoidance of lard may make bread or ice-cream prohibited, and no alcohol or pig meat may be consumed. During the month of Ramadan (or Ramadhan) no food or drink may pass the lips during daylight hours. Ramadan commemorates Mohammed being sent the Qur'an (or Koran), Islam's sacred book. It follows the lunar calendar, and so occurs ten days earlier each year.

SIKHS
Believe in one God, and freedom and equality for all. Sikhism is an offshoot of Hinduism, but rejects its caste system. Last names are 'Singh' for men and 'Kaur' for women, even after marriage.
Traditions and prohibitions: Men wear long hair and turbans. Their undershorts (*kachh*) and bangle (*kara*) may not be removed routinely. No alcohol, tobacco or other intoxicants.

In Asian religions young women are usually expected, for the sake of family honour, to avoid imprudent social contact with men.

Hindus, Jews, Muslims and Sikhs all reject a secular basis for ethics. They regard moral laws as essentially religious, and based on the detailed teachings of their sacred books. They reject, or at least have a distaste for, sex education since it is separated from these moral laws.

8 Classroom management

Teacher-student relationships

Good teacher-student relationships are based on mutual respect. The student respects the teacher for his or her teaching skills, personal qualities, knowledge and professionalism; and the teacher respects each student as an individual, and that student's attempts to learn. It is important to realise that respecting each individual student is not the same as some kind of generalised respect for the class as a whole; and that the teacher's respect must be shown as well as felt, otherwise the student will be unaware of it.

Rapport takes time to establish, usually passing through two phases. In the first phase you achieve a position of power by virtue of your role as a teacher. If your students are never likely to challenge your authority, offer a brief prayer of thanks, and skip this topic by moving on to the next section on 'establishing rapport'.

David Hargreaves, a social psychologist in the education field, suggests that a teacher starting with a new class must insist that the students accept his or her 'formal authority'. Teachers must convey that their authority is legitimate, that it exists to maximise learning; and they must show confidence in their ability to enforce their authority.

You cannot expect students to like you from the first lesson; you have no mutual experience on which to build a personal relationship, so – like it or not – you will start in a formal relationship with your class. Being a teacher confers on you certain duties, but with these duties come rights; grasp them with both hands! You have the right to be obeyed on matters of work and behaviour. You have the right to silence when you are speaking. Some learning teachers feel uneasy in this position of power, perhaps because they are unfamiliar with it, and the first time a student obeys one of their orders they can barely hide their surprise. Why should you feel shy or apologetic about the use of the teacher's formal authority, if you are using it for the students' benefit? You are there to teach, and you cannot teach without order; use your authority.

How do you develop and use this formal authority? This depends on your teaching situation. If your students are not cooperative, then you may well find yourself in the following fix: your students will only accept your authority if you apply it with confidence. However, you will only begin to feel confident when they accept your authority. An unfortunate 'catch 22'.

You never get a second chance to make a first impression. To begin with, you must act. Stride about the room as if you are absolutely confident of your ability to control the group. Appear to be self-confident, relaxed, and in control – especially when you are not! This is particularly important in your first few lessons or when coping with a difficulty.

A staff-room adage: 'Never smile before Easter'.

Formal authority is sustained by non-verbal methods. Stand up straight, shoulders back, face students squarely, give orders with a confident tone of voice and expect to be obeyed. If you ask a student to do something, don't hang around with an anxious look on your face wondering what will happen next. Give your order with confidence. If the student has not done what you asked in reasonable time, be confident and emphatic; you might show a puzzled surprise at the impertinence, but *never show that you are flustered.*

Authority is conveyed principally with body language. For example, compare these two ways of dealing with a student who is not working:

1. Not facing the student, and at five metres distance saying: 'I want you to stop talking and start working now, Paul.'

2. Walking confidently but unhurriedly up to the student, putting both hands on his desk to lean over and face him, looking him in the eye for three seconds, then saying 'Why aren't you working?' confidently, still holding his gaze.

These two methods produce startlingly different effects on the student; ask a friend to try it on you if you don't believe me!

Of course, you don't need to be quite so extreme in giving every order, but remember that when giving instructions the effect on the student is increased, not by shouting or anger, but by:

Proximity: the closer you are, the greater your effect, especially if you invade the students' 'personal space' and adopt a commanding posture.

Eye-contact: that is, sustained eye-contact while you are speaking, and for enhanced effect after you have spoken.

Posing questions: it is often more powerful to put the student 'on the spot' by posing a question than to deliver a lecture. However, this is sometimes best done when you have the student alone.

The above three enhancements can be remembered by the mnemonic 'PEP' – **p**roximity, **e**ye-contact, and **p**osing questions. Using them well, you can 'pep up' your message. Usually, proximity and eye-contact are enough without posing questions; they should certainly be tried first, with a positive statement such as 'Come on, let's get started.', before combining them with questions.

If you use the PEP approach effectively, you will barely need to raise your voice to maximise the effect of your instructions. In fact, you will make at least as big an impression by *lowering* your voice.

If you expect trouble, *never* sit behind the desk; move around the class, and use plenty of eye-contact. You don't have to be tall. The most effective disciplinarian I have ever seen was a woman no more than five feet high; she just stood up straight and looked confident! Don't over-rely on enforcing formal authority in this way, though; interesting lessons, good relations, and proper classroom management are much more effective in keeping order, as you will see in the next few pages. If you have problems, some of the advice on discipline later in this chapter may help. Don't be afraid of making short-term enemies; you must show that you are not afraid of becoming unpopular, if you are to become popular!

Rapport and personal authority

Phase two in developing student-teacher relations is a gradual shift from this formal authority towards the teacher's personal authority. A teacher who wields formal authority fairly and effectively, and shows some skill in teaching, will earn the respect of the students. If all goes well, given time, the relationship may shift so that it is based on personalities. The source of the teacher's power becomes the desire of the students to please the teacher, and to build their own self-image through the teacher's approval. This is called 'personal authority'.

How does this personal authority evolve? It takes months rather than weeks; obviously teachers will gain their students' respect by being effective teachers, but the following will also help:

- Showing a genuine *interest* in each student's work, and making a point of using praise – especially in recognising a student's individual contributions or attempts to learn, regardless of their previous attainment or innate ability.

- Having a clear set of rules and applying them fairly and consistently, without bearing grudges from one class to the next.

- Using the students' names.

- Showing ordinary polite respect for students by saying 'please' and 'thank you'.

- Never using put-downs, or sarcasm.

- Having a professional approach to your teaching and its organisation, e.g. well-planned and organised lessons, good timekeeping, tidy appearance, etc.

- Being patient.

– and perhaps, a little later:

- Showing an interest in students as individuals, e.g. smiling, using eye contact and speaking to them 'one to one'. Recognising each student's individuality, e.g. their personality traits, interests, style of dress etc.

- Choosing teaching methods which allow students to make personal contributions, and reacting positively to these when you can.

- Showing an interest in students' attitudes, feelings and needs.
  'What do you think of the new library, then?'
  'Are you worried about the mock exams, Andrew?'
  'Are you clear on that now, or would you like me to go over it again?'

- Developing a relaxed and confident style that is not too formal, using humour where appropriate (this includes being prepared to have the occasional laugh at your own expense.) Relaxed humour conveys confidence.

Much of the above is simply showing a genuine interest in students' work, feelings and individuality, without trying to be 'one of them'. If you succeed in establishing rapport your job will be made very much easier, as well as more enjoyable. The main rewards of teaching are in a teacher's relationships with his or her students.

'Remember that a man's name is to him the sweetest and most important sound in the English language.' – *Carnegie, How to Win Friends and Influence People*

Do you find it hard to learn names? I did; but I had a colleague who knew the name of every student she taught within the first week of a new academic year, so I asked her how she did it. Remember that 'frequency and recency' are the clues to all memory learning. She made a plan of the class, with each student's full name written in the place they sat. She read through this a number of times every day, even if she couldn't remember the face to go with each name. She spent a few minutes with her plan before each lesson – and especially after it, while she could still remember the faces. She openly referred to her plan in the class, and always used her students' names when she talked to them. (Students are not offended if you make a few mistakes, or ask their name, in your first few lessons.)

Unless rapport is established, a 'psychological barrier' is created which stops students taking part in discussions, asking questions, or asking for help. It also detrimentally affects student motivation and classroom management. Names, smiles and equal treatment are the most effective ways of ensuring this barrier does not develop.

Don't try too hard with rapport. Be patient. You will be disliked if you are desperate to be liked. And don't expect too much; your students don't want you to become a best friend or confident. They have these already. All they want is that you should be effective in your teaching and classroom management, that you should be approachable, and that you should have a genuine interest in their learning.

You will never establish a rapport with your class unless you can manage the class effectively, and this is the subject of the next section.

Some don'ts

Canadian university students were asked to say which were the teaching habits they most disliked. Their answers were:

- Ignoring students.
- Discouraging and restricting questions.
- Ridicule of a student's contributions.
- Sarcasm, belittlement, hostility or anger.
- Arrogance.
- Interrupting a student's contributions.
- Failure to promote discussion or questions.

This research was not specifically about rapport, but notice that all the disliked teaching habits are in effect expressions of the teacher's lack of respect for, or interest in, the students.

Creating a working atmosphere in the classroom

'Students are the beneficiaries, not the victims of effective classroom control.'
– *Michael Marland*

One day during my first term of teaching, I was walking down a school corridor when I noticed that one of the classes was in uproar. Students were standing on the tables and bellowing at each other, books were flying through the air, and two boys were fighting in a corner. With my heart in my mouth I stormed through the door, put on my sternest expression and bellowed, 'Sit down quietly and wait for your teacher.' The remark was greeted with a roar of laughter from the class; they glee-fully pointed to their teacher, who was tucked into a corner with the two students in the class who *were* trying to work.

Some teachers have terrible discipline problems, while others create an atmosphere in the classroom that is conducive to learning, with little apparent effort. How do they do it? The bridge from chaos to order in the classroom has four spans, each of which must be in place if you are to guide your class across. These are:

- effective lessons based on a well-conceived curriculum;
- good organisational skills;
- good teacher/student relationships;
- effective discipline (which is almost impossible to achieve unless the first three conditions are satisfied).

The first of these points must not be overlooked. Most of the 'discipline' diffi-culties experienced by teachers in the classroom were created before the lesson started; they were inherent in the lesson plan. The factors involving motivation should have been given very careful consideration. The student's work should be interesting, involving plenty of varied student activity. There should be something for every student to do all the time, and the standard of the work should not be too difficult or too easy for any student in the class. There should be ample and prompt reinforcement, such as praise and encouragement, for students' efforts. This is a tall order, but who said teaching was easy!

Practical help in achieving this balance can be found elsewhere in the book; for the moment, we shall be looking at the other three spans of the bridge.

I am assuming in what follows that you are interested in how to deal with a fairly 'difficult' class; if you teach adults or very motivated students, some of what follows can be toned down, or may even be wildly inappropriate – unless you are interested in parenthood, where many of the techniques are very relevant!

Organisation in the classroom

Experienced teachers don't deal with problems, they prevent them occurring. This is why student teachers whose classes are reminiscent of the Sorcerer's Apprentice look in vain for the 'tricks' used by teachers who are able to keep 'difficult' classes working. Good classroom organisation allows the lesson to run smoothly, so that good relationships can grow through positive experiences.

Rules and regimes

Every teacher has rules and regimes, even if they are not overtly stated. Think them out carefully, express them clearly, and enforce them consistently. Do you want work handed in on Mondays or Thursdays? Do you want students to put their hands up to answer a question? During practical sessions, are students allowed to talk to their neighbour, to students behind them, or to students at the other end of the room?

Your rules and regimes will take time to establish, and should be based on educational, safety, and moral grounds, not on personal idiosyncrasies. Despite getting my own back on two occasions, I still harbour a smouldering resentment against a teacher who made me rewrite an essay because I had written it in green biro!

Exactly what is allowed in your lessons will be decided by what you do, not by what you say. If you say that there should be no talking when you are talking, but do not enforce this, then the rule becomes inoperative; and should you then 'jump' on a student for talking inappropriately, your inconsistency will be resented. 'Why pick on me, I'm not the only one.' If you consistently refuse to accept contributions from students who call out, but accept them from students with raised hands, then hand-raising becomes a rule.

Whether or not you make your rules explicit, expect them to be tested, and be consistent in their enforcement. This may seem irritating and time-consuming at first, but it is a vital investment in future order. Rules and behaviour are governed by case law, which will only be established by ruthless consistency. Sometimes rules have exceptions, but not many. Be sure you are being fair, then be very firm.

A very effective and experienced teacher once gave me this tongue-in-cheek advice: 'Listen to excuses with concern, interest and compassion – then ignore them!'

It is sometimes worth negotiating rules and regimes with students: 'Would you prefer to hand in work on Mondays or Thursdays?' Some teachers go further and bring problems to the group. 'I'm getting lots of trouble with students not handing their work in. What's the problem? Is the work too difficult?' Be equally consistent in enforcing rules decided by the group. Once the rules are established you may be able to bend them a bit, but be fair and consistent even here.

As far as possible, there should be a similar approach to rules and regimes from all the teachers whom the students experience.

Here is a set of rules and regimes I use for 17-year-old students. Many other sets would be equally valid.

- Absolutely no talking if I am talking. (I try not to go on too long, though!)
- No running in the classroom.
- When working individually or in groups, students can:
  talk to their neighbour about work;
  move out of their place to talk about work with another student.
- Work is handed in on the same day each week. Absence for more than one day is an acceptable excuse for a *delay* in handing in a week's work.
- Students are not allowed to pack away their folders until I say so (whatever the clock says – however, I will accept a reminder about the time if I have overrun).

Ask to observe classes in your school or college, so you get a feel for the sort of behaviour which is acceptable. If your expectations are the same as those of other teachers, this will make your life much easier.

Before they arrive

Arrive before your class, and make sure you have everything you need (and that everything works). If you are a science teacher, you should already have rehearsed any experiment/procedure you or your class will be carrying out. Lay out anything you may need for the lesson neatly, so you can find it, and prepare the overhead projector or the blackboard for the first few minutes of the lesson.

When the students arrive, you may like to greet them at the door and watch them as they take their places; appear confident and relaxed, but businesslike. Start on time;

waiting for students who are late is unfair on those who have arrived on time, and encourages late arrival in the future.

Getting silence

Gaining and maintaining silence is very important. It is worth being pedantic about this when you first meet a new group; time spent at this stage will be an excellent investment. If you don't get silence in your first lesson you probably never will, and even if students can hear you in subsequent lessons, they will not be listening.

Ask for silence and then WAIT for it, however long it takes. If necessary, repeat your call for silence, and use the techniques below to obtain and enforce it. Don't start until there is a conspicuous silence and all students are looking in your direction. NEVER start your lesson over the class's noise. If you do, students will be given the impression that it is permissible to talk whenever they like; as a result even students who were initially quiet will start talking, and before long virtually the whole group will be talking over you.

If waiting makes you feel panicky, don't show it; never be cross or abusive, as this is counterproductive. It gives the impression you are not in control. Instead, make it seem they are missing something when they make a noise:

> 'Everyone's waiting to hear what Sandra has to say.'
> 'No, I'm sorry, we can't start yet because we're not quiet enough.'

Having achieved silence, let it sink in for a second, and then begin saying what you want to say. If someone talks when you are talking, stop in mid-sentence, and look at them until they stop. They are likely to find this an embarrassment, and will probably soon stop; but if necessary use their name, or ask for silence again. Only when you have re-established silence should you continue talking, going back to the beginning of the sentence which was interrupted. Should talking start again, do exactly the same. Soon most students will realise that they cannot talk without immediately drawing attention to themselves, and they will stop trying.

If there is a persistent offender, explain that it is impossible to talk and listen at the same time, stand close to them, and if necessary threaten to move them. Other techniques are dealt with below, but whatever you do, do not give up. However, don't expect *too* much; some groups can literally only concentrate on teacher talk for about two minutes, or even less. If you have a group like this, don't rely on teacher talk to the class as a whole. Talk to them in small groups, and communicate with the board or overhead projector (OHP), also using worksheets.

Gaining silence is a common problem for inexperienced teachers, but the approach above will work if you are persistent.

At the start

The first five minutes of any lesson is crucial in setting the atmosphere for the rest of the lesson. If you want to enliven a sleepy class, then start with a bang; if you want to quieten a noisy group down, start quietly.

If a class is particularly noisy, try making the first activity one where the students are working alone without needing input from you. They could be copying a diagram off the OHT/board, doing an exercise from a textbook, or finishing off something from the last lesson. You can then concentrate one hundred percent on getting quiet; settling the class into a quiet working atmosphere; and dealing with Lucy who has arrived late, having lost her folder. Once the class has been really quiet for five minutes, you have set the atmosphere for the rest of the session.

Giving instructions

Get silence first, and make sure the class are all looking at you. Some teachers, especially those who must compete with noise from machines, have a routine way of attracting attention such as clapping three times. Be brief, clear and positive. The tone should be firm, confident and pleasant. If you are asking the class to change positions, ask them to remain still until you have finished the instruction. When you have finished, give a summary. Here's an example:

> [The teacher claps hands a few times] 'OK, can I have everybody's attention, please. – Julie... – Robin, look this way, please. Now, when I tell you, I want one person from each group to collect its apparatus from the front bench, and another to pick up a power-pack from the back of the lab. Whoever's left in your group will be preparing a table for the results. OK? One set of apparatus, one power-pack, and one prepared table. Off you go.'

If you often require movement to the front of a class for a demonstration, it is worth considering having fixed positions for students to move to.

'Tell them what you are going to tell them – tell them – tell them what you have told them!'

Don't make repeated generalised complaints, e.g. 'Come on, everybody, start work.' Give the generalised instruction ONCE, then pick on individuals who are not obeying, by name or by eye contact: 'Come on, Paul, get started!'

Those who give instructions should set a good example. If you want students to be neat and methodical in the way they lay out their work, then take your own advice when writing on the blackboard. If you want them to use certain safety procedures, then use them yourself. Don't allow your students to leave before the end of a class; it sets a difficult precedent. If they have completed your activities, try a revision quiz.

'With-itness'

'He has eyes in the back of his head.' A sixty-year-old deputy headmaster finished off some excellent advice on how I should treat a new class by saying, half seriously, that I should keep my eyes on the reflections of pupils in the glass doors of the cupboards that lined the laboratory. If I saw in the reflection a student misbehaving, I should then turn my back on the student before beginning to tell him off. 'It really unsettles the little blighters when they think you know what they're up to with your back turned!'

Inappropriate behaviour soon spreads unless it is dealt with promptly; this is called the 'ripple effect'. Students are quick to think 'Why should I behave if no-one else is?', and before long you may have a riot on your hands.

Whatever you or your students are doing, you must make your presence fill the room – every corner of it. Students some distance from you will not feel so strongly under your influence; walk close to them occasionally, and scan all the faces in the room with eye-contact from time to time. Be vigilant and be mobile, *don't* sit behind the desk. Which way are the students facing? Are they listening? Have they got pens in their hands? If particular students are not being productive, give them sustained eye-contact; if necessary, walk over and stand close to them. This can be done with no disruption to your teaching, and will usually be enough to stop the inappropriate behaviour.

If you are writing on the board, half-face the room and scan the class every now and then, every five words if necessary. If you are talking to an individual student, don't relax your vigilance; always position yourself so that you can see most if not all of the room. Whilst talking, scan the room frequently, all of it. Vigilance has a way of preventing misbehaviour before it starts: students gain little by behaving inappropriately if they are picked up for it straight away. Who bothers to steal helmets off the heads of policemen?

There are circumstances where it is best to pretend not to notice misbehaviour – harmless silliness that is already settling down. With experience you will know what is best ignored, but you will find yourself ignoring very little.

It is difficult to remain vigilant while teaching; it takes practice. If it seems impossible at first, don't worry; it's like changing gear whilst steering a car – you will soon be doing it automatically. You must also notice *appropriate* behaviour, for students who are working should be reinforced.

Fire-fighting

If inappropriate behaviour begins, it must be stopped as soon as possible, for three reasons:

- to stop the behaviour spreading to other students;
- because it is easier to stop behaviour that has hardly started;
- to prevent the student gaining from the misbehaviour.

Students talk when they shouldn't because they enjoy a chat. If they usually manage to get half a dozen sentences in before you deal with them, then they might begin to feel their chats are worth your displeasure. On the other hand, if they never manage to finish the first three words of the first sentence, they have gained nothing of value from their inappropriate behaviour, and they will soon decide that it is not worth trying.

Knowing the student's names is crucial to effective fire-fighting. You probably remember this technique from your school days:

> 'In those days Genoa was a thriving commercial port – wasn't it, Samuel? It wasn't a very big city...'

Even if the name is not said with a disapproving tone, Samuel knows why he was 'picked on', and it is nearly always enough to stop the inappropriate behaviour.

Give the work of offending students some attention. If your vigilance and fire-fighting succeeds in getting them back to work, find something to praise in their work if you can: 'This is better, now you are getting down to it!' Research shows that praise of appropriate behaviour is more effective than criticism of inappropriate behaviour.

The power of praise

In a famous piece of research* students with 'a high frequency of problem behaviour' were observed for 20 minutes a day, three days a week from November till June. Their behaviour was recorded as 'appropriate' or 'inappropriate' every ten seconds during this time. At the start some students behaved inappropriately as much as 70% of the time, despite having a competent and experienced teacher.

The teacher adopted various strategies to make the students behave well. Telling them the class rules had little effect; and ignoring inappropriate behaviour made them worse! However, if the students were given the class rules, and their inappropriate behaviour was ignored *but appropriate behaviour was praised*, these very difficult students began to behave well 90% of the time.

* Madsen, Becker and Thomas (1968), *Rules, Praise and Ignoring*

---

9 Discipline and problem-solving

I encountered a young pupil called Mandy in my first year of teaching; she was thirteen years old, but I lived in dread of her. I put her in detention once for blatant defiance, and I told her to write me a letter there to explain her behaviour. Her explanation was fulsome, and included the comment: 'Most teachers are very strict about behaviour; others are not. Mostly I like teachers that are strict about work.' I was astonished by this comment. How could such a badly-behaved pupil prefer strict teachers?! I had a lot to learn; in this respect she was the rule, not the exception.

In the previous chapter I argued that order in the classroom was created by a combination of four factors: effective lessons based on a well-conceived curriculum, good organisational skills, good teacher-student relationships, and effective discipline. Here we deal with the last of these four; prevention may be better than cure for the vast majority of 'behaviour problems', but it does not deal with all of them.

> Only unobservant teachers have no problems.

Finding the root cause of the problem

If students are bored because their work is too simple, no amount of juggling of rewards and punishments will solve the problem. Even if vigilance and threatened punishments keep the behaviour within tolerable limits, the problem is likely to resurface in a new guise, which may well be even more difficult to deal with. If the root cause of the problem is inappropriate work, then the solution is obvious. Unhappily the diagnosis of behaviour problems is sometimes very difficult, and occasionally impossible.

The 'adult to adult' chat style is perhaps the best method for finding problems and their solutions. Use it one-to-one after the class.

1. *Find* the real problem. This is best done by *listening*. Even if your first instinct is to strangle the student, assume in the first instance they are willing and able to solve the problem by themselves. Do not jump in with advice or judgments at this stage. You may give another's point of view, but without implying that you yourself hold that view. Show acceptance non-verbally. You

are looking for the reasons for the behaviour you want to change. A key reason-finding question is: 'What do you find most difficult ...' E.g. 'What do you find most difficult about working with the other students in your group?'

2. *Agree* a solution. Give the student the problem and ask them for a solution. 'So what are you going to do about this problem?' If a solution is not forth-coming, suggest one yourself, but ask the student if they can think of a better one. Ask for an agreement to *carry out* the solution, if this is not offered.

3. A *target* is set. E.g. 'So we agree that you will talk to Philippa about your disagreement before next lesson?'

4. **An *evaluation* will follow, to see whether the target has been reached.** The student is made aware of the fact that the agreed solution is to be checked: 'Good, let me know before next lesson what you and Philippa have agreed between you.'

If you want to give the student time, omit the target and evaluation, and perhaps talk again later. The most unlikely students respond very well to being treated like adults, even if they don't deserve such treatment! Here's an example. A student is a long way behind with his work despite exhortations. The teacher has listed the outstanding work; the student says he is still positive about the course. The first letters of the four key elements in an 'adult to adult' kind of chat (find the problem, agree a solution, set a target, evaluation afterwards) spell 'FATE'. See if you can identify each of the FATE elements in the dialogue:

Teacher	So what's the problem?
Student	I don't know. I'll just have to work harder, won't I.
Teacher	Is the work too hard, too easy, too boring...?
Student	No, not really.
Teacher	What do you find most difficult about completing homework?
Student	Finding the time, really.
Teacher	Why is that hard?

[The student tells the teacher that he works in a pub three nights a week, and that when he finds time for college work he is often too tired to concentrate. The money, it seems, is needed to finance the student's car.]

Teacher	So what do you plan to do about this problem?
Student	Cut down on the pub work – maybe I could just work weekends.
Teacher	What about the money for the car?
Student	I'll ask my mum if I can get a motorbike, but she's not keen on them.
Teacher	OK, talk to your mum and tell me on Monday what you have decided. But don't tell your mum I said you should have a motorbike!

[On Monday the student says his mother will lend him money to finance his car, if he will work for her during the summer holidays.]

One advantage of this method over a 'telling off' is that the *real* problem is much more likely to be discovered, and students are committed to the solution because they suggested it. A further advantage is that it fosters independent problem-solving in the student.

Beware of expecting too much from this technique, if the problem is deep-seated. If the evaluation shows the student has not responded, try making him or her feel guilty: 'I'm really disappointed in you, Charlie. I thought you were the sort to keep your promises...' But be ready to believe Charlie if he makes another promise.

Common causes of persistent 'discipline' problems

Don't let the following alarm you; you may never experience any of them, but awareness of the problem is often enough to avoid it, so I make no apologies for mentioning them.

Inappropriate work

Satan finds work for idle hands to do. Is the work too easy or too difficult? Is it clearly defined? Has the task been going on so long that students are bored? Does the student finish very quickly? You must do your best to make sure every student has something to do all the time, and that you are available to give help where necessary.

Students testing the teacher

This is 'playing up' the teacher. Often students tend to behave increasingly inappropriately until your response is sufficiently firm to prevent further deterioration. They are experimenting to find out where you draw the lines. The 'case law' which results defines what they can 'get away with'.

Be strict but fair, and *never appear flustered* even when you are angry. If you deal confidently, consistently and firmly with this playing up, it will soon lose its attraction for the students. Consider carefully the contents of this and the previous chapter.

If you feel uncomfortable about being assertive, then read the following canon immediately before and after every lesson for a week!

1. It is entirely appropriate for me to use my teacher's authority, as long as I use it in the interests of my students' learning.

2. If I use my teacher's authority effectively, I may well upset some students for a short time. If I use it *in*effectively, I will upset them all for a long time.

3. If I do my best to be strict but fair, eventually I will succeed.

If you are challenged, or find yourself in a difficult situation, try hard not to over-react – or under-react. You may find it helpful to make it clear that:

- You have a right to be obeyed: 'I am the teacher here, and what I say goes.'

- You are acting in the learners' best interests: 'I am moving you because it is clear to me that you, and the rest of the class, will learn much better if you sit over here.'

Try also to make it clear that your final statements are not negotiable, but that you are prepared to discuss any matter with a student in private after the lesson. You may find the 'broken record' technique helpful here. Keep repeating what you have decided, in a calm but very positive and determined way. It helps to acknowledge the feelings of the student, even if you don't sympathise with them, but keep repeating your decision. Remember to 'PEP' up what you say with proximity and eye-contact. Here is an example:

Teacher	John, I asked you to pack the equipment away.
Student	Phil will do it, miss, it's his turn.
Teacher	He's still doing his graph. I want *you* to pack it away.
Student	But it's Phil's turn!
Teacher	Even though it's Phil's turn, I want you to pack the equipment away.
Student	But only ...
Teacher	*[Faces the student with constant eye contact, confident posture, and close proximity.]* If you want to discuss this matter, see me after the class. Meanwhile, pack the equipment away.

Once students realise you do not easily change your mind, you will find the broken record even more effective, and eventually almost unnecessary.

This dogged persistence usually works, but if it does, don't gloat – you will only make enemies, and in any case it is more impressive to take the victory for granted. If it doesn't work, wait in determined silence for a few seconds, then simply walk away (removing the immediate pressure sometimes allows the student to back down without losing too much face). If you do walk away, write something down for a few moments without paying too much attention to the student (though he or she should know you are recording the interchange). Don't say in detail what you are writing. If the student has still not complied, say very confidently and sternly (do not say 'please' or 'thank you') that you will see him or her after the class.

Throughout the conversation you must appear, certainly relaxed and confident, maybe stern and determined, perhaps almost menacing, but never flustered or rattled. You should try never to lose that inner stillness that conveys authority. A tall order? Yes, it is! But anger is nearly always counterproductive; it tends to produce an angry response from some students, leading to a situation which is out of control. When you are more experienced, you may be able to put on a stately anger that maintains your dignity and sense of authority; until then it is better to avoid appearing anything more than very stern. If you don't get angry, it's no fun 'playing you up', and you are less likely to be 'tested'.

Give yourself time and space when dealing with problems; don't leap to judgments. Leave difficult situations till the end of the class, and deal with the students on a one-to-one basis when you are both calmer.

Don't worry too much about outright defiance. It is very rare if you are firm, fair and confident.

Attention-seeking

Attention-seeking students are usually extrovert, and seem to enjoy the attention of the teacher and the class even if this attention is negative. Classmates may call such students 'show-offs', while teachers who can't think beyond the inconvenience caused to themselves may categorise them as 'buffoons' or 'class clowns'.

The best strategy is to accept the need for attention, but encourage the student to get this attention through 'legitimate' means. Give lots of attention for learning-related activities, and as little attention as possible for the disruptive attention-seeking behaviour. The latter is difficult, but the former isn't.

Such students can be very difficult to deal with, though their craving for attention makes them easy to 'bribe':

'That's quite a good start, Cynthia – a good opening sentence... When you've finished up to question three, let me know and I'll mark it straight away.'

'Good diagram started here, Cynthia, I'd like to have another look when it's finished.'

'I would like someone from your group to take notes on your findings, and report them back to the rest of the class. OK, Cynthia, you can do it if you like. Make sure you keep good notes, so you can tell the rest of the class what your group decided.'

[After giving a neighbour of Cynthia some conspicuous attention for having completed a task] 'Now, Cynthia, have you finished too? No?' *[Walk away]*

Show a meticulous fascination in every aspect of the student's work and anything that relates to it, and react as little as possible to attention-seeking behaviour. The main difficulty for the teacher is that you must give valuable time and attention to a student that you may dislike. Such students give teachers a stark choice: give attention for legitimate activities, or they will steal it for disruptive ones.

The seating position of such students should be thoughtfully considered. They are best placed well away from admirers, and next to students who ignore them.

Remember that for all students being able to sit where they like is a privilege, certainly not a right. Experienced teachers have no hesitation in moving students; inexperienced teachers tend to fear the temporary disapproval this engenders, and so make life much more difficult for themselves.

The teacher uses formal authority ineffectively

If your response to the kind of 'testing' mentioned above is not vigilant or firm enough, you may experience rudeness, open lack of respect and even outright defiance. You may also notice that many students who once behaved reasonably well are beginning to join in, and the riot syndrome – a negative 'ripple effect' – causes the misbehaviour to spread.

This is alarming for the teacher concerned, but it is often just an extreme example of 'testing'. If you are strict in your consistent application of classroom rules, and you refuse to get really rattled, you will eventually establish control. Nevertheless, tell someone you are having difficulties, and seek help and advice. Everyone experiences difficulties from time to time. I certainly have. You needn't feel it is an admission of failure to seek expert advice. We all need help when we are learning! If you hit a problem, re-reading this chapter and the previous one may help.

There is a breach of discipline but no culprit

Who threw that paper dart? Who said that swear word? You can try to avoid this problem by 'with-itness'; but if it does happen, what do you do if no one owns up? Don't over-react by punishing the whole class, as this will be deeply resented. Don't accuse someone unless you are certain.

Quieten the class and then ask who did it; when (as is almost certain) no-one admits to the misdemeanour, do your best to use this to your advantage:

'If you haven't got the nerve to say it to my face – don't say it at all.'
'I see, so the culprit hasn't got the courage to stand up for what they've done.'

In this way the perpetrator is seen to be sheepish and cowardly rather than smart, so repeat performances are less likely. Someone might even own up; if they do, thank them for their honesty and deal with them as you feel fit, preferably alone. If there is still no admission, it is usually better to move on and forget it; you can do nothing without cast-iron evidence. But increase your vigilance – you can't afford to let it happen again straight away.

Dealing with problems that won't go away

Before explaining the strategies that can be used to deal with really persistent problems, I will deal with some of the techniques that may be useful.

Talking to students one-to-one

If a problem is persistent, one should obviously talk to the student about it. But how? Try the straight-talking 'adult to adult' style first, even if your every instinct is to tell the student off (if not strangle him). Anger is rarely your best adviser.

However, there will be times when an 'adult to child' approach is more appropriate.

'Adult to child' style

There are times when a student needs a good telling off! How should this be done? Enormous pressure can be put on a student in this way; the technique needs to be used with care, and in conjunction with problem-solving techniques. (If the student cries, relax the pressure and if possible revert to a more 'adult to adult' style – though this might be better accomplished the next day.)

Talk alone. Remember the 'PEP' technique from the previous chapter. Face the student squarely, move too close for comfort, use almost constant eye to eye contact. Don't act in an aggressive way, and don't touch the student. If you are flustered, hide it, and think through carefully what you are going to say before you say it.

Ask questions in a stern and extremely self-confident manner. Don't be afraid of silences after your questions; they create a great deal of pressure on the student. Don't launch into a tirade of criticism; your body language and your questions put much more pressure on the student than anything you can say. Never be venomous or sarcastic in anything you say, and relate your criticism to the student's learning or safety.

Make it absolutely clear you are doing this for the student's own good, not to 'get your own back' or for any self-centred reason. If you are sure the telling off has been effective, it sometimes pays to extract a promise and then try to end up on reasonable terms. Here is an example.

Emma (13 years old) threw a pencil after being told not to. She was then asked to see the teacher after the class. The teacher speaks more slowly than usual, and tries to appear absolutely in control. Remember, it's the body language that does the real talking.

Teacher	Let's get this straight. If I tell you not to do something – you don't do it. Is that clear?
Student	*[Silence]*
Teacher	Is – that – clear? *[Silence with sustained eye contact; then:]*
Student	Yes, Miss.
Teacher	Do you know why I don't want pencil-throwing in my classes?

Student	Because we're not supposed to throw things, Miss.
Teacher	Yes, but why ?
	[The student can't think of anything, but you leave a long silence with constant eye contact]
	... Well? ... Safety, Emma, safety. I am responsible for your safety and that of the class. Now, what's wrong with throwing pencils?
Student	Could get in someone's eye.
Teacher	That's right. And what effect would that have?
Student	*[Silence]*
Teacher	*[After some time with constant eye contact]* What effect would that have?
Student	*[Silence]*
Teacher	How would *you* feel if *your* eye was damaged by someone throwing a pencil?
Student	*[More silence - but Emma is clearly upset]*
Teacher	*[In a more friendly style, but still firmly]* OK. How about a promise?
Student	*[Still no response yet]*
Teacher	*[Quietly]* Well? Will you promise not to throw pencils in future?
Student	Yes, Miss.
Teacher	Good. And you'll do what I say in future?
Student	Yes, Miss.
Teacher	*[In a friendlier tone]* OK then, Emma, you can go.

NEVER touch a student during 'adult to child' talk; the student may interpret it as an attack and strike you in 'retaliation'. DON'T show aggression. Never allow a student to walk away or turn away: 'Look at me when I'm talking to you.'

This technique puts far more pressure on the student than any punishment, or any 'lecture', but if you find yourself relying on it then you are failing to diagnose the real problem. If you talk to a student like this in the class, make sure they have their back to the class or they might 'play to the gallery'. They may also resent the 'put down' in front of their peers, and respond badly. Older students will certainly resent this technique if taken too far. If you are fairly sure a student will 'answer back', don't use this technique, especially in front of a class. Instead, use the 'broken record' technique to emphasise indisputable fact or a well-known class rule. Many students will try to draw you into an argument – don't be tempted. Stay on ground where you know you can't lose, by repeating the fact or rule:

'But I was explaining fractions to Paul!' – 'You know very well you are not to talk when I'm talking.'

In an exchange like this, a good natured laugh or smile can drop the temperature and show your confidence. Criticise behaviour, never criticise the student.

A 'chat'	A 'word'	A 'telling off'
Non-directive adult to adult style	**Parent to adult style**	**Directive parent to child style**

Teacher's implied message:
'I think you are willing and able to solve your own problems.' 'I respect you as an individual and have some sympathy for your difficulties.'

Teacher's implied message:
'I think you need some pressure to solve your own problems.'

Teacher's implied message:
'You are a perishing nuisance and I don't like you.' 'You can't solve your own problems.'

Technique:
ask probing questions and LISTEN: 'What do you find most difficult ...?'

Technique:
set clear targets; tell the student the consequences if the target is not met; evaluate the achievement of the targets. (A persistent series of meetings may be necessary.)

Technique:
'PEP' – proximity, eye-contact, pose questions and/or use 'broken record': 'Why haven't you...?' 'Do you realise the consequences of this behaviour?'

Style and body language:

supportive/encouraging
non-judgmental
accepting
listening

Style and body language:

— [Continuum] →

Style and body language:

dictatorial
judgmental
directing
telling

Likely student reaction:
co-operative

Likely student reaction:
compliant

Likely student reaction:
resentful but compliant

A summary of three approaches

The box above shows an expanded summary of what we have been discussing. Three separate approaches are distinguished, but really they form a continuum: for example, the adult to adult example on page 83 was a mixture of a 'chat' and a 'word'. To respond appropriately, you must choose the right approach to fit the student and the situation. Beware if your personality gives you a strong bias to a particular approach.

Escalate your response to repeated inappropriate behaviour

If you have a persistent problem with a class or individual, your response to that problem may be ineffective. You must change the response if it doesn't work! This idea is simple but critical, and often overlooked. If you find yourself saying 'For heaven's sake, how many times have I told you not to...?!!', then stop and think: why are you using a response you have proved does not work? A response to misbehaviour should not be tried more than two or three times consecutively with the same student. After this, change or escalate your response, or threaten to do so.

> If you're in a hole, stop digging!

If you habitually respond in the same way, the students will begin to feel secure about repeating the inappropriate behaviour: 'He only tells you off if you talk, so I'll have another chat with Mandy.' You must gradually increase the severity of your response, until the gain the student experiences from the inappropriate behaviour is no longer worth the unpleasant consequences of being caught at it. Only steady escalation will help you discover what is a sufficient deterrent.

> If you always do what you've always done,
> You'll always get what you've always got.

Teachers who are very good at maintaining control often have a wide range of reactions to inappropriate behaviour. This means they are rarely at a loss, and are always able to move to a new reaction if a previous one did not work. The list below is roughly in order of severity; it would, of course, be up to you to choose which techniques are appropriate in any given situation. I certainly do not suggest that you work mechanically through the list in every case, but if the strategy you are using is ineffective, try one a little further down the list. (You may like to make up your own list, using this one as a guide.)

- Look at the student.
- Sustain eye contact.
- Move towards student maintaining eye contact.
- Remain close to the student
- Shake your head or frown while looking at the student.

(All these first five techniques can be used without interrupting teacher talk etc.)

- Stop talking and look at the student until they notice your attention; sustain eye contact in silence, then continue.
- Point at the student (e.g. during a class practical).
- Use the student's name without explanation: 'Then, *[John]*, I'll look at Act II.'
- Ask the student a work-related question.
- Ask the student to explain some aspect of the work to the rest of the class.
- Stop what you are doing, and ask the student in a firm voice to stop the behaviour. This can be done in public, but is best one-to-one.
- Do the above with more non-verbal pressure – e.g. sustained eye contact in silence, stern voice, while standing close to the student. Ask the student a question about the behaviour.

- Speak to the student after the class, using 'adult to adult' style. Set targets and evaluate these. Repeat as necessary.
- Punish the student by giving him or her an irksome task, preferably not work-related. Make sure the task is done alone.
- Threaten to move the student.
- Move the student.
- Put the student 'on report' – that is, he or she must show work done to you at the end of the lesson, or after every lesson in the week.
- Threaten to report the student to a higher authority / to his or her tutor.
- Report the student. Keep the higher authority updated verbally on the student's subsequent behaviour. Tell the student this. (Don't be afraid to ask for help from experienced staff or from your teacher education tutor. It is not an admission of failure to ask for advice.)
- Threaten to move the student to an isolated position in the room.
- Move the student to an isolated position.
- As the student's behaviour has not improved, keep the higher authority to whom you have reported up to date on the student's behaviour – do this on paper, and make it clear you keep a copy. It may prove helpful. Tell the student you are doing this.
- Threaten to ask a senior teacher to talk to the student.
- Carry out the above threat.

- *In response to misbehaviour that has been constantly repeated, despite every attempt to stop it:*

  Stop what you are doing. Move away from the student if you are close, and get a piece of paper; ask someone for the date and the exact time. Coolly write down the behaviour on the piece of paper, saying: 'OK. I've had enough. If this is the way you want it, so be it.' *Do not say what will happen to your piece of paper.* If asked, be studiedly vague: 'You'll see.' This will almost certainly stop the student misbehaving. Give a copy to the tutor responsible for the student.

- *In response to outright defiance:*

  As immediately above. This removes you from the confrontation, and some students will 'back down' almost as soon as the pressure is released. It is essential that defiance is reported. It is widely accepted in the profession that you should not be expected to teach students who are not prepared to accept your authority in the classroom, for safety reasons if for no other.

- Contracts. The student agrees, in writing, to a code of behaviour. The student should then be 'forgiven' and fully accepted back into the fold.
- In addition to all the above, your school or college may have standard forms of punishment.

Exactly what you do is less important than the fact that you increase the severity of your response, and that you appear confident and in control at all times. Changing tactics leaves the student uncertain of the consequences of repeating a misdemeanour. This uncertainty acts as a deterrent.

Never physically handle or hit a student. Do not send a student out of a class unless you have been told this is acceptable. If you do send a student out of a class, you are responsible for anything the student does in class time.

Don't bear grudges. Try very hard not to *show* resentment towards a student who is causing you trouble. I know this is very hard, but if you show resentment the student may retaliate. A student who believes you dislike him or her will make your job much more difficult.

Having threatened a student, you must carry out this threat to the letter if the student persists; otherwise, your credibility will go down in the eyes of the students, and should you make another threat it will not be taken seriously. Only consistency will give your authority credibility. For this reason, it is very important not to get so angry with a student that you deliver a threat that you regret, or that you could not carry out! Long before you get really angry, pretend that you have reached the end of your tether and 'act angry' with the student; that way you are more likely to appear in control. *Use* your temper, don't *lose* your temper.

Sometimes it is better to say 'I will see you about this after the class.' than to rush to hasty threats or punishments. This gives you time to think, and the student time to reconsider.

Make sure you have your facts right before you reprimand a student.

ABC

ABC stands for antecedent – behaviour – consequences. Behaviourist psychologists suggest that inappropriate behaviour is triggered by a situation they call the antecedent, and that the behaviour usually has desirable consequences for the misbehaving student. Behaviour can be changed by changing either the antecedent and/or the consequences.

Avoid the antecedent that triggers the behaviour. If students squabble when they collect equipment, give the equipment out yourself or elect a student to do so. If students arriving late disrupt the teacher-talk introduction to your classes, start the lesson with group or individual activities. If a class cannot maintain concentration for longer than two minutes, then don't talk for longer than a minute and a half at a time. I followed this approach with a particularly difficult group: I communicated with an overhead projector (OHP), with handouts, by talking one at a time to a series of small groups, and with the blackboard which I prepared before the lesson.

This transformed the lessons. I wasn't frustrated by students' poor concentration or their interruptions; and secondly, these methods of communication released me from teacher talk, so I could give my undivided attention to firefighting and to praising and encouraging students who were working well.

Avoid situations you know cause problems. Why struggle over a wall when you can walk round it?

If you can't change the antecedents, see if you can change the consequences. If you repeatedly come across a problem, ask yourself 'What are the students getting out of this inappropriate behaviour?' – then try to remove these gains. For example, suppose you are having difficulties with students packing up their folders five minutes before the end of the session. You can't change the antecedent, which is that the lesson is near its end, so what are the consequences *for the students*? They do less work! You could change this consequence by asking students who pack up early to summarise the main points of the lesson for you, or to answer searching questions on the lesson. If packing up early begins to mean *more* rather than less work, then this type of work-avoidance behaviour will naturally disappear.

Sandra was repeatedly late to my classes, and she played the class clown when giving excuses for her lateness. The consequences for her were that she got attention from the class. I made it clear that from now on I wanted written excuses for lateness, and the behaviour disappeared. If students don't gain from their misbehaviour, then the behaviour usually ceases.

However, the problem with denying needs is that, however successful in the short term, it leaves those needs unsatisfied, and the student may seek their fulfilment in some other way. Attention seekers and students who are bored, frustrated or angry are not easily put off; if you close one door, they will soon find another. Can you discover what these students really want – perhaps attention, or an opportunity to be a leader – and give this to them in a legitimate activity?

> Student teachers often complain of the lack of attention of some students in their class while they are talking. What are the antecedents and the consequences for this behaviour? Can you think of solutions to this problem? There are answers in the box at the bottom of page 96. (No, don't look – think the answer out for yourself first!)

Authority without resentment

There is a difference between authoritarianism and the vigorous use of legitimate authority. The former is resented and the latter is not. Suppose your ship sank on a cruise, and you and the other passengers were marooned with the captain on the proverbial desert island. What principles should be followed by the system the captain might use to maintain 'law and order'? Most people would suggest the following guidelines:

■ **There must be equality before the law.**
The objective of the law must be to protect the interests of all its subjects equally. It should not be used to the unfair advantage of a privileged minority or those in authority. If subjects believe the law benefits the law-makers and law-keepers, rather than themselves, then they may well revolt (the 'revolution' syndrome). The law, including case law, should be widely understood.

■ **The law must be effectively policed.**
Ideally the policing should be conspicuous and effective, and transgressors should know they stand a good chance of being caught. If a law is not enforced effectively, at least some members of the community will consider the law inoperative. (For example, it is illegal to travel at 75 mph on the motorway, but many travel at this speed, believing the police will not charge them.) If policing is conspicuously absent, then law breaking can become widespread; even the usually law-abiding may then take advantage and join in the lawless behaviour (the 'looting' syndrome).

■ **Policing should be seen to be fair.**
If an element of the community believes it is being 'picked on', harassed, or kept down by policing, then respect for the law and its enforcement diminishes, and it can even be seen as an instrument of oppression.

> During difficulties in Toxteth in 1988 the police started 'saturation policing'. This caused resentment in the black community, who complained of being harassed. Eventually resentment at this perceived injustice caused serious riots, and millions of pounds of damage was caused.

■ **Subjects should have a right to a fair trial.**
Subjects should have a right to a fair hearing, and the decisions of the court should be seen as impartial, consistent, and equally fair to all subjects.

> In Los Angeles in 1992, a court saw a widely broadcast amateur video showing four white policemen beating a black motorist, Rodney King, whom they had pinned to the ground. The man sustained nine fractures to the skull and was in intensive care for some time. The court found the policemen not guilty on all charges. Riots ensued in which 60 people died.

■ **Punishment should be fair and sufficiently onerous.**
Likely punishments should also be well known, and they should be severe enough to have a deterrent effect. Where possible, punishment should attempt to achieve rehabilitation of the transgressor. After accepting punishment, the subjects should be welcomed back into the fold without bitterness.

> At the end of the First World War the German people were made to give up German land, and to pay reparations to the allies. Most historians now recognise this as a dreadful if understandable mistake. The German people were seething with resentment at the reparations; they saw them as a humiliation, and looked round for someone to restore German pride. This led to the rise of Hitler, and to the Second World War. If a punishment is perceived (eventually) by the miscreant as being fair, it is effective. If it is perceived as being unfair, it may actually encourage further law-breaking.

Law and order in the classroom

If the general principles above are applied to the classroom, class rules should be based on educational, moral and safety criteria only. They should not be seen by students as being primarily for the teacher's benefit. The rules and their purposes should be well understood. The rules should be equally applied to all students. It may help to emphasise that the rules are there to benefit the *students* in the class, not just the teacher. Some teachers involve their students in rule-making and the maintenance of order.

Policing

Make sure you are constantly 'on the beat', enforce the rules conspicuously, and be vigilant. However, don't harass individuals. It is perceptions that count here. If a student *feels* harassed, or 'picked on', he or she might rebel, making future class management more difficult. It makes little difference if students are wrong in feeling picked on (unless they can be *persuaded* they are wrong); it is not reality that determines behaviour, but perceptions.

If a student feels picked on, tell other students off for the same offence (preferably within earshot) before repeating a criticism of the 'harassed' student. Escalating your response can avoid the need to nag a student for repeating a misbehaviour.

Fair trial and punishment

Don't punish unless you are clear about the facts. Listen to excuses, don't punish in anger, be consistent. Only those who have transgressed should be punished; don't punish a whole class. After punishment, *show* that you don't bear grudges, e.g. by showing an interest in the student's work, smiling etc.

Suggested answers to the problem on page 94

The antecedent is that the teacher is using teacher talk, so use teacher talk less often, and for shorter periods. The consequence of inattention is that the student avoids work. If every student who shows inattention is asked a question, then the behaviour actually *increases* work rate - and so should die out!

Unsolvable problems

> God, give me the grace to accept the things I cannot change, the courage to change the things I can – and the wisdom to know the difference.

Don't blame yourself for failing to deal with difficulties caused by factors beyond your control – for example, severe local unemployment, or family and emotional problems. Those that are unloved become unlovable; all we can do is try to treat such unlucky creatures as professionally as we can.

> *From an NSPCC poster:* 'He drinks, he smokes, he spits at his teacher... What he needs is a damned good cuddle.'

Many criticise our educational system because it recognises and rewards intellectual skills, but in comparison ignores, for example, manual skills, creative skills and personal skills, even though these are of great personal and economic importance. Students with these non-intellectual skills feel undervalued, and as a result tend to reject the system they feel has rejected *them*. Many 'behaviour' problems are really curriculum problems.

It is beyond the scope of this book to look into this problem in any detail, but here is an exercise to make the point. Mark each type of skill listed below out of ten, first for use and then for value.

N.B. 'Use' = usefulness in the real world, e.g. in commerce and industry, or at home.
'Value' = value and reward given them by schools and by post-school education.

Use   Value

Intellectual skills: Academic skills in any subject: arts or sciences, humanities.

Manual skills: Any skills that involve coordination of hands and eye: woodwork, metalwork, electronic assembly, dressmaking, etc.

Creative skills: Ability in design. Ability to create, in the visual and other arts. Ability to think up new ideas or use established ideas in a new way. Ability to be proactive rather than reactive, e.g. entrepreneurial skills.

Self-organisational skills: e.g. being organised and dependable, able to work unsupervised.

Interpersonal skills: Ability to work well in a team; ability to lead or to motivate others; sensitivity to others; caring skills; ability to cope with difficult emotional situations, being 'good with people'.

Vocationally specific skills: Knowledge and capability specific to a vocation or profession.

Comment on any discrepancy you find between the marks for 'use' and 'value', and its effect on learning – bearing in mind that success is a prerequisite for learning, and that students will tend to value an education which values their skills.

This simple exercise raises more questions than it answers; for example, how teachable or examinable are these skills? To some extent the problems raised are beginning to be addressed, with the moves towards vocational education and common or core skills.

If, with some groups, discipline is a problem even for experienced teachers, then there is something wrong. Often the problem is that the students do not see the educative experience as being in their own interest. Frankly, they are sometimes correct in this perception. If a curriculum consistently condemns a student as a failure, then the student may well retaliate by condemning the curriculum and those charged with delivering it. The solution for such problems lies in developing a curriculum that is perceived by students as being in their own best interests. This may be done in part by valuing every student's attempts to learn, and by developing a curriculum which recognises such a wide variety of skills that most students have a chance of having some of their abilities recognised and valued.

> 'My argument is that our present secondary school system ... exerts on many pupils ... a destruction of their dignity which is so massive and persuasive that few subsequently recover from it'. – *David Hargreaves*

Don't, in your difficulties, lose sight of your most powerful ally, the use of re-inforcement for good behaviour. An American-inspired system called 'assertive discipline' has recently been introduced in some British schools. In outline, six rules are displayed in every classroom. Pupils are told they must arrive quietly and on time for lessons; bring everything they need; remain seated unless asked to move; follow instructions the first time they are given; raise their hand before speaking; and treat others, their work, and their belongings with respect. There is nothing surprising here, so why are teachers using the system almost universally enthusiastic? Why does it work? Because of reinforcement. Students who obey all six rules get an 'R' for reward in the teacher's register every class. Six letter Rs earn a 'Bronze' letter of commendation, noting their high standards of behaviour, to take home to their parents. Silver and Gold certificates can be earned for more 'R's.

This was a school-wide initiative, of a kind which you will not be in a position to institute by yourself. But the principle is what counts: reward good behaviour with recognition, encouragement and praise.

At the top of the next page is a 'mind-map' for the topic of discipline. (You might like to ask your students to prepare mind-maps for the topics you teach; research shows they aid understanding and memory.)

- Clear and concise
- Educational justification
- students see rules as for maximising learning
- Punishment known in advance

Rules

- Tasks are interesting, varied and student-centred
- Clear attainable objectives

Effective lessons

Praise good behaviour

Good Organisation

- Clear directions
- Everyone has something to do

- Alertness or 'with it-ness
- Rapid response
- Assertive reaction: proximity, eye contact, 'pep' pose questions
- Consistent; 'firm but fair'

Policing rules

Discipline

Good rapport

- Patience
- Individuals are praised often
- Names and smiling
- Equal opportunities
- No apparent likes or dislikes
- Interest is shown in students as individuals
- Humour and fun

Trial and punishment

- Innocent until proven guilty
- Clear case law
- Not vindictive - the aim is seen to be to maximise learning

Targets
- Attainable and short term, plus:
- Stretching targets for the able

Reinforcement
- Praise
- Rapid feedback after success

Motivation 'SPERT'

Enjoyment
- Interest
- Fun, curiosity
- Challenge and competition
- Student relevance and human interest
- Variety

Success — Attainable goals

Purpose
- Point of study is clear
- Study is related to 'outside world'

This 'mind-map' summarises the last few chapters. Try using mind-maps in your teaching.

Exercise: 'Problem page'

Can you solve these real-life problems? They have all been experienced by learning teachers. Some suggested answers follow.

1. 'My class is very difficult to get started at the beginning of a lesson. They are noisy and unsettled every week, and won't concentrate on what I say. I think it's because they have Mr Jones just before.'

2. 'The class are reasonably OK when they are doing written work activities, but as soon as they start a practical activity they go barmy.'

3. 'I was telling a girl off for being late when there was a comment I didn't hear from someone in the class, and she then collapsed into a fit of giggles.'

4. 'I teach firemen first aid. They seem to think it is a blow to their dignity to be taught by a woman, and they do everything they can to question my authority.'

5. 'One student in my computer class always finishes before the others; then she causes problems by distracting others in the group.'

6. 'Whenever I dismiss the class, Paul always runs out at breakneck speed to get to the coffee machine first. I tell him off, but it makes no difference.'

7. 'Kevin is a pain. He wants attention all the time, and he keeps bossing the others about. I've tried but I can't stop him. He's quite able, but can't concentrate for more than a few minutes. When he finishes the task he distracts me from helping the less able students in the group.'

Further reading

Gray and Richt, *Classroom Responses & Disruptive Behaviour*, Routledge (ISBN 0–415–08428–8)

Answers to the exercise

I am assuming that the lessons are well planned and interesting, and that there is plenty of reinforcement for success. These are skeleton suggestions only.

1. Don't use teacher talk at the start of the lesson. Give them something to do and go round firefighting, praising, and setting them.

2. Talk to the class about it, and ask for their cooperation; it sounds as though they enjoy the practicals. Plan activities with great care, and threaten not to use friendship groups. Open a really interesting practical by threatening to withdraw it if they are noisy. Firefight at the start of the practical, praising individual groups for sensible behaviour.

3. Never start a battle you may not win. Tell her you will see her after the class, and try to settle down, then do your best to ignore her.

4. Tell them your qualifications. Act in a calm, relaxed and confident way. If you teach well, sooner or later you will get their respect.

5. Give the class an interesting, stretching, 'fun' activity to do when they have completed the routine work.

6. Change the antecedent. Dismiss the class in order of completing the last task, or by rows. Alternatively, dismiss Paul if he runs.

7. See the section on attention-seeking. Give his work plenty of attention while he is doing it. Can you get him to help the others when he has finished his tasks?

10 What kind of teacher are you?

Here is a questionnaire designed to evaluate yourself as a teacher, according to a specific method of analysis. The background to the questionnaire is explained later. Think of your teaching situation or intended teaching situation, and answer the questions from your 'teacher's' point of view. Answer the questions honestly; don't try to guess the 'right' answer. There is no need to tell anyone about your score.

Teacher's self-analysis questionnaire

Tick the appropriate column to show your opinion:

YES! =	emphatically yes	yes =	on the whole, yes
NO! =	emphatically no	no =	on the whole, no

	YES!	yes	no	NO!

1. On the whole, students come to school or college reluctantly.

2. Most learners can do well on an appropriate course if the teaching is good.

3. The subject I teach is rewarding and interesting to learn.

4. Most learners don't like their work being appraised by the teacher.

5. Learners can be divided into two groups: those who want to get on, and those who want to get away with as little work as possible.

6. Most learners can be motivated by an effective teacher.

7. Every learner works best with plenty of individually-given praise and positive reinforcement.

8. Learners are reluctant to learn unless they are firmly directed.

9. Most students like an orderly, well-managed environment in which to work.

10. Bright students are difficult to control.

11. It is only natural for students to do as little work as possible.

12. There is always a reason for the way students behave.

13. 'What's in it for me?' is a legitimate question for learners to ask about a course.

14. On the whole, if learners fail to learn it is the fault of the teacher, the school, the curriculum, or poor resourcing.

15. Most learners learn to their maximum.

16. What learners want and what teachers want is different, therefore they can never see eye to eye about work rate.

17. Work of a low standard deserves strong criticism.

18. Teachers should be prepared to put their foot down if necessary, even at the risk of temporary unpopularity.

19. It encourages inattention if the teacher helps students who don't listen the first time.

20. Teachers should go out of their way to behave positively towards students whom they know do not like work.

21. The subject I teach requires natural flair – either you can do it or you can't.

22. Students should be threatened with punishment if they do not work.

23. Learners nearly always accept constructive criticism, as they know it helps them improve.

24. Students welcome work if they are given a chance to succeed.

Scoring

For each question number, please circle the mark corresponding to the answer you chose in the questionnaire. E.g. if you answered 'no' to question 1, score 3; if you answered 'YES!' to question 5, score *minus* 5.

	YES!	yes	no	NO!		YES!	yes	no	NO!
1.	-3	0	3	5	13.	5	3	-2	-3
2.	5	3	-3	-5	14.	5	5	-3	-3
3.	5	5	-3	-5	15.	-5	-2	2	5
4.	-3	0	3	5	16.	-3	-3	3	5
5.	-5	3	3	3	17.	-5	-2	3	5
6.	5	2	-5	-5	18.	5	3	-3	-5
7.	5	3	-3	-5	19.	-5	-3	2	5
8.	-3	0	0	0	20.	5	3	-3	-5
9.	5	2	-3	-5	21.	-5	-3	3	5
10.	-5	-3	3	5	22.	-2	2	0	0
11.	-5	-3	3	5	23.	5	3	2	-2
12.	5	3	-3	-5	24.	3	5	-2	-3

Positive score [   ]   Negative score [   ]

TOTAL SCORE [   ]

1. Add all your positive scores together and put the total in the positive score box at the bottom.
2. Add all your negative scores together and put the total in the negative score box.
3. Combine your positive and negative scores by addition. E.g. +75 -25 = +50.
4. Read off below the findings which are appropriate to your final score.

-100 to -40 Your attitudes are likely to produce learners who do as they are told and nothing more. Please read chapters 5, 6 and 7.

-39 to zero Your attitudes are likely to produce learners who only rarely show genuine interest in their work. Please read chapters 5, 6 and 7.

zero to +40 Your attitudes are likely to produce an average bunch of students who will do well on the whole; many of the more able will show some interest and enthusiasm for their work.

+41 to +100 You will produce students who are committed to learning (and to you), and they will find their work enjoyable and rewarding.

If you are unhappy with your score, reread the chapters on motivation and praise and criticism.

Background to the questionnaire

The questionnaire is very loosely based on Douglas McGregor's analysis of management styles in his book *The Human Side of Enterprise*.

Broadly speaking, teachers have two different assumptions about human nature. We can label these assumptions 'Theory X' and 'Theory Y'.

Theory X

- The average learner dislikes work and will avoid it if possible.
- Learning is difficult and not very interesting.
- Because learning is basically lacking in interest, most people must be coerced, controlled, directed, and threatened with punishment in order to learn satisfactorily.
- The average learner is passive, unambitious, and prefers to be directed rather than show initiative.

Theory Y

- In most learning situations learners only work to a fraction of their full capacity.
- Learning is rewarding and interesting.
- Learners have social, self-esteem and egoistic needs which they want to satisfy by their learning. They achieve this satisfaction by gaining respect and recognition for their successes.
- Students do not dislike work. Laziness, and lack of motivation or ambition, are not inherent human characteristics; they are reactions to unsatisfactory learning conditions.
- Learners can become committed to the goal of self-improvement.

Theory Y does not preclude the setting of targets, nor should it encourage low standards. According to Theory Y, the successful teacher must satisfy the self-esteem needs of the learner through activities directed towards the teaching aims. According to Theory X, the learner must be directed and coerced into carrying out these activities. In a strange sense both of these theories are correct. They both have a tendency to work as self-fulfilling prophecies. Theory X teaching can make students bored, passive and demotivated. Theory Y teaching can be inspiring, motivating students into self-improvement. To some extent, what the teacher thinks will happen is what the teacher gets.

Of course, students also have theories about teachers. Theory A is that the teacher is only in it for the money, and basically dislikes the students and the subject they are teaching. Theory B is that teachers are interested in students, in their efforts to learn, and in their subject. If a Theory Y teacher meets a Theory A class, it can take some time to turn the situation into one where learning is productive.

2 The teacher's toolkit

INTRODUCTION TO PART 2

In order to make an informed choice of teaching method, and in order to be adaptable and have a variety of activities for lesson planning, the teacher must know:

- what teaching methods are available;

- what are the strengths and weaknesses of these methods;

- what purpose each of them can serve;

- how each should be used in practice.

This is the purpose of this section of the book.

Which is the best teaching method? You might as well ask a carpenter which is his best tool; he chooses his tool depending on whether he wants to make a hole, remove a screw, or cut a piece of wood in two. Every tool has its uses, and good carpenters not only know how to use each tool, but are able to assess which is the most appropriate in a given circumstance. Teaching methods, like carpenters' tools, are chosen on the basis of fitness for purpose. As we will see in the chapters on lesson planning, the teacher should first clarify the purpose of the lesson and then choose an activity to achieve it.

What teaching methods do students prefer? This is not a deciding factor, but it is certainly an important one. Better for students to have 80% concentration on a moderately effective method than 10% concentration on a very effective one.

M. Hebditch asked 11- to 18-year-olds what teaching methods they preferred. The answers to his questionnaire are tabulated on the following page. Look at them carefully before reading on: what do their preferences have in common?

Students' preferences on teaching styles

Preferred styles	Like %	Dislike %	Neutral %
Group discussion	80	4	17
Games/simulations	80	2	17
Drama	70	9	22
Artwork	67	9	26
Design	63	4	33
Experiments	61	11	28
Options (choice allowed)	61	4	33
Computers	59	22	20
Exploring feelings (empathy)	59	11	30
Reading English literature	57	9	35
Practical ideas	52	9	37
Laboratory work	50	11	37
Library research	50	24	26
Charts, tables etc.	46	15	37
Craftwork	43	17	39
Fieldwork	43	20	35
Open-ended work	43	20	37
Themes	41	11	48
Creating products	41	11	43
Working alone	41	26	33
Invention	39	20	41
Organising data	37	20	43
Empathy	35	30	35
Observation	30	13	57
Worksheets	28	17	52
Reading for information	26	30	43
Using technology	24	26	46
Deadlines	24	50	26
Time schedules	17	41	41
Analysis	17	35	46
Theories	15	39	43
Essays	13	28	54
Lectures	11	70	19

Data collated from questionnaire submitted to students from 11 to 18 years and provided by M. Hebditch, Gillingham School, Dorset. 1990.

Students like action: talking in groups, making things, being creative, doing things. Passive methods get an emphatic thumbs-down; bottom of the list is 'lecture'. So don't fall for the commonly-believed myth that students are fundamentally lazy, preferring activities which intrude as little as possible into their daydreaming. In general, the more active and engaged students are, the better they like it.

Many teachers develop one or two teaching methods and stick to them. This is a mistake. A variety of methods – as well as increasing student attention and interest – gives you the flexibility to deal with the wide range of challenging and infuriating problems which teachers inevitably encounter. It also helps you deal with the increasing demands of the ever-changing teacher's role. In modern education, as in evolution, the motto is 'adapt to survive'.

There are other reasons for developing a varied set of tools in your teacher's toolkit. Students learn in different ways and only a variety of activities will ensure all students fulfil their potential. Variety also helps to make teaching a more stimulating and enjoyable experience for *you*. One-method teachers bore themselves as well as their students.

When it comes to trying out new teaching methods one could hardly do better than to take Sir Arnold Bax's advice: 'You should try everything once – except incest and folk dancing.' Teaching being what it is, though, you need in fact to try everything *three* times to find out if it works for you. Once may be an accident, twice could be a coincidence, but three times begins to look like a pattern.

Try as many teaching methods as you can. Be bold; as the chapter on learning by experience makes clear, it is only by risk-taking experimentation that you will discover which methods suit your purposes.

Don't be worried if you find that you can't make the methods work well the first time, or that students are initially reluctant to vary their diet. Keep practising and you will soon make them work. And remember, if you don't have the occasional disaster when you are learning how to teach, you are not experimenting enough.

Teacher talk

> 'If telling were teaching, we'd all be so smart we could hardly stand it.'
> – *R.F. Mager*

Teacher talk involves the teacher standing in front of the class and giving a verbal input. A teaching session may, of course, include many other activities besides teacher talk, but we will consider this teaching method in isolation here.

Teacher talk is the most commonly used teaching method, on average occupying at least 60% of most lessons. Certainly, it can help to provide explanations and 'doing-detail'; but crucially, it cannot provide for corrected practice and the other learner's needs outlined in Part 1. Devoting 60% of a lesson to teacher talk is clearly far too much. Good teachers know when to shut up!

Teacher talk is a teacher-centred or 'didactic' teaching method. What are its main advantages and disadvantages?

Advantages

- It is a convenient method for delivering an explanation.
- Unlike a book, it can be adapted to the correct 'level' for the class, and the content can be tailored to the needs of the class.
- It can be inspiring.
- Little preparation or resourcing is required for the experienced teacher.
- It is a rapid method of presenting material.
- It is a more personal method of communicating than written methods.

Disadvantages

- The teacher must go at the same pace with the whole class.
- Inexperienced teachers tend to deliver material too quickly.
- There is no feedback on whether understanding has taken place.
- It can be boring.
- There is no active student involvement.
- Backup is required to ensure that information is understood and remembered.
- Students' concentration span is shorter than for other learning methods.

- It assumes consenting students.

- Students are not given the opportunity to use the ideas being taught.

> 'When all can read, lectures will be unnecessary.' – *Ben Jonson, 1573-1637*

The talk trap

Most people talk at about 100 to 200 words per minute. At that rate, a one-hour lecture could contain up to 12,000 words – a short book!

Here is a simple calculation that compares the rate of delivery of material using teacher talk, with the rate of student comprehension:

> Even at a moderate rate, a teacher could read aloud to a class the whole of a typical GCSE textbook in about 10 hours, covering the entire syllabus in this time. The average GCSE course includes about 200 hours of teaching time. This means that, very roughly, teacher talk can deliver (even very appropriate) material at about twenty times the rate at which students are expected to learn it!

Is it any wonder that inexperienced teachers often 'lose' their classes when they use teacher talk? Teaching with teacher talk is rather like herding cows in a Lamborghini.

Imagine going to an evening class to study GCSE biology, and finding that the teacher simply read from a textbook, or sounded as if he or she was doing so. Why would this be unsatisfactory? Our short term memory would soon be swamped; with no time to process the new information, it would never become structured enough to pass into the long term memory, and so it would quickly be forgotten. Nor would we have any chance to practise *using* the ideas that we were learning. There is much more to teaching than telling.

Concentration span

While listening to teacher talk, the concentration span of some students is less than five minutes; that of undergraduates and sixth-formers is perhaps 15 to 20 minutes.

> 'A lecture is an event where information passes from the notes of the lecturer into the notes of the student, without passing through the minds of either.'

This short concentration span puts the near-exclusive use of teacher talk in some educational circles into a rather alarming perspective. Many former university students will remember the eerie experience of revising from lecture notes that are entirely unfamiliar, but in one's own handwriting!

109

Remember that, in effect, the short term memory soon gets filled up, and any new material simply replaces earlier material. Even if a teacher talk session is of moderate length, the teacher cannot guarantee the concentration of all the members of the class all of the time. During a ten-minute teacher talk session, almost every student will 'dream off' at least once, perhaps at a crucial point in the explanation. If you don't believe me, try maintaining 100% concentration throughout a thirty-minute radio documentary.

You must imagine that, for any given student, it is as though your teacher talk session has had sections cut out of it at random: from that student's point of view, your performance is rather like watching a video that is 'on the blink'. Yet your lesson *must* make sense to them, despite these random omissions. Clearly repetition of the most important points will be necessary – though these repetitions should of course be disguised as far as possible, to avoid boring the students who do listen well. Our inability to sustain 100% concentration is one reason why students appreciate summaries, especially at the end of a lesson or topic.

Teacher talk technique

As we have seen, many teachers use teacher talk too much; but most teachers use it a good deal, so it is worth looking at how to improve your technique.

It is fascinating to watch really effective teachers use teacher talk. Often they owe their effectiveness not to what they say but to the *way* they say it – in particular, their use of body language. They never sit behind a desk or bench, but stand close to the class unless they are using the board a great deal. They move around the classroom, facing first that group, then this, constantly making direct eye contact with students. The pitch and the volume of the voice changes a great deal to add emphasis, and there is much use of gesture and facial expression.

If a student should start to talk, they move over to stand next to them and stop them talking without a break in their delivery. Their presentation *appears* to be 'off the top of their head'; they will not be found reading with their face buried in a sheaf of papers. A new sentence or a new paragraph is usually signalled by a long pause, and often a change of posture or position.

Inexperienced teachers, by comparison, are self-conscious and rather flat in their presentation until they gain in confidence.

> Experienced teachers – indeed, able public speakers of any kind – tend to vary the pitch and volume of their voice at least three times as much when 'perform-Ing' as when they are not.

Hills (1979) found that when we are depressed we talk more slowly than usual, and with a lower pitch; when we are excited we talk faster and higher. If you want to convey enthusiasm you must be prepared to use your voice for that purpose. Listen to David Bellamy, David Attenborough or some other effective communicator – but don't listen to what they say, listen to *how* they say it. They have an excellent voice technique, they vary pitch and volume enormously, they convey enthusiasm by their lively delivery. Try to learn from these examples, but note that their style is natural and informal. Don't put on a formal 'announcer's voice'; this tends to distance you from the students.

> Hypnotists can put people to sleep with a monotone.

A problem many learning teachers have is that they repeat, over and over again, phrases such as 'OK?' or 'All right?', or they 'um', 'ah' or 'er' too much. To 'er' is human, but try not to overdo it. I once caught students recording with a five-bar gate the number of times a student teacher said 'Right, then.' They told me they had counted 82 in their one-hour lesson, but they were disappointed – it wasn't a record! Gestures or verbal habits that become mannerisms can be very distracting, but you may need someone to observe your teaching before you become aware of them.

Don't stare down at your boots or at the ceiling. Students feel 'included' if you look at them and if you face in their direction (eye contact and body-pointing). This requires that you rake the class with eye contact, and change the way you are facing from time to time – one reason why it is not a good idea to read from notes. If you must use notes, put them on the OHP or on the board before the lesson. The students will think you put them up for their benefit, when really they are there to jog your memory.

Without eye contact the class feels rejected. I remember a story, which I hope is an exaggeration, of a history lecturer at Edinburgh University who delivered a lecture to 200 students with his eyes closed throughout. It was a mannerism of his which he thought gave him the air of someone deep in intense concentration. At the end of the lecture, he found the students had all gone!

Clearly, *interest* must be considered very carefully when preparing for teacher talk, which most students agree tends inherently to be the most boring teaching method. This topic was dealt with in detail in Chapter 5 on motivation, where techniques such as human interest, student relevance, curiosity and puzzles were described.

Humour is greatly appreciated by nearly all students, except when they are the butt of your jokes. You don't have to be a professional stand-up comic to make a class laugh. I have heard them roar with laughter at the following:

> 'King John was a sod.'
> 'I will now demonstrate how to rip your arm off with a lathe.'

Don't hide behind a dour style; try rhetorical questions, humour, anecdotes, quotations, catch phrases, exaggeration, understatement – and don't be afraid to experiment!

Making the material easy to understand

First of all, make sure you avoid unexplained jargon and an oversophisticated general vocabulary – we looked at this in Chapter 4. Try to become familiar with the working vocabulary of the students you are teaching; alarm bells should ring when you go beyond this. Most teachers have at least twice the vocabulary of the average 16-year-old. (Of course, you should not be afraid to *teach* the meaning of unfamiliar words if they are genuinely important.)

Enhancement

Teacher talk can be made very much more effective by the use of visual aids: blackboards, overhead projectors, models, or other objects brought into the classroom. These are dealt with in later chapters.

One of the main methods of enlivening teacher talk is the use of questioning. This involves the students, and so overcomes some of the disadvantages of the basic teacher talk technique (see Chapter 15).

How do you know if your teacher talk is effective? As we saw in Chapter 4, this can only be decided by feedback from the students. What is their body language? Are they attending, or staring out of the window and shuffling in their seats?

Questioning also gives instant feedback on whether students are understanding you.

☑ Checklist

☐ Do you know your students' concentration span, and do you avoid exceeding it?

☐ Do you make your voice sound lively?

☐ Do you use eye contact and body-pointing?

☐ Do you use straightforward words in short sentences?

☐ Do you use humour, and human interest?

☐ Do you use student relevance?

☐ Do you appeal to curiosity with paradoxes and puzzles?

☐ Do you stand close to students and move your position occasionally?

☐ Is your voice loud enough?

Exercises

1. Listen to how professionals in the media use their voice; pay special attention to variation of pitch, volume etc.

2. Try testing the vocabulary of your students by giving them the list of words in Chapter 4 (you will find it on page 28).

3. Comment on the efficiency and use of the university-style lecture.

12 The art of explaining

Early in my teaching experience I encountered a student in my tutor group who regularly complained that one of her teachers had very poor explaining skills:

> 'If you ask him to explain, he just says the same thing over and over.'
> 'When I say I don't understand, he just says, "You should have listened the first time." – but I *was* listening.'

Most students on the course complained about this same teacher. One day I made the mistake of pointing out that the teacher was exceptionally well qualified in his subject. I was astonished by the anger in her reply: 'I'm sure he knows his stuff, but his brain doesn't appear to be connected to his mouth.'

Her frustration and bitterness demonstrated to me two points that are confirmed by almost every teacher's experience: that students consider explaining skills to be perhaps the teacher's single most important skill; and that a teacher's subject knowledge alone will not make him or her into a good explainer. So when your students don't understand, don't complain that they are 'thick'; develop your explaining skills.

> In the 1930s, Hollis asked 8000 pupils what characteristics they most valued in their teachers. Very near the top of the list came 'the ability to explain difficulties patiently'.

But how does one learn to explain? Let's look at some examples of explanations to discover what makes them effective – or ineffective! Compare these two (correct) explanations of how to get to Charles Street:

Explanation 1:
'Straight on to the roundabout, where you take the *third* exit signposted to Durham. Half a mile later, fork right, and it's the first on your left. So it's *right* at the roundabout, *right* at the fork, then first on the left.'

Explanation 2:
'Charles Street is right off Comberton Street. That's if you're travelling towards the City Centre, so it will be left as you approach it. So, carry on past Carringtons, they've got a sale on now, actually, three-piece suites for less than £500 – worth going to; past the railway station, that's not the *main* railway station, of course, it's

Farringdon Street, you know, that one on the Euston line. Keep going on the same road until you get to the Bull Ring, about a mile before the town centre, you know. Turn right. Then on your right you'll see the floodlights for the football ground – they call it the stadium, heaven knows why – anyway... after that you're in Comberton Street, I explained earlier how to get to Charles Street from there.'

What are the good and bad features of these two explanations?

The second: has *redundant information* which lengthens and confuses the explanation. It also *assumes knowledge in the learner* – e.g. that the learner will recognise 'the Bull Ring'. It isn't logically ordered, as the last direction is explained first.

The first: is *logically ordered, concise,* and includes a *summary* of the more important points; particularly important points are emphasised.

A good explanation should:

1. contain *only* such information as will be sufficient to give a reasoned, logically ordered description of the point being explained.

2. be exclusively built on knowledge that the student already possesses.

3. be tailored to the intended audience, *even if this means missing out what an expert on the subject (such as a teacher) might call important detail.*

4. be carried out persuasively and patiently.

It is important to recognise that a statement of fact such as 'When starting a car from rest, the clutch should be released slowly.' is not an *explanation*. Understanding requires that the student knows the 'why' as well as the 'what'.

Explaining is a skill that you must prepare for, and practise – on your own as well as in the class. There follow some techniques for you to practise. Throughout, I assume the teacher is attempting to explain a concept or idea that students tend to find difficult to understand.

Start from the student's existing knowledge and experience

This is harder to achieve than one might think. It requires an intimate knowledge of the subject being taught, as well as of the learner's ability and previous learning. It also requires careful planning.

The diagram at the top of the next page illustrates the point that a new understanding is built on old learning. But remember that the process shown in the diagram goes on inside the student's head. Explanations that do not relate to our foundation of present knowledge are not just inadequate, they are meaningless.

Simplify

During an explanation, the teacher's enemy is often the limited size of the student's short term memory. Don't feel you have to mention everything you know about the subject; only include information *vital* for understanding the point being explained.

Don't be afraid to simplify to the point where you are distorting the truth somewhat. You can always mention the exceptions and oddities later, once the basic idea is understood.

Extreme simplification is often used by teachers of science and mathematics to establish a principle. Here is a teacher explaining the equation:

$$distance = speed \times time$$

Teacher	Say you were travelling at 20 mph. How far would you travel in one hour?
Student	20 miles.
Teacher	How far would you travel in 2 hours?
Student	40 miles.
Teacher	And how far in 5 hours?
Student	100 miles.
Teacher	Good. How did you work that out?
Student	Multiply the speed by the time.
Teacher	Very good! So distance = speed × time.

If the teacher above wants to mention how Donald Campbell got the land speed record, or the speed of the fastest running mammal, it should be done after the basic idea has been explained and understood; or beforehand, as part of the introduction. Explain new ideas very, very simply, preferably getting learners to persuade themselves rather than be persuaded by you; *then* fill in the detail. **Warning:** simplification is a very difficult technique for the teacher; it needs careful preparation.

> On being asked whether the theory of relativity was too difficult to explain to a school pupil, Einstein is said to have replied that any scientist who cannot explain what he is doing to a reasonably intelligent fourteen-year-old is either incompetent or a charlatan.

Level of complexity

Simplicity requires that we avoid unnecessary complexity. One way of achieving this is by thinking in terms of 'black boxes'. One is aware of what goes into each box, and what comes out of it, but one does not worry about how it works inside. A child, an unmechanical adult, an amateur car mechanic, and a professional mechanic all see the car at different levels of complexity. However, no individual understands a car in its entirety; an expert on the thermodynamics of combustion may not understand the ergonomics of seat design. Most things, for most people, are understood in terms of 'black boxes'. So do not try to give every detail about what you are trying to teach; choose a level of complexity that is as simple as possible, while still being sufficiently detailed for your explanation.

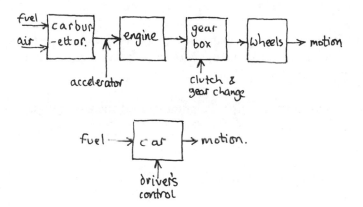

The car, in two different levels of complexity

Simplification can only be achieved by careful thought and planning before the lesson.

Focussing

When a speaker is confusing we often think, 'What is the point of what they are trying to say?' We might understand each sentence, but we are left unsure of where the sentences are leading.

Even a fairly concise explanation might last ten minutes, in which case you will deliver over 2000 words. Are all these words or sentences of equal importance? A student struggling with a new idea often has difficulty in isolating the point you are trying to make from the explanation you are giving in support of it. Even if students are intelligent and motivated, without help they may well miss important points amongst the detail.

Depending on the nature of the explanation you may need to focus on a key phrase, a list, or a chain of reasoning.

Key phrase

Can you boil down your explanation to a simple sentence or formulation that is the kernel of the teaching point(s) you are trying to make? Don't be afraid to use the vernacular; it gives students confidence if the idea you are trying to teach them can be stated in simple language. It is essential to prepare this 'key phrase' in advance, and to repeat it to the students often. Here are some examples:

> 'Voltage is the push on the electrons.'
> 'If we don't shutter trenches, we may end up digging our own graves.'

To focus attention on this key phrase, you can use:

> ■ emphasis ■ gesture ■ repetition ■ silence before and after the phrase.

You can write the phrase up on the board or OHP; and leave it there during the discussion; give the phrase in handouts or in notes; or say, 'Listen to this carefully – it is very important...'

Use questioning to check whether the point you are focussing on has sunk in.

A list

Many explanations are best summarised as a list. For example:

The Overhead Projector

Advantages over the black- or white-board are:

- Transparencies can be prepared in advance.
- Transparencies can be updated and kept for future use.
- Accurate drawings can be presented immediately.
- 'Overlay' and 'reveal' techniques can be used.

[etc.]

Emphasise and display the list during the explanation, as with the key phrase.

Chain of reasoning

If an explanation cannot be summarised as a list or as one key phrase, it can usually be summarised in a chain of reasoning. For example, when a science teacher is explaining why hot air rises she might focus on, or 'point' to, the following reasoning:

> A gas expands when it is heated.
> This expansion reduces the density of the gas.
> Less dense materials float in more dense fluids (like cork in water).
> Therefore hot air floats in the surrounding cold air.
>
> That is to say: 'Hot air rises.'

Each of the four statements needs explaining carefully in its own right, but in order to understand why hot air rises, the overall chain of reasoning must be understood. After convincing or reminding the students of the four separate statements, it is necessary to repeat this chain of reasoning in its shortened form a number of times. It is as though all four statements need to be understood separately, and then need to be in the short term memory together, for the students to be able to connect up the chain of reasoning and 'understand' why hot air rises.

Whether you summarise your explanation as a key phrase, as a list, or as a chain of reasoning, it is important to *emphasise* and *repeat* your summary. This is sometimes called 'pointing'.

> 'His speech was like a tangled chain; nothing impaired, but all disordered.'
> – *A Midsummer Night's Dream*

Structure and orientation

Suppose you were asked to study a play entirely on your own. You have seen the play twice, and read it twice; you are anxious to do well in an examination on the play in two days' time. How would you prepare for it?

Most effective students would write organised notes, with headings and sub-headings, mentioning the most important features of the play. These notes could be in time sequence, they could be broken down by character, by events in the play, by acts and scenes, by plot and sub-plots; or perhaps each theme in the play could have its own heading. Different students will choose to organise their notes in different ways, but effective learners *will* all organise them.

We need to impose a *logical structure* on what we want to understand and remember. It is as though our long term memory is like a filing cabinet, requiring information to be divided into drawers, files and sub-files. Even students who do

119

not resort to pen and paper are likely to 'structure' the play in their understanding in some way. Only structured material can pass from the short term into the long term memory.

Good explainers make sure their students have the explanation in a structured form, usually by doing the structuring for their students, but alternatively by ensuring students develop their own structure.

Explainers make it clear at all times where they are in the structure; this is called 'orientation'. For example:

> 'We have been looking at the reasons for the introduction of compulsory schooling in Britain. So far we have isolated a number of economic reasons for compulsory schooling: shortage of clerks, shortage of skilled labour and so on. But economics did not provide the only reasons for compulsory schooling. Let's have a look at some of the others.'

The diagram below shows how information can be shown in a *tree structure*; the headings and subheadings in this chapter could also be displayed in that way. Such a structure makes information easier to remember.

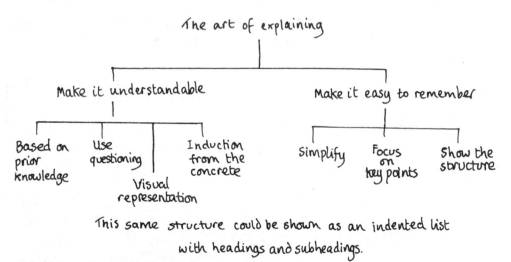

Orientation and structuring avoids the explanation becoming a vast, seamless, incomprehensible mass; and it breaks the argument up into easily understood and assimilated portions. Structure can be shown on the blackboard or OHP, or in headings in the students' notes.

It also often helps to start an explanation by saying what you are going to explain – and *why*, if this is not obvious. E.g. 'I'm going to explain the difference between a "state" and a "nation", as this has important implications in the history of Ireland which we will study next week.'

To conclude this section, then, a good explainer makes plain both the structure and the hierarchy of importance in the content of an extended explanation.

Abstract and concrete explanations

How would you explain the meaning of the word 'superstition' to an eight-year-old? Would you say, 'A superstition is an untrue belief, based on the idea that certain actions can affect our luck by magic.'? Whilst the eight-year-old might understand all the words in that explanation, I am prepared to bet that they would not understand the sentence. It is an *abstract explanation*: 'superstition', which is itself an abstract idea, has been explained in terms of other abstract ideas such as 'luck', 'magic' or 'untrue belief'.

Hopefully you would also explain the idea of 'superstition' with a *concrete* explanation; that is, by means of concrete examples of superstitions, preferably those with which the eight-year-old is familiar, such as:

'It is superstitious to:

- cross your fingers in the hope it will make a wish come true.
- believe a rabbit's foot can help you pass your examinations.
- expect trouble on Friday 13th.

[etc.]'

Non-examples are also very helpful – e.g. 'It is superstitious to cross your fingers before crossing the road, but it is *not* superstitious to look both ways.'

Learners feel a strong need for concrete examples (and non-examples) of abstract ideas. This seems to be the way they like to form new concepts. Another way of putting it is that they like to move from the particular to the general.

Interestingly, a child who has learned to use the concept of 'superstition' correctly may not be able to explain it! Concepts seem to be formed in the right half of the brain, which is non-verbal. In learning at all levels understanding comes first, and the ability to verbalise the understanding comes later. This in itself should warn us against explaining purely through abstract explanation.

For learners of all ages, the ideal introduction to an abstract idea is often through concrete specific examples from their own experience, with an abstract explanation to summarise. *Good explainers use both abstract and concrete explanations.*

The fact that learners and experts prefer to think in different ways during explanations explains why experts are often bad explainers; they cannot make themselves think from the concrete to the abstract. The diagram at the top of the next page presents this idea in visual terms.

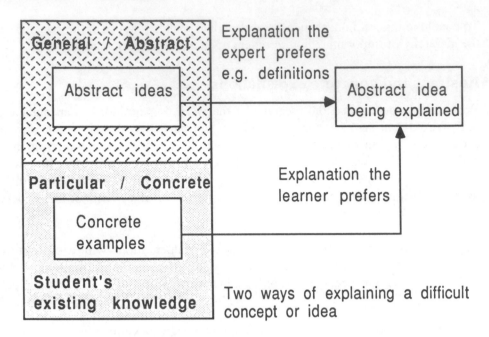

Two ways of explaining a difficult concept or idea

The strengths and weaknesses of concrete explanations

Concrete explanations are easily assimilated, but inexperienced teachers often omit them; they think it is 'talking down' to give concrete examples of phrases like 'adequate precautions' or 'protein-rich foods'. But experienced teachers would give (or ask for) examples to make the meaning of such abstract phrases clear.

Consider the concept of friction: 'Friction is a contact force which opposes motion.' We can view a concept as a kind of mental box in which we keep examples. In our 'friction' box we might keep:

> Friction is rubbing hands; it stops bike wheels from turning for ever;
> it makes it hard to pull a box on level ground... (and so on)

The box labelled 'friction' is useless to us until we have something to put into it! Also, we begin to see what the examples in the box have in common, apart from the opposition to motion:

> Friction is reduced by wheels, by oiling or by ball-bearings;
> friction causes heating;
> friction causes wear etc.;
> it provides grip;
>
> (and so on)

The best way to develop this new 'box' in students' minds is to give them plenty of things to put into it. A good explainer helps students to 'fill their concept boxes'.

How would *you* teach the concepts of 'a raising agent'; 'mean and mode'; or 'cash flow'?

The strengths and weaknesses of abstract explanations

Abstract explanations tend by their nature to be concise, accurate and widely applicable, and so are much prized by teachers. For example: 'A psychological complex is a group of (repressed and forgotten) ideas or impressions to which are ascribed abnormal mental conditions and abnormal bodily conditions due to mental causes.'

Definitions are abstract explanations, using abstract concepts. If the concept being explained is 'difficult', the learner will usually feel such an explanation is vague, or even completely meaningless. Definitions are often an *end point* rather than a starting point for the teacher.

Learners prefer to form a concept by induction, and then test and improve their concept by using or testing it:

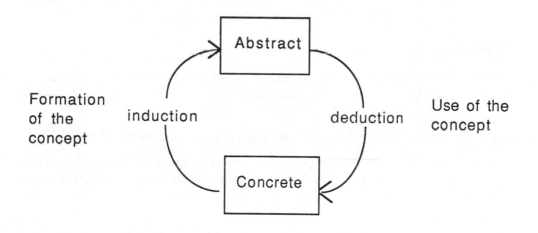

If I were trying to explain a psychological complex as defined above, I would not *start* with the definition. Instead, I would give examples of complexes, and ask students if they could see the similarities between them (induction). That would form the concept, and enable us to draw out the definition. Then I would ask students to use this definition to categorise other examples as either 'complexes' or not (deduction). This would require students to *use* the concept, so that I could *check* they were using it correctly (and thus infer that they had understood it). So we have involved both the abstract and the concrete, both induction and deduction.

Questioning

Questioning is a very powerful way of bringing about understanding; it is also a vital technique for checking that learning has taken place. (It is dealt with in detail in Chapter 15.) *'What would happen if...'* questions are particularly helpful when explaining. For example, when teaching the process of making bread:

> What would happen if I didn't use strong flour?
> What would happen if I poured the boiling water over the yeast?
> What would happen if I used twice as much yeast?
> What would happen if I covered it in a dry cloth instead of a wet one?

Tools for explainers

Analogy and comparison

These are much loved and much used, but they require careful preparation. Students like them, and they remember them. They have no difficulty in understanding that analogies sometimes break down. Just a few examples:

> 'Sweets are tooth enemies, apples are tooth friends.'
> 'This floppy disk can hold the equivalent of the Encyclopaedia Britannica.'
> 'An electrical current is a bit like water flowing along a pipe.'

Reductio ad absurdum

This is a method of 'unteaching' an erroneous idea, by showing it leads to a clear absurdity. The last sentence gave an abstract explanation of an abstract idea, and no doubt you will find a concrete example helpful! So here goes:

Suppose a student thinks that $4 \times 0 = 4$. (This is a common misunderstanding.)

Explanation: 'I have a fleet of cars that carry four people each. How many people can be carried by two cars?' *($4 \times 2 = 8$)* 'How many people can be carried by one car?' *($4 \times 1 = 4$)* 'How many people can be carried by zero cars?' *($4 \times 0 = ?$)*

This technique is particularly useful in science and mathematics. Here is a science example. A student states that the smaller the diameter of a chimney, the faster the smoke in it rises. The teacher knows this is only true up to a point, not as a generalisation. So she replies: 'Suppose I had a chimney with a near-zero diameter. Your theory suggests the smoke would rise at a huge speed. Is that likely?'

Visual representation

Even abstract ideas and relationships can be represented visually – a mode of communication that has a very powerful impact and is easily remembered. It is considered in detail in Chapter 31 on visual aids.

Expressing yourself unambiguously

Words such as 'it' and 'they', and phrases such as 'the system' or 'the method', all refer to a word or phrase mentioned earlier, usually in the same sentence. This can be confusing or even ambiguous, so for maximum clarity in worksheets and in verbal communication, they should be avoided. For example, in the last sentence 'they' could mistakenly be taken to mean 'worksheets', but is actually intended to relate to 'words and phrases used for referring back to something mentioned earlier'.

Some general advice

Try to hear what you are saying through your students' ears. Use simple language in short sentences, explaining all your jargon, and remembering that what is jargon to the student may be everyday language to you. Watch out for body language clues indicating 'lost' students: if someone is finding it hard to understand, they may lean forward and frown. Try to devise more than one way of explaining difficult ideas, and don't forget that explanations are never enough in themselves. Students must *use* the concepts or ideas being taught before they will really understand them. Don't go on too long.

Giving summaries

These help to consolidate learning by giving an overview of the main ideas and their structure. For example:

> An explanation should be based on the student's existing knowledge and vocabulary. It should be concise and logically structured, and this structure should be made clear. The explainer should focus on the vital components of the explanation by 'pointing', and should use both abstract and concrete explanations.

☑ Checklist

- ☐ Do you base your explanation on existing knowledge?
- ☐ Do you give your explanation a logical structure and make this clear to the student?
- ☐ Do you focus on the crucial points by 'pointing' – e.g. emphasis, repetition etc.?
- ☐ Do you simplify, adding detail later?
- ☐ Do you avoid unexplained jargon?
- ☐ Do you use the concrete, giving examples and non-examples?
- ☐ Do you use the abstract, but do so referring to the concrete?
- ☐ Do you give analogies and visualisations?
- ☐ Do you use questioning to explain and to monitor learning?
- ☐ Do you give students a chance to use the ideas you are teaching?

No one sets out to be a poor explainer, but many become one. Good explainers improve their explaining by clarifying their ideas, inventing explanations, and evaluating their effectiveness. They also tend to blame poor understanding on themselves, rather than on their learners. There is more advice on explaining in the later chapter on questioning (Chapter 15). Persuading is dealt with in Chapter 35.

Exercises

1. **The dictionary game.** Get a friend to read out the definitions of reasonably well-known words from a dictionary, and try to guess the word being defined. You will find it harder than you think; this shows that our understanding of concepts is not verbal, and consequently that abstract definitions are poor *explainers*. At times, definitions are so poor at explaining that we don't even recognise an abstract definition of a concept that we understand very well.

2. How would you explain the following to a seven-year-old: 'communication', 'irrational'?

3. In your own subject, choose a concept or topic that is difficult to explain. Look back over this chapter, and use it to prepare two alternative explanations of this topic or concept.

13 The art of showing

Demonstrating physical and intellectual skills

Perhaps the most natural way to learn is by imitation. This, after all, is how children learn to speak their first language – and the method is almost 100% successful! How can teachers make use of this method of learning?

If we accept that a demonstration is 'showing how' by example, then it is clear that this method can be employed by a teacher of any subject. As we saw in Chapter 3, it can be used to teach physical (psychomotor) skills, such as how to fillet a fish or weld mild steel; but it can also be used for intellectual skills – such as how to use Pythagoras' Theorem, how to write an appreciation of a poem, or how to analyse critically a theory in sociology. Most demonstrations will of course be followed by an opportunity for student practice. This chapter considers the demonstration of physical and intellectual skills separately.

Demonstration of a physical skill or ability

Learning teachers are often terrified of demonstrations; they remember the science teachers whose experiments never worked, and expect a similar humiliation. But there is nothing to fear if you have practised in advance.

The aim of most demonstrations is to provide students with a concrete example of good practice to copy or adapt. This provides the 'doing-detail' that, as Chapter 3 showed, is so vital for learning physical and intellectual skills: it shows how the task is carried out, what the task achieves, to what standard it should be carried out, the indicators that the task has been carried out successfully, and so on.

'Doing-detail' can occasionally be provided by an exemplar (i.e. a model of good practice); for example, a typing teacher can show students a well laid out table of figures, and a catering teacher can show a well presented dish. Examples of bad practice can also be useful. 'Here are two business letters; they each have four layout mistakes in them. See if you can find them!'

Science teachers sometimes demonstrate a phenomenon by experiment. The intention here may not be to encourage the learner to imitate the teacher; indeed, that might be dangerous. These demonstrations should be carried out in much the same way as is described below.

Preparation

Make sure the students are ready: have they been introduced to the necessary background information, and do they know what the demonstration achieves? If the demo is likely to be long and involved, can it be broken down into parts to be learned separately?

It is nearly always necessary to move students for a demonstration, but even then, will the whole class be able to see? If not, it would be better to break it into smaller groups. Will you let students arrange their own positions, or will you direct them? Whatever you decide, get them as close as is practicable. Some teachers who often do demonstrations have a routine position for students around the demonstration bench – for example, the students from the front row on the teacher's right, the second row to the left, and so on. This avoids students jostling for position. If you are in a science laboratory, decide in advance whether some students will be allowed to sit *on top of* the bench immediately in front of the demonstration bench. If this is allowed, arrange for the front row students to sit in front of that bench, rather than in their usual places behind it, to avoid the other students sitting on their folders etc.

Student placement for a demonstration in a science laboratory

Will there be a mirror image problem? Students will see your left hand on their right. This is not normally a difficulty unless you expect students to copy you *while* you are demonstrating, as some keep-fit or dance teachers do. If this is the case, demonstrate the movements in mirror image so that students see you as they would see themselves in a mirror – see the illustration at the top of page 129. (Are you left-handed, or are any of your students left-handed, and if so will this make any difference?)

How will you involve your students? This can be done by asking questions, but a student can also be asked to copy or adapt your demonstration in front of the rest of

The demonstrator as a mirror image

the class, before the general student practice session. In science experiments, students can be asked to take readings.

Always practice a demonstration before doing it in front of the class, and make a note of all the equipment you need, including any extras you may need to repeat the demo if this is necessary. Can you talk and work at the same time? Does the demonstration take longer than you expected? If so, you may need to use the *Blue Peter* trick: 'Here's one I prepared earlier.'

It is important to decide in advance on the key points you want to make during the demo; these can often get lost in the welter of detail. Have a summary ready for the board or overhead projector. Finally, are you certain that you have considered all the safety factors carefully?

Execution

Arrange the equipment in advance, well away from any confusing clutter, so that it is facing the students if at all possible. Once students are aware of what they are about to see, and why, move them into their new positions. Don't start until they are all settled.

Explain as you demonstrate if you can, preferably using questions. 'What should I do next? Why am I doing it like this? What should I be careful of here? What would happen if...?' Make sure your students understand the purpose of each action; they should understand the 'why' as well as the 'how'. Emphasise your key points carefully.

Do it slowly, and if necessary do it at a more realistic speed later. If there is more than one method and you wish to demonstrate them all, it is usually better to show only one at a time. Show the other method(s) in a separate demo if necessary. It is very difficult to demonstrate, talk, question, and use eye contact with the group at the same time – but *try*; if you can do it, this will increase the impact of the demonstration enormously.

Ask questions to check on understanding before sending the students back to their places, and if necessary repeat the demo. If students are about to have a go themselves, ask them to look out for particular points which will show whether or not they are doing it properly. These 'performance indicators' are important: here's a woodwork teacher finishing off a demo on planing wood. '...You should hardly need to push at all; the shavings should be so thin that you can see light through them; and there should be no score marks left by the plane.' This is important 'doing-detail', because it helps students to check and correct their own work.

If you make a mistake, laugh it off and if possible make a teaching point out of it. 'You see how important it is to do it slowly! You will have more time, so I will expect a better job from you!'

Learning by imitation or 'modelling' takes place even when you don't intend it. It is well known that students take more notice of what teachers *do* than what they say. If you tell your students to turn off the powerpack before changing their circuit, or to wash their hands, or to be courteous to patients – then do so yourself. If you want your students to employ safe practice, to lay out work tidily, or to be thorough or enthusiastic, you must do the same! Think carefully what a teacher in your subject area needs to model, and make sure you set a good example.

Some techniques you might like to try are:

The silent demonstration: Here the teacher explains that the coming demonstration will be without explanation, and asks the students to watch carefully, as they will later be asked exactly what was done, and why. This can often create intense student concentration, especially if some aspect of the technique is unexpected or puzzling.

The 'how NOT to do it' demonstration: We can certainly learn from deliberate mistakes, but be careful that your students do not become confused, or learn the wrong technique. The students are of course asked to watch out for the mistakes. If safety is involved, this technique should be avoided. With humour this method can be most effective, a good example being the John Cleese videos showing how not to behave at an interview. (Those videos show, incidentally, that it is not just practical skills that we can learn by example.)

☑ *Checklist for demonstrating a physical skill*

☐ Did you ensure that they could all see?

☐ Did they know what they were seeing and why it was done that way?

☐ Did you involve students by question and answer?

☐ Did you have everything you needed?

☐ Did you do it slowly enough and a sufficient number of times?

☐ Did you consider safety?

☐ Did you give performance indicators so students could self-check during their practice?

Demonstration of an intellectual skill or ability

If you teach intellectual skills or abilities you can still teach by showing. This method of teaching is under-used and under-estimated by many teachers of intellectual skills. There are two main methods of 'showing how'.

Showing by exemplar

The teacher shows a model of good practice from which students can copy, adapt or learn technique. You can show your students good essays, intelligent critical appreciations, well-constructed computer programs, good assignments, worked solutions, effective designs... The source of these may be the teacher, books, former students, or even peers. The exemplar is then examined carefully by the learners. With care they can learn from both good and bad examples. (However, don't use a *student's* work as a bad – or even a good – example, if this will cause embarrassment or offence.)

Showing the exemplar is often not enough. The student must be clear how it was done, and understand *why* the exemplar is effective. Discussion and questioning may bring this out, but if not the teacher must provide all the information. Sometimes it is helpful for students to prepare checklists of criteria defining good practice, based on the examples.

Give some thought to the number of examples you will show your students. Usually it is a case of 'the more, the better'. If the examples are very different, so much the better, as this helps the student see what the examples have in common, and how to use the skill in different contexts. It is particularly helpful for students

131

to study an exemplar solution of a task soon after completing an identical task: an exemplar laboratory report, or translation, for example; or an 'A' grade essay on the same title as a recent assignment.

Showing by demonstrating

The skill or ability being taught can be carried out by a teacher in front of the class. For example, a mathematics teacher might demonstrate how to solve a problem in geometry; an English teacher might demonstrate how to write a critical appraisal of a poem; or a doctor might carry out a diagnosis. Demonstrating an intellectual skill like this usually requires that the teacher 'thinks out loud'. This takes practice. Watch a good mathematics teacher at work; not only is the correct thinking shown, but students are warned against common errors, and the class are often involved in the process by the careful use of questioning:

'I bet some of you think the answer is simply 12. But it's not! Can anybody see why? ...'

'What should I do next? I can't find the height h, so it looks like I'm completely stumped. Or am I? ...'

After showing by demonstration, many teachers 'do one on the board' in a different way – by following instructions from the students. This enables students to practice the skill under close supervision, before a 'solo flight'. Mathematics and science teachers often do 'worked examples' in this way, using questioning to elicit instructions from the students: 'Right, so I've found the relative molecular mass; now what?...'

'Learner case studies' are excellent methods of teaching by showing. They are commonly used in the teaching of professionals. For example, nurses being trained in a new care technique can report back to their study group on how their use of the new technique is going in practice. This can generate valuable discussion, and each student's experience can be used to demonstrate to the others on the course how to use, or how not to use, the technique being studied. The nurse trainer can also offer practical help as her students use the care technique they are studying.

Teaching by example is a most effective and inspiring way of giving students 'doing-detail'': what students should be able to do, and how they should best do it. Many poor teachers leave students to work this out for themselves. Able students often do well, despite poor teaching, precisely because they are bright enough to guess what the teacher wants. Indeed, students often spend some time discussing 'doing-detail' amongst themselves: 'What does he want? ... How long does it have to be? ... Is this OK, do you think? ... How have you done it?' These are questions best answered by showing how.

Teachers of social sciences, English literature and a number of other subjects must develop their learners' ability to create their own informed opinion. Even high-order cognitive skills such as this can be learned by showing. Indeed, they are taught almost exclusively, if unconsciously, in this way. Exemplar opinions can be studied and criticised – for example, the views of experts or peers, opinions from a textbook, etc.

Alternatively, the teacher can argue out loud whether such and such an opinion is consistent with the facts, explaining why it is or is not valid, and showing why a different view is not tenable. From this students can learn the characteristics of a well-argued opinion, and so develop their ability to create their own informed opinions. Much of this learning is done unconsciously; it is then called 'modelling'. However, try to make a conscious use of the technique, 'thinking out loud' to exemplify these high-order thinking skills.

If you are involved with this form of teaching, it would help your students enormously to explain and make explicit the criteria for a well-reasoned opinion. Science students are not left to discover for themselves how scientific laws can be induced from experimental data. Science teachers rightly regard the laws of scientific reasoning as far too subtle and difficult to be left solely to self-discovery. Yet humanities students are often left to divine the much more complex laws of reasoning in their subjects completely unaided.

Showing and telling

Showing is not always necessary. If the skill or ability is a straightforward adaptation of a well-practised technique, then simply telling students the 'how' of the skill may be enough. If the technique is well practised, they already know the 'doing-detail'. (Students who are practised at algebra may be happy with 'Divide the two equations and then solve for the unknown.' Those less practised would like to see one done on the board.) However, if the skill is complex, or must be developed over an extended period of time, then 'showing how' is important.

Showing and telling are not really equivalent methods of giving the same information. The two techniques involve the learner in quite different mental processes. *Showing* is concrete and holistic; it involves the learner in analysis of the examples, and looking for similarities in the examples of good practice. It involves learning by induction. In contrast, *telling* is abstract, and involves the learner in synthesis and learning by deduction. Cognitively they are mirror images of each other; they probably even involve different halves of the brain.

As was mentioned in the previous chapter on the art of explaining, when we are learning a concept we like to be given examples of its use; the definition is not enough. We like to be *shown* how to use the concept, as well as being *told* how.

Learning seems to require both the concrete and the abstract, both induction and deduction (though it is possible that some learners learn better from one than from the other).

Don't ignore learning by imitation; it is immensely powerful. Incredibly, we can learn complex skills such as grammar or the laws of reasoning in this way, without being told – or even formally understanding – the rules that govern these processes! Perhaps the reason for the power of this kind of learning is that our species learned to imitate before it learned to speak. Have our brains perhaps evolved to learn best in this way? Who knows; but no teacher can afford to ignore its power.

☑ *Checklist for demonstrating the use of an intellectual skill*

☐ Do you show your students examples of good practice?

☐ Are the examples you show numerous and varied?

☐ Do you 'think aloud' to your students to show the reasoning in your subject?

☐ Do you let students examine bad as well as good examples?

☐ Can you make use of case studies to show how the ideas you are teaching are used in practice?

☐ Do you 'do one on the board' while thinking aloud?

☐ Can you make explicit the laws of reasoning in your subject?

Exercises

1. Work out methods for teaching the following by demonstration:

    How to use inverted commas.
    How to use apostrophes.

2. Practise 'thinking aloud' while showing how, and then make use of the technique in one of your classes.

14 Supervised student practice

We owe almost all our skills and abilities to corrected practice, so this is an obligatory teaching method. Here are some examples:

- Students completing a series of exercises from a worksheet or textbook.
- Students carrying out an experiment.
- Learners in an adult education dressmaking class, making a garment chosen by themselves.
- Engineering students practising a welding procedure.

Note that students in the same class may not be doing the same thing. In the dressmaking class, for example, there is an element of personal choice, so that the individual interests of the students and their differing attainments can be accommodated. This is very motivating, but it is not always possible.

In this chapter we will look at the practice of practical and intellectual skills separately, but before doing so, some considerations are common to both. (An alternative approach to student practice is the discovery method described in Chapter 24.)

In terms of the EDUCARE? elements, at the very least this activity lets the students *'use'* the skill, and gives an opportunity for a *'check and correct'* phase; it also offers students a chance to get their queries answered (the *'?'* phase).

Supervised practice makes students work harder than any other learning method, so the cynical might expect it to be unpopular. However, if it is well prepared and managed, students enjoy this method of learning more than most.

Preparing for the activity

If student practice is to be used effectively, before the activity starts:

- The students must have been adequately introduced to the activity, so that they understand the aim of the work they have been set. They must be fully aware of 'doing-detail' (what they are expected to do, and how best to do it). They will also need to know why things are done this way.

- The activities must be at the right level for all the students. (This might involve different activities, or different expectations, for different students – for example, stretching activities for students who finish early.)

- Students should have had the opportunity to ask questions about the activity.

- If the activity consists of a series of tasks, these should usually be available to the students in a written form, and broken down into sub-tasks. For example, 'When you have finished, write a report.' may be too vague for many students; try itemising sub-tasks – e.g. what the report should contain.

Preparing for and managing a practical activity is dealt with separately, later in the chapter.

Managing the practice of an intellectual skill

The crucial first few minutes

Describe the activity with care, giving it to the students in written form. Before allowing anyone to start, ask if there are any questions; when everyone seems clear, summarise the activity one last time before they start. For almost any activity, each student's work should now be checked as soon as possible after the start of the practice, to make sure no one is completing it incorrectly. Communication in the classroom is so tenuous that, however carefully you explain, in most groups at least one student will get the wrong end of the stick, or will have no stick at all, or will not be aware there is a stick!

> I once saw a student maths teacher set his class a series of exercises on fractions. The class seemed to be working well, and the teacher moved about answering queries. About forty minutes later at the end of the class, the work was handed in, and the teacher noticed that one student had completed all the exercises incorrectly. Understandably the student felt frustrated, angry and demotivated. What was more, she had spent forty minutes practising an incorrect method which might be difficult to unlearn. A quick initial check avoids such disasters.

Students' work can be checked by moving systematically round the class, looking over their shoulders; by asking students to self-check or peer-check; or by giving the answer to the first few questions. This initial check is important, and should usually take priority over answering individual queries. It also establishes that everyone is working!

Here is a teacher of geometry four minutes into a twenty-minute activity. She has stopped the large class and asked for silence:

'Just about everybody has finished the first question now, so let's make sure everybody is on the right lines. I want you to check three things. First: does your construction fill the page? Second: is it labelled like the one on the board? Lastly, did you get 8.7 metres as the answer to question one? See me if you have any queries.'

Even better, she could ask the students to supply the checking criteria, and having established these, ask students to use them to check their own or each other's work.

Once you are under way

Once you have established that all students are working along roughly the right lines, the role of the teacher is to be permanently available to help students with any difficulties, and to continue the checking process. In some classes, it is also important to check on the work rate of all the students.

Unless the activity is very short, it is often wise to check *every* student in the class briefly from time to time (though in large classes this can be very difficult). Apart from allowing monitoring of student work rates and prompt correction of errors, the checking process also gives students positive feedback; this provides motivation and gives them confidence in what they are doing. If you are positive about criticism and use plenty of praise, students will enjoy the attention of regular checks, and find them motivating.

Never ridicule a student's work. However silly or appalling their mistake, do not even show surprise, let alone laugh, or you will discourage help-seeking in the future. For the same reason, discourage students from ridiculing each other's work. We all make mistakes; we could hardly learn without them. Of all the attributes of able teachers, the most prized by students is – *patience*. Not that effective teachers are really patient; it's just that they learn not to show their irritation. Cultivate the ability to smile through clenched teeth, and keep a punch bag in the staff room!

Reluctant learners

Try:

'When you have finished down to question 4, let me know and I will mark it for you straight away.'

Instant knowledge of results like this is very motivating even for students whose work rate is usually very low; mark with the student present, and find something to praise if possible. Students enjoy your undivided attention as much as the marking. If the class is large, then offer to mark part of the work on the spot, or the work of those individuals who are least motivated.

**How do you deal with students
whose work rate is low because of low motivation?**

- Check work-rate often. You may need to make a mental, or even a written, note of where students have 'got up to' in their work at the beginning of the work session.

- Use eye-contact between checks.

- Praise what you can in their work.

- Set targets: 'I'll come back in five minutes, and I'll expect to see question four completed.' Make sure your targets are realistic, that you remember to check whether they have been met, and that you praise their achievement.

- In extreme cases, put students 'on report' – that is, they must bring their work to you at the end of each lesson.

- Read the chapters on motivation and praise and criticism in Part 1!

You may need to keep an eye out for trouble. Scan the whole class from time to time, and as you move round the class or give individual help; try to arrange yourself so that you face the majority of the class.

Helping students 'one to one'

How should you correct a student's error? There are all manner of approaches: the wrist-slappers, the shoulder-shruggers, the move-over-and-let-me-do-iters.

When a stroke victim is left paralysed down one side, they must relearn how to carry out such everyday tasks as opening a jam jar. Seeing someone who is struggling to open a jam jar produces in most people an overwhelming desire to 'help' by opening it for them. But the families of such stroke victims are told that to help is to hinder. To become independent, they must be left to practise by themselves, no matter how long it takes. Sometimes it is most helpful not to help.

Inexperienced teachers often over-teach when sorting out a student's difficulties: their approach is to say, 'No, do it like *this*.', and then to take over. It is much more effective to encourage students to recognise their problem and to work out their own solution. The aim here is to make students independent of the teacher, by developing their ability to *evaluate* their own performance, *diagnose* problems, and *solve* them on their own. Such skills are crucial if students are to learn how to improve their performance. The aim is to produce a 'reflective practitioner', that is, a student who reflects on his or her performance with a view to improving it.

In general, when correcting students' work, try to get *them* to do as much of the correcting as possible:

- Ask if they have any questions or difficulties, and listen carefully to their reply.
- Try to get the students to recognise the root cause of their difficulty, using questioning if necessary.
- Ask the student to offer a solution.
- Only when this fails should you explain and demonstrate how the error should be corrected.

It has to be said that with large classes there often isn't time for this process – especially if you are besieged with queries because the work is too difficult or the class is not well prepared!

> Do you want your students to help each other, or should all difficulties be referred to you personally? Most teachers encourage peer tutoring.

If a lot of students have similar troubles, get them in a group; this can save you the trouble of saying the same thing over and over. You can say:

> 'Quite a few of us are having trouble with question seven. If you'd like some help with this one, gather round the board; I'll go over it with you. The rest of you can carry on.'

Students find working alone hard work, and although this activity can often go on for very long periods, beware of tiring them out.

Worksheets

Worksheets are duplicated sheets consisting of a series of exercises or practical tasks for the students. They may also include summarised notes.

Commercial publishers market worksheet masters with a copyright waiver, which usually authorises the purchasing institution to photocopy the sheets for use within that institution. However, most worksheets are produced by the teacher for his or her own use. (See the section on handouts in the visual aids chapter.)

When writing your own handouts:

- Graduate the work very carefully. Students need more than one question to practise a difficult idea, and they like to climb one step at a time.
- Make the first few questions very simple to give confidence.
- Whenever possible, break tasks down into sub-tasks, giving each a unique question number. Order tasks with great care.

- Worksheets should give students the opportunity to demonstrate the skills and knowledge they have been learning in a straightforward way. Don't aim to catch students out. Leave the more difficult questions until the basics have been well established and practised. Success is the key to motivation.

- Make at least the last question *open*, so that students who work quickly don't end up with nothing productive to do.

- Consider student relevance, human interest puzzles, challenges etc.

- Make your worksheets as attractive and interesting as you can. Type them; include diagrams and photographs; don't cram too much into them. (Look carefully at commercially produced worksheets and see how they do them.)

Don't rely too heavily on worksheets, especially if other teachers on your students' course use them widely. Overuse makes for tedium. If you are provided with a coursebook or a large collection of worksheets for a course you are teaching, don't feel tyrannised into using them to the exclusion of all else.

Checking progress

In most teaching situations the work can be marked by the teacher. If so, the results should be given to the students as soon as possible, as this maximises motivation. In subjects such as mathematics, where there is often only one correct answer, students can be asked to check their own answers; however, don't over-rely on self-checking. Always mark some of the work yourself to check on work rate, methods used to obtain answers, copying etc. Copiers are easy to spot, especially if you collect and mark work in classroom seating order; they use identical layout and make identical mistakes. But some copying is genuine collaboration, so investigation may be necessary. Regular testing, such as in 'mastery learning', soon uncovers those who copy and those who collaborate.

I will probably be shot for saying this, but if the student work rate exceeds your ability to mark it, then consider marking only a sample of each student's work – for example, the last four questions of the worksheet only. Ideally everything should be marked, but ideal practice also requires that you are given adequate time and resources. Teachers in Britain are expected to teach considerably more hours a week than teachers in civilized nations!

'Has anybody any queries?' is better than 'Is anybody stuck?' In learning, errors are both inevitable and necessary for advancement, so try to adopt a shoulder-shrugging 'no blame' policy towards them.

Some teachers use individual student practice almost exclusively – for example, those teaching the use of standard computer application packages through workbooks; or practical classes such as dressmaking, where students are working on their own projects. Over-reliance on any one teaching method can be tedious for the students, so try hard to introduce variety. The dressmaking students will enjoy grouping round each other's work and hearing from the teacher about each other's special difficulties, techniques employed etc. The computer students will benefit from seeing demonstrations of practical uses of the application they are learning, or learning some general background to the equipment they are using.

The plenary

'What have we learned from this activity? What are the key points?' The plenary helps students see the wood as well as the trees. Students usually need to reflect on the activity, and to discuss it; summary notes are often given after this process.

After work has been marked it is of course vital that you, or preferably the student, correct any errors; and that you go over any common difficulties with the group.

Managing a practical activity

At their best, practicals are an enjoyable and active 'hands on' experience. At their worst, they are frustrating episodes where not even the teacher knows what is supposed to be happening, and where half the equipment is malfunctioning or missing. As with so much in teaching, success depends on planning.

Are the students well prepared for the activity? Will they be following a procedure defined by you, or using a 'discovery' approach (Chapter 25)? Will they be working separately, or working in groups (Chapter 17)?

However you elect to organise a practical activity:

- it will take much longer than you think, so allow *plenty* of time.
- unless the activity is very routine, try out the practical yourself (with the equipment the students will use). Try to see it from the students' point of view, making a note of the following:
  - the procedure, and *all* the equipment required.
  - what can go wrong.
  - any 'performance criteria'.
  - (especially) any safety precautions.
- order the equipment well in advance (before anyone else 'bags' it!)
- ask experienced teachers for tips, tricks and traps when handling practicals.

If you have a shortage of equipment, divide students into groups and either extract groups from a class activity to do the practical, or have a 'circus' of different activities (see Chapter 17). If students are extracted from other activities one at a time to use specialist equipment, then student number five will benefit from watching student number four, and so on.

Decide on exactly what you hope to achieve in the lesson, and then plan the activity with more than usual care. Is there anything you especially want your students to notice? Do you want them to write up the activity in any way? Will the students need a demonstration? Have you emphasised safety considerations? Make sure everybody has something to do all the time; you might like to consider an open-ended stretching activity for those who finish early.

Unless a discovery method is to be used, put special emphasis on clarity of instruction; make sure the activity is described for students in written form on a worksheet, board or OHP screen. These instructions will not be read unless they are concise, and are best written up before the class.

If preparation is critical – e.g. whisking egg whites before adding to a soufflé mixture, or setting up an electrical circuit before starting a science experiment – it sometimes pays to get the learners to check their preparation with you before switching on or making a start.

As soon as the activity is underway, check each individual or group has started correctly. Are they getting the results you would expect? Pay special attention to safety factors. While supervising the activity, especially if safety or misbehaviour is likely to be a problem, try to remain facing most of the group even when talking to individuals. Scan the whole class with eye contact every few seconds.

The plenary session is often very important in practical work. What should the students have learned? What conclusions can be drawn? Can any anomalous experiences or results be explained away? Students often appreciate a summarising note at this stage. They may also profit from seeing each others' work, and discussing it.

If you expect practical work to be written up, make it clear how this is to be done, and let students see good examples of such write-ups. Allow plenty of time, with the accent on repetition which should be deliberate, accurate and unhurried. It is not strictly true that practice makes perfect. Practice only makes perfect if the practice *is* perfect! Partly for this reason, 'doing-detail' should include performance indicators where these are appropriate, so that students are in a position to self-check their own work.

When teaching a physical skill it is important not to teach too much at once. A complex task is best broken into a chain of steps that are each learned separately. Particularly in the case of a physical skill, these steps should then be practised *slowly* and *accurately* until the required speed is attained. Then the steps can be chained together to make up the complex task. For example, a music teacher might teach a student to play a complex four-bar passage in this way, perhaps one bar at a time. (Chapter 2 also deals with the teaching of a practical skill.)

Experimental work in science

One cannot imagine science being taught satisfactorily without experimental work; but however necessary, such work is not sufficient. Students also require an opportunity to use the scientific idea you are teaching to solve problems, and to answer questions verbally and on paper. It is one thing to understand an experiment involving, say, 'diffusion' and then write a laboratory report. It is quite another to be able to use the concept of diffusion to answer, say, examination-style questions. This latter skill can only be developed by corrected practice in question-answering. Such practice provides the teacher with feedback, so that errors and omissions in the use of the concept can be corrected.

When used well, experimental work is active, fun, enlightening and engaging. However, if used badly it can result in bored and confused learners. Research shows that even directly after completing a conventional practical exercise, many learners cannot say what they did, why they did it, or what they found out!

Uncritical and unfocussed use of experimental work has received heavy and well-deserved criticism in the Association for Science Education's journal. (See Hodson, D, 'A critical look at practical work in school science', *School Science Review*, 1990, Vol. 71, No. 256, pp. 33-40; and 1992, Vol. 73, No. 264, pp. 65-78.)

It is crucial to be clear about your objectives when using experimental work. These may include learning:

- about a particular example of a scientific fact, principle or concept.
- how scientific investigations are carried out.
- how to interpret data, e.g. how relationships between variables are discovered.
- how to deal with anomalous results.
- how to carry out error analysis.
  [etc.]

Especially early on in a science course, learners are sometimes expected to cope with all these objectives at the same time. This can overwhelm or at least confuse all but the most able. There is a lot to be said for at least *introducing* each of the above objectives *one at a time*, with an activity which allows the clear and unambiguous exploration of the objective. This introductory activity may or may not involve experimentation.

Scientific concepts and principles can be developed by providing students with a variety of concrete examples of the concept or principle. Methods for providing such examples might include practical demonstrations, teacher talk, discussion of students' suggestions, textbooks, computer simulations, videos etc., as well as experimental work.

It is important to be sure that your science practicals do not always involve your students in blindly following a procedure laid down by you as the teacher. Constant use of this 'recipe' method bores students, as it reduces their need to think. If they are to develop skills in planning and designing experiments, they must practise those skills! Try asking students what they expect the experiment will show before they carry it out, then comparing the results with their expectations.

Try to avoid time-consuming repetitive work; it is often possible to share out sections of an experiment. Different groups can investigate different variables, or different values of the same variable, and then report their findings back to the class. For example, each group can find the solubility of a salt at a different temperature, and the result can then be combined on to a master graph.

Even if students are carrying out identical experiments, there is something to be said for this reporting back of results to the group. It is motivating, and encourages students to take responsibility for their work. The averaging effect of taking all the results from a class can also produce more reliable results.

Make sure you leave time to tidy up and collect in the apparatus, and for a plenary session. This plenary is vital for experimental work. Make clear what the student should have learned from the experiment, explain any anomalous results, and drive home the objective with a will. Make sure the students are aware of the laws of valid inference from experiment.

Common problems for inexperienced teachers

Work too difficult

Are you surrounded by a forest of hands? Are you saying the same thing over and over? Have you decided the class is a bit thick? Don't worry; setting work that is too difficult is a very common mistake for learning teachers! Get advice on the level of work from teaching colleagues and teacher-tutors. Make sure the students really know *how* it should be done, and *why* it is done that way. Show them plenty of examples – i.e. do a demonstration. Compare the work you set with the level of work set by their other teachers. Don't assume knowledge or skills the students lack.

Task too vague

Are they missing things out? Are they 'doing it all wrong'? Does everyone look bemused?

Break the task down as far as it is possible to do so; write it down very clearly in simple language.

Some students finish early and have nothing to do

Make at least the last task 'open-ended', and perhaps a little more demanding.

Everything takes them MUCH longer than you expected

This is quite normal! As long as they can cope and are not wasting time, you probably don't need to worry.

☑ Checklist for managing student practice

☐ Are students prepared, e.g. are they aware of the 'doing-detail'?

☐ Did you ensure that the necessary resources and sufficient time were available?

☐ Is the task sufficiently broken down, achievable, and clearly and concisely defined in writing?

☐ Did you check and correct each student at the very start of the activity?

☐ Can you help students without 'doing it for them'? (See Chapter 15.)

☐ Did you look out for safety and discipline problems by facing the majority of the class as you checked and corrected, helped and circulated?

☐ Do you *always* have a plenary, so that no student is left in doubt about what they should have learned?

For experimental work

☐ Will students get paper practice and other opportunities to develop the scientific ideas you are teaching?

☐ Do you avoid constant use of the 'recipe' approach? (See Chapter 15.)

15 Questioning

Most experienced teachers use questioning a great deal, in talking to classes and groups, as well as when talking to individual students. Questions are of course used in both verbal and written form; but this chapter will focus on the teacher asking questions verbally. Many experts on education, including many experienced and effective teachers, consider verbal questioning to be one of the teacher's most potent tools. Why is this?

To help us answer this question, let's compare two teachers developing the same teaching point. They are both teaching students of catering how to display cakes in a self-service cafeteria.

The first teacher's approach is to use teacher talk.

Teacher   Now, in cafeterias it is important to make sure that the cakes on display do not go stale over a period of time. This is particularly important if there is a large selection of cakes, or where the cake is kept in warm conditions. Unfortunately, warm conditions are all too common where food is being cooked and served. So we must pay a great deal of attention to the display of cakes in a cafeteria environment.

When choosing a cake for cafeteria display, bear in mind that it should be an iced cake, as these go stale less quickly. Also, it should not be left near an oven, coffee urn or other source of heat. It should be covered, of course, and a cake display cover like this one could be used to good effect here. So, during your practical this afternoon, I want to see cakes in suitable display conditions.

The second teacher uses questioning to develop the same teaching point.

Teacher   Why does fruit cake go stale?
Student 1 Currants go off, miss.
Teacher   Currants keep for years, actually.
Student 2 Flour goes off, miss?
Teacher   No, flour keeps for ages too!
(Silence)
How would you tell fresh cake from stale cake?
Student 3 Fresh cake is nice and moist, and stale cake is all dry.
Teacher   Good! So if stale cake is dried-out cake, how could we store cakes to stop them going stale?

Student 1	Put them in a plastic bag, or an airtight tin... *(Teacher nods and smiles)*
Student 2	Or use one of those glass covers.
Teacher	That's right, like this one. Now – plastic bags, air-tight tins, glass covers... Why would these all stop the cake going stale? ... Tracy?
Student 3	Because it stops the cake drying out.
Teacher	Good. And what effect would icing a cake have on the staleness?
Student 1	It would stop it going stale so fast, because it covers most of it up.
Teacher	Good, so going stale means drying out. Now, in our practical this afternoon, would you choose an iced or an un-iced cake for display?
Students	Iced.
Teacher	And where would you store it?
Student 2	Away from the oven.
Student 3	Away from anything hot.
Teacher	Yes, away from the oven, the heated display counter, the coffee urn and so on. Because... ?
Student 3	Because heat dries cake out, makes it stale.
Teacher	That's right! Well done.

There is a crucial advantage to the questioning approach, and that is that the knowledge gained in such a lesson is 'transferable'. Imagine asking the two classes who experienced these lessons the following question:

'How should bread be stored overnight to prevent it going stale?'

The class who were given the 'teacher talk' lesson would probably say, 'We haven't done bread.' (One hopes they would not suggest icing it!) However, the class taught to *understand* the process of going stale would probably have some correct suggestions; they would be able to transfer their understanding to this unfamiliar problem. It is important to teach for understanding, rather than just for knowing. Questioning teaches students to think for themselves.

Does anything else strike you about the differences between these two approaches? Most people would agree that the questioning approach would be more interesting for the students; they are actively involved rather than passively listening, and the questioning style tends to stimulate the students' curiosity – why *does* cake go stale? Also the students are made to *think* in the questioning-style lesson; the logic of the subject is exposed and they are encouraged to use it: 'How could we store cakes to stop them going stale?'

The emphasis in the questioning-style lesson tends to be on understanding rather than simply knowing. In the teacher talk lesson, the students were simply told what they had to know; they were not encouraged to understand it, and less likely to remember it.

As a result of the questioning, the students had their assumptions and prior knowledge challenged and corrected. Beforehand, some of the students had thought that 'going stale' meant 'going off'; but in the course of the lesson they found out it means something closer to 'drying out'. This process of having incorrect assumptions corrected is sometimes called 'unlearning': as we have seen in earlier chapters, correction is a vital part of the learning process. Many students come to our classes with incorrect assumptions and 'common non-sense' notions that need challenging. Questioning helps enormously here.

Notice also that the teacher who used questioning was being given instant feedback on the understanding of the students, while the lesson proceeded.

More teacher questioning

A history teacher has asked her students to discuss in pairs the problems that land owners might have experienced immediately after the Black Death (a plague that killed a high percentage of the adult populations in Britain and elsewhere). One group has realised that landowners would get less income from their cottages because some of them would be empty, but they are now 'stuck'; they cannot think of any other economic consequences the plague might have had for a landowner.

Teacher	What do landowners do with their land?
Paula	Hunting?
Teacher	Yes, anything else?
Emma	Grow wheat and stuff. They would farm it.
Teacher	Good. Now, what problems would farming landowners have after the Black Death?
Paula	No-one would want to work on their farm, because they would catch the plague from the other workers.
Emma	No, the plague is over now.
Teacher	That's right, but Paula is half right in a way. The landowner would find it difficult to find workers, but not for the reason that Paula gave. It's obvious, really.
Paula	Some of them have died. There are fewer workers.
Teacher	That's right; well done, Paula. Now, what would the landowner have to do to make sure he got workers to bring in his harvest? *(Silence)* All the other farmers need workers too, but there's a shortage.
Emma	Pay good wages?
Teacher	That's it. And would the landowners be pleased about that?
Paula	No!
Teacher	So, what are you going to write down on your list of effects of the plague? Get it right – I'm going to ask you to explain it to the rest of the class in a bit.

Knowing only involves remembering – understanding requires that students 'own' the reasoning.

There is another crucial advantage of using questioning as a teaching technique. When we were considering motivation, it was pointed out that students need to know they are making a success of their learning. Nothing motivates quite as much as the glow of satisfaction that a student gets when he or she answers a question correctly, and immediately gets warm praise from the teacher. Remember that psychologists studying stimulus-response learning found that an immediate reward encouraged learning. Remember also that students are motivated by success. Questioning motivates students not just because they find it to be an interesting activity generally, but because it gives an immediate reward for their endeavour, and demonstrates their success in learning.

To summarise, then, the advantages of questioning as a teaching method are that it:

- displays the 'logic' of the subject and passes it on, encouraging understanding rather than rote remembering.
- produces transferable learning.
- gives instant feedback on whether learning is taking place (to teacher *and* student).
- ensures the lesson moves at the student's pace.
- is an active and interesting activity for the students.
- gives students practice in *using* the recently acquired ideas and vocabulary you have been teaching.
- uncovers incorrect ideas and assumptions, allowing 'unlearning' to take place (i.e. it supplies the *'check and correct'* elements of learning).
- can be motivating, as it gives students a chance to demonstrate their success in learning.
- offers, in one-to-one questioning, a chance for the teacher to diagnose the difficulty a 'stuck' student might be having.
- can be used to discipline a student.
- allows the teacher to evaluate learning.
- encourages the development of high-level thinking skills.

The disadvantages are that it:

- can be a time-consuming activity.
- makes it difficult to involve all students in the group.
- is not an easy technique for the teacher to master.

Questioning technique

How should we use questioning? A good questioning technique should encourage *all* the students in the class to think. It should avoid an 'I'm trying to catch you out.' atmosphere, and should give students a chance to get some positive feedback demonstrating their success in learning.

After posing a question, wait; most of the students should then be trying to puzzle out the answer. When they have had reasonable time to think, ask someone to answer. If you nominate someone to answer *before* posing the question, the rest of the class will be mentally in neutral, if not actually asleep! A helpful mnemonic is: 'Pose – Pause – Pounce!' The longer you pause, the more thinking the students do, and the longer their answers will be when they come.

Encourage responses to your questions by asking simple ones at first, especially with a new group. Without going overboard, show that you are grateful for the responses you are offered, and *always praise correct answers*. If an answer is given in a quiet voice, repeat it to the class.

How do you deal with incorrect responses? Reread the example at the beginning of this chapter, and see how the teacher involved dealt with the problem. She did not ridicule the incorrect answers; instead, she tried to show the reasoning that would have given the correct answer. If a response was incorrect, she simply stated why it was wrong (without giving away the answer), and then asked another question to get the student(s) on to the right track. She also used the incorrect answers to correct misconceptions.

It will take practice for you to develop your questioning skills to this level. But in time it *will* happen, and you will enjoy doing it.

This technique of leading students through the reasoning can also be used if they are unable to answer a question at all. Here is a driving instructor's response to an error made earlier by one of his students. Look at his technique carefully. You might like to cover this dialogue with a sheet of paper and reveal it line by line, thinking of questions the teacher might ask before revealing what he actually says.

Teacher You started signalling too early just then. Say you wanted to turn right, when should you start signalling?
Student *(No response)*
Teacher Can you signal right too early?
Student Not sure... I suppose so.
Teacher What would happen if you signalled right a mile before the junction in a city centre?
Student Other drivers would think you were turning right before you really were.
Teacher That's right, so when should you start signalling if there are lots of junctions about?
Student Just after the junction before?
Teacher That's right!

The student's confidence is boosted by the praise and smile from the teacher, and a potentially negative experience for the student is turned into a positive one. You might not have asked the same questions, but that does not matter, as long as your questions would make the student think out the reasoning for himself.

Distributing questions

When questioning a class, try to distribute the questions as widely as possible:

> 'How about someone on the back bench answering this one?'
> 'Have *you* any idea, Simon?'
> 'How about someone who *hasn't* answered a question yet answering that one.'

The plan of a classroom shows what is sometimes called the 'arc of vision' of the teacher. Students within this arc are more likely to feel involved in the lesson, and are therefore more likely to answer a question.

Students who do not want to participate in a lesson choose to sit out of the teacher's arc of vision. You may remember from your school days the scramble for seats at the back of the class in the less popular lessons!

It is too easy to ignore quiet students at the back of the class. Try to include them. Responses can often be obtained from reticent students by 'body-pointing' or by eye contact. Suppose, for example, two students on your left have not yet answered a question. If you move closer to them, and keep looking from one to the other after you have asked the question, one of them will answer if they can.

Don't be afraid to leave plenty of time for students to think; this is not wasted time. Smile while you are waiting, if you are worried about putting too much pressure on them.

Teacher: 'Why did we go to war; as a merchant, how would you feel; and how was your trade affected by the Napoleonic War?'

What answer do you think the teacher got? I expect you guessed; he got no answer at all. Make your questions short and simple – and ask them one at a time!

Avoid questions which are so vague that there could be any number of correct answers. I have heard many novice teachers ask such 'guess what I'm thinking' questions. Here is an example. A keep-fit teacher had asked a student to demonstrate an exercise to the rest of the group, to review what the students had

151

learned the previous week. The teacher noticed that the student had her arm in the wrong position, so she pointed vaguely to the student and asked: 'What do you see here?' The question was so vague that no student felt confident enough to answer. A better question would have been: 'Can anyone see anything wrong with her position?' The question 'What do you see here?' was not a genuine question at all, but an invitation to guess what the teacher was thinking. She would have been cross if one of the students had – correctly – answered this question with: 'Susie in a green leotard.'

If a question leads into a conversation between you and a student, use eye contact and body-pointing to include the other members of the class. Give your own comments to the whole class, and repeat the student's points if they are made too quietly for all to hear.

If students are reluctant with their answers, then first make sure your questions are simple enough, that you wait long enough, and that you praise or thank students for their responses. If this doesn't work, ask them to discuss answers in pairs before giving their response. This gives students time to think, and to check their answer with their partner.

Experienced teachers usually pepper their teacher talk with between one and four questions per minute. When explaining a difficult point that involves reasoning, their presentation is often virtually 100% questioning.

Varying the type of question you use

Open and closed questions

Closed questions have only one satisfactory answer, which is usually very short.

> *Examples:*   'Should it be "Yours sincerely" or "Yours faithfully"?'
> 'Is there a danger of the plant drying out?'

Open questions require a more detailed response, and there is often more than one correct answer.

> *Examples:*   'What did merchants have to gain from this war?'
> 'How could we improve the apparatus to make our
> experiment yield a more accurate value?'

Open questions make students think, and tell the teacher much more about what the students have learned. By contrast, closed questions such as 'yes/no' questions usually require little thought. They are likely to be guessed with at least 50% success, and so have low 'diagnostic power' – that is, the teacher cannot assume for certain that a correct answer means that successful learning has taken place.

152

Some students can manage a 100% success rate on 'yes/no' questions without understanding the first thing about the subject of the questions. Their technique, perhaps unconscious, is to put on a thoughtful expression after the question has been asked, and then shake their head from side to side to give the impression they are about to say 'no'. Whilst doing this they look carefully at the teacher's expression. If the teacher smiles and raises his or her eyebrows, the student completes the answer as a 'no'. If, however, the teacher lowers the eyebrows or shows no expression during the student's head-shaking, the student feigns a sudden flash of insight and converts the answer to a 'yes'!

A similar student technique is to give an immediate answer, for example a 'no', and watch the teacher's non-verbal reaction. If this is unfavourable, the answer is immediately changed before the teacher has had a chance to respond verbally. Most students use this second technique quite unconsciously. If you don't believe me, try the following. Ask students some reasonably difficult 'yes/no' questions. On receiving a correct answer, say nothing, and make no facial expressions or other bodily movement – just wait. Unless the student is very sure of the subject, I will wager that within three seconds he or she will have changed the correct answer to an incorrect one!

Questioning levels

'What are the names of the bones in the upper arm?'
'What would happen if human beings didn't have a skeleton?'

Some questions simply require that students recall facts. Such questions certainly have their uses: reinforcing earlier learning, practising recall, 'pointing' to the most important facts in a topic, and informing the teacher of what students can and cannot remember.

However, there is more to learning than remembering. Even the most hard-boiled teachers would acknowledge that most examination syllabuses award less than half of their marks for the recall of facts. The majority of marks are awarded for higher-order skills, such as the ability to comprehend and apply the concepts and principles associated with the course of study. Although it is not recognised formally, marks are in effect also awarded for more general 'thinking skills', such as the ability to sift through the memory and choose only the information relevant to a particular question.

Fact questions do not by themselves develop understanding, and they do not let students apply their knowledge, let alone practise the higher-order thinking skills. There are plenty of types of question that are more demanding.

Trevor Kerry (1982) listed a number of different question types. His suggested categories are shown in the table at the top of the next page.

153

Question type	Example
Data recall	What is the capital of France?
Naming	What is the name of the bone in the thigh?
Observation	What colour was the litmus paper?
Control	Will you sit down, John?
Pseudo-question	*(An open question but the teacher expects only one answer)*: What do you see here?
Speculative hypothesis	What would happen if all the trees in the world were cut down tomorrow?
Give reasons	Why do people in the Third World choose to have so many children?
Evaluation	What evidence is there for the existence of an after-life?
Problem-solving	How can we drill the wood without overheating it?

While facts are often soon forgotten, higher-order thinking skills tend to be retained, because such skills are more generally applicable, and therefore more often used. The dates of Henry VIII's reign, for example, will soon be forgotten unless recalled from time to time. In a culture such as ours, the importance of higher-order mental skills can hardly be overstated; once developed, such skills can be applied in any field of human endeavour. For the majority, who find little direct use for most of the factual knowledge gained during their education, these skills are the main benefit of their many years in school or college. These precious thinking skills can only be developed by the effective use of questioning.

Education is what remains when you have forgotten what you have been taught.

Sadly, research shows that 70% to 80% of questions asked by teachers require only factual recall. Researchers suggest that many teachers are simply not skilled enough to ask higher-order questions.

The uses of questioning

Questioning can be used whenever either reasoning or recall is needed, but it has little use if the students are being given *new* factual material.

In terms of the EDUCARE? elements of learning, questioning can be used to provide students with an *explanation*, to let them *use* the knowledge you are teaching, and of course to *check and correct* and indeed to *evaluate* their learning. It can also be used to *review* or revise earlier work.

An explanation should display the logic of a subject and pass this thinking on to the student; questioning is an excellent method of doing this. Here is an example of the

154

If you have trouble thinking up thought-provoking questions, try those which start with 'why', or 'how'. Putting one of these words in front of almost any statement can help change it into a question. 'What would happen if...' is also a useful phrase for the start of a question. Try making the following statements into questions:

Rain tends to fall in mountainous regions.
Thomas More was executed.
Increasing the temperature increases the rate of the chemical reaction.
This bacteria needs air to survive.
Jesus told parables.

It is often possible to make more than one question from each factual statement. For example, you could ask 'Why was Thomas More executed?', 'How was Thomas More executed?', 'What would have happened if Thomas More had not been executed?' etc.

use of questioning to give a student an explanation for hot air rising. The student has already studied density and expansion.

Teacher Why does cork float on water?
Student Because it's less dense than water.
Teacher Good. Now, when you heat air, it expands. What effect does this expansion have on the density of the air?
Student It makes it less dense.
Teacher That's right. So, what happens to hot air when it is surrounded by cooler air?
(Silence)
Well, what happened to the less dense cork when it was surrounded by water?
Student It floated.
Teacher Yes, so what will happen if hot air is surrounded by cool air?
Student It will float too.
Teacher Good; and why?
Student Because the hot air is less dense than the cold air.
Teacher Well done. So *hot* air floats in *cold* air. Can you think of an example of this 'convection' happening?
Student A hot air balloon?
Teacher Exactly. And that's why we say 'hot air rises'.

The teacher could of course give this reasoning by teacher talk. However, there are a number of advantages in making the student provide the steps in the logic. The explanation is done at the student's pace; there is an opportunity for the student to use the ideas, and have the use checked; and when the student eventually 'gets it right', the success is motivating.

It is important to realise that the interchange on hot air rising could have been carried out with a class as a whole, with a group, or with an individual student.

Questioning can be used to evaluate the learning of students. This is perhaps most frequently seen where a teacher meets a group of students for the first time, and wants to establish their existing knowledge before proceeding with new material.

Questioning can also be used to wake up an inattentive student. Paul is gazing out of the window:

Teacher So, how would you tell a good précis from a bad précis? ... Paul?
Paul What? *(Some laughter in the class)*

Another important use of questioning is in the diagnosis of a student's difficulty. When students are 'stuck', how should a teacher respond? It is tempting to help them over their difficulty as quickly as possible by *telling* them what to do, but it is better teaching to find the cause of the blockage and put this right – or better still, let the student *discover* how to put it right. Questioning students is perhaps the only way of discovering the misunderstanding or knowledge gap that has caused their difficulty. The driving instructor dialogue we looked at earlier is an example of this use of questioning.

Teaching by the use of questioning only is sometimes called the 'Socratic method'. Socrates claimed he knew nothing (this may partly explain why he never wrote his ideas down); he simply questioned his students in order to show up any inconsistency in their beliefs. He was not rewarded for this humility, however, but was put to death for 'corrupting the young'. Moral: don't ask questions that are too difficult!

Questioning does not come naturally to most people, because novice teachers are used to thinking in terms of answers rather than questions. As a result, many novice teachers find it very difficult to sustain a lengthy bout of questioning, requiring as it does the ability to 'think on your feet' in order to field an unexpected answer and turn it into the next productive question.

It is advisable to think out in advance the questions you are going to use in a lesson, especially the thought-provoking ones. However, it does not take long before you are able to think up questions 'on the spot'.

Trevor Kerry (1982) thought the main faults inexperienced teachers showed when using questioning were that their vocabulary was too complex; they did not leave enough time for students to answer; they did not use enough reinforcement (e.g. praise); and they were often unable to prompt a student into producing a useful response by, for example, using a simpler question. Most learning teachers are unaware of these faults, so it is advisable to start by over-compensating: make your questions very clear and concise, leave more answering time than you think necessary, and give more praise than you think necessary.

> Groisser (1964) said questions should be clear, purposeful, brief, stated in a natural and simple language, thought-provoking, and distributed widely; there should be a balance between 'fact' and 'thought' questions.

Summary and checklist

Questioning is of paramount importance. It would be impossible to develop genuine understanding, or other higher-order mental skills, without it. It teaches students to think for themselves, and produces high-quality, transferable learning.

It allows students to practise using the concepts and principles they are being taught, and it gives the teacher the opportunity to check immediately and correct this use. It also gives teachers feedback on whether learning is taking place, and ensures that they do not 'lose' the students.

Students tend to find questioning an active and enjoyable activity, especially as answering correctly gives them confidence and a feeling of success. Even the students who are not chosen to answer the question will gain in confidence if they are able to think of the correct answer for themselves. This confidence and success, along with the praise and approval which should accompany it, fuels motivation.

However, questioning is an unfamiliar technique for most of us at first, though after a little practice it soon comes quite naturally.

☑ *Questioning skills checklist: The 'ten commandments'*

☐ 1. Do you ask questions which students can answer successfully?

☐ 2. Do you leave time for students to think?

☐ 3. Do you use body language (eye contact, smiling, raising the eyebrows, nodding etc.) to encourage responses?

☐ 4. Do you always praise or otherwise acknowledge correct responses?

☐ 5. Do you avoid ridiculing student's answers?

☐ 6. If no answer comes, are you able to ask a simpler question that leads to the answer to the original question?

☐ 7. Do you make questions short and clear, using straightforward language?

☐ 8. Do you avoid using solely fact-based questions?

☐ 9. Are you able to distribute questions widely around the class?

☐ 10. Are you able to ask questions, say, twice a minute during teacher talk?

Exercises

1. Take a simple teaching point that needs only a minute or so, and requires reasoning, and try teaching it entirely by questioning. Prepare your questions in advance. Use 'why', 'how' and 'what would happen if...' questions.

2 Think of a process or skill you know well, which requires reasoning to explain it – say, wiring a three pin plug, or repotting a pot-plant. Think of a series of questions that could be used to teach a student the skill.

3 Write down five ways to encourage answers from reluctant or shy students.

4. Write down five ways to help distribute questions widely around the class.

16 Discussion

We all love a discussion. The media has been quick to catch on to this, even if some teachers have not: it is hard to avoid discussions now on radio or TV, be they panel-based, phone-ins or involving a studio audience.

Discussion is used as a method of teaching more often than you might realise. It involves a free-flowing conversation, giving students an opportunity to express their opinions and ideas, and to hear those of their peers. Some teachers use short spontaneous discussions as a natural extension of their questioning technique, but this chapter concentrates on their deliberate use in a class or large group.

When to use discussion

Discussions are generally considered to be of value in the following situations:

- Where the students' opinions and experiences need to be known by the lecturer, or are valuable and interesting to the other students in the group.

  e.g. In a workshop where experienced Health Workers are evaluating old methods of working and considering new methods.

  In an English literature class discussing bullying.

- Where the topic involves values, attitudes, feelings and awareness, rather than exclusively factual material.

  e.g. While exploring sex-stereotyping or racism.

  While trying to develop or change attitudes to safety in an engineering workshop.

- Where it is necessary to give students practice in forming and evaluating opinions.

  e.g. Discussing the character of Hamlet in an English literature class.

  Discussing some effects of unemployment in a sociology class.

Uncontroversial fact-based topics are of course not suitable for discussion-based learning. It is important to recognise that many teachers are in effect encouraging their students to develop their own informed opinions about the material being studied. This is where the discussion comes into its own. Opinion-forming and persuasion are considered in Part 4.

Imagine you manage a high street chain store, a job you have held for eight years. Your Head Office sends you on an updating store management course, and one of the sessions concerns intentional and unintentional racism in your staff's attitude towards customers. What would be your reaction if the session involved:

1. A lecturer being critical of the racism he has discovered in his researches, and prescriptively describing in detail how store managers should change their practices in order to improve matters.

2. A discussion where a lecturer first details factual material concerning intentional and unintentional racism in stores, and then asks *you* and your fellow participants what you feel about it as store managers, and what could be done about it.

Many people would react to the first session I have described by rejecting the implied criticism. 'What does he know about running a store?' 'The lecturer is just a careerist on a bandwagon.' The result would, if anything, be a hardening of attitudes – quite the opposite of the lecturer's intention.

The reaction to the second session is likely to be more positive, and not only because students enjoy expressing their opinions. If students' views are accepted with interest, they will respond by being open-minded rather than threatened and defensive. They are then more likely to change their opinion and practices, especially if they find other course participants do not agree with them.

It might be objected that a discussion will only encourage students to express 'wrong' opinions. However, 'wrong' opinions can only be changed if they are challenged, and for this they need to be out in the open. (You might, though, want to make an exception in the case of a very personal topic such as personal hygiene.)

Using discussion as a teaching method carries a hidden message – the teacher is in effect saying to his or her students: 'I value your experience and I am interested in your opinions.' By contrast, the unspoken message of a lecture in teacher-talk style is that the students know nothing of value about the topic.

Well-managed discussions are interesting, absorbing and active. They produce a safe environment for students to examine their opinions, and where necessary change them (although opinion changes often occur later, as a result of reflecting on the discussion). There is an opportunity for students to use high-order cognitive skills such as evaluation and synthesis. They are useful for affective education; for example, establishing empathy, examining social and moral values etc. They also offer an opportunity for students to get to know each other, which is important if they are to feel at ease and become communicative.

Make a list of topics for discussion in your teaching situation.

Planning a discussion

For anything other than a short ad hoc discussion, the discussion leader needs to have objectives that he or she hopes to achieve during the session. Having decided on these, a plan must be produced; the plan may simply take the form of an ordered list of key questions.

Some discussions are genuinely open-ended, and the teacher will be more interested in listening to the students' ideas than in achieving predetermined learning. For example, a teacher may start a weekend gardening course by asking each student to describe their own garden, with the aim of learning a little about each member of his group. Similarly, a teacher of English Literature might ask students to discuss the motives of a character in a novel. Open-ended discussions like these are dealt with under 'opinion-forming' in Part 4. It is still worthwhile to prepare a list of questions in advance, though you probably won't stick to them.

Other discussions have clear objectives. Consider a discussion on safety at work, designed to establish the main risks to health and safety in an engineering workshop, and how these risks can be minimised. In discussions such as these, a list of questions will not of themselves ensure that the objectives are achieved. There will be important conclusions that need to be reached during the discussion, and it is advisable to write these conclusions down as they are made, preferably in a place where the students can see and refer to them. You certainly need to prepare a clearly-worded summary of each of the key ideas you want to get across.

Choosing appropriate questions

As we saw in the previous chapter, there are two types of questions:

Closed questions have only one appropriate answer, as for example in 'yes/no' questions.
> E.g. 'Is spilt oil a risk?'

Open questions require a more detailed and more personal response.
> E.g. 'When do you find yourself most tempted to take risks?'

Clearly open questions are more useful for getting a discussion going. If a student gives a short answer to an open question, use eye contact and nodding etc. to encourage a longer answer.

Make sure the sequence of questions and conclusions leads you to fulfil the objectives that you set for the discussion. If the discussion is not planned, then it will degenerate into an aimless airing of views; the students will learn nothing of value, and the experience will be a waste of time for all concerned. The discussion plan needs to be written down; no-one minds a discussion leader having a prompt sheet in front of them setting out their plan (they do it on TV, so it must be OK!)

161

> **Which of these questions would be suitable for inclusion in a discussion on safety in the workplace?**
>
> 1. Is safety important in the workplace?
> 2. Could anyone tell us about any unsafe practice they have seen in the work-place?
> 3. In your opinion, is too much importance placed on safety procedures?
> 4. What would you think are the greatest risks to health and safety in your working environment?
>
> To produce the best response, try *open*, *controversial* and *personal* questions. Question 1 is closed, impersonal and uncontroversial, and is therefore hopeless for a discussion. Question 2 is personal, question 3 is personal and contro-versial; both would be suitable for a discussion as long as 'yes-no' answers were not expected. How would you classify question 4?

Effective discussions are usually structured very carefully, though the participants may not be directly aware of this.

> **Example of a plan for a discussion with 17-year-old science students, as part of an introduction to study skills:**
>
> *'To start with, I would like each person to describe briefly how they expect to prepare for this summer's exams.'*
>
> *'What activities do you find helpful during revision?'*
> (Reading notes, reading textbook, doing questions from past papers, writing summaries, seeing other students or teachers about problems etc...)
>
> *'How long should revision sessions be?'*
>
> *'Does anyone draw up a revision plan for examinations?'*
> (Example revision plan)
>
> *'Has anyone any ideas on how to cope with exam nerves?'*
> (Adequate preparation, past exam paper questions, clearing up difficulties with other students or teachers, plenty of sleep, rest and relaxation, talking with friends, realistic understanding of own ability, e.g. read last year's reports...)
>
> *'What should you remember to take into the examination room with you?'*

How to lead a discussion

Give the topic, and then sit back and wait until it is all over? No! It takes skill to develop a successful discussion, especially if specific objectives are to be covered.

First consider seating; participants need to be able to see each other's faces easily, so the circle is the best seating arrangement. If this is out of the question (because of fixed benches, for example) try one of the seating plans below, where most students only have to change the way they are facing.

Conventional seating   Discussion seating

Or you could permanently rearrange the seating in this discussion style.

Seating plans for discussions

The start

Has relevant factual material been presented? Opinion should be consistent with fact! Starting a discussion is sometimes difficult, especially if the participants are shy and reticent because they have not met before. It often helps if the leader of the discussion produces some factual material to start it off. If the topic is a matter of dispute, the introduction should be as unbiased as possible; give both sides of the argument, for example by reading a few paragraphs from relevant sources. Don't give away your own opinion on the matter, as this may inhibit students from expressing the opposite opinion.

163

After this initial input it is helpful for the leader to ask a question. The question should be open, clear, and concise, not a jumble of related questions. In order to make sure the discussion 'warms up' quickly, it helps if the first question is either controversial, or requires an answer from each member of the group, as in the examples below:

> 'Would each of you in the group just like to explain briefly the responsibilities you have in your company?'

> 'Do you think revision is a waste of time for a good student?'

Don't ask vague questions like: 'Well, you have most of the important facts now; what do you think?'

Questions which require answers from every member of the discussion group are called 'rounds', and can be used at any stage of a discussion. E.g.

> 'How would *you* deal with this situation?'

> 'What most troubles *you* about this procedure?'   [etc.]

Make sure you respond positively to the contributions.

In large groups there is a tendency for the more self-confident students to dominate discussion. For this reason, some teachers split their students into smaller groups. With more than about 12 students, it is difficult to run a discussion where most students contribute. However, short discussions can still be valuable in such larger groups.

Too often discussions are like a game of ping-pong, with comments passed back and forth like this:

> teacher - student - teacher - student - teacher ......

Ideally student-student communication should also take place.

You can encourage responses from students non-verbally:

- While a student is talking, use eye contact and nod your head.
- When a student appears to finish, leave a silence with sustained eye contact to encourage a longer contribution.
- When you are talking, scan *all* the members of the group with eye contact.
- When you have finished asking a question, fix an individual who has not contributed yet with eye contact, and wait. They will feel a strong pressure to answer.
- *Don't* talk in a quiet, restrained manner. This 'drops the temperature'. Use a strong voice, and show interest and enthusiasm!

> **You can also encourage responses verbally by controversial questions, and by:**
>
> - Saying 'That's interesting – can you explain that more fully? ... What makes you feel that way? ... Could you say a little more about that?'
> - Playing devil's advocate or exaggerating a student's opinion (with a smile): 'So you believe even whites with non-white marriage partners are racist?'

If discussions tend to go badly with a group, talk to them about it directly – ask them why. If they find that everybody in the group is as nervous as they are, this sometimes helps. Ask them how students should behave in order to make discussions fun. Get a list of this behaviour, then ask the group members to promise to try it out!

> **Credit the source of ideas during the discussion:**
>
> 'As Paul said, there is no point in...' This shows you genuinely value contributions, and encourages participation.

The style

Most people distinguish between a debate and a discussion. In a debate, the style is competitive; in a discussion it is, ideally, non-competitive and exploratory. There should be a cooperative attempt to come to a mutually-held conclusion, and members of the group should not attack each others' views in an adversarial style. Unlike a debate, a discussion should leave people free to speculate, and to change their point of view.

You may like to establish ground rules with your group, such as: no interrupting; no-one speaks for more than one minute at a time; all points of view must be respected; everyone should express their opinion; no smoking.

> If all the students are in agreement, it is sometimes hard to get a lively discussion. Try being a 'devil's advocate': express an opposing opinion regardless of whether or not you hold that opinion yourself. This often enlivens discussion:
>
> 'But if other nations manage without nuclear weapons, why can't we?'

The role of the discussion leader during the discussion

You can include yourself: 'What do we think about...?'; or exclude yourself: 'What do you think about... ?' During the discussion, it helps if you watch out for the points in the following checklist:

☑ **Discussion checklist**

☐ Do you make sure only one person speaks at a time?

☐ Do you clarify what someone has said if it was not well expressed?

☐ Do you encourage decision-making, and summarise the main points as they are covered or agreed?

☐ Do you move on once consensus is found, or when a point is exhausted?

☐ Can you ensure that one person does not dominate the discussion, and that everyone feels involved even if they don't make a contribution?

☐ Can you make sure there is no verbal bullying?

☐ Do you keep your eye on the clock and on the objectives?

☐ Do you encourage participation by praise and acceptance, and by non-verbal means?

☐ Do you listen hard, and summarise and conclude the discussion at the end?

The summarising role is very important, to ensure that students are clear about what they have learned during the discussion; the main points should be reinforced by note-taking or by handouts, otherwise they will soon be forgotten. For similar reasons, discussions lasting more than half an hour are of questionable value.

Some people find it difficult to 'shut up' students who hog the discussion, but you will gain everyone's respect if you are brave enough to intervene on the group's behalf. Be polite: 'Clive, you've made some interesting contributions already, but I'm anxious to hear everyone's opinion...' Try nominating someone who has not spoken to answer the next question; or just say, 'How about someone who hasn't contributed yet?' Some teachers advocate doing a 'round' of all the students who have not contributed at the end of a discussion. If students know this will happen, it encourages them to get involved before the end.

It is almost always best for you not to express your opinion on the matter under discussion until the very end, if at all. It is considered unprofessional to give away your political opinions during a discussion.

Summary

Discussions are fun. They can involve students in high-order cognitive skills such as evaluation, and can be used to develop their opinions, attitudes and values. They can be left open, but usually need to be structured, perhaps by means of a series of questions. The questions should be open, personal and controversial if they are to elicit strong responses, and they should be clearly and concisely stated.

Student response can also be encouraged by praise, interest and acceptance of their opinions; and non-verbally by eye contact, waiting at the end of a response, or nodding.

If a teacher uses discussion, this demonstrates that he or she values the students' knowledge and opinions. Therefore it is a vital method for use with adults, and for attitude changing in any age group. Avoid verbal bullying, time-hogging and clamming up, by making it clear you value *all* opinions and want everyone to contribute.

Encourage decision-making and summarise the main points as they are covered or agreed, moving on once consensus is found or when a point is exhausted.

Summarise at the end, perhaps with an aide-mémoire.

17 Group work and student talk

Why use groups?

Think of an activity you really enjoy, and I will wager it either *requires* other people, or would be made more enjoyable by involving them. Think of an activity you hate; and I am prepared to bet that doing it in company would make it less odious. *Homo sapiens* is a social animal, and even that arguably distinct life form *studens quasi-sapiens* enjoys working in groups – so long as the teacher is able to direct activities meaningfully.

Peer through the window into a science lesson, or into a primary classroom, and you are more likely to find learners working in fours or fives than being taught as a whole. Why do teachers use groups? Is it just fashion and fun? Let's look at some examples of teachers splitting students into groups. See if you can guess the teacher's motives.

Case A
A humanities teacher has just explained the principal factors affecting the growth of European towns during the Industrial Revolution. She splits the class into groups of four, giving each group the details of a different fictional town. 'OK, I want you to use the ideas we have been talking about, to prepare an argument that will convince the rest of the class that *your* town will grow fastest. You have just five minutes to prepare your case.'

Later, one person from each group shows the map of their town, and argues the case for its growth to the class.

Case B
Some maths students have just completed a graph. 'Now,' says the teacher, 'remember the ten points to look out for when drawing a graph? In a moment I want you to work in your groups to check each other's graphs against those ten points. If you find an error, explain how to put it right.' Later the teacher asks the groups which errors they discovered. A similar graph is set for homework.

Case C
An accountant is running a one-day course for middle managers in a newspaper business. He has just described two alternative accounting procedures. He asks

the course participants, working in groups of four, to write down the main advantages and disadvantages of these two systems.

Later, the teacher gathers the class together and asks each group in turn to give one advantage and one disadvantage, until he has been given all the suggestions. During this process he accepts legitimate points and summarises them on the board.

Group work is active. It gives the students a chance to *use* the methods, principles and vocabulary that they are being taught. Shy students who will not contribute to the full class can usually be coaxed into contributing to a group. What is more, there is a built-in self-checking and peer-tutoring aspect to most group work, where errors in understanding are ironed out in a relatively supportive atmosphere.

Group work involves learners in task-centred talking. As well as being an enjoyable activity in itself, this provides huge opportunities for learning. It requires that learners process the new material, and make personal sense of it. Group work tends to hand the responsibility of learning over to the student.

In terms of the EDUCARE? elements, bearing in mind 'peer-tutoring', group work provides all but the aide-mémoire of these learners' needs (and could be adapted to provide even this). Students get a chance to practise high-order mental skills such as creativity, evaluation, synthesis and analysis. They also practise 'common skills' such as the ability to work with, and communicate with, others.

In addition, group work gives students a universally welcomed opportunity to get to know each other. It can also arouse group loyalty, especially if there is an element of competition; this can produce strong motivation (as in Case A above).

The teacher is given an opportunity to make use of the views and experiences of students. Consider the middle managers' lesson. Students in groups are more likely than individual students to think of all the major advantages and disadvantages of the accounting system; and more likely to get them right. Partly because of this self-checking factor, group members have confidence in group suggestions, and so offer them for discussion more readily. If the teacher had asked for individual contributions presented to the whole class, he would have been given fewer suggestions, and these would have been less well thought out.

In group work, students' opinions are being valued and accepted; in teacher talk they are being ignored. This has important implications for all teachers, but especially those who are teaching professional people, or those trying to change attitudes, values or prejudices. The 'hidden curriculum' underlying group discussion, as against that for teacher talk, was examined in the previous chapter on class discussion.

Most of the activities in Cases A, B or C above could have been carried out individually by students, but a high proportion of the advantages outlined would then have been missed. Group work is an adaptable and powerful teaching strategy with marked advantages; it is an essential feature of almost all modern teaching.

Limitations of group work

Some things are best done alone. Some would argue that creativity is an essentially personal process, requiring uninterrupted private thought. Perhaps the same could be said of some learning. Groups can go off in the wrong direction, and they can be hijacked by a determined individual. Some group members may become passengers, letting others take the lead, though assigning particular roles to each group member can sometimes overcome this difficulty.

Like all teaching methods, group work becomes ineffective when used indiscriminately, or when used too often or for too long.

> 'Garrulousness far from guarantees insight..'
> – *Mike Ellwood in an article in the TES*

Group work activities

Single tasks

Groups are asked to carry out a task or sequence of tasks – for example, an experiment; a question to answer; a series of calculations to carry out and check; a set of books to research for specific information etc. The task needs to be very clearly stated, and broken down if necessary.

170

Same, selected and different tasks

The task can be identical for each group, or selected by the group from a list of options. Alternatively, different related tasks can be entrusted to each group. For example, each of six groups can research the main manufacturing industries in one of six different cities; their findings can then be reported back to the class as a whole. Students often respond well to the trust implied in giving them a unique task to carry out for the class.

Open-ended tasks should be used – or at the least, one open-ended task should be given as the last activity. For example, after finding the manufacturing industries for their city, the students could be asked to 'find out what else your city is famous for'. If the task is 'closed', you may find one group will have finished and have 'nothing to do', before other groups have even worked out which way up to hold their pencils!

Group competition

Each group has the same task; the aim is to see which can do it best, or fastest, or simply to compare the different approaches. The task could be designing an experiment, or producing a notice-board display on a given topic; or it could be as simple as answering a set of multi-choice questions. After the work is completed, it can be judged by you or by the class; or less competitively, each group can simply present its work. Competition needs to be handled with care. Ideally effort should be rewarded at least as much as achievement (see Chapter 6 on praise and criticism).

The circus

The 'circus' is routinely used in science lessons, but is now finding extensive use elsewhere. A set of tasks is carried out by each group in a different order – thus at any given time, each group is carrying out a different task; but by the end of the circus, all the groups have completed all the tasks.

This allows classes to complete tasks for which full class sets of materials are not available: science apparatus, for example, or computers, or reference books. The two matrices at the top of the following page outline examples of how this system can be used with three groups A, B and C. The first matrix involves three tasks of equal duration; the second accommodates five tasks, one of which takes twice as long as the others.

The matrices may look complex, but they work easily in practice.

> Libraries will find a selection of books on a given topic for you if you give an indication of the level of work, but they will need adequate notice. You can then use these as reference materials for tasks.

Group	Task number		
A	1	2	3
B	2	3	1
C	3	1	2
	15 minutes	30 minutes	45 minutes

Three tasks of the same duration with a change-over every 15 mins

Group	Task number					
A	1	1	2	3	4	5
B	2	3	4	5	1	1
C	4	5	1	1	2	3
	15 minutes	30 minutes	45 minutes	60 minutes	75 minutes	90 minutes

Task 1 takes thirty minutes, the other tasks take 15 minutes. There is a change-over every 15 minutes.

Circus tasks can be of different durations if this is planned for carefully.

'Buzz groups'

Students are asked to discuss (usually in pairs or threes), in order to answer a question, solve a problem, draw up ideas for a design, decide on their attitudes to a scenario, etc. It is usual for the teacher to provide relevant factual material, and perhaps to outline the main arguments as an introduction. As with any discussion, the topic should not be purely factual.

Make sure the topic is clear, concise and structured. Asking buzz groups to 'discuss safety on the building site' is too vague to be productive, even if the students have had some experience of building sites. Break the task down:

1. Has anyone in your group heard about (or experienced) an accident on a building site? If so, tell your group.
2. What safety procedures are apparent in your place of work?
3. What do you think are the five most common accidents on building sites?

The task breakdown should be displayed for students during the group work; it could be written on the board, provided on a handout or card, etc. If the task is too vague or too abstract, the discussion may 'stall' or become directionless.

Try asking different but related questions of each group, with the group's findings to be reported back to the class. This is motivating, as it gives each group a special responsibility. For example, different groups of trainee teachers could discuss when to use questioning; how it should be used; its advantages as a teaching method; and its disadvantages.

Arrange seating so that students are facing each other. Buzz group sessions usually work best when they are kept short – a maximum of five minutes. It is usual then for the teacher to ask for feedback; students will be interested in expressing their findings and in hearing those of the other groups. As students have had time for critical appraisal of their ideas, the quality of their responses will probably be quite high, certainly higher than in question and answer; but if you are disappointed try not to be too critical of the responses. Accept those you can, perhaps summarising them on the board or OHP. It is very important for the teacher to reflect on and summarise the main points at the end of such a session – though indeed this is true of all group work.

> Some teachers ask buzz groups to produce outline answers to old examination questions. Students appreciate the practice.

Buzz groups are named after the noise made when a class starts discussing; so don't be alarmed. If the discussion is task-centred, what you are hearing is the sound of learning. However, if you are dealing with reluctant learners, make sure you have established a relationship with them before using this method.

> If some group members are time-hoggers, try to invent activities which share group discussion time out among the group's members. You can say, 'Start with each group member expressing their ideas in turn. Talk for about a minute each, without interruption. Then embark on a general discussion.' You may also like to devise ground rules for group discussion with the class.

Buzz groups are very popular with students, but use a time constraint; if you wait for everyone to finish you will be there for ever. Don't be afraid to keep it short; some simple questions can be quite deeply discussed in no more than one or two minutes. Buzz groups are an excellent method of reviving a dying lecture.

'What's your theory?': This type of buzz group session is highly adaptable. Rather than the teacher telling the students the accepted theory or 'correct' opinion on some matter, students are asked to discuss their own opinions in groups, and then report their ideas back to the class as a whole. Only then are the textbook ideas introduced. For example, trainee managers could be asked to draw up guidelines on how to run a good meeting, before a lecture on the topic. The group can write their findings on an overhead projector transparency, or on 'flip chart' paper, for later display to the class.

Pyramiding or snowballing

This is a way of extending buzz groups. After a buzz group session in pairs, two pairs combine to make a foursome in order to complete a related activity. If necessary these groups of four can then combine again to create groups of eight.

Here's an example; a mechanical engineering lecturer has just described ARD, a new method of creating plastic mouldings:

5 minute buzz groups: Working in pairs, trainees isolate the likely problems with the ARD production process.

For 10 minutes: After joining pairs to make fours, the trainees combine their list of problems into a master list, and then think of ways of overcoming two of the main problems they have isolated.

For 5 minutes: Combining groups of four into groups of eight, the trainees compare the work they have done in fours, and then decide whether or not to recommend the adoption of the new production process, or to recommend its adoption with reservations.

Pyramiding works best if the activities at each stage are more than just combining lists, and (as in the example above) develop in a logical sequence.

Brainstorming

Brainstorming is a method of producing a large number of creative ideas for *subsequent* evaluation. The rules are that:

- All ideas are welcomed, however offbeat or daft (wild ideas can often suggest more practical ideas, or be tamed to produce useful contributions).
- The group aims for quantity, not quality.
- *Judging* ideas is not allowed.
- Ideas are common property; combining or improving previous ideas is encouraged.

The first time you use brainstorming, you must explain the philosophy very carefully, and an example session can help to establish the idea. Get your class to think of as many uses for a house brick as possible. Initially you will get suggestions like 'doorstop' and 'support for shelves'; when you get suggestions like 'anaesthetic' and 'window remover', you know they have got the right idea!

Once brainstorming is understood:

1. Carefully define/agree the problem, issue or topic to be brainstormed:
    e.g. 'How could a retail store increase sales at Christmas?'
2. Brainstorm for ideas, writing them down on the board or flip-chart. You could ask your students to take turns at doing this writing, as it is a full-time job! Everyone should be able to see the suggestions:
    advert in the paper; give the stuff away; Christmas tree outside the shop; give people free coffee; offer a Christmas present ideas service; ...

3. If they flag, give them a one-minute 'incubation' period and then start up again.

4. Once the brainstorming session has dried up, choose the most useful ideas. If there is no consensus, choices can be made by each student ticking their favourite five, or by awarding points (rather like the Eurovision Song Contest).

   Alternatively ideas can be chosen for satisfying agreed criteria. E.g. 'Must be cheap to implement; must not require special training; must not involve extra staff' etc.

5. Now the ideas themselves are brainstormed to decide how they can be implemented in practice:
   '*How* would a 'Christmas present ideas service' work?'
   '*How* could the store go about giving people coffee?'

6. There is a vote for the two daftest or funniest suggestions, e.g. 'give the stuff away'. Now ask, 'Is there *any* sense at all in this suggestion?'

   Discussion might then lead to the idea of giving away one free present to anyone spending more than £20.

7. Evaluation of the ideas is best done on another day.

Brainstorming is great fun, but surprisingly, research shows that people can produce almost twice as many effective ideas when working alone (Taylor et al: 'Does group participation when using brainstorming facilitate or inhibit creative thinking?', *Adm. Sci. Quart.*,1958, 3, pages 23-47).

A simplified version of the above, where there is just one brainstorming session, is sometimes called a 'bull session'. (See also Chapter 25 on creative work.)

Peer-tutoring and peer-checking

Peer-tutoring involves students helping or teaching each other. This goes on informally much more than most teachers recognise; finding a whole class with an identical misconception in a piece of homework is not uncommon. On the whole, most teachers look on peer-tutoring very positively. It allows the faster learners to teach the slower, and gives the slower ones a chance to query misconceptions without embarrassment.

Peer-checking is one method of peer-tutoring, and is an under-used activity. Immediately after completing a calculation, a diagram, or some written work, students are asked to check each other's work in pairs or in small groups. The students must of course be very clear on how the work should be evaluated. An example might be:

'Now each of you check the other's letter – are the addresses both in the right place? Is it dated? Has the right ending been chosen? Is it well placed on the page?'

Asking students for a list of criteria to check each other's work is in itself a very useful activity. Peer-tutoring or peer-checking encourages students to develop *and use* the skills required to check or evaluate their own work, and to clarify in their own minds the criteria that need to be met for the task at hand – prerequisites for future improvement.

If prior warning is given that an activity will be peer-checked, this can concentrate students' minds wonderfully. The activity is usually carried out in a very good-humoured way; if you find it is not, don't use it.

Group seminars

Each group researches a different topic and makes a presentation to the class. The 'research' could be extensive in both time and scope, or as simple as a five-minute group discussion. The presentation usually involves one member of the group, or indeed all of them, explaining the group's conclusions to the class with the aid of notes written on an overhead projector transparency. (See Chapter 20 for more on seminars.)

Advocacy

A debating topic is argued in pairs. After three minutes or so, the pairs are asked to switch 'sides' in their argument. Clearly the topic must be contentious if this activity is to be a success. Here are some possible examples:

'Euthanasia could never be reconciled with a nurse's professional duty.'
'Who was responsible for the death of Romeo and Juliet?'
'Unless there is a global ban on nuclear weapons, one day they will fall into the hands of someone ruthless enough to use them.'

Unless the group is very able, it is important to ensure that its members are acquainted with at least some of the relevant arguments, and of course the relevant facts. It is often worth telling students which point of view they will be arguing, and giving them time to prepare notes before the persuasion session.

Some topics are best approached by describing a scenario or a case study to a group, and then asking it to debate a point arising from this. For example, after describing details of Mr Jones's behaviour and his treatment by his employer, you could ask them to debate:

'Was Mr Jones wrongfully dismissed?'

Optionally, the pairs can feed back to the class any new arguments or debating points for class discussion. The session can end with a vote. This activity could also be carried out in groups of four, with two people taking each side at any given time. If they are able students, it is fun for the teacher not to warn the students that they are going to be asked to change sides halfway through. This is an excellent activity where students need to be aware of the arguments on both sides of a contentious issue.

A variant of this game is for students to take turns in picking a statement out of a hat and then defending it against the rest of the group. Usually some preparation is necessary.

Empathy

You can ask buzz groups to create a detailed empathy profile of someone – e.g. nurses discussing how a new arrival on a surgery ward might feel, or teachers considering the possible feelings of someone returning to study after twenty years.

Alternatively, each person in a group takes on a character, and the other members of the group interview these characters in turn. This is a useful activity for any topic to do with human interaction: aspects of management, work in the caring professions, character analysis in English literature, etc. Here is an example:

A case study concerning strike action is read out. Groups of three are formed, and each member of the group is allotted a character: the employer, or the union official, or a 'blackleg'. The case study is then read out again, and students are given time to make notes about how it feels to be the character they have been allotted.

Each character is then 'interviewed' by the other members of the group. The other group members can either keep their roles during the interview phase – or better still, they can take the role of a sympathetic outsider or newspaper reporter. (See also 'role-play' in Chapter 20 on games and simulations.)

J'accuse

This is similar to advocacy. The class is divided into four groups: A, B, C, D.

A and B are prosecution and defence in one 'case'; C and D are prosecution and defence for another. The 'cases' involve accusing a person (or process) of something or other, e.g.

'Bach is accused of being a mechanical and soulless composer.'
'The box construction girder bridge is accused of being an outmoded design.'

While A and B are acting as lawyers, C and D act as jury – and vice versa. One person can be appointed judge. Taking this further, there can be 'expert witnesses' who have researched a particular aspect of a case in detail; cross-questioning and points of order are allowed. It's fun to think of a humorous sentence if a conviction results.

Groups will need substantial preparation time, and this preparation needs to be checked by you before the 'case' is tried.

'J'accuse' is ambitious, but active and fun; students remember what they have learned, as the activity usually makes a big impression.

Any more ideas?

The only limit to group activities is your imagination. (Many more suggestions can be found in Chapter 20 on games and simulations.)

Planning the activity

First decide on your objectives, and be sure these can be genuinely met with the use of group work. Choose an activity that your students can complete with only very infrequent help from you. Don't overestimate them. Is there some preparatory activity that will make the group work easier and more productive?

Choose short activities at first; if you are going to have a disaster, it may as well be a small one! Group work can often last as little as a minute. Make sure the task involves putting something down on paper, so that you will have something to check.

Make sure your activity is concrete, clear, concise and structured.

Collect and prepare your resources. Group work is an admirable opportunity to use books, magazines, videos, and specialist equipment that students would not other-wise see. Don't forget to leave time for the plenary, where the activity (and what was learned from it) is discussed and summarised.

The plenary

It is usual for the class to reflect on the tasks as a whole, and to summarise what has been learned. Commonly the scribe from each group reports back their findings, and these are written on the board by the teacher. Occasionally it is possible to summarise with each group individually, immediately after the completion of each task.

178

Grouping

What size should your groups be? This may depend on the activity.

The *larger* the group:
- the greater the confidence the group will have in its findings, and the more likely it will challenge the tutor's opinions.
- the more likely it is that the group will interpret the task correctly.
- the more experience the group will have to draw on.
- the less time it will take you to visit all the groups.
- the slower the decision-making process, and the greater the difficulty in achieving consensus.

The *smaller* the group:
- the more activity there will be –
  and therefore:
- the less passengers there will be.
- the faster decisions will be made.

Groups of between two and five are very common. Groups greater than about four tend to require or develop leaders. Groups larger than about seven tend to become increasingly unwieldy, and passengers become common unless very specific roles are allotted. Up to six and many hands make light work; over eight and too many cooks spoil the broth!

How do you decide which student goes into which group?

Random grouping E.g. allot each student a group number by counting and pointing round the room: 1,2,3; 1,2,3; 1,2,3 ...

Random groups might be a little shy with each other at first – which may or may not suit your purposes.

Friendship grouping Students will soon group themselves if you ask them to; but be clear and firm about the maximum group size.

This is popular with students, but friendship groups may not share your lesson objectives, and they can be resistant to awareness-raising or attitude-change. There is often no gender or race mixing, and cliques or exclusions can develop. Students will not increase their pool of acquaintances.

Achievement or experience grouping This could be strictly by achievement, with a top, a middle and a bottom group; or those with a specific weakness (e.g. maths) can be grouped together so that they don't become (maths) 'passengers', and can together be given the specific help they might need. Shy students are sometimes grouped together for similar reasons.

*This approach allows the groups to go at their own pace; it **can** produce rivalry and resentment, but this is by no means always the case.*

Deliberate mix   You may want a mix of experience, backgrounds, ages, genders or abilities.

This is useful in preventing bias, and allows students to learn from each other's experiences. It is helpful, too, for awareness-raising and attitude-changing. Mixed ability groups can create an opportunity for peer-tutoring.

Proximity grouping   This is the most commonly used method. But don't choose groups of people who sit beside each other; make groups of those who sit behind and in front of each other. This makes it easier for the group to arrange itself so that members can see each other's faces, which is most important. Grouping like this can be carried out in a lecture theatre or laboratory, as well as a classroom.

Managing group activities

Bear in mind the chapters on classroom management. If you use groups a great deal you may like to rearrange the furniture, but check with others who use the room, or finish the class by putting it back as you found it. If you do decide to move furniture, give *very* clear instructions before allowing any movement.

You may need a chairperson or scribe for each group. Ask for 'someone who hasn't done it before', so that everyone gets a turn. Make sure the task is clearly explained, and draw the attention of the class to the all-important summary which should be permanently available to the group. Don't allow any activity until you say so, and give a time limit: 'Right, off you go; you have five minutes.'

To begin with, leave them to get on with it but remain obviously in attendance. Unless the activity is only going to last a minute or two, it then becomes important to visit the groups. (If the activity lasts more than three minutes, this is vital.)

- Check that genuine progress has been made:
  - what has the scribe written down?
  - have they interpreted the task correctly?
  - have they missed some important points?
- Ask if there are any queries.

Don't talk to the entire class during group work unless it is unavoidable. If it is, then stop all activity; make sure you have everyone's attention; and make your point clearly and concisely. Groups dislike being interrupted.

180

Body language

As you visit, make sure you don't get stuck with one group, however interesting their work might be. Body language is important.

Get your head down to their level, and smile to signal cooperation rather than judging. Some teachers ask each group to leave a spare chair for them. Position yourself so you can see the other groups.

After the activity ask at least some groups, and preferably all, to report back at least some of their findings. The groups will usually be interested in each others' work. It is *vital* to reflect on any outcomes, and to summarise what you hope they have learned from the activity.

Inexperienced teachers often ask groups to carry out tasks for which they are not prepared; they may also define group tasks insufficiently clearly, and neglect to visit groups.

☑ Checklist on use of group-work

☐ Do you define the task very clearly, and leave a summary of the task on the board?

☐ Do you visit each group as it is working, to check on progress and help where necessary?

☐ Do you ask each group's scribe to summarise the group's ideas to the class?

☐ Do you acknowledge the ideas of each group – e.g. by putting them on the board?

☐ Do you hold a plenary to summarise what students should have learned from the activity?

☐ Do you use group work as often as you could?

18 Games, simulations, role-play: active learning methods

During my schooldays, learning was regarded as a serious and difficult process; if laughter ever burst from a classroom, passing teachers would peer in with anger and suspicion. Yet games can produce intense involvement, and a quality of concentration no other teaching method can match. What is more, the increase in interest and motivation produced by a short session of game-playing can produce positive feelings towards the subject (and the teacher) which last for weeks.

The basic assumption of this chapter is that learning and enjoyment are not mutually exclusive. A 'further reading' section at the end of the chapter directs you to subject-specific games, of which there are many. But I will start by considering 'games for all seasons'; that is, games which may be adapted to almost any topic or subject area. Most of these games can be played by students as individuals, or in groups. There were other examples of games and active learning techniques in the previous chapter, on group work.

If cards need to be made, remember that any photocopier will copy on to thin white or coloured card in the usual way. Then you can guillotine these copies to cut your game cards to shape.

Games for all seasons

Decisions, decisions

This game is much more fun than it sounds. It is best done in pairs or perhaps threes, and can be played as a race or as an accuracy competition. In each case, the teacher needs to prepare in advance a set of special cards for each group, which they are required to sort, classify or match. A numbering code can be used on the cards, to allow quick identification of the correct answers by the teacher if necessary. The game is best described by giving a few examples:

- Groups are given a set of about 30 cards, each of which has a different phrase with an underlined word: for example, 'The fox ran quickly into a hole.' Students must sort the underlined words into nouns, adjectives, adverbs etc. Each group has the same set of cards. The first to sort them correctly wins.

Similar games can be devised for students to practise classifying:
> metaphor, simile and personification;
> conduction, convection and radiation;
> igneous, sedimentary and metamorphic rocks;
> valid and invalid arguments for the increased crime rate in cities;
> (and so on).

■ Groups of social workers and probation officers on an AIDS awareness course are given cards on which are described various sexual practices. They are to sort them into two piles: 'safe sex' and 'unsafe sex'.

■ Business studies students are given a set of cards, each of which describes an activity which prepares for the launch of a new product. The students are to sort the cards into the correct chronological order. Similar activities can involve, for example:

> Chronologically ordering the process of fitting a new central heating system.

> Working with given scenarios: for example, the ordering of necessary responses to a medical emergency (and the rejection of unnecessary responses).

'Matches' is a variant of 'Decisions, decisions' – some examples might be:

■ Science students are given a set of cards describing energy transformations, and another set describing processes. They have to match each 'process card' with the appropriate 'energy change card'.

■ Geography students are given a map of France and a set of labelled pointers: 'Paris', 'Lyon' etc. Once these are correctly positioned, they must be matched with another set of labels saying such things as 'Wine-producing area', 'Border with Italy', 'Fishing industry is active here', etc.

Most of these games can be made more difficult by 'spurious' cards which must be rejected – for example, a 'Geneva' pointer for the French map. Clearly, only your imagination limits the adaptation of such games to any conceivable topic or purpose. If the race or competition aspect is removed, the game is made rather more sedate, though it is still a very engaging activity.

The quiz

Quizzes are usually arranged as a competition between groups; they are a popular means of enlivening revision. Most commonly the teacher asks the questions; alternatively, students can make up questions for their competitors to answer, though these questions need to be cleared by you to ensure fairness.

Split the quiz up into different sections, along the lines shown overleaf.

183

- Groups answering questions in turn. (Will conferring be allowed? Will unanswered questions be offered to another group?)

- Questions for individuals (two points for a correct answer, one point if there is conferring with other team members).

- Questions for groups, where challenges from other groups can gain them double points if they challenge correctly, and a loss of a point if they challenge incorrectly.

- Difficult questions for the first raised hand (with referring to notes allowed), etc.

- Questions which are very difficult to begin with, and then become progressively easier (but score less points) as more information is given.

In a more elaborate version of this activity, groups make up questions for each other on a given topic, with model answers. These questions and their answers are checked by you as you visit the groups. Then the groups ask each other their questions in turn in a quiz format; you do the scoring. Make sure you decide on the rules about conferring etc. before the quiz starts.

Agree the format and scoring system in advance, and stick to it! Try to do the quiz in a spirit of fun.

The competition

Each student is either a 'competitor' who prepares work for presentation, or a 'judge' who evaluates the competitor's work after deciding on the judging criteria. Once work has been presented to the judges, they hold a 'fishbowl' discussion to evaluate the work. (Only judges are allowed to speak, but competitors are allowed to listen. Judges are usually arranged in a circle in the middle of the room.) For each piece of work, the judges can be asked to say what they liked about it, and to suggest one way in which it could have been improved. Eventually a winner or winners can be declared; these may get a small prize, or their work can be displayed. Two competitions can run simultaneously, with each student being a judge for one competition and a competitor in the other.

Students enjoy such competitions greatly, as they provide a sense of occasion and a clearly defined goal. Don't underestimate how much the judges learn from the process. After carefully deciding criteria, and using them to judge the work of others, they will subsequently use them to judge their own.

Alternative systems may use the teacher, or an impartial expert from outside the class, as the competition judge; or a national competition can be entered. Examples might be:

- a poster to show the effect of cash crops on Third World economies;

- a poetry, photography or short story competition;

- competitions to design an experiment to measure local air pollution, or the packaging for a new breakfast cereal.

Modified TV/radio games

Students often find it amusing to play an adaptation of a well-known TV or radio game show. Some examples might be Blockbusters, A Question of Sport, Any Questions/Question Time, Gardeners' Question Time – all offer formats which may be adapted to your subject area.

For example, I once saw the Gardeners' Question Time format (where a panel of experts answer questions from the floor) being used to great effect on a management training course. Course leaders formed the 'expert panel' on the first day; but on the last day of the course the panel were course participants, and the course leaders were among the audience.

The challenge

Almost any activity can be made into a game by turning it into a challenge:

'Can you separate the following chemicals without using filtration?'

'Can you devise a computer program to do the following, in less than twenty lines?'

'Out of three elastic bands and a cereal box, can you make a vehicle which will carry a matchbox 10 cm over a table top?'

'Five factors causing urbanisation are mentioned in the video – I bet no-one gets them all!'

Treasure hunt

A search for information can become a simple game by making it into a race, or a competition – e.g. 'Find as many examples of the use of percentages as you can in your newspaper. Let's see which group can find the most!'

Activities and games for teaching social skills

Two groups are each given an identical pile of 'Lego' building blocks. They are instructed to build a tower which is both as high as possible and as light as possible. They will gain three points for every centimetre the tower rises above the ground, and will lose one point for every brick used.

185

One observer (not a group member) is allocated for each group. It is made very clear that this is a competition, and that the only rules are the scoring system stated earlier; a time allocation is made.

The groups soon forget their observers, who are instructed to observe how their group makes decisions (democratic, dictatorial, etc.), who takes charge, to whom group members make their suggestions, to whom they defer, and so on. The game generates a great deal of heat! In the excitement rows often break out, and groups steal each other's bricks or even knock down each other's towers! (Tower-bashing and brick-stealing are not outlawed in the rules.) The aim of the game is to act as a focus for a discussion on groups, assertiveness, leadership and decision-making. The discussion begins with a detailed report from each observer on the behaviour of his or her group.

Thousands of games and activities have been produced to help teach social and management skills, human relationships etc. This is just one example. Those interested in finding more should find the *Active Tutorial Work* scheme (Longmans) a mine of useful ideas; another excellent source is Hopton and Scally: *Lifeskills Teaching*.

Ice-breakers

Games or activities are often used to introduce members of a new class to each other. Here is one example often used for the first meeting of an adult education group (though it could be adapted for any class):

> The class is split into pairs. The members of each pair ask each other a prepared list of questions: 'What is your name? Where do you live? Why did you come on this course? Where do you work? What are your hobbies? Have you any children?' and so on.

> The pairs then form into foursomes. Each person in each pair then introduces their partner to the other pair, giving the partner's answer to each of the questions. Fours then form into eights; each pair introduces the other pair in their foursome, and so on. This develops listening skills!

Another icebreaker is to ask each person to find someone in the room with a particular characteristic: someone who is a vegetarian, who doesn't like coffee, who sleeps without pyjamas, who has been to Africa... These will need to be on a handout, and at least a few should be slightly silly!

Board games

Commercially-made board games on many topics are available from educational publishers.

Role-play and simulations

In this activity, learners take on roles and act out a given scenario. For example:

- Trainee teachers are split into pairs. One takes on the role of a student with persistent attendance problems; the other takes the role of the student's teacher. Later the teachers swap roles.

- Trainee hotel receptionists take on the role of a receptionist dealing with an irate couple whose room has not been cleaned. Other students play these customers. The rest of the class watch, taking turns to be the receptionist.

- Three students take on the roles of characters in a novel they are reading. They are interviewed by the class about their motives.

- Two students take on the roles of Moslem women, talking of their fears about sending their five-year-old sons to school for the first time.

Role-play is very useful for developing the 'interpersonal skills' of learners – e.g. for training in the caring professions or the retail trades, for management training, and so on. It gives learners an opportunity to practise skills in a risk-free environment. It is also useful as an empathy activity where feelings and attitudes are being explored. (The last role-play activity listed above is an example of this.)

Role-play is often a single performance viewed by non-players and the teacher. Alternatively, several groups of students can carry out the same role-play activity simultaneously. The latter has the advantages of reducing stage fright problems, involving the whole class, and giving every student practice in the skills. It is sometimes possible to give everyone in a class a part or observing role in a single role-play activity.

Planning the role-play activity

Be clear about what you are trying to achieve, and design the activity towards these ends. If a skill is being practised – for example, interviewee skills – you could explain any background information or techniques to participants first, and perhaps show them an example of good (or indeed bad) practice.

Alternatively, you could use the discovery method, and learn entirely from the role-play activity itself. If you are using role-play as an empathy exercise, then research and group discussion can be used to develop a profile of the players before the role-play itself begins.

The scenario is best provided on paper; different versions are usually required for each player. Emphasise the goal for each role, and make the instructions brief; the players will enjoy filling in the detail. Don't define characters; the players will feel more involved if they do this themselves. Avoid stereotyped or extreme characters. Consider providing supporting documents such as mock letters or newspaper articles, to give background.

Can you give every member of the class a role in the play, or a special observing role? Observers can be assigned a particular player, or given some other specific observing brief – for example, they might be given a checklist. These observations can then be used as a focus for the debriefing session.

Clearly, the players will need to be given background details about the scenario being played out, perhaps including briefing on what they know about the other characters. In empathy-related role-playing, the background research might be considerable.

Running the role-play activity

Give players time to study the scenarios, and don't start until they are ready. If well planned and prepared for, role-play activities should run themselves; indeed, you should intervene as little as possible. However, you might like to add new information while the activity is running – for example, a memo or message could arrive for one of the players. Such interventions can be designed to prevent the action becoming too one-sided, but usually need to be prepared in advance.

Consider allowing a character the opportunity to stop the role-play activity at any point. This 'time out' can give the person concerned time to consult others, or to think out how to proceed. Once the student is ready, the play continues from where it left off.

If skills are being practised, and the players are reasonably confident and used to role-play, you could consider videoing the session. This allows for self-evaluation, and supplies detail for the debriefing session; but it may inhibit the players.

Debriefing or plenary session

Debriefing should be done straightaway if possible. It is usually the most important and time-consuming part of the activity. The aim is to reflect on the role-play, and to reach some general conclusions. You might like to prepare a list of questions to be considered by individuals and/or groups, and then by the class as a whole. For example:

Skills practice: What went on? Why did it go like that? How could it have been done differently? In what way was it realistic – and unrealistic? Can you relate what you saw to theory or technique? How did each player feel as the play progressed; what were their motives, and were they justified? ...

In the case of skills practice, it will be necessary for learners to criticise themselves and each other. Handle this carefully. When evaluating each performance, try asking the class for 'two goods and two improvements' – that is, two creditable aspects of the performance, and two ways in which it could have been improved. You must tease out from the experience both good and bad practice, and thus move towards generalised criteria for future success. Chapter 27 on learning from experience has more detail on this.

If the experience has been intense for any player, or for the group as a whole, feelings should be discussed. Ask players how they feel on a one-to-one basis, while the rest of the class are preparing for the debriefing session; and give any support they might need.

Drama

Try giving students an opportunity to prepare a short dramatic piece in groups, to present to the rest of the class. This is a very popular activity which is excellent for exploring emotive issues. Give each group a different brief; or better still, let them choose their own.

Simulations

An elaborate role-play activity is often called a simulation. Examples include war games; playing Chancellor of the Exchequer with a computer simulation of the British economy; flight simulators; and business in-tray games. Micro-teaching is another example, where trainee teachers deliver a short lesson to their peers.

Simulations can introduce an element of realism into our teaching, perhaps giving students experiences it would be impossible for them to have 'for real', and allowing them to develop skills without suffering the real-life consequences of their errors. By condensing time, and by eliminating non-essential distractions, they often provide powerful tools for teachers. They are now widely used in teaching and training in business studies, economics, stock market operations, political science, and medical diagnosis.

Simulations can be home-made, or obtained commercially – see the references at the end of this chapter.

Simulations inevitably simplify, and students need reminding of this.

Using games in practice

There is too much seriousness and not enough levity in most of our lives, so be brave and try using games. If the group are used to a very dull diet, they may get a little overexcited: try gentle games first, such as 'Decisions, decisions'. But do persevere. You may encounter initial reluctance from a very apathetic class, but be enthusiastic and absolutely insistent, and don't even *seem* to listen to the students who say they don't want to play. You will win them over eventually.

Further reading

Graham Gibbs, *Learning by doing*. FEU
Learning in Groups. Croom Helm
Lewis R and Mee J, *Using Role Play: an Introductory Guide*. National Extension College, Cambridge
Hopson and Scally, Life Skills Teaching Programme

SAFSET (the Society for the Advancement of Games and Simulations in Education and Training) has a journal, *Simulations and Games for Learning*, and produces resource lists for different subject areas.

19 Games to teach language and communication skills

I feel very envious of teachers of foreign languages. Almost any activity they fancy will be educationally valuable, so long as it involves the use of the language they are teaching. So why not play games? They produce an overwhelming desire to communicate, and so are excellent teaching methods. The following games can be used to teach any language, but there are thousands more games and activities; make up your own, or look for more in books on Teaching English as a Foreign Language (TEFL). The games in this chapter, then, are just to get you started; they may seem tame on paper, but once you have tried teaching languages with games, I promise you will never abandon the idea. Unless otherwise stated, it is assumed that learners will speak only in the target language (i.e. the one they are learning).

Picture recognition

Cut-out pictures from colour magazines are spread out on a table at one end of the classroom. Arrange the class into groups, and place them away from the table; identify each group as A, B, C... etc., and number each group member 1, 2, 3... etc. No. 1 from each group is shown by the teacher one of the pictures on the table; the teacher makes a note of which picture has been allocated to which group. The No. 1s then attempt to describe their picture (in the target language) to their group. Meanwhile, the picture placements on the table are shuffled by the teacher.

No. 2s then go to the table and attempt to choose the correct picture. They can if they wish go back and ask questions of No. 1 (who for the moment must *leave* the group). When they feel sure, the No. 2s bring the picture they have chosen back to their group (which No. 1 has not yet rejoined). If the group agrees this is the right picture, it is submitted to the teacher.

If their decision is correct, No. 2 is shown a new picture to describe; and so on round the group. Groups race to finish, say, two circuits round the group members. This game can generate real excitement and an intense desire to communicate. Students run excitedly to and fro (so check there are no floor obstructions).

Depending on the similarity of the pictures, this game can suit any level from elementary to advanced students. I have seen advanced students of sign language use this game to describe head and shoulder portraits of men and women in formal dress; they found it a difficult and hugely enjoyable challenge.

Variations

Sedate version: Each student is given a magazine picture in an envelope, which they are not allowed to show the others. Each describes their picture to their group. When the descriptions are complete, the pictures are shuffled and placed on a table, and identified with a letter. The group must work out whose picture was whose.

Advanced sedate version: The game can be made more difficult by requiring every group member in turn separately to identify each picture.

Stories

Chain stories

With the group sitting in a circle, the teacher or first group member gives the first line of a story, provided from a card. The next student in the circle makes up the next line, and so on round the circle. Very simple 'stories' are used – e.g.:

> 'He liked the picture very much.'
> 'It was a painting of his daughter.'
> 'His daughter didn't like the picture; she said it made her look ugly.'
> 'One day the daughter threw the picture away.'

Variation: A more difficult variation is for the beginning line and the end line of the story to be given. The group then provide one line at a time, until they link the two lines logically. This can be hilarious if the lines are amusing and/or have no obvious connection – e.g.:

> *Start:* 'The dog was learning the trumpet.'
> *Finish:* 'My grandmother hates spaghetti.'

Mime stories

The teacher mimes a simple story. The students then take turns to describe the story as it is mimed. For example:

> He was eating a meal. He dropped some food. He called the dog.
> The dog ate the dropped food. He patted the dog.

The whole class repeats the story at the end. The teacher claps *once* if the class is to repeat only the last line; *twice* if he or she wants the whole story repeated from the start, with students taking a sentence each.

Card stories

Each student has a story in English on a card, and must translate it to the class or group. The class/group must repeat the story back to him in English, sentence by sentence. Use simple stories.

The pyramid

Students work in pairs to find out, for example, how many brothers or sisters their partner has. The pairs now make groups of four. Each person then tells the group how many brothers and sisters *their partner* has. Then the groups of four make groups of eight...

I Spy

A student chooses an object in the room, revealing only its first letter. Other students ask questions about the object: 'What colour is it?' 'Is it bigger than my briefcase?' When a student guesses correctly, it's his or her turn to think of another object, and so on. This game can be made into a competition by dividing the class into groups, and giving each student an 'I spy' object on a card (an identical set of cards is given to each group). The first group to guess all its objects wins.

Variation: The teacher describes an object, and the students have to guess what it is. E.g. 'It is heavy.' 'It is made of glass.' 'You could put it on a table.' – and so on.

What's My Line?

A student thinks of a job, or is given a card with the job title. Other students ask questions: 'Do you have to travel?' 'Do you earn a lot of money?' The same competitions and variations can be used as for 'I Spy'.

Dice, board and card games

Simple dice games are excellent for teaching numbers. Here is a game for threes. You will require counters or tickets, and one or (usually) more dice for each group.

Student 1 throws the dice, and the other two attempt to be first to say the total number thrown correctly. The student who first correctly says the number picks up one counter; however, if he or she makes a mistake, one counter is *forfeited*. The dice are then thrown by student 2, and so on round the group of three. When all the counters are gone, the student who has the most wins. This game generates more excitement than you might think, and teaches numbers in no time.

Variations on this game: Students can take turns to say the numbers thrown, which gives them more time. Also, where two or more dice are used, the students can either say all the numbers separately, or add them to practise higher numbers.

Cards can be used to teach vocabulary. Pairs of students are given about fifty cards, with target-language words on one side and their translation in smaller writing on the other side. Each card is revealed in turn, target-language side up, with the translation hidden from view by a blank card. The first student in the group (including the dealer) who gives the correct translation gets that card. If students make a mistake, however, they must give a card to their opponent. The student with most cards at the end wins.

Variation on this game: The pile of cards is placed in the centre of the table and students take turns, round a group of three or four, to give the correct translation for each card; if they get it right the card is put on the bottom of the pack. If they get the card wrong, they keep the card and must learn it during the rest of the game. At suitable intervals, each student gives his or her pile of cards to a neighbour who reveals them one by one; the students who previously got these cards wrong must now attempt to get them right. If they still get it wrong, they continue to keep the card. The student who has the fewest cards at the end of the whole game is the winner.

It helps to have piles of cards on different topics (numbers, money, months and days, the kitchen, shopping etc.); then groups can swap packs of cards.

Student presentations

Each student must give a short talk on his or her interests, hobbies, favourite music, favourite dish etc. to the group. This helps members of the class get to know each other better. Give learners a week or so to prepare.

Objects

All the students are asked to bring an unusual object into the classroom the following week. They show the class their object, and the class have to guess what it is. Students usually bring something to do with their hobbies or interests.

Discuss a news story

Students choose a story from a recent newspaper, and report it to their group. They prepare this during the week. Optionally, the group can then discuss any issues the story raises.

Interpreter

One person must use the first language only, another only the target language, and the third interprets between them. The two single-language speakers take on parts – e.g. a French speaker wishes to find the way to the local railway station, and an English speaker is asked to provide the directions.

Video

A video is played with the sound turned down, and learners take it in turn to add a radio-style commentary.

194

Just a Minute

Many radio or TV games can be adapted to teach languages; 'Just a Minute' is only one example. Students pick a topic out of a hat, and then speak about it without marked hesitation or repetition. Students usually appreciate being given time to prepare for their 'minute'.

Variation: This game can be made into a competition between two teams, as in the radio version, with a referee changing the speaker to one from the opposite team if hesitation or repetition takes place. The speaker left speaking at the end of the minute wins a point for their team.

Granny's basket

The group sit in a circle or horseshoe. Students take turns round the circle to repeat objects given in previous turns, whilst adding one more – e.g.:

> 'In Granny's basket I found a banana.'
> 'In Granny's basket I found a banana and a bottle of wine.'

In a large group this can be a real test of vocabulary and memory.

Role-play

Role-play was considered in more detail in Chapter 18; it has obvious value for students of a foreign language. The teacher can give each of a group of students a role, which they then act out. For example, one student could be a hotel receptionist, with another playing a speaker of the target language who wants to make a booking. Group members can take turns to play each role.

Posters

The class is shown a poster or large photograph with plenty of detail in it. The teacher then asks questions based on the poster: 'Where is the dog?' 'What is under the table?' The class or individuals respond appropriately: 'In the field.', etc. (If you wanted to focus on grammar rather than meaning, you could ask for full sentences, e.g. 'The dog is in the field.') To practise past and future tenses, a card with 'YESTERDAY' or 'TOMORROW' on it could be pinned below the poster.

What am I doing?

Best done in groups. A student is given a card describing an activity – for example:

> 'You are ironing your wedding dress for your marriage tomorrow.'

The student then mimes the activity to the rest of the group, who must guess what is being done by asking questions which only require a 'yes' or 'no' answer.

Drills

Repeated hearing (and repeated use) of a particular language item is very helpful in language learning. As a form of repetition, drills enable us to focus sharply on particular points of grammar, vocabulary or pronunciation; and they can be fun, especially if you are lively and enthusiastic about drilling, and you don't do it too slowly. Give the word, phrase or sentence, and then let the class respond to you. Repeat each item up to six times only, and then give something new to drill. Never drill for more than 1-2 minutes, and keep this method for really useful learning.

You can ask individuals to respond rather than the whole class; if so, don't go round the class in a predictable order.

To provide variety, some of the following ideas can be helpful.

Changes

Make up a sentence that can be changed very easily. For example, 'Where is the butter?' The teacher gives the sentence, and the class repeats. Then you change the noun, e.g. 'Where is the cat?' Alternatively, go round the class with each student adding their *own* noun at the end of the sentence.

Ping pong

The teacher gives a sentence. The students must reply with an appropriate question:

'I went to the cinema.' – 'Did you enjoy going to the cinema?'
'I rode my bicycle.' – 'Did you fall off your bicycle?'

Teaching new vocabulary

Try to teach new words by using them in sentences. The students learn them much more easily this way. Teach new vocabulary items in groups. For example, you can group things found in the kitchen together:

'Where is the dishcloth?' 'Where is the mixing bowl?' 'Where is the spoon?'
'I need a new kettle.' 'I need a new saucepan.' 'I need a new ...'

Make sure you teach the words that the student really needs. Revision is essential.

Flash cards

There are published sets of these, but you can also make your own. Each card has a picture on it. Students respond to what they see on the card, with words, phrases or whole sentences. Try to make them so that they get harder and harder: 'Small dog', 'Big dog', 'Black cat', 'White cat', 'Small white cat' and so on. Good for revision.

196

Your own games and drills

New games and drills can be invented to suit your particular groups, and your own style; the activities described here are only a start. Try asking students to invent their own, or invent them yourself.

Wherever they come from, though, **do try games**; they create that intense desire to communicate which is the prerequisite for learning any language. And they make your lessons fun.

However, don't play any one game too often, or for too long.

20 Seminars

A 'seminar' is a timetabler's word, not a teaching method. It is an opportunity for between eight and twenty students to have a searching intellectual discussion on reasonably well-defined subject matter. It is not usually intended to be a wide-ranging general discussion; and it should not be confused with a tutorial, which is usually an opportunity for individual students to clear up personal or intellectual queries or difficulties.

Be clear what you are trying to achieve, and choose activities to suit. Teaching methods described elsewhere will work very well in seminars – particularly discussion; groupwork (especially buzz groups); games (notably 'Decisions, decisions'); and role-play or simulation. Some other methods are shown below. Beware of turning the session into a mini-lecture; the main aim of the seminar is usually to allow students an opportunity to arrive at the personal meanings which are the products of real learning. This requires that students should have corrected practice in forming their opinions. The process is necessarily slow, and requires student activity.

Student or group presentation

This is the most common seminar activity. An individual or group can be asked to make a presentation to the class; define the topic with care, and give references. It is usually very important to discuss the group's findings with them before they make their presentation. The presenter(s) may need help preparing the presentation – and some emotional support! An overhead projector transparency is a useful prompt for the presenter, and handouts circulated before the presentation can considerably improve any subsequent discussion.

In the discussion which usually follows the presentation, the presenting students may feel confident enough to lead; if not, however, they could offer statements for a discussion to be led by you.

This method is useful for exploring different aspects of the same topic, one aspect being taken by each group. You could ask third-year students to present to first-years. If presentations are to be assessed, ask students to take part in this by filling in, for each presentation, a questionnaire based on previously agreed criteria.

Agreeing 'statements worth making'

In 'Teaching in groups', Jaques suggests asking the students who lead a seminar to formulate 'six statements worth making' about the topic under study. These should be well grounded, non-trivial, and not obvious; they should aim to be concrete and useful, rather than vague and abstract. The statements should be agreed with the tutor before the seminar.

The student introduces the statements to the class, and a free and informal discussion follows. Then the student who has made the statements attempts to get unanimous agreement for each statement in turn. The student or the tutor may need to suggest amendments; the aim is to satisfy critics and retain support, and yet leave a statement which is worth making. If compromise proves impossible, the dissident members are left to compose a 'minority view' statement. One student is charged with writing up the minutes of the discussions, making notes of statements and who agreed with them. This process requires students to make decisions about the topic under study, and so increases involvement.

You against the rest

As a variant of 'statements worth making', the lecturer can refrain from being involved at all while the group members are deciding their statements. As well as the student presenter and scribe, another student is appointed to chair the discussion. Make it clear that the group must be absolutely agreed and committed to clear written statements; but don't join in the discussion.

Once statements have been agreed, however, you play devil's advocate for all you are worth. A few deceitful arguments will help to raise the temperature! It is now 'you against the rest', and if the students are genuinely committed to reasonable statements, a very lively and reasonably evenly-matched discussion should ensue. The session will need a plenary.

Especially if they fear assessment, students can collude in avoiding any forceful criticism of each other's presentations or ideas, preferring to leave this to the lecturer. 'You against the rest' should minimise this tendency. Some seminar leaders would suggest that the lecturer leaves the room during the students' discussion; this heightens the 'us against the lecturer' atmosphere.

It helps to agree ground-rules and discuss difficulties with a seminar group. How long should presentations, handouts or discussion contributions be? Who should lead discussions? Have disagreements been genuine, or due to personal rivalry? Some sensitivity may be required here!

21 Learning for remembering

This chapter looks at techniques you can use to ensure students remember what you have taught them. The ability to recall given information is a simple skill, and like all skills is learned by corrected practice. Reading notes or listening to summaries is not enough; it is *practising recall* that counts. Intellectual and physical skills are also best retained by reuse, rather than by more passive methods.

Have you ever played 'Kim's Game'? Players are shown a tray of objects for a minute, and then try to recall as many of them as they can. If you are like me, you will not be able to remember all the objects; but when you are shown the tray again at the end of the game, *you always recognise the objects you were unable to recall*. The memory was in your mind somewhere – you were just unable to find it! The mind is rather like a library, with our memories as the books. The book is in the library somewhere, but an index system is needed in order to find it. For a given memory, the mind's index system is only established by sufficient recall attempts.

Think of the process of learning a poem by heart. It often takes many failures to recall a line before we can recall it at will. Don't think of these failures in a negative way; they are a necessary part of the learning process. Some learning occurs only after two failures; more difficult learning might take ten or more. The mind is developing its index system, and the failed attempts are needed in order to establish or correct it.

Research suggests that anxiety and effort can hamper memorisation. When you set learning for homework, tell your students to settle down with some music and browse over revision notes in a relaxed frame of mind. They should keep attempting recall until they achieve success. It is not *effort* that counts; more important is the *time* spent in corrected practice of recall. One might even claim that anyone can remember anything, if they have tried to recall it often enough!

Some psychologists believe that we never truly forget anything – we simply lose the ability to recall it. The brain surgeons Penfield & Rasmussen found in 1950 that if the exposed brain of a conscious patient is stimulated by a mild electric charge, the patient can recall incredibly detailed memories of long-forgotten events, only ever experienced once. Similar experiences occur under hypnosis. (However, I do not suggest that you try either of these techniques in the classroom!)

If the ability to recall given information is seen as a skill, then the learner's needs for corrected practice apply:

Explanation: In order to remember, we must first understand. Otherwise, recall can only be achieved with very great difficulty, and what is recalled is of little use to the learner.

'Doing-detail': Students like to know exactly what they should be able to recall, and in what detail. This is obvious to you, but not to them. They cannot be expected to recall every word you say, so key facts for learning must be limited and very carefully defined. Specific learning notes can provide this detail. Once key facts are recalled, they act as reminders for associated information.

Use: Students must practice recalling. Many learners believe that reading and rereading their notes is sufficient, but corrected practice of recall is vital.

Check and correct: The recall must of course be checked for completeness and accuracy; if 'doing-detail' is carefully enough defined, this can be done by the learner.

The need for an **aide-mémoire**, and for **review, evaluation** and **queries** is self-explanatory.

As with all teaching, it is vital to set achievable objectives and reward achievement well. But beware – don't turn learning for remembering into a mechanical process; if new material is not understood it will be forgotten very quickly, so teaching for remembering should take place after the material is already well understood. Also remember that learning requires arousal and involvement, not *just* repetition; anything you do to make learning interesting and active will hugely increase recall ability. Bear this in mind when looking at the following ways of increasing the ability of students to recall what they have learned.

Research suggests that students learn a large number of new words (e.g. the names of the bones in the hand) more quickly if they say the words out loud.

'Within 24 hours of a one-hour learning period at least 80% of detailed information is lost.' – *Tony Buzan, author of Use your Head*

Continuous review

Good teaching programmes provide some of the necessary revision by using knowledge and skills taught earlier to help in the teaching of *new* knowledge and skills. In this way, previously-gained knowledge is maintained without sacrificing time for new learning. Review should be *integrated* into a course of study, to make sure that earlier learning is not lost. Otherwise, rather like trying to fill a bath when the plug is out, our students will forget old material almost as quickly as they learn the new. Repetition and reminders do work, up to a point, but review should involve students in *actively* searching their memories for previously-learned facts, and *actively* reusing their previously-acquired physical and intellectual skills and knowledge.

> The Japanese regard repetition of learning experiences as vital. In mathematics, the average 15-year-old Japanese student achieves an equivalent of the British A-level standard. They have an average IQ of 111-115, and 10% have an IQ of over 130. The other side of the coin, however, is that Japanese education has been accused of putting less emphasis on understanding, and on higher mental faculties.

The advantages of this 'review as you go' strategy are:

- More learning is retained.
- You save revision time, enabling more productive activities to be carried out at the end of the course.
- More reliable use can be made of old learning to aid new learning.
- Students are more likely to see the course/subject as an integrated whole, and more likely to see the patterns and similarities which are important for deep understanding.

Given the forgetting mechanism of the human memory, you might expect this 'review as you go' strategy to be in common practice. However, many teachers teach Henry V while their students forget about Henry IV. It seems that review is rather like death: it may be unavoidable – but everyone is against it. A teacher of any subject needs to plan for 'review as you go'. Look out for ways of teaching new ideas by using old ones. Allow time for review in your schemes of work and lesson plans.

Some teachers advocate a 'spiral syllabus' in which, rather than finishing off a new topic at once, topics are returned to again and again throughout the course, each time at greater depth.

You will meet teachers who tell you that they do not have time for review. Yet it only takes a minute to review what it took an hour to learn. And would these same teachers plant out new seedlings, saying that they have no time to water the ones they planted last week? If there is no time to revise, there is plenty of time to forget.

> Wright and Nuttall (1970) investigated 62 variables which they thought might influence teacher effectiveness. Two of the five teaching techniques that turned out to improve learning most were: ►providing an informative *summary* at the end of a discussion (rather than at the beginning); and ►providing comprehensive *revision* at the end of lessons. (The three other factors involved asking clear questions, spreading them widely, and thanking students for their responses.)

Summaries

Students can't be expected to remember every word that every teacher says in their thirty-lesson week – so *get students to remember only key facts*. This is crucial to understanding as well as memory. You can prepare key facts for them in summaries, or get them to prepare their own (though these will need checking). Key facts act as reminders for lesser facts, because our memories work by *association*. Once a key book in the library has been found, other associated books can be found next to it. Every memory does not need to be indexed separately.

Some teachers advocate summarising the last lesson before each new lesson, and the last topic before each new topic. This is all excellent practice, especially if it is done with questioning so that student recall is involved. Research shows we remember most from the beginning and the end of a lesson, so summarising at these times maximises learning.

Some people like the idea of 'mind maps'. These make use of association, and present information in a partially visual way which mimics the way our memory works. Colours and shapes can be used to classify key facts, and diagrams used to represent information visually. Have a look now at the example at the end of Chapter 9. Get your students to make a mind map for each topic you do.

Some students like to prepare revision cards – one card for each topic, containing, say, five or six key facts.

Review questions

Quizzes are always popular; they are enjoyable, arousing and involving – all of which serves to increase their effectiveness. Some teachers of examination subjects choose a past paper and get their students to work through it, question by question, in the course of the year. The questions are chosen to review former learning. This has the added advantage that it makes clear to students what they should be able to do, and familiarises them with the examination. Students recognise the importance of doing past-paper questions, and experience a feeling of achievement if they can answer them correctly.

In Harbin, China, Gou Yan-ling once memorised more than 15,000 telephone numbers. Bhandanta Vicitsara recited 16,000 pages of Buddhist canonical text from memory in Burma in 1974.

Revision tests

You can also ask students to learn for a short test: this works best if the 'doing-detail' is very precise. For example, don't say 'Revise for a chemistry test next week.', but 'I want you to learn the formulae for the following chemical reactions for next week....' I often tell students in advance what the questions in their learning test will be; then there is no excuse for failure! If the learning task is *well defined*, is *achievable* by the great majority, and is based on *well-understood* work, the chances of success are high. This success should of course be well rewarded with praise and recognition. Students get a real feeling of achievement from success in learning tests, and this fuels future motivation.

Try producing a summary learning sheet for tests. I produce a set for my GCSE physics students; it summarises the key points of the whole syllabus on six sides of A4. Here is an extract covering about two weeks' work. (I ask older students to produce their own revision sheets – but I check them.)

Springs

The bigger the load on a spring, the bigger the extension. **Hooke's Law** states that the extension is proportional to the load. A graph of load against extension will be a straight line (as every extra newton produces the same increase in extension).

When a spring is stretched beyond the **elastic limit**, it does not go back to its original length, and the graph is no longer a straight line.

My summary sheets include important reasoning and example calculations, not just facts. Don't forget that visual information is easier to learn than verbal. I test the learning from these sheets by two- to five-minute tests, where I verbally ask simple questions such as 'What is Hooke's Law?' or 'What is the elastic limit of a spring?'. At first students mark their own papers; this gives them feedback on what they can recall. Then they prepare for a test where I note the mark each student gets.

Summaries indicate key facts that students must be able to recall at will; they are much shorter than 'notes' or the aide-mémoire. They also consolidate learning, and if students understand a summary, they are left with a feeling of confidence about that topic.

Mnemonics

'Richard Of York Gained Battle In Vain' can be used to remember the colours of the rainbow – red, orange, yellow, green, blue, indigo, violet. Make up your own mnemonics. Students too enjoy making up their own, but unless you are unshockable, don't ask for them to be repeated to you!

More adventurous review methods

These are all straightforward review methods, but there are plenty of more adventurous ones. How about using some of the methods in Chapters 17 and 18, on group work and games respectively?

'Old learning is never completely lost. Relearning efficiency is the virtue of education.' – *Bugelski*

Choosing activities for learning facts

Here is a 'topic plan' for teaching students about the human eye. Note that it stretches over a number of lessons which might also involve other topics not mentioned here. It is a somewhat simplified scheme for readers who are not biologists!

TOPIC PLAN TO TEACH THE FORM AND FUNCTION OF THE HUMAN EYE

Objective: Students should be able to draw a diagram of the eye, and to state the names and functions of the main components.

To present material to be learned: Teacher talk, OHT, model, video of dissection of a bull's eye, students take down a note, etc.

To give familiarity and understanding: Verbal question and answer. Student groups are given little cardboard pointers labelled 'retina', 'iris' etc. which have to be placed correctly on a diagram of the eye.

Student groups are also given a set of cards with names, e.g. 'eye lens', and another set of cards with 'functions' e.g. 'to focus light on the retina'. They must match the appropriate names and functions. This is checked by reading out the answers.

Questions to check understanding (written): E.g.'What would happen if the pupil contracted?' 'How would the iris respond if you stepped into the dark?' etc.

Next lesson:
Students practise and self-check recall: Students are asked to draw and label an eye, and to write down the functions of each part. The answers are then given for them to self- or peer-check. They are told a mastery test next week will test their ability to do this.

Next week:
To assess each student's learning of the objective: Mastery test where students are asked to 'Draw a diagram of the eye', and state the names and functions of the main components.'

Other activities could be used: making posters, quizzes, homework activities, reading and so on. Note that recall is practised and tested.

Some teachers persist in believing their sole role is to present new material – don't become one of them! Ask yourself: why am I teaching these facts? What are students supposed to be able to do with them? Usually you will find that they need to be able to *use* facts to *make decisions, solve problems, answer questions requiring more than recall, explain other facts,* etc. The phrases in italics involve higher-order abilities than simple recall, which themselves require corrected practice.

Warning

Students accept that not all learning can be fun. However, don't alienate them by intensive and over-ambitious review programmes; this will only demotivate those who can't keep up, and do considerably more harm than good.

> Victorian educationalists were rightly criticised for an over-emphasis on factual learning. Charles Dickens mocked them in *Hard Times*:
>
> > 'Now what I want is, Facts. Teach these boys and girls nothing but Facts. Facts alone are wanted in life.'
>
> Many educationalists still believe that the modern curriculum is too fact-oriented, and places too little emphasis on skills which are less likely to be forgotten – thinking skills, for example.

People sometimes think that students will find summaries or other forms of review boring, but in my experience they will appreciate review activities, especially if they are successful at them. But do try to make review less necessary – make your lessons interesting, active and fun, and less will be forgotten!

☑ Checklist: learning for remembering

☐ Is the teaching involving, arousing, and active?
☐ Do students gain an understanding of key facts before they are expected to be able to recall them?
☐ Is what students must commit to memory clearly defined – by learning notes, for example?
☐ Do students practise recall (not just read, or hear it over again)?
☐ Do they have their recall individually checked and corrected (by themselves or others)?
☐ Is failure to recall tolerated as part of the learning process (as long as satisfactory progress is being made overall)?
☐ Is sufficient time allocated to learning for remembering on a 'little and often' basis?
☐ Is all relevant previous learning, and all current learning, reviewed?
☐ Have you tried mind maps, revision cards and similar techniques?

Exercises

If you believe that review is unnecessary, or its importance overstated:
Summarise this chapter without rereading it, and then go back over it, seeing how much you missed.

If you believe review is important:
Devise a review strategy for the next topic you teach!

22 Projects and assignments

Projects and assignments are the big guns in the educator's arsenal. They can have a powerful effect – if correctly aimed. Few teaching methods enable the teacher to develop a greater range of skills; and few offer greater opportunity to waste time in ill-directed activity. If you are going to involve students in an activity that takes (say) ten hours, then it had better be well thought out! Projects and assignments are very fashionable at the moment. The discovery method and group work were fashionable before them, and like these, assignments and projects are sometimes overused; used indiscriminately; and even thought to be self-justifying.

What exactly is a project or assignment? It is a task or set of tasks for students to complete – usually individually, but sometimes in groups. Usually the students can exercise considerable autonomy over how, where, when and in what order the tasks are carried out. Projects are usually more open-ended than assignments.

Terminology varies, but the following is common:

0 to 2 hrs	an exercise
2 to 12 hrs	an assignment
12 to 60 hrs	a project
over 60 hrs	a dissertation or a thesis

The rest of this chapter mentions only assignments, but applies equally to projects. Assignments give the students an opportunity to use – that is, to practise and to apply – their skills and knowledge; often this is in a fairly realistic context.

Assignment type	Example
A series of academic exercises	*Carry out a series of calculations.*
A design or development problem	*Design a self-watering flowerpot and produce a prototype.*
A literature search	*Research and write a report on owls.*
A work-related or real-life practical activity	*Design and make a range of cosmetics and market them within the college.*
Skill practice	*Make a bowl on a wood lathe.*
Creative activity	*Design an advertisement for a specified computer.*

Assignment type	Example
Problem-solving	*Suggest methods for reducing wastage in an industrial process.*
An encounter with the real world	*Visit a builders' merchant and interview staff on modern developments in building materials.*

Combinations of these and other activities are commonly used in single assignments.

Unlike many learning activities, assignments give the students an opportunity to use higher-order intellectual skills such as creativity, lateral thinking, evaluation, synthesis and analysis, etc. There is also an opportunity to practise 'self-management', 'study skills', 'problem solving skills' and other 'common skills'. (If you are not aware of it already, you will soon discover that these skills are not called 'common' because everybody *has* them, but rather, because everybody *needs* them. They are 'common' to a vast range of work-related and other human activities.)

Devising an assignment or project

Writing an assignment is a creative process. It is not possible to be precise or prescriptive, but the process will usually involve the following:

- **Decide on objectives:** What do you aim to achieve with the assignment? Be sure that an assignment really is the best way of achieving your objectives.

- **Consider resources:** Is there enough time? Are specialist equipment or rooms available where these are necessary? Will all your students be clamouring for a limited supply of specialist books? If so, warn the library, and arrange for relevant books to be put on 'desk loan'. The library removes the relevant books from the shelves, and students inquiring at the library desk may borrow the books but cannot remove them from the library. You will need to give your students a list of the books available on desk loan.

- **Consider skills needed:** Do your students know how to research in a library? Do they know how to approach an assignment? Are they adequately prepared for all the tasks?

- **Devise activities:** Make sure your activities achieve your objectives. Most assignments benefit from being very carefully described, with tasks broken down and sequenced where necessary. Demotivated students tend to do best with short assignments.

209

Motivation was considered in detail in Chapter 5. Ensure the activities:

- **interest the students.** Make the activity genuinely useful; relate it to their interests, and make it intriguing or unusual.

- **offer an opportunity to practise skills in 'real-life' or work-related circumstances.** Develop realistic scenarios or case studies; give students roles; get the students out of the classroom into the real world; involve them with visits, or in having visitors.

- **are active and varied.** No-one wants to spend three weeks researching in the library. Aim for a number of contrasting tasks in a long assignment or a project.

- **are well defined, so students are confident that they know what you expect.**

- **set an achievable target which is rewarding to meet.**

Students don't enjoy activities which produce a negative result, even if this is technically useful. So don't ask students to investigate whether or not it is possible to measure sugar concentration using a pH meter, if this cannot be done.

You may like to give staff and students roles: e.g. Mrs Smith is the design house manager, Mrs Brown is the customer commissioning the design, students are the designers and have daily meetings with both Mrs Smith and Mrs Brown. If students are working in groups, do you need to define their roles (leader, scribe, journal keeper, etc.)?

Problem-solving assignments

Problem-solving should go through the following series of stages. If you plan to set a problem-solving assignment, tell students about this process, and use it as a guide to the tasks included.

Define the problem → Brain storm for sources of help → Research and analyse the problem → Brainstorm a range of solutions ↓

Test and evaluate the solution ← Develop the solution ← Select the best solution

Those affected by the problem and/or the solution should usually be consulted throughout.

Note: 'Brainstorm for sources of help' may sometimes be omitted, but this can lead to 'reinventing the wheel' or to impractical solutions. If, for example, the problem is to reduce wastage in an industrial process, brainstorming may suggest talking to the relevant machine operator, contacting the makers of the machine, etc.

Why not have some tasks or assignments that are student-devised but negotiated with you? This allows learners to follow their particular interests.

Devising the assessment schedule

I remember the first time I set an assignment. My class of 14-year-old science students hummed with contented activity for hours. I was delighted – until they handed it in. One lad, and he was not the only one, had made an appalling attempt at the meat of the assignment, but had produced a magnificent front cover. He had meticulously copied illustrations from the box of books the library had provided, combining them into a breathtaking piece of artwork. I pointed out it was a science, not an art, assignment and gave him a low mark. He (correctly) pointed out that I had asked for illustrations, and was incensed. Now I use assessment schedules! This is common practice in further education (but, sadly, not always elsewhere).

The assessment schedule tells students what skills are being tested in some detail, and what criteria you will use in assessing the assignment. It must be given to the students before they start work on the assignment.

An example assessment schedule for a chemistry assignment

Distinction: The water content is measured to an accuracy of plus or minus 3%. The report is well written, and includes a clear indication of all the main sources of error and how these could be reduced.

Merit: Plus or minus 5% accuracy of analysis. Clear indication of the main sources of error, and some idea of how some of these could be reduced.

Pass: Plus or minus 8% accuracy of analysis. Adequate report; the student needs help in determining all the sources of error and their means of reduction.

Refer: If the above criteria are not met, the assignment will be handed back to the student for completion.

Common skills: *Use of computers.* The assignment is to be written up on computer; marks will be awarded for use of **bold**, <u>underline</u>, and similar effects. Text should be well laid out and fully formatted.

Self-management. Marks will be awarded for finishing on time, and keeping adequate records.

*If you don't like this format, design your own, but **tell** students what you expect.*

Assessment schedules increase student motivation markedly, and they ensure that their time and effort is focussed in the direction you intend. Also, if students know what to aim for, they are more likely to be successful; this is as important for long-term motivation as it is in achieving the objectives of the assignment itself.

If students are completing assignments in groups, should each group member get the same mark? Some teachers advocate letting the students decide whether this would be fair or not; whatever you decide, this must be made clear from the start.

Why not get students to evaluate their own performance as part of the assessment – or each other's performance? Students certainly enjoy looking at each other's work, and can learn a great deal from the experience.

Debriefing and reflection sessions

It is vital that after – and preferably also during – the assignment, students are able to evaluate their performance, decide how it could be improved, and come to firm conclusions about what they have learned. This is true both for common skills, and for subject learning.

Reflection can be arranged in a number of ways. It can occur during a debriefing session after the activity, where the teacher and class mine their experience for learning. Alternatively, students can reflect individually with the teacher; or one task in the assignment can be for students to reflect individually or in groups, and report their findings to the teacher.

Designing the assignment briefing sheet

Every assignment needs to be described to students in detail and in writing. This is usually done on a typed handout containing:

- A clear statement of the aims and objectives of the assignment, though not necessarily in formal language.
- A clear statement of the tasks, broken down where necessary.
- A clear outline of what will be assessed, and how.
- Background notes, e.g. roles of staff, references, desk loans available etc.; debriefing session.
- The launch date and date for completion; usually with a penalty for late completion (e.g. maximum of half marks).

Planning for evaluation

How will you decide whether the assignment was a success, and whether there are ways of improving it? Keep a monitoring copy of the briefing sheet in your folder, on which you can write suggested improvements as they occur to you. You will never get an assignment right first time.

Role of the teacher during assignment work

You have devised your assignment and briefed the students on it. 'OK,' you say, 'you can start.' The students enthusiastically make their way to the library, and you are left in a classroom which is empty except for two students who are discussing how to approach the assignment. It's a strange feeling. Can this be right? What exactly *is* the role of the teacher when students are working on assignments? There is more to this than answering queries, assessment, debriefing and evaluation of the assessment's effectiveness. The teacher must become a learning manager and a facilitator, rather than just an instructor. Students who are going to the library should be asked to write their names on a dated class library sheet. But then what?

If students are left entirely to their own devices, it is very common for them to misinterpret, misread, or fail adequately to read the assignment. Also, you may not have described the tasks as clearly as you hoped. If you do not check on the students' progress, they may proudly offer you inadequate assignments after many hours of hard work. This is very depressing and demotivating, for them and for you. Check work is up to standard while it is being done, and request improvement straight away where necessary; then all work will be successful and motivating.

Except for short assignments, it is common to arrange an appointment system so that you can check on each student's progress; otherwise some students will be missed. This is a good motivator, especially for those students who find it difficult to sustain effort over a long period.

Procrastination

Parkinson's law says that a job expands to fill the time available; in the case of an assignment, this might better read 'one and a half times the time available'! Procrastination is sometimes caused by a lack of confidence on the student's part; this can be overcome by praising or accepting the standard of work in progress.

Some teachers advocate a 'reciprocal supervision' arrangement for long projects. Each student supervises one other student, but not a close friend. The supervisor can be given a fairly detailed brief, and made partly responsible for the prompt submission of the work, or simply asked to meet occasionally to discuss progress.

To be fair on the students who have submitted their assignment on time, it is common practice to deduct marks from those handed in late. Prior warning of this arrangement needs to be given.

Integrated (or integrative) assignments

BTEC, the Business and Technician Education Council, oversees many vocational courses in further education in Britain. It has done much to promote assignment-based learning strategies, and especially integrated (sometimes called integrative) assignments. One of the aims of such assignments is to encourage students to 'experience their programme of study as a coherent whole, in which all the parts are well related to each other.' (*Assignments Help Students To Learn,* BTEC, 1986). Of course, schools also make use of assignments.

A student on a construction science course may study a number of 'subjects': materials, science, surveying, technical drawing, mathematics, and so on. An assignment to design a small bungalow would enable students to integrate the skills and knowledge gained in these different 'subjects', and to practise and develop common skills.

It is usual for the course team to develop an integrated assignment in such a way that every part of the curriculum is adequately represented. The assignments are often realistic and work-related; and indeed for students on work experience or on day release, the assignment may be suggested by their workplace, and wholly or partly carried out there. Otherwise, a realistic scenario or case study underpins the assignment.

Such assignments have obvious merit. However, they may require staff visits to the workplace, and they do demand extensive staff meetings to develop, monitor, and assess and evaluate the assignments. A college's finances are all too finite, and in practice lecturers often report that the necessary resources are not made available.

The limitations of assignments

In the flurry and excitement of devising projects, it is easy to forget that they only rarely provide all of the EDUCARE? elements discussed in Chapter 2. This is especially true of common skills. For example, students often fail to complete assignments on time because they have not developed the skill of self-management or time management. It is not enough to give students repeated practice in this skill. That may simply allow them to learn their mistakes. The skill needs to be actively taught with the use of all the EDUCARE? elements. They need:

An explanation: 'When you first get an assignment, draw up a timetable allotting times to each of the tasks. Plan to finish one day early. Refer to this timetable as the assignment progresses...'

A demonstration to show them by example: 'For example, let's draw up a time-table together for your present assignment. How long do you think each task will take? ...'

As well as **use,** the student needs a **check.** You can provide this during the assignment: 'We are halfway through the assignment now; are you keeping to your timetable?'

You may feel students can do without an aide-mémoire, but they will need **review** and **evaluation** until the skill is developed.

The same principle goes for skills other than common skills: completing a task does not in itself guarantee learning. For this reason, most teachers combine assignments with other teaching and learning methods. Although careful use of assignments can avoid most of the disadvantages mentioned above, it must surely be a mistake to base an entire course on them. Students need variety.

☑ Checklist for using assignment-based learning

☐ Was the assignment well defined in writing, with tasks broken down in sufficient detail?

☐ Was assessment transparent, and were criteria given in advance?

☐ Was it enjoyable, with a clear purpose?

☐ Were students adequately prepared for the tasks?

☐ Were resources adequate?

☐ Did you check on, and encourage, both general work-rate and the content of the student's work while it was in progress?

☐ Have you got an annotated monitoring copy of the assignment?

☐ Did all students succeed in completing it satisfactorily?

☐ While marking, did you comment on both good and bad features of the work, as well as awarding a grade? (See the next chapter for further discussion of this point.)

☐ Did debriefing confirm what students should have learned?

23 Essays

Have you ever written what you thought was a great essay – only to get a really low mark? I am prepared to bet that you felt resentful, and wondered what the teacher was looking for.

Essay writing must be taught directly. Students need an explanation of how to go about writing an essay, and they need to know exactly what is expected of them – in general, and for each particular essay. They need to read and discuss good examples; they need practice; and they need informative, constructive feedback on the strengths and weaknesses of each of their attempts.

In short, essay writing is a skill, and it therefore needs the elements in the mnemonic EDUCARE? (see Chapter 2).

Imagine your students asking you 'What do you want me to do?', and 'How can I best do it?'

What do you want me to do?

Everything that was said about projects or assignments in Chapter 22 also applies to essays. For example, I would argue strongly for detailed guidance notes, and that assessment criteria should be made clear before the essay is started.

There is an example of an essay set with guidance notes and assessment criteria at the top of the following page.

Guidance notes focus student effort in the direction you consider most productive; they can also be changed from year to year to minimise the occurrence of common misunderstandings or omissions. Guidance notes and assessment criteria tell students what to include, not what to leave out, so they are unlikely to be so prescriptive as to hamper an original approach to an essay. Optionally, the teacher can afterwards give each student separate feedback on each of the criteria.

Some teachers believe their students are more in need of autonomy than guidance, and may prefer to use general guidance notes similar to those at the bottom of the following page. These are perhaps best generated through discussion with your students. Time spent in clarification of the points listed, early on in a course, will be an excellent investment.

```
Module 4: Assignment 8

Write an essay on the theory of learning, relating it
directly to your own subject area, and to your own teaching
experience so far.
Suggested title: 'How theories of learning inform practice
in the teaching of ..........'

Guidance notes:
1 Deal with each of the theories of learning covered in
  classes; if you find one or more of them less than
  useful, explain why.
2 Include a brief summary of each of the theories in your
  own words.
3 Describe how some or all of the theories inform the
  choices you make in planning and executing your lessons.
  Give some concrete examples of this.

Assessment criteria
1 Evidence of having done your own reading from this
  module's reading list. (Relevant reading outside this
  list is required for a distinction.)
2 A concise and accurate explanation of each of the
  theories, with concrete examples of good practice clearly
  related to the relevant theory.
3 Evidence of having used the theories in practice, with an
  evaluation of the experience.

Less than 800 words should suffice.
```

(Which would you prefer as a student: 'Write an essay on the theory of learning.' or the above? Which would you get most out of, and in which would you be
most likely to succeed?)

You or your students may well disagree with the ten points below. If so, draw up
your own list and pass it on formally to your students. This can also make criticism
easier: e.g. 'Pay special attention to 4 and 7.'

```
Guidance on writing essays

1  Read the question or consider the title very carefully
   throughout the writing process.
2  Order material logically.
3  Keep to the point, and make your points as persuasively
   as possible.
4  Be concise.
5  Be clear.
6  Generalise with great care and with full justification.
7  Represent the opinions of others fairly and accurately.
8  Think for yourself, and express your own opinion.
9  Have a strong opening and ending.
10 Include a bibliography.
```

How can I best do it?

Make sure you discuss the process of essay writing with your students. College students are often recommended to follow a process similar to that outlined below. A simpler version could be devised for younger students. (It is assumed that the students have already been introduced to the source material.)

```
The process of writing an essay

1  Whilst you are reading (and subsequently) make a rough
   set of notes,in any order,of the key ideas and any points
   you want to make. Keep this with you at all times, so you
   can add new ideas as soon as you think of them. Read
   through these notes often, to allow your subconscious to
   work on the topic. Give the matter some thought on the
   bus and in the bath!

2  Reread lecture notes and important passages in the texts.

3  Arrange your essay note ideas in a logical order. Leave
   for at least a day.

4  Draft the essay, then leave it for at least a further
   day.

5  Continue to draft and redraft the essay until you are
   happy with it, leaving it for at least a day between
   drafts.

6  Plan your essay-writing timetable so that you hand it in
   on time!
```

Note that the short breaks between stages allow some distance to develop between the writer and what is written, so that weaknesses can more easily be seen. They also allow time for reflection and changes of mind. The process lends itself to the use of a word processor, if the student has reasonable typing skills. Of course, some students already have strong ideas about how essays should be written, so be ready to defend your ideas in any discussion!

If the teacher takes this process seriously, essays should be set well in advance, and plenty of time should be given for their completion. You might like to take students through these stages for their first few essays, looking at their notes or drafts and consulting with them briefly after each stage.

An alternative view of essay writing may be taken by following the ICDIP phases outlined in Chapter 25.

Marking essays

A pep talk on how to write an essay, although necessary, is not sufficient to develop the essay-writing skill. Constant detailed feedback is vital. This can be provided through students reading each other's essays and discussing them in class, as well as through your marking. The university tutorial and seminar methods are often in part opportunities for students to get feedback on their essays, and the thinking behind them.

Too often, students' essays are just given a grade, with perhaps a brief comment. Ruth Beard (1970) suggests writing two lists of comments at the end of student's essays under the headings 'good' and 'could be improved'. She reports that this causes students to improve steadily, whereas those who are simply given grades for their essays maintain an almost unvarying standard of performance.

> Try putting one tick in the margin for an important point, and a double tick for a well-made point. Detailed feedback facilitates improvement. Also try getting students to read each other's essays, in pairs, before submission to you; ask them to isolate two strengths and one weakness.

From time to time, especially early on in a course, students benefit from reading and discussing a particularly good essay immediately after completing their own on the same topic. Make sure you point out why the essay is good, with reference to your guidance notes and/or assessment criteria. If you don't want to embarrass a student in the group by choosing their essay, write your own, or use one from a student in a previous year.

> 10% of articles submitted to the quarterly *Journal of Experimental Psychology* are judged to be so unintelligible that it is not possible to decide what experiment (if any) has been carried out! If mature research students find difficulty in expressing themselves, don't expect your students to pick up the skill without help.

Coda

In most areas of study, students must understand the rules of clear thinking if they are to write an effective essay – that is, what is and what is not evidence; when generalisations can be made, and when they cannot; the dangers of oversimplification and bias, and the tyranny of labels; and so on. Reasoning is a hugely difficult skill – nobody fully masters it!

There seems to be an invariable law in education that the time spent teaching a skill is in inverse proportion to its importance. We spend a great deal of time teaching facts that can easily be looked up in reference books. We spend very little time developing creative thinking and problem-solving, though our students will be involved in these activities all their lives. But the importance of reasoning is so great that it is usually not taught at all! (See 'The skill of opinion forming', starting on page 308 of this book.)

☑ Checklist for essay learning

☐ Was the essay well defined in writing, with guidance notes?

☐ Was assessment transparent, and were criteria given in advance?

☐ Were students adequately prepared for the essay?

☐ Have you discussed the essay-writing process with your students?

☐ Do students see exemplar essays (not *too* wonderful), preferably after attempting an essay on the same title themselves?

☐ How would you change the title or guidance notes if you set the same essay next year – have you made a note of these suggestions?

☐ While marking, did you comment on both good and bad features of the work as well as awarding a grade?

☐ Did a debriefing session confirm what students should have learned?

24 The discovery and guided discovery methods

Welcome to an educational mine-field! But before considering the case for and against discovery learning, let's look at what this teaching method involves.

In teacher-centred (that is, 'didactic') teaching, learners have the concepts, principles or techniques explained to them, and then they are expected to use and remember this new material. In discovery learning, however, the learners are expected to discover the principles or techniques for themselves – though usually with some guidance or special preparation.

Let's consider some examples. How could a discovery approach be used to teach the following?

1. For a circle of any size, the ratio of the circumference to the diameter is 3.14 ($= \pi$).

2. The time for small swings of a simple pendulum depends on the length of the pendulum, but not on the mass of the bob or the width of the swing.

3. The main motives of adult learners enrolling on adult recreational courses are to develop skills important to their life or career; to gain intellectual stimulation; to follow a hobby or interest; and to enjoy social contact and a change from their home environment.

4. The advantages and disadvantages of laser and dot matrix computer printers.

5. How to use French railway timetables.

6. How to solder electrical components on to printed circuit boards.

Let's take each of the above topics in turn:

Topic 1: Assuming the learners are familiar with the concepts of circumference and diameter, the teacher could say: 'Measure the different-sized circles I have given you, and see if you can see any patterns in your data.'

Topic 2: The teacher could ask learners to guess what variables might affect the time for one swing of a pendulum; and to devise an experiment to investigate each variable in turn, and so discover how they affect the time for one swing.

Topic 3: The learners could be asked to devise and administer a questionnaire to investigate the motives of adult learners.

Topic 4: The learners could be asked to use such printers themselves, and to survey advertisements in computer magazines to discover the advantages and disadvantages.

Topic 5: The learners could be given copies of French maps and railway time-tables, and challenged to discover without help how to travel from Calais to Burgundy.

Topic 6: Learners could be asked to experiment with different types of solder and soldering iron, and with different techniques; and to use this experience to draw up guidelines for soldering.

Which method would *you* prefer to be taught by: the didactic or the discovery approach? (Note that searching out information from books is not discovery learning.)

Discovery activities are usually carried out in groups. They require high-order thinking skills in order to puzzle them out, and because learners are developing their own meanings, learning is of a high quality.

> Discovery methods are used by many primary teachers, and by many science teachers – for example, the Nuffield Science programme has made extensive use of the method. However, discovery can be used by teachers of all disciplines.

Effective use of the discovery method

When well devised and managed, the discovery method offers active learning and an achievable challenge which engages interest. Consequently, discovery activities motivate all but the most apathetic students. They are also very effective in developing the learners' understanding. However, it must be stressed that if the activities are poorly thought out, or ineffectively managed, the result can be lack of learning, confused and frustrated students, and a waste of time and good will.

How should the method be used? The following are the most important considerations:

- **Learners must have any essential background knowledge and techniques they need in order to make a success of the discovery activity.**

- **Learners must understand exactly what is expected of them.** It usually helps to have the task precisely and concisely written on the board.

- **The great majority, if not all, of the learners must be able to make a success of the activity.**

This effectively means that guidance must be given where necessary. For example, before starting their soldering activity (topic 6 above), students could be shown how to test a soldered joint. By means of question and answer, the class could also be introduced to the factors which may affect the soldered joint: size of soldering iron bit, where it is placed, time it is in contact, type of solder used, whether flux is used, and so on. The teacher could even suggest experiments for the class to carry out in detail.

This is 'guided discovery'. Too much guidance, and the students feel cheated of the chance to make their own discovery; too little, and they are floundering in frustration. Clearly you must know your students' capabilities before using this teaching method. Often some groups need more guidance than others, but don't leap in with guidance until the learner(s) have had a chance to think things through for themselves.

In practice, nearly all discovery is guided; it is just a matter of how much guidance has been given. If it took science 2,000 years to arrive at Galileo's ideas about dynamics, one can't expect 2B to do it in an hour and a quarter!

■ **Students' work must be carefully monitored.** Because of their inevitable lack of understanding at the start of the activity, students can spend hours on fruitless activity if left entirely to their own devices. Ask them what they have decided to do. If the method is unsatisfactory, it is usually best to use question and answer to improve it. Here is a teacher who has found a group trying to measure the circumference of circles by following it with a ruler.

Teacher How accurate is that method?
Student Not very, it's hard to do.
Teacher Try measuring the same circle twice, and see if you get the same answer.
(A little later)
12 cms and 15 cms for the same circle? That's miles out, isn't it! Can you think of a better way?
Student Use string? John says we should cut the circles out and roll them...

It sometimes helps if students bring their ideas to the teacher before embarking on them. This gives you the opportunity to check that methods are feasible, and to ensure vital steps or data are included. Alternatively, visit each group in the first few minutes to check they are on the right track.

Sometimes students learn a good deal by being left to see the consequences of their own errors, but this can be counterproductive; guidance is often the safest option. If they waste hours chasing a wild goose with a clutch of red herrings, guess who will be blamed when they find out!

- **Choose a topic where students are very unlikely to know the answer already.** It is galling to outline a discovery activity, only to have one or two students shout out 'the answer', even though the activity may still usefully consolidate and confirm their prior knowledge. If you suspect some students do have such knowledge, ask them to keep their ideas to themselves for the sake of the others. If you can, develop a 'stretching activity' for those who finish quickly.

- **Leave plenty of time.** About twice as much as you expect should do!

- **Summarise what students should have learned at the end.** This is critical. Some 'discoveries' will lack clarity, and others may be entirely wrong-headed. It is crucial that you summarise the main teaching point(s) of the activity, explaining it fully by reference to their findings. If you want students to write their own summaries, then try: 'When you have agreed your conclusion, tell me about it before writing it up'.

Students used to teacher-centred methods may need a little practice in the discovery method before they can use it to its full effect.

Strengths and weaknesses of the discovery method

The discovery method has been criticised for leading students to discover 'the wrong thing', and for leaving learners confused. This, however, is a criticism of the way the method is implemented, not a criticism of the method itself. If students are confused or misled after being taught this way, either there was very poor implementation or it was not a suitable method for achieving the teacher's immediate objectives.

Every method has such traps, and it is the business of the teacher to avoid them – though it must be said that this method is one of the more difficult for an inexperienced teacher to use. If you are worried by this, show your plans to an experienced teacher or to your tutor/mentor, especially if you have had limited previous contact with the group you will be teaching.

The method is slow, but even this disadvantage can be largely overcome if enough guidance is given.

A far more important limitation of the discovery method, often ignored even by experienced advocates, is that it is never adequate in itself. To teach an intellectual or physical skill or procedure, students need to have their new learning explained in terms of previous knowledge and experience. The discovery method is excellent at meeting this important need. However, students also have other needs, outlined in the mnemonic EDUCARE? (Chapter 2). After the discovery, students will need to find out what they are expected to be able to do with this new learning; to practise this 'use'; and to have that practice checked and corrected, etc. It is one thing to 'discover' an equation describing the oscillation of a simple pendulum; it is another thing to be able to use the equation to predict a pendulum's behaviour.

At the end of this chapter, you will find a diagram which shows a whole range of teaching methods in their approximate positions on a continuum stretching from heavily teacher-controlled activities at one extreme down to largely student-controlled ones at the other.

The main advantages of the discovery method, appropriately used, are that:

- It is active, involving, motivating, and fun.

- It develops a sound understanding of the subject matter in terms of earlier learning and experience.

- It involves the students in high-order thinking: evaluation, creative thinking, problem-solving, analysis, synthesis etc. By contrast, teacher-centred methods often only involve the learner in low-order skills such as attending and comprehending.

- As with other student-centred teaching methods, students are encouraged to see learning as something they do to themselves, rather than something that experts do to them. Some teachers believe this 'hidden curriculum' is the method's most important attribute.

- It allows students to enjoy the fun of puzzling things out for themselves, and so arguably it develops their intrinsic as opposed to their extrinsic motivation.

The method does have some limitations. It can be slow, and there is no practical way of using it for some topics; for example, simple fact-based topics, or those where the student is highly unlikely to be able to make the discovery required. As in much group work, there is also a danger of 'passengers' – students who watch rather than participate. However, if the passengers are attending well to the discussions in their group, they can gain almost as much as those actively participating.

> The discovery method is still very popular amongst learning theorists; for example, Ausubel believes that new learning requires appropriate background knowledge, and must be organised by the learner and then integrated into his or her existing knowledge. He sees discovery learning as an excellent method of producing this integrated learning.

Recent controversy

Recently it has been argued by politicians and the media that 'modern teaching methods' such as the discovery method are a trendy throw-back to the permissive sixties, and are wrong-headed. The discovery method is criticised for not providing enough guidance, and seen by the critics as confusing for learners. Teachers, it is argued, should go back to 'chalk and talk' methods.

The discovery method was first advocated early this century by educational theorists of the 'cognitive school', who were deeply critical of 'rote learning' – by which they meant memorising without understanding. Rote learning methods were widely employed at that time, because knowledge of facts was considered the main gift of education. Once facts and procedures were memorised, it was argued, any understanding that was necessary would come later.

It is important to distinguish between learning by rote and learning by repetition. Rote learning means memorising facts or procedures *without understanding*, or with very partial understanding. Research confirms the common sense view that learners are unable to make use of such learning.

For example:

Teacher	What are three fours?
Paul (*a seven-year-old*)	Twelve.
Teacher	Good. Now, suppose I had three boxes and each box had four oranges in. How many oranges would I have?
Paul	I don't know.

Learning tables by repetition is fine – indeed, it's the only way. But the *concept* of multiplication needs to be understood if this learning is to be useful.

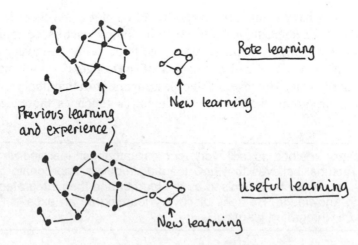

The circles show concepts, facts, principles, and experiences, etc. The links show reasoning between them.

In order to make use of new learning, connections must be made from it to existing learning. This enables the learner, for example, to reason with the new learning, or to apply it in a different but related situation – 'learning transfer'. In the discovery method, students use their previous knowledge and experience to develop their own understanding of the new learning. As a result, they create *for themselves* the important connections between new and existing learning.

In rote memorisation (without understanding) the links are not available, and a learner who has memorised Newton's second law of motion will be unable to explain applications of the law, or use it to solve problems.

> Those in the cognitive school think highly of bafflement. They suggest that bafflement motivates the learner to utilise previous learning to come to an understanding.

Cognitivists, however, believe that rather than simply committing facts and procedures to memory, education involves developing thinking ability – that is to say, 'cognitive skills'.

Most of the facts we are taught are forgotten, because we don't make repeated use of them. What thirty-year-old, for example, remembers the principal exports of Belgium, or the industrial method for the production of sulphuric acid, unless this knowledge has been used since being taught? However, the *skills* we used while gaining this knowledge are largely still with us, because we make use of such skills almost every day of our lives. I refer to thinking skills such as the ability to learn new ideas and express them concisely; to order and structure our knowledge and understanding; to puzzle out a procedure so it can be expressed in terms of previous knowledge and understanding; to problem-solve and evaluate; and so on. These, of course, are the very skills used in discovery learning.

> 'We think of the mind as a storehouse to be filled when we should be thinking of it as an instrument to be used.' – *J.W. Gardener in* **Self Renewal,** *1963*
>
> 'Education is what survives when what has been learned has been forgotten.' – *B.F. Skinner*

Early cognitivists argued that education should concentrate on teaching learners concepts, relationships, creative thinking, problem-solving and other thinking skills, and should not simply teach facts. They warned against rote methods which, though they might get quick results initially, were soon forgotten and did not produce genuine understanding. Dewey (1859-1952), the champion of learning by doing, said that 'mechanical drill' would 'strengthen traits likely to be fatal to reflective power.'

Bruner (born 1915) expressed the view that 'expository teaching' deprived students of the chance to think for themselves. He said the modern curriculum should strip away all but the bare facts, and leave time for teaching thinking skills. He thought intelligence was the 'internalisation of cognitive tools', and believed it could be improved by appropriate teaching. (IQ scores have been shown to be increased by education, though most research has concentrated on younger learners).

The cognitivists were hardly expressing a new idea. For centuries, an education in classics was considered suitable preparation for almost any employment, on the grounds that it 'trained the mind'; and the Civil Service has always recruited graduates of any discipline. Perhaps one day we will have a curriculum based on cognitive skills, rather than an exclusively knowledge-based curriculum.

> Why are people who do well in intelligence tests usually better learners than those with excellent memories? (IQ tests measure the abilities of pattern recognition, non-verbal and verbal reasoning, and problem solving.)

The Gestalt school of psychology entered the debate, stressing the importance of insight. Kohler carried out experiments to discover how chimpanzees solved problems. Chimps would put boxes on top of each other, or join together poles like fishing rods to get bananas which were out of their normal reach. He said their learning required the imaginative leap from present facts to future possibilities; and that they needed to see the problem as a whole in order to solve it.

He found that the chimps' solution:

a. comes quickly, often after trial and error and considerable thought.
b. can subsequently be repeated without error.
c. is long remembered, and is transferable to different problems of similar type.

Gestalt psychologists believe that perception and learning are dynamic processes where the individual actively makes sense of the environment. This is illustrated by the famous 'inkblot' experiments. It requires creative thinking to form these insights which, when remembered, constitute learning.

Soon many educationalists came to believe that useful learning:

- was not the same as remembering facts and techniques.

- must be organised by the learner and then integrated into the learner's existing knowledge.

- involved developing cognitive skills such as the ability to reflect critically, to evaluate, analyse, to think creatively and to solve problems.

So what are we as teachers to make of the controversy between guided discovery and direct instruction methods? Research suggests that teaching by discovery may well be better retained and more easily transferred. The recent 'Cognitive Acceleration through Science Education' research project (CASE) was specifically designed to develop thinking skills through discovery learning. It was shown to improve examination results markedly. Interestingly, the improvement was not just in science subjects, but in mathematics and English as well. Despite this success, the ideas developed in the project have not been adopted in the National Curriculum.

Didactic or 'reception' learning has improved a great deal since the 1930s, with less emphasis on mechanical drill, so one could argue that this overcomes the cognitivists' criticisms. On the other hand, the discovery method is fun, it is motivating, and it develops thinking skills in our learners – and research seems to show it has value. You must decide for yourself, but most informed opinion now considers that what happens in the learning 'process' is at least as important as its 'product'.

Teacher controlled

Rote memorising

Lecture or demonstration

Questioning

Practicals

(The positions of the teaching methods on this continuum are only approximate, as they depend on context.)

Individual work

Discussion

Group work

Guided discovery

Reading

Discovery

Student controlled

25 Creativity, design and invention

Ask reasonably motivated students to make notes on the dangers of drug abuse, and they will politely comply; ask them to design a leaflet on drug abuse for distribution in their college or school, and they will be fired with enthusiasm. Creative activities are fun, and increase the learners' sense of self-worth. Whatever your subject discipline, you cannot afford to ignore their motivating effect.

Creativity is often seen as the exclusive territory of the creative arts; yet just stand in a modern department store and look around you. You are surrounded by the products of the creative imagination. In the 'real world' creative skills are vital. They are required for product initiation and design, marketing, packaging, management, child care, teaching, engineering, house decorating and housekeeping, architecture, cooking, writing, research and development, entrepreneurial development, window dressing, store layout... Indeed, creative skills are necessary for anyone involved with thinking up new ideas and techniques, or with problem-solving. Creativity is a vital cognitive tool, not a subject discipline, *and it needs exercising*.

In most learning the learner is expected to receive knowledge, skills, techniques and opinions developed by others. Creative work is the important exception, but it is often misunderstood and undervalued by teachers and others.

Creative work is important for the teacher of any subject, for three main reasons:

- **To develop our students' ability to think creatively.**

- **To increase motivation.** Creativity satisfies a deep human need to make something and to gain recognition for this. Maslow's hierarchy of human needs places emphasis on self-esteem and self-actualisation, both of which can be satisfied by creative work. Being creative is fun.

- **To provide an opportunity to explore feelings and develop skills in self-expression.** There is more to education than learning facts and work-based skills. Students need to exercise their imagination, and explore feelings and perceptions. They need to make personal meanings of their experiences, and to express these to others.

A New York school was dismayed by discipline problems so extreme that armed guards were employed to roam the corridors. They consulted a curriculum expert who suggested they introduced creative work into the school. The students were encouraged to paint, put on plays and musicals and do other creative work. Within a year there was no need for the guards.

Planning for creative work

Whilst creativity is a mysterious process, it is not beyond understanding or influence. With the right preparation and activities, the quality of your learners' creative work can be massively improved.

What are the needs of learners when they are involved in creative work? First they need an introduction to the use of the basic tools and skills. They need to know how to use the wood-lathes, paints, or inverted commas that will be the medium for their creative expression (though the creative work itself can of course be used to develop these skills further). Let's suppose this initial need has been at least partially met.

Encouraging creativity

The creative process is complex and variable, and only a simple outline of activities which can improve creativity can be given here. The process can be seen as consisting of five phases: **i**nspiration, **c**larification, **d**istillation, **i**ncubation, and **p**erspiration (producing the mnemonic ICDIP). In the course of producing a single piece of work, each phase may be encountered many times, and not in any particular sequence. However, at any given time the learner will usually be concentrating on one phase or another. Let's examine the phases in turn.

Inspiration

This is the research phase, and involves an uncritical search for ideas. The process is uninhibited and is characterised by spontaneity, experimentation, intuition, untrammelled imagination, and risk-taking improvisation. Very much as in the first stage in brainstorming (see Chapter 17) the idea is to develop as many ideas as possible, however off-beam or impractical they may initially seem. In the field of the creative arts this phase is often associated with a search for an individual voice, and with an attempt to conjure up deep feelings of (for example) sympathy, spirituality, or empathy with the subject matter.

If students 'can't think of anything', they could be having difficulty with this inspiration phase. Encourage them to try out 'any old thing', without being in any way self-critical. This is not the stage for worrying about form, composition, practicality, rhyme or metre etc.; the aim is to think up as many imaginative ideas as possible. If most of the ideas produced are workable, not enough risks were taken.

I believe it was Monet who was said to spend a little time each week experimenting with something that both conventional wisdom and his own intuition suggested would *not* work. He explained that 98% of the time he was right, but 2% of the time the experiment suggested strikingly original ideas.

Clarification

The idea here is to clarify the purpose or objective of the work. It is characterised by the question: 'What am I trying to say?' (or, 'What am I trying to do?') When a student is stuck for the next sentence in an essay, try asking 'What do you want the line to say?' Often they have no idea, and rather than dreaming up a stream of alternatives they need to consider carefully where the paragraph or essay is going. A similar argument holds for other forms of creative work. In this phase the student is being logical, analytical and critical; and has his or her eye on the horizon.

Distillation

Here the ideas thrown up by the inspiration phase (or the perspiration phase – see below) are sifted through and evaluated, perhaps in the light of the findings of a clarification phase. The best ideas are chosen for further development. This is a self-critical editing phase. It requires cool analysis and judgment rather than spontaneous idea generation. However, it should not be so critical as to inhibit productivity entirely.

Incubation

It is often difficult to achieve this in practice, but ideally there should occasionally be a few days of inactivity between the phases outlined above. This gives time for the subconscious to work on any problems encountered, and provides the learners with a chance to get some distance between themselves and their ideas, so that they are better able to evaluate them. 'Incubation' is particularly useful after an 'inspiration' or a 'perspiration' phase, or if a problem has been encountered. Whilst there is no formal activity during this phase, learners should be encouraged to mull over what they are doing. Creative people rarely snatch at their first idea, and they are content to let half-baked ideas, loose ends and inconsistencies brew away in their subconscious until 'something turns up'.

> Whenever Sir Isaac Newton had a particularly thorny problem, he worked on it just before he went to sleep. He said, 'I invariably woke up with the solution.'

Perspiration

Once ideas have been chosen, they are then amended and developed towards completion, though this may well involve further 'inspiration', 'clarification' and 'perspiration' phases, usually with many drafts and redrafts.

> 'Genius is 1% inspiration, 99% perspiration.'
> – *Thomas Edison*

Remember that though the first letters of the five phases can usefully be ordered to spell ICDIP, this does not imply that they always occur in that particular order; and each phase may be experienced many times in a given piece of work.

> One of the main difficulties of the creative process is that the different phases require radically different 'mind-sets'. These are described below:
>
> **Inspiration :** uncritical, deeply involved, spontaneous, risk-taking, intuitive, joyful, 'slap-happy' and improvisational, subjective. Not judgmental.
> **Clarification:** critical, analytical, logical, impartial.
> **Distillation:** self-critical, objective, analytical, judgmental
> **Incubation:** developing a disinterested distance
> **Perspiration:** mainly uncritical persistent effort.
>
> Many people find it very difficult to switch from one mind-set to another, especially if they have an overpoweringly prevalent mind-set.
>
> If a student approaches a phase with the wrong mind-set, they are almost bound to be ineffective. It is no good being critical and perfectionist when searching for ideas, and it is no good being uncritical and 'slap-happy' when choosing from alternative ideas. It is common to find learners who are strong in one phase and weak in another. One student will be full of ideas, but unable to work on them critically; while another will have a dearth of ideas on which to apply their good judgment.

Learners and the creative phases

In contrast to the complex process described in the phases above, 'uncreative' people will tend to latch on to the first idea that comes to them, and quickly and uncritically bring it to completion without serious thought about what they are trying to achieve. How can we encourage learners to go through all the phases mentioned, and so increase their creative potential?

One of the teacher's roles during creative work is to help learners manage whichever are their weaker phases. This is done by choosing activities which help them cure their creative constipation or design diarrhoea, and by *explaining and discussing the creative phases with them*. Make it clear that their first idea will not necessarily be their best; that ideas can be worked on; that it is important to have a clear idea of what one is trying to achieve; and so on.

'Imagination is more important than knowledge.' – *Albert Einstein*

Encouraging the inspiration phase

Sometimes one can provide students with an activity which helps them generate ideas. This is often best done at the start of the creative session. For example, if students are expected to write some prose about the sea, they could browse through books relevant to the subject, or look at paintings or photographs of the sea, noting down as they did so any words, phrases or observations which struck them – without any preconceptions about whether or how these ideas would be used. They could be asked to recall personal experiences, or read examples of good writing on the subject.

Word association is another method for generating material. Students could be given two minutes to write down as many words or phrases as they could think of on the subject of the sea. A variant of this is to write down word chains, where each word is suggested by the *previous* word in the chain – for example 'Sea, saltwater, tears, cry, shout, danger...' Carefully looking at such chains can suggest useful ideas and associations; this process is particularly useful for creative writing.

An uninhibited personal brainstorming session often generates useful ideas.

It often helps if the inspiration phase forces students away from what would otherwise be the conventional-thinking route to an obvious or clichéd piece of work. 'Kick start' material with only an oblique relevance to the subject matter is often surprisingly productive, as it encourages a more unusual approach. A magazine article about a tidal barrage, or a coastguard safety leaflet, will suggest more original words or approaches to the sea topic than examining a description of the sea in a novel. The more material the better; rifle the library!

More advanced students can try lateral thinking techniques pioneered by Edward de Bono. These techniques may seem oddball and most unlikely to produce ideas with any merit; but all I ask is that you try them seriously yourself for half an hour. Further recommendation from me will then be unnecessary! Here are a few of them:

Random association

This has the advantage of throwing one off well trodden paths. Words are chosen at random from the dictionary, and then word association is used to work towards the desired subject matter. Here is an example of this technique as used by a student who is looking for ideas for the subject of a painting, to be entered for a competition in the category 'Human Group'. The words on the left are those generated at random from the dictionary

recite → poem or reading → group as an audience at a poetry reading

revelation → religious revelation → angel appearing to group of shepherds

glove → hand → handshake → group of people meeting for the first time

glow → fire → group of people round a camp fire

Encourage students to generate as many ideas as possible.

This technique can be used in almost any creative work, whether devising the plot for a short story, problem-solving, or dealing with design problems. In the following example, a student uses the technique to consider ideas for a device that will automatically water plants when the owner is on holiday:

spark → fire → fires can be thermostatically controlled; could a plant pot have a humidity detector that automatically turned on a water supply when a certain level of dryness was reached?

impale → spike → could a spike or pipe which slowly releases water be stuck in the soil?

purse → money → paper → soggy paper; could some kind of highly absorbent material be soaked and placed under the flowerpot to prevent it from drying out? ...

There is no end to these random and oblique-relevance approaches:

To look for colour combinations for a wallpaper pattern, try throwing cut-out shapes from magazine pictures on to a white background.

Try cutting out lots of words and phrases that appeal to you from a newspaper, and then randomly ordering them to produce ideas for a story or poem. (David Bowie has used this technique when writing lyrics.)

To find interesting shapes for a fabric design, try looking at photographs of microbes.

Beethoven is said to have used the rhythm of the hooves of a running horse passing his window, when writing a movement of a piano sonata. Using random or oblique sources for inspiration ensures that one escapes the obvious. Why not encourage relatively advanced or motivated students to keep a journal or scrapbook of ideas that interest them? This can then be used for inspiration.

CAP

This stands for Consider All Possibilities. For example, if one 'did a CAP' on how the automatic plant waterer could be powered, one might come up with electricity, elastic band, gas, compressed air, clockwork, compressed spring, hamster wheel, petrol, battery, wind, gravity... Every possibility is considered, feasible or not. Each idea suggests a different approach to the design, some practical, some not. CAP forces one to consider possibilities which would otherwise be passed over for no good reason. A musician could 'do a CAP' when working out what bass note would best harmonise a short melodic passage; a whole series of notes would simply be tried in turn.

Po

'Po', as used by de Bono, stands for Provocation. A provocative statement is made which is clearly ludicrous but would be very convenient or interesting. Rather than rejecting the statement, it is worked on to see if it yields any useful or productive ideas. For example:

> *'Po: suppose the plant could water itself.'* After a little thought, this leads to the possibility of water transpiring or evaporating from the plant's leaves being put back into its soil. This might lead to the idea of putting a plastic covering of some kind over the plant, so that water would not be able to escape from the plant and pot.

'Po' is particularly useful in group work.

Backtracking

If one is at a dead end it is often helpful to go back a few paces and take a different route. To take the plant-watering example again, if the design team was experiencing difficulty developing a cheap electrical design, they could 'backtrack' and look at a gravity-fed design which would probably be cheaper. This may seem an obvious strategy, but it is often ignored in practice, as one does not like abandoning an idea in which there is a large investment of time or emotion.

When encouraging inspiration, concentrate on novelty and quantity. The ideas will generate more ideas, and sooner or later something useful comes up. The vast majority of the material generated will be rejected, but what remains is likely to be sound, as well as imaginative.

Encouraging the remaining phases

The other phases in the creative process are more easily encouraged; one simply needs to set appropriate tasks:

Clarification phase: 'I want you to produce a clear statement of exactly what you want your leaflet to achieve. When your group has agreed it, write it down, and show it to me.'

Distillation phase: 'Now rifle through your notes and decide on your best ideas; then see if you can choose which ones you want to work on.'

Incubation phase: Here it is simply a question of making the necessary time available – though with crowded curricula, 'simply' may not always be the right word!

Perspiration phase: 'Now you have decided which ideas you like, see if you can develop them.' 'Look at what you have produced and ask yourself what is the weakest aspect of it; see if you can set about improving this.' ...

'In some cases creativity has been abused by being allied with a vague permissiveness, with the notion that whatever happens in the classroom should be allowed to happen without the constraints of moral, critical or imaginative judgments. In other cases, teachers, with a primitive conception of inspiration, have urged children to write spontaneously but without consideration of an attentive audience. This may, of course, be a way of beginning – but if imaginative work stays at this level it will quickly deteriorate into mass cliché and private rhetoric.'

– *Peter Abbs in* **Root and Blossom**

Creative work never follows a strict pattern, so it is not easy to plan for. However, consideration of the ICDIP phases can help to make your creative lessons more productive. Let's look at some case studies that make use of ideas in this chapter.

Even if the case studies are not in your subject area, you can still learn from the teacher's general approach. You might like to work out your own approaches to the cases before seeing the teacher's solutions:

Case 1. An embroidery class with adult learners who are reasonably experienced at 'embroidering by numbers'. Their teacher, Valerie, is keen to get the class to generate their own ideas, despite their lack of confidence in design. She wants each student to develop his or her own simple abstract design.

Case 2. An English language class of fairly able students. Their teacher, Hilary, has allowed each student to choose a title for a poem about an animal, or to make up his or her own title. We will take Clive as an example; he has chosen the title 'On finding a dead fox'. The other students in the class will follow a similar process with their titles.

N.B. In a third case study at the end of the chapter, creativity is considered as a skill rather than as a process.

Valerie's class (Case 1)

Clarification and 'doing-detail': Valerie shows the group five pieces of original embroidery work and asks them to work in teams of 'judges', as if they are judging a competition. Each group is asked to agree what constitutes a good abstract embroidery design. Eventually, each student uses this as a basis to draw up a personal design brief (e.g. bold simple shapes, strong colours, ... etc.)

Inspiration: The next week she takes to the class a number of photocopies of a photograph of a stairway. This high-contrast photograph looks almost like a complex geometrical design in itself. She shows the students how to place two mirrors on their photocopy so as to produce a kaleidoscope effect. Moving the mirrors over the photocopy generates a very wide variety of symmetrical designs Others cut out a small rectangle in a large piece of card, and move this over the photocopy to generate unsymmetrical designs.

She asks each student to use the mirrors and/or the card to produce four designs, and to sketch these out roughly.

Distillation: With the help of their design criteria, students choose the best of their four designs.

Perspiration: They are then asked to isolate this design's main weakness, and to modify the design to put this right. (This takes time in many cases.)

Inspiration: Students look through colour photographs of garden flowers, lichen, shrubs, wild birds etc. to get ideas for a colour scheme for their design. The first draft of the design is then produced, using paints and paper.

Hilary's class (Case 2)

Inspiration: Clive is asked to go to the library to find books containing colour photographs of foxes. He is told to read about his subject matter, and make notes of facts, ideas, words and phrases that appeal to him. He is also asked to do a word association list using the words suggested by his title: 'dead', 'fox', 'find'. He finishes up with two pages of words and phrases.

Clarification: After the class has studied some poems with clear central ideas or messages, Clive and the rest of his class are asked to read through their notes and decide on a central idea or message for *their* poems. They are asked to produce three different ideas (but Clive is only able to produce one that he is keen on).

Distillation and Perspiration: He is asked to take his favourite idea and produce four opening lines, making them as striking as possible; to do this he makes use of some of the best ideas from his two pages of words and phrases.

Creativity as a 'how to' skill

Some people consider creativity to be an unteachable gift. This is nonsense. Whether the medium is painting, fabric design, engineering design, creative writing, original experimental work, musical composition, creative problem-solving, creative management or some other field of creativity, learners can improve their skill. This requires attention to both process and product.

Learners certainly need to become aware of the creative *process* that I have tried to describe in this chapter, and must learn to manage it effectively. But they also have to learn about the the medium in which they are working, to discover how to make an effective painting, poem, design or whatever. This is a 'how to' skill, so it is useful to examine the elements in the mnemonic EDUCARE? (see Chapter 2) to see how it could be developed.

- **Explanation:** Students need the theory of the medium in which they are working. For example, they may need some notion of the ideas of form, structure and rhythm in poetry; composition in painting; economy, boldness and simplicity in engineering design; etc. Do they understand something of their discipline, along with its traditions and schools?

- **'Doing-detail':** Concrete examples of good practice (e.g. the work of experts/masters in the chosen field) can be analysed to good effect. From this, students should be encouraged to discover the general principles of good practice in the medium they are studying. They will need your guidance here. Students may not all agree on these principles, of course; but if they develop their own ideas, so much the better. Even the great masters learned from, and were inspired by, previous great masters. Students can also learn what *not* to do from bad practice!

- **Use:** Learners need time to experiment and develop their ideas.

- **Check and correct:** It is even more important in creative work than in other forms of learning that learners criticise and correct their own work. However, a teacher can obviously help enormously, especially in technical matters. It helps if the teacher and the learner are both aware of what the learner is trying to achieve.

- **Aide-mémoire:** This often helps to clarify techniques and principles.

- **Evaluation:** Learners gain immeasurably from evaluating their own and each other's work, especially in open discussion with peers and/or a teacher. Appeal to general principles should be encouraged, rather than simple statements of taste. Severe criticism of each other's work is probably counter-productive.

- **?:** As always, it is helpful to be able to share difficulties and queries in a supportive atmosphere.

In a further case study, let's examine an example of how EDUCARE? might be used to choose activities for a design class.

Case 3

Students are to produce a new design for a supermarket's carrier bag.

Explanation: The functions of carrier bags must be explained or discussed.

'Doing-detail': A varied selection of 'concrete examples of good (and bad) practice' are examined critically by the class. This process is then used to agree on some criteria for good carrier bag design: e.g. strength of handles, simplicity and boldness of graphics, biodegradable plastic... This makes really clear what is expected of the design – and of the learner.

Use: Students produce some designs.

Check and correct: Students are asked to evaluate their own, and perhaps each other's, designs against their design criteria.

Aide-mémoire: The design criteria are likely to be written down.

Review: What relevant ideas can students use from previous learning?

Evaluation: Ideally, learners should be involved with the evaluation of their completed designs, to sharpen their critical faculties – and therefore their *self-critical* faculties. Perhaps there could also be a public showing of the work, with a comments book?

?: The atmosphere should be supportive, with learners able to get their queries answered.

It is not enough to give students the brief and then leave them to it! Creative work rarely follows a smooth path to completion, and people like to work in different ways. As a result, it is impossible to be prescriptive about the process, but I hope that the ideas above will at least help you to devise useful activities.

☑ Checklist for encouraging creativity

☐ Have you explained the ICDIP phases and their associated 'mind-sets' to your students?

☐ Do you make conscious use of the ICDIP phases in your lesson plans?

☐ Have your students been shown, and carefully examined, work of a high standard in order to learn the general principles of good practice?

☐ Are students encouraged to use general principles when creating their own work?

☐ Are students encouraged to use general principles in the criticism of their own work, and the work of others?

Exercises

Use the EDUCARE? mnemonic and the ICDIP phases to develop learning activities to help students do one of the following:

1. Develop a T-shirt design for the 'Grannies for Fitness Campaign'.
2. Write a short story with the title 'Ambush!'
3. Design a jar opener for people with arthritis.
4. Think of ways of collecting money for a local charity.
5. Design an experiment to measure air pollution.

26 Reading for learning, and information searches

You would not be reading now if you did not believe one can learn from the process. A decent textbook can be a gold-mine of varied and useful activities, but this chapter concerns itself specifically with students who are reading in order to gain knowledge and understanding.

The use made of reading as a teaching method is increasing, but very variable. In many schools and colleges some learners never trouble their library, and some textbooks are issued only to be returned unopened a year later. Other textbooks are so extensively used that they could do with annual replacement. Until recently, however, reading for learning has often been regarded as old-fashioned outside higher education. Now, partly due to the move towards assignments and project work, some teachers are using it very widely.

It is best not to approach this topic with starry-eyed idealism. Reading does not guarantee learning. We have all had the experience of reading something for some time, only to realise with irritation that we have learned nothing from the process because of a lack of concentration. I hope it is not happening to you at this moment!

Marton and Saljo have identified two distinctive approaches to reading:

- **Surface-level processing,** where students take a passive approach and are concerned with:

  - covering the content.
  - how much they have learned.
  - finding the right answers.
  - assimilating unaltered chunks of knowledge.
  - learning verbatim.

- **Deep-level processing,** in which students take a mentally active approach and are concerned with:

  - the central point.
  - what lies behind the argument.
  - the whole picture.
  - what it boils down to.
  - what it is connected with.
  - the logic of the argument.
  - points that are not clear.
  - questioning the conclusions.

Deep-level processors were shown to be more successful in exams and to be more versatile. I would add a third level:

- **Zero-level processing,** where the learner simply goes through the motion of reading the text, believing that understanding will automatically follow by some osmosis-like process. The student is concerned with:
  - getting it over as quickly as possible.
  - what's for tea!

How can teachers maximise the chance that students will learn from their reading? In Chapter 1 it was pointed out that learning involves producing a *personalised* meaning for the information presented to the learner. Reading should be an active process, where learners interrogate the text to form this personalised version of its message. This can be encouraged by, for example:

Interesting reading activities: A challenge to discover something that is puzzling or intriguing from a good book is more motivating than 'Read Chapter 23.'

Expecting reading notes: Ask your students to produce a précis, a summary, a set of key points, or even a full set of notes. This should require more than blind copying.

Reorganising the material into a different form: For example, a text which looks in turn at the function of different agencies in a process could be reorganised to give the information chronologically.

Reading for information: Ask students to look for specific information, e.g. the answers to specific questions; this information should preferably need to be 'dug out' of the text.

Reading for criticism: Ask students to take a critical view of the text they are reading: what is the author's point of view, what is the evidence for and against this point of view? What's missing? What would other authors or theorists think of the points of view expressed?

Expecting to make a presentation: Ask students to read different material in groups, and make a presentation to the rest of their class. In higher education, students are expected to present and defend their views on what they have read to a 'seminar' consisting of fellow students and an experienced tutor. Similar techniques are used in FE and in schools. Students can be expected to produce reading notes for their fellow students, perhaps checking these with the tutor before duplication.

Reading requires that the learner takes responsibility for understanding and learning, and it has many of the advantages of individualised learning. It allows learners to study at their own pace, so that the keener can go further and deeper, and the weaker can take their time with a text personally chosen for simplicity.

It also:

- develops the very important skill of learning from reading, which will never be accomplished without practice.

- helps to develop library and book-searching skills.

- acquaints learners with their textbooks and with other important texts, which they are then more likely to make further use of in their private study.

Whatever you teach, there are bound to be some excellent texts available, and you are ignoring a valuable source if you don't encourage your learners to make use of them. If the texts you would prefer are not available in the quantities you would like, it may be possible to devise a group-work 'circus' where texts circulate, and groups carry out different activities with each of the texts (see Chapter 17). Don't forget non-book material such as journals and newspapers.

> Some research has shown that university students given a textbook, enrolled on a course and told the exam date have done as well as those attending lectures.

For most classes, it will be necessary to make sure the reading activity you set has actually been carried out. This can be done, for example, by observing student presentations; or by requesting summaries, précis, reading notes, essays or other written projects or assignments; or by tests.

Reading is an essentially solitary activity requiring quiet concentration. Many students find it difficult to read for more than a few minutes in class, preferring to read at home or in private study. It is an excellent homework activity, as the ratio of learning value to marking effort is high.

> Try producing a reading guide for your students. This should list useful books, with comments from you such as 'Dull but thorough' or 'Better on X than on Y'.

Library and information searching skills

A university biology lecturer told me that she once set an essay on hawks for first year students. She provided a book list including a 2,000-page alphabetical reference guide to birds in Europe and North America. When she asked for the essay from one student he replied, bleary-eyed, that he was still working his way through the booklist, and was currently reading the previously mentioned reference guide. He explained sheepishly that so far he had only read up to 'E'!

In her excellent book *Teaching and Learning in Higher Education*, Ruth Beard describes annually finding science and mathematics students researching topics in psychology books by meticulously searching from page to page. 'A suggestion to consult the index invariably caused initial surprise, and some of these postgraduate students needed to be told where to find it!'

It is tempting to laugh at such students, but the derision is better directed at their schools and colleges. Every student should be taught information-searching skills, including how to use a library; this is perhaps best done by a tutor librarian. There is a good deal more to research than using card indexes nowadays; for example, most colleges have an encyclopaedia and the *Times* newspaper on CD-ROM computer disks (similar to music CDs), which can be searched using keywords. Have your students been taught to skim, or to speed-read?

> 'The lecture is the primrose path to intellectual sloth.'

Making full use of your library

If they are given sufficient notice, most libraries will assemble a box of books on a given topic for you to take to your class. They may also have a 'desk loan' system where books in great demand are removed from the shelves, and can only be borrowed for use in the library.

> You may like to consider writing digests or summaries of some texts for your students – but why not get your students to do this for themselves? Some university lecturers organise 'reading deals' where students share out the reading list, and then share their reading notes.

Readability

Are the books you recommend easily readable by your students? There are a number of methods for estimating the readability of text, usually based on the average sentence length, and the average number of syllables per word. These methods can only give a rough idea of the readability, so it is still desirable to supplement them with the use of your own judgment. The 'Fog index' is an example; this calculates the reading age as follows:

- Select a passage of continuous text of about 100 words, containing a number of complete sentences 'S'.

- Find the average number of words per complete sentence in this passage.

- Find the number of words of three or more syllables, 'W', in exactly 100 words from the passage.

- Calculate the reading age by: *Reading age = [0.4 × (S+ W)] + 5.*

For somewhat greater accuracy, select *three or four* passages from the book, and compute the reading age from each to obtain an average.

Reading techniques

Some commentators suggest that reading should follow the 'SQR³' process:

Survey: Skim-read the chapter, noting content and organisation.

Question: Before reading each section, stop and ask what is being covered, and what you want to extract from it.

Read: Read the text, but think about the material as you do so, and try to answer the questions mentioned above.

Recite: At the end of each section, stop and recite the major points to yourself.

Review: At the end of the chapter, review the whole of it, paying special attention to the way the author organised the material.

☑ Checklist on reading for learning

☐ Do you encourage students to make use of their textbooks?

☐ Do you set reading that encourages students to *process* information rather than simply read it?

☐ Do your students know what books are available, and their strengths and weaknesses?

☐ Do you evaluate whether reading has been done, and whether learning has resulted?

☐ Have your students been taught information-searching skills?

Making use of reading: some case studies

Reading is particularly valuable where the syllabus is too large, or where student experience is mixed:

Case 1

Jane finds that there is a large discrepancy in the background knowledge of the students on her 'improvers' photography evening class. Rather than spend the class's time going over basics, she gives her students a condensed set of notes outlining what she expects them to know, and a reading list.

Case 2

Reading assignments in the field of the arts and social sciences are common, but they can also be used in the sciences. I ask my A-level physics students to study a descriptive topic without the aid of explanatory lectures. I give them this assignment:

Nuclear Physics and Radioactivity Assignment

Write your own notes on the topics in the title by reference to suitable texts. I will expect to see your notes, in progress, and when they are completed. There will be a test on the work in the usual way. Some time will be given in class to clear up any queries; all quantitative aspects of the topic will be covered in full during lectures.

Your notes should cover:

The nuclear atom and an understanding of Rutherford's alpha particle scattering experiment (qualitative only): proton, neutron, atomic number and mass number, isotopes.
Simple nuclear equations.

Fission and fusion reactions and the energy changes involved (binding energy is not on the syllabus).

Radioactivity
> **Alpha, beta and gamma radiations.** Typical sources, mass, charge, penetrating power, ionisation effect.
> **Detection of radiation**: cloud chamber, Geiger Muller tube. Experimental determination of charge and penetrating power of α, β, and χ.
> **Radioactive decay**, decay constant and half life. Effect on the nucleus.
> **Hazards** and precautions in the safe handling of radio-active substances.
> Some examples of the uses of radioactivity.

Assessment:
Marks will be given for:
> Comprehensiveness and clarity of the notes, including clear diagrams where necessary.
> Use of more than one source in your research (please give a bibliography).

Interim tutorial: Week beginning 4th Feb.

Final submission: 3rd March

27 Learning from experience

In his history of the First World War, A.J.P. Taylor graphically describes the terrible carnage resulting from wave after wave of allied assaults on the heavily defended German trenches. The tactic, though fruitless, was repeated by the generals with chilling determination. A.J.P. Taylor concludes that 'Nothing had been learnt from previous failures except how to repeat them on a larger scale.'

Experience in itself does not guarantee learning. In order to learn from experience we must reflect on our experiences; try to relate them to theory; and then plan how we might do better next time. After carrying out this plan we need to reflect again – and so the process continues. This cyclic 'experiential learning' process is much the same whether we are learning military strategy, coronary care, or how to write essays. We also learn to *teach* by following this cycle.

The 'experiential learning cycle' was first suggested by Kolb. A learner can start the cycle at any point, but the stages should be followed in sequence.

Let's illustrate the cycle with an example. Suppose you wanted to grow prize carrots. You might start on this learning process by **(2) reflecting** critically on your carrot-growing achievements to date. This would lead on to **(3) abstract conceptualisation**, where you consider your experience in the light of theory, e.g. soil type, soil pH, spacing, variety of carrot grown etc. This would lead you to a plan of how to grow better carrots next year; that is **planning active experimentation (4)**. You then have the **concrete experience (1)** of carrying out this plan, which again is reflected on **(2)**, and so on.

Note that the learning process is cyclic, and can go on indefinitely. Whether consciously or not, virtually all successful learning from experience follows this cycle. Let's look at an example of a teacher choosing and ordering learning experiences to follow the experiential learning cycle. This should maximise the learning that takes place from experience.

A case study

A catering lecturer is teaching students how to organise a restaurant kitchen. The students experience one four-hour session every week working in a training restaurant, preparing meals for members of the public. This experience is realistic – and intense!

After a session in the training restaurant **(1)** the teacher holds a debriefing session where students discuss this practical experience. The teacher starts by encouraging the students to reflect on the experience **(2)**. First, facts are established: how did the practice go? Then discussion moves on, with students addressing such questions as: 'What were the group's successes and failures? How did you all feel during the practical session? What would have happened if.....? How did you feel at the time? Did you work well when you were rushed? Was anybody resentful about their role?' – and so on. The aim is an honest but non-accusatory evaluation of performance, where mistakes are seen as inevitable and even valuable. It's all right to fail, if you (and others) can learn from your mistakes.

In Chinese the word for disaster also means opportunity.

Having reflected, the teacher steers the discussion on to 'abstract conceptualisation' **(3)**. What are the general principles that the group can learn from their experience? The teacher may well need to act as midwife here, establishing principles from apparently unconnected events, such as 'If a task needs doing, someone must be made responsible for it.' or 'Unless preparation is comprehensive for each dish, serving will be delayed.' – and so on. In practice, great stress should be given to these 'learning outcomes'. General principles like these should find their way into the students' notes and, more importantly, should be adopted by them in future practice.

The next stage is active experimentation **(4)**, where the students are asked to plan how they will organise themselves for the next session. The design could be carried out in some detail, with students assigning themselves responsibilities for the session, and personal action plans being devised. For example, John agrees to read up the recipes in advance, Paula resolves to be less shy about asking for help when she knows she is behind, and so on.

A discussion such as this is a time-consuming process; ten minutes of concrete experience can generate hours of reflection, abstract conceptualisation and planning active experimentation. Sometimes it is necessary to restrict discussion to one or two themes.

> Could it be that some slow learners miss out one or more of the stages of the experiential learning cycle?

The four stages are now examined in more detail.

1. Concrete experience

Experience can be realistic – for example, students using a woodwork lathe, or work experience programmes. Alternatively, the experience offered can be a substitute for a 'real-life' one. Here are some examples of the latter:

Observing an experienced practitioner (live or on video), e.g. a trainee shop assistant observing someone serving in a shop.

Case study, e.g. doctors discussing case notes, or management trainees discussing the strike record of a company.

Students discussing each other's experience, e.g. interviewing each other about how they approach essay writing; listening to each other's experience of work-shadowing; etc. (Student diaries or log books are sometimes helpful for this activity.)

Games and role-play, e.g. students of industrial relations acting out an industrial dispute, in which they take the parts of employers and employees.

Simulation, e.g. nurses working on a computer simulation for intensive care.

Demonstration, i.e. the students experience a teacher demonstrating a procedure.

'Concrete experience' should be used by students to test out ideas, methods and plans, rather than to repeat well-known procedures mindlessly. For example, when students are writing a poem, welding a joint, or observing an experienced social worker, they should be trying out a new technique or approach, or looking for something they have not paid particular attention to before. Ideally the 'concrete experience' should be informed by sessions of 'planning active experimentation' (stage 4).

Learning from work experience

Gibbs in his excellent book on experiential learning, *Learning by doing*, suggests that substitutes for direct work experience are useful in order to:

- practise skills in safe contexts.
- illustrate theory in action.
- develop interpersonal skills.
- increase personal involvement in learning, and enliven topics.
- derive theory or general principles from examples.
- prepare learners for work experience.
- focus attention on experiences which are difficult or impossible to provide in any other way.

---

2. Reflection on experience

Reflection involves a systematic objective evaluation of the student's 'concrete experience', perhaps along with an examination of his or her feelings at the time. This may largely be undertaken by or with the teacher at first, but the long-term aim should be to get the students to carry out the process by themselves.

Reflection through self-assessment

There is a danger in students relying solely on their teacher for the evaluation of their performance. If they are never trusted to evaluate their own experience, they will not acquire the habits and skills of reflecting on their performance, and so they will not develop the ability to improve themselves. The aim must surely be to produce a student who has the confidence and skill to reflect and evaluate independently of the teacher. Give students confidence in their ability to learn from their own experience, and when your teaching finishes, their learning continues. The student becomes a 'reflective practitioner'.

Self-assessment can be encouraged during debriefing sessions by asking questions such as 'What were the main difficulties your group had?' rather than saying, for example, 'Lack of preparation was your main problem.' Try to avoid the temptation to help too much.

You can also encourage self-assessment by asking students to draw up a self-assessment checklist, preferably in advance of the experience. This serves the dual purpose of aiding reflection, and focussing the student's efforts in the right direction. It also encourages the student to analyse the process carefully, and to ask questions. For example, before carrying out a welding operation students could write a checklist of objectives that define a satisfactory weld. This could be checked by the teacher. The student then carries out and assesses the weld. Students are often harsher in evaluating their own performance than the teacher would be.

A self-assessment checklist by a student learning how to chair a meeting

1. Did I stick to the agenda?
2. Did I maintain everyone's interest?
3. Did I prevent red-herrings?
4. Did everyone get a fair share of the time to express their views?
5. Was I able to summarise the decisions?

Self-assessment encourages reflection and purposeful activity towards useful goals, as well as encouraging learners to become responsible for their own learning.

Peer-assessment

Peer-assessment is another means of encouraging reflection. Checklists can be used in a similar way as for self-assessment, and the advantages of peer-assessment are similar to those of self-assessment.

Diaries

Here is a further way of encouraging students to reflect on their experience. They are encouraged to record facts first, and then their personal emotional response to their learning experiences. Diaries are perhaps particularly useful where such emotional responses are strong, as for example with students of social work, teaching or nursing.

After completing a day on a geriatric ward, a student nurse could record factual material about her experiences and then her emotional responses: what she found difficult or rewarding; what made her feel uneasy; what she felt her strengths and weaknesses were. Before starting the 'concrete experience' it sometimes helps if students agree probing questions which they will answer in their diaries.

These diary entries can then be used later at a debriefing session with other student nurses. It's amazing how much students forget after they complete placements or work experience; diaries are a useful way of salvaging experience for later use by the student, or the group as a whole.

The importance of trust

An atmosphere of trust between teacher and student is usually necessary before students are prepared to evaluate and reflect on their strengths and weaknesses honestly. For this reason, the reflection process must be separated from any assessment of the student.

3. Abstract conceptualisation

The aim in this stage is for *the student* to relate his or her 'concrete experience' to theory. A learning teacher might ask why students were more motivated in one of her lessons than in another; a design student might ask why a circuit does not behave as expected; a graphic designer might ask why his new design is particularly effective.

Whatever the student is learning, the questions are much the same, though they take less time to ask than they do to answer:

> Why were the successes a success? Why were the failures a failure? How should it be done? Why should it be done in this way? What would happen if it were done in a different way?

Students may well need to change the way they think about the process that they are learning. Alternatively, their concrete experience may simply confirm their ideas about theory, in which case this stage may not take long.

4. Planning active experimentation

Having reflected on past experience and attempted to relate this experience to theory, the learner's next task is to ask *'How can I do it better next time?'* The answer to this question can then be tested during a subsequent 'concrete experience'. No-one gets better at doing anything, other than through this process.

If the student's area of study involves human relations, this stage may require some conscious risk-taking. Trainee doctors may need to ask questions of their patients that make them feel uneasy; student teachers may need to try unfamiliar teaching methods; trainee social workers may need to use more assertive techniques. In many areas of study, it is a matter of 'nothing ventured, nothing gained'.

It is often helpful for students to put ideas down on paper. This can take many forms: an action plan, a list of objectives to be achieved, a design for a biology experiment, a checklist of criteria to be used later for the self-assessment of an interior decoration project. These are all ways of setting targets for 'how to do better next time'. Here are some more detailed examples:

Case 1

Students learning how to program a computer-controlled metal cutting machine write out an action plan based on what they have learned from previous attempts.

Here is their action plan:

1. Examine the drawing and decide on the cuts necessary to fashion the required shape.
2. Decide on the best order of these cuts.
3. Decide on the depth and speed of each cut.
4. Work out the coordinates for each cut.
5. Write the program.

Case 2

Students learning how to design a newspaper advertisement draw up a list of criteria to be met by the design. This could come from self- and peer-assessment of previous attempts, or from looking at examples of good practice.

Advertisement should:

1. be uncluttered and eye-catching.
2. include the company logo in a prominent position.
3. have an attention-grabbing phrase in largest type.
4. have an explaining phrase in the next largest type.
5. have the minimum possible number of words.
6. have a design style in keeping with the company image.

Further learning experiences

Some students may decide that in order to do better next time, they need certain learning experiences. They may decide they have had enough of the present activity and want to move on, or that they need more practice in some other activity. Adult learners especially enjoy having some control over their learning.

Stages 2, 3, and 4 in the experiential learning cycle sometimes merge into one another, but there should always be a clear statement of 'how I will do it better next time' as a plan for the next 'concrete experience'.

Conclusion

Experiential learning is as old as learning itself, though it is only recently that theorists have made the process explicit, enabling teachers to choose and to order learning experiences which follow the cycle. Adopting experiential learning techniques need not require a revolutionary approach to teaching and learning. However, the techniques require that students admit their mistakes honestly and willingly, and have the courage to try out new ideas. This is demanding of the learner and requires sensitive teaching.

The reflective learning cycle also describes how you will learn to teach, whether consciously or not. The emotional demands mentioned above also apply to you as a learner. How will you fare in learning from experience? Chapter 40 (on evaluation) considers this, and there is a questionnaire to help you discover in which phase of the experiential learning cycle you are likely to be weakest.

> When I first started teaching I asked a senior member of staff how I should teach a certain topic. It turned out to be bad advice, and a head of department berated me for taking it. I defended myself by pointing out that the teacher whose advice I had sought had had thirty years experience of teaching. 'He has not,' said the head of department crossly. 'He's had one year's experience thirty times.'

Designing training

A great deal of training, especially in the professions, is limited to the 'abstract conceptualisation' phase of the cycle. Theory is taught without relating it directly to the learner's concrete personal experience. In such circumstances the trainee cannot apply the theory in practice, even when it is well understood.

Some trainers address this problem by designing exclusively practical courses. Here the student is likely to accept techniques uncritically, without any understanding of why they are used or what the alternatives might be.

In short, many teaching programmes concentrate almost exclusively on one or two of the stages of the experiential learning cycle, instead of recognising the importance and interdependence of them all. The strength of the experiential learning cycle is that it develops in the student an understanding of how theory and practice are linked.

I once oversaw a novice teacher who was training experienced working nurses in a new care-plan for diabetics.

She met her trainees for a short session half a dozen times over a period of some months. She described the new plan, and asked them to try it out on some of their patients.

Each did so, and reported their experiences back to the teacher and the other trainees. The trainees suggested ways of overcoming each other's problems, and congratulated each other on their successes. The teacher put right any misunderstandings, answered queries and gave concrete advice on how to overcome difficulties.

Theory and practice were welded into one, and the learners soon became confident in the use of their new techniques. All the reflective learning cycle was there; all the learners' needs for corrected practice were met. Compare this with a two-day lecture course!

☑ Checklist for experiential learning

☐ Is your students' concrete experience realistic and productive?

☐ Can skills be practised wherever possible?

☐ Do students evaluate their own performance?

☐ Is this evaluation checked by the teacher?

☐ Are successes and failures related to theory and 'how to do better next time'?

☐ Are students encouraged to experiment bravely and systematically?

☐ Do students draw up checklists of criteria for success?

☐ Do students use theory to work out how to do better next time?

☐ Are students supported emotionally if risk-taking or painful reflection is necessary?

☐ Are mistakes seen as opportunities to learn?

☐ Do students take responsibility for their own learning?

Exercise

Plan a series of learning activities which follow the experiential learning cycle for:

- Someone learning how to do a 'three point turn'.
- Students developing their essay-writing skills and techniques.
- Students developing their study skills.

28 Private study and homework

Some call it homework, some private study, some 'prep'. Others have no name for it and don't formally request it – but expect it to be done nonetheless.

When I was a student I hated homework, and when I became a teacher I saw no reason to revise my opinion. At the end of an evening marking classwork, preparing for lessons and dealing with a mountain of administrative work, the last thing I want is thirty homework assignments to mark. Then, one year, my new timetable involved me in teaching eight classes of 25 students. Every week I would be setting and marking two hundred pieces of homework; at ten minutes each, simply marking them would take me 33 hours a week! Slowly it dawned on me that the aim of homework is to get the *student* to work at home, not the teacher.

Many learning activities are best done alone, and are therefore much more suited to private study than to work in the classroom. Ideal homework:

- should involve the student in a genuinely useful activity that is best done alone – or at least does not require teacher support.
- should be of a kind which makes it possible to check that it has been completed satisfactorily.
- should require a minimum of teacher effort.
- should (usually) provide a mark.
- should not be too onerous.

Which student activities best fit these criteria?

Reading: Most, or even all, homework could simply be reading the textbook; but take note of the chapter on reading and set a specific series of pages to read. Give a short five-question 'slip test' to check that the material has been read and understood. If students mark each other's papers, the test need only take three minutes. Reading familiarises the student with the textbook, and provides general book learning practice as well as direct subject learning.

Preparation for a lesson: This may take the form of reading, revising relevant material covered earlier, or answering questions which orientate the student. For example, learners might be asked to consider the purpose of stock-taking, before a lesson on the subject.

Preparing revision notes: Summaries, mind maps, mnemonics or revision notes are often best produced by the learners themselves, and make an excellent activity at the end of a topic. Revision notes don't take long to mark.

Learning revision notes: Nearly every subject has basic factual material which must be remembered by heart; vocabulary in language subjects, formulae, definitions, procedures etc. Make sure students understand what they are expected to learn, however – see Chapter 21 on 'learning for remembering'.

Revision: An often neglected activity which is usually too vital to be left to the whims of student motivation. (See Chapters 21 and 37 for further discussion of review and mastery learning.)

Whatever the homework, if it is set it must be seen, marked or tested by the teacher, otherwise it will be evaded. (Do you need separate homework marks for reports or record cards?)

Finishing off classwork is the most commonly set homework, but it is often not the most suitable. It will not be appropriate if the student is likely to get stuck, or needs special books or equipment unavailable at home; or if separate homework and classwork marks are required. It is a useful way of ensuring that slower students catch up, but it doesn't require anything of students able or fast enough to complete the work in class time.

In general, don't set anything more difficult than the students have practised in class. If you do, some will get stuck, and others will use the difficulty as an excuse for not doing the work even when they can.

Try to follow a rigid regime for the setting, collecting and marking of homework. It is advisable to require students to write something as part of the homework activity – and for you to have thought out a response for the following:

> 'Sorry, miss, I forgot.'
> 'Sorry, miss, I didn't know there was any homework.'
> 'Sorry, miss, I left it at home.'
> 'Sorry, miss, I spent all evening taking my Granny's budgie to the vet...'

☑ Checklist on homework

☐ Are you aware of the homework policy and practice for your school or college?

☐ Do your homework assignments combine maximum learning value with minimum marking effort?

☐ Are they genuinely useful?

☐ Are you rigorous about setting, collecting and marking homework? And do your students' *parents* know this?

29 The aide-mémoire

Earlier chapters, in considering the EDUCARE? mnemonic, have explained that students regard 'aide-mémoires' as vital. The aide-mémoire is usually a summarised record of what is being learned. This may be provided by textbooks or handouts; alternatively the teacher can use dictation, or students can copy written notes from the board or overhead projector. The aide-mémoire is needed to clarify what has to be learned, to compensate for the fallibility of memory, and to provide material for revision (though ideally you should also provide a separate, very concise set of notes for students to commit to memory – see page 204).

When students are learning an exclusively practical skill such as bowing a violin, an aide-mémoire may not be necessary, but even here many teachers like to offer one to prevent the student getting into bad habits during unsupervised practice.

Have you ever tried writing and listening at the same time? Sadly, many teachers (especially in higher education) still leave their students to write their own notes during lectures. As a result, universities and polytechnics are full of students who cannot concentrate in their lectures because they are too busy writing over-detailed and inadequate notes. At bottom, the justification for this practice is: 'If it was good enough for me, it's good enough for my students.' A wider application of the same argument would have kept us in the Stone Age. If a lecturer provides a summary, students can concentrate on the lecture itself.

Allowing students to write their own notes is a questionable practice for all but the brightest students or most straightforward topics. If you don't believe me, ask for your student's notes to be handed in from time to time, and look at the notes of the least able students. I guarantee you will be shocked by what you see. But if you want to teach note-taking skills, leave uninterrupted time for your students to compose their notes – perhaps one or two minutes after each fifteen-minute topic. This improves concentration and comprehension, as well as the standard of their notes.

Most teachers communicate their notes directly; let's see how they do it.

Aide-mémoire by textbook

If a well-written, readable textbook or handbook comprehensively covers every aspect of the course you are teaching, this may well fulfil all your student's aide-mémoire needs. You are also very lucky! If the textbook is too comprehensive, it is sometimes possible to indicate to students which sections they may omit, or better, they can be asked to mark the sections of the textbook relevant to what is currently being studied. If you are going to use a textbook like this, ask students to bring it to your sessions and refer to it in class.

Most teachers do not have the luxury of a text that suits all their needs, or prefer their students to have a personal record of their studies.

Writing notes for your students

Writing notes for your students has many obvious advantages, though it can be very time-consuming. Whether they are communicated by handout, by writing on the board/OHP, or by dictation, make them:

- **concise**. A summary is better than a full explanation. Refer to textbooks (giving page numbers) if necessary.

- **simple**. Don't try to impress by an over-formal style. Use as simple a vocabulary as you can, and explain all technical terms. Keep your sentences shorter than twenty words whenever you can. (See Chapter 12 on the art of explaining.)

- **attractive**. Take care with layout. Use clear, simple diagrams whenever you can. Try to get your handouts typed, or better still 'desktop published' on a computer. Don't overcrowd the page; unattractive handouts are not read.

Making your notes clearer

Avoid words such as 'it' or 'they' where the reference may be unclear, replacing them with the word to which they refer, e.g. :

    NOT: 'Place the disk in the disk drive, keeping it label uppermost.'
    BUT: 'Place the disk in the disk drive, keeping the disk label uppermost.'

(Students may think that 'it' in the first sentence refers to the disk drive.)

Avoid complex sentence constructions.

Avoid negatives; positives are often clearer, e.g.:

    NOT: 'Seldom does the machine fail to jam when the cotter is not
             lubricated.'
    BUT: 'Lubricate the cotter or the machine will probably jam.'

Aide-mémoire by handout

Handouts save valuable teaching time, and can be made to suit your needs exactly; however, they can be very time-consuming to produce. Students collect handouts assiduously, but rarely read them unless they are introduced to them during the lecture.

It is common for teachers to give out handouts, and then to find that students are reading rather than listening. If possible, give them out after the topic has been covered, and talk students through the handout as a way of summarising the topic for them.

Alternatively, students can be led through the topic with constant reference to the handout – but make sure you have their attention when you need it.

Whatever you do, make sure you have *used* the handout with the students. Some teachers produce uncompleted handouts: diagrams that are not labelled, headings with missing text, questions without answers, and so on. Completing the handout then becomes a useful lesson activity, which 'personalises' the handout for the student. Encourage students to annotate their handouts with their personal notes.

Death by a thousand handouts is a common fault of many courses for professionals. Don't try to write a textbook – write references to other people's books instead. Don't give out more than one double-sided A4 handout per hour; any more will be treated with exasperation. And do get your handouts copied double-sided rather than single-sided. Modern photocopiers can manage this entirely automatically, and if all teachers did it, we would collectively save at least one tropical rain forest a year.

Using the board or OHP for notes

Note-taking need not be a passive, fruitless activity. Prepare your own notes in advance; you should, of course, use simple language and make them clear and concise. Teach the topic before giving the note, and then use note-taking to summarise what you hope the students have learned. Involve the students in composing the note.

Suppose, for example, a science teacher is about to give the following note on power after teaching the topic:

POWER

Power is the rate of transforming energy, and it is measured in watts. One watt is one joule per second. So, for example, if an electric motor used 18 joules of energy in three seconds, the power would be 6 joules per second or 6 watts.

$$\text{power} = \frac{\text{energy transformed}}{\text{time taken}}$$

After writing the title, the teacher can ask the class for a definition of power, with its unit. A satisfactory answer should give the first sentence of the note, which can then be read out and written up. Then the teacher can ask, 'What do we mean by a watt?' This should give rise to the note's second sentence. Next the third sentence can be written, up to 'the power would be ...'; and the teacher can then ask someone to complete the sentence. Finally, the teacher can ask, 'What is the equation for power?', and a correct answer completes the note. Students enjoy being involved in composing their notes, and it gives them confidence in their learning when they are successful. Try to use their wording where you can.

If an OHP is used, the note could be progressively revealed as students answer the questions and complete the sentences. Alternatively, it can be written up at the time, which is more likely to give the students a feeling of involvement with the process.

Dictation

Dictation is the *bête noire* of teaching methods, but students often find it quicker and easier than copying. However, dictation is a disaster for slow writers and bad spellers – and for students whose pen has just been lost! Nevertheless, the status of great dictator is not as difficult to achieve as the history of the Third Reich suggests. The solution is to dictate the note while it is being written on the board or screen.

'Speak sweetly, man, although thy looks be sour.' – *Richard II*

Use a slower, more deliberate voice than usual, and give the punctuation; students can check their own spellings from the board.

What are notes for?

Don't give notes if your students will never need to use them. Give them sections of notes to learn, and then test them (see Chapter 21 on learning for remembering).

Don't overdo notes. If you find yourself spending more than five minutes every hour on them, or your handouts get longer and longer, then you should give reading references instead. Notes should be a summary only.

30 Visitors, visits and other methods

Visitors and visits are the best remembered teaching methods, and they do most to benefit the teacher-student relationship – *provided* they are well planned. They motivate students, and allow the real world into the teaching and learning.

Visitors

Studying urban crime? – why not ask a policeman to visit? Studying careers in retailing? – why not arrange a visit by a supermarket manageress?

Choose your visitors carefully; the students should be enthusiastic, or the visit is likely to be a failure. Put the students in control: who will meet the visitor? Who will make her coffee? Who will introduce her?

They should spend at least one session arranging such details, including what questions to ask the visitor, and who will ask them.

Visits

Talk to the school or college management to resolve such issues as insurance, consent forms and other paperwork. It is sensible to take students on a visit only if you have the close cooperation or agreement of a senior member of staff in your school or college.

Here are some other important points to consider:

- Are you visiting an institution that has student material already prepared?
- Have you researched the venue, and decided what you hope your students will gain from the trip?
- Is it worth devising a worksheet or set of questions, or asking the students to look out for something specific?

Other teaching methods

In this book, I have concentrated on discussing the commonest teaching and learning methods. However, there is really no limit to the possible range. The most important thing is to include adequate variety within your classes. Never be afraid to try an experiment – but always analyse the results to check whether it was a success.

For visits and visitor ideas, see The Resourceful Teacher's Handbook, ed. FitzHugh, Macmillan, ISBN (1994–5) 0–333–61600–6.

Teaching aids

31 An introduction to visual aids

The verbal channel of communication is the one most used in teaching, but for many purposes visual information is more effective. Research shows that information enters our brain in the following way:

Try to display information visually.

The main advantages of visual aids

- **They gain attention.**
  You cannot teach without the attention of your students, no matter how carefully prepared your lesson may be. A new picture on a screen is difficult to ignore – a new sentence in a speech is not. Gaining attention in the television age is not easy, and we need all the help we can get! Also, while the student is looking at your visual aid, he or she is not distracted by competing visual stimuli – the view out of the window, for example.

- **They add variety.**
  Visual aids add variety and interest.

- **They aid conceptualisation.**
  This is a major advantage of visual aids. Many concepts or ideas are understood visually rather than verbally – for example, 'practical skills' like soldering. If knowledge is understood and remembered visually, you should transmit it visually. How a table is laid for a seven-course dinner is best shown by means of a picture, or better still the real thing. Most novice teachers realise this; but they often fail to grasp that many *abstract* concepts such as 'fractions' or 'cash-flow' are also best conveyed and understood in a visual way. This idea is explored in more detail below.

- **They aid memory.**
  Research shows that most people find visual information easier to remember than verbal information. For example, mind maps (see pages 98 and 203) display verbal information visually, and so aid learning.

- **They show you care.**
  Going to the trouble of preparing visual aids shows students you take their learning seriously.

Displaying non-visual information in a visual way

Non-visual abstract ideas can be displayed by a huge variety of methods. The illustration on the following page offers an 'idea bank' of techniques for representing information visually.

Next time you are planning a lesson, check through it for ideas. (Consider also maps and tables of figures.)

Look at magazines, textbooks, newspapers and TV documentaries for more examples, and make a note of any methods you could make use of.

Try displaying the following ideas visually in as many ways as you can.

1. 87% of information enters our brain through our eyes, 9% by ear, and 4% via the other senses. (There was one possible version of this on page 265.)

2. For germs to grow on food they need warmth, moisture and time.

3. The fact that an Act of Parliament starts as a Bill produced by the Government, and must pass through the House of Commons and the House of Lords before becoming law. Once it is law it is interpreted by the courts.

The advantages of the visual channel to teachers are enormous, but you would be surprised how often poor teachers ignore it.

Venn diagram

Decision Flow chart

Why won't my car start?

Have you run out of fuel? — Yes → Get some!

no

Does the engine turn over? — yes → Is fuel getting to the carburettor? — no → etc...

no — yes

Do the Lights work well? — no → Your battery is flat!

yes → etc

etc. yes

etc

Pie diagram

urban / forest / farmland.

Bar chart

Line graph

Tree diagram

computers

micro   mini   main frame

IBM   APPLE   BBC

1991   1993

Tree planting schedule

Pictorial representation

costs   time   personnel

contract

other resources

Arrow diagram

Flow chart

Cartoon

Labelled diagram

Series of diagrams

model   board   video

visual aid

posters   overlay

OHT   reveal

Mind map

	cost	time	toilet
train	£20.	2HR	✓
coach	£10.5	3HR	✗

A matrix

Chablis   Claret   Sauternes

dry ←———————————→ sweet

A continuum

Types of visual aid

1. Handouts

Modern photocopiers can reproduce newspaper articles, including photographs. They can also increase or decrease size to suit any requirement. If you want a poster-sized copy of a postage stamp, or an architect's drawing reduced to the size of a postcard, it can be done. With careful use, they can cope surprisingly well with faint masters, often making copies which are better than the original. Some photocopiers will automatically print on both sides, collate and staple. You can photocopy on card, or on coloured paper. Colour photocopying is also now available (though still expensive as yet).

Masters for worksheet handouts can be obtained commercially, and these are often excellent value for money. The masters are supplied with a copyright waiver allowing the purchasing institution to photocopy the masters, for use within that institution only.

Making your own handouts

Handouts can give information, or they can be in the form of a worksheet; sometimes they combine these two functions. You can cannibalise magazines and brochures, and photocopy diagrams from textbooks, adjusting the size if necessary – but beware copyright restrictions, and acknowledge sources. Then this material can be 'cut and pasted' together with linking text in type or neat handwriting, to produce a handout with impact.

- Try 'gapped handouts', where space is left for students to answer questions, fill in words and phrases, or label a diagram.

- Don't forget that OHP transparencies (OHTs) can be photocopied as a handout, or handouts made into an OHT.

- If you can, get your handouts typed 'on computer' (modern word-processing programs can produce very good results), or even 'desktop published'. (But don't be afraid to draw your own diagrams – I have for this book!)

- Write clearly in black; use a print style rather than your usual handwriting.

- Leave a minimum of 2 cm at top and bottom, and 1 cm at the sides, for photocopying; if holes are to be punched, then leave at least 2 cm on the left hand side (2 cm on both sides if copying both sides).

- Don't overcrowd; if handouts are unattractive they will not be read. Pay attention to layout, e.g. use indenting and bullets as in this list. Will it help to present your handouts in the form of a booklet?

- If your school or college has an agreement with the Copyright Licensing Agency (CLA) there will be notification of this displayed near the photocopier. It usually allows you or your students to copy for any one course in one academic year:

- up to 5% or one complete chapter of a book published in stated countries.
- a single article from a journal or periodical.

You should only make enough copies to provide one for each student, and one for yourself. Check before copying, as it is an offence to break copyright.

Using handouts in class

Talk your class through the handout, or ask them to use it for individual or group work. Ask them to highlight important parts of the text. In this way they will become familiar with its contents; otherwise they are unlikely to be read later.

Handouts can save a great deal of time, for you and your students, but don't overuse them. Even for professional presentations, it is inadvisable to give out more than one or two A4 double-sided handouts per hour. If you feel more information may be required, refer students to books or journals.

One last word: save trees by using handouts only when they are necessary, and always copy on both sides.

2. The overhead projector

The overhead projector has many advantages over the blackboard or whiteboard.

- You can present complicated overhead projector transparencies (OHTs) that you would never have time to prepare on the board during a class.

- You can keep your prepared transparencies to use over and over again. (You can store them in plastic document wallets in an A4 ring binder, together with your notes.)

- Techniques such as overlays often make difficult concepts easy to explain.

- It saves you a great deal of time in class, enabling you to concentrate on more pressing matters.

- You can face the class while writing on the projector, maintaining eye contact. (Not the case with a blackboard, and particularly useful with a 'difficult' group.)

- Professional-looking transparencies can be made easily by hand, photocopier, or computer (using a laser printer); alternatively, they can be obtained commercially.

- You can photocopy directly off an OHT, or directly on to one. Subject to copyright restrictions, OHTs can be made from diagrams, photographs or pages in books in this way, enlarging during the photocopying process where necessary. (Beware! A special transparent heat-resistant photocopying material must be used. Ordinary transparency films will, rather expensively, melt in the photocopier to cause considerable damage.)

- Complicated diagrams may be drawn to a high standard of accuracy, using drawing instruments if necessary.

- You can show X-rays direct (and even your own photographs, if special transparencies are produced). You can also project silhouettes of objects such as skeletons of the hand, etc.

- It is possible to project an image of the contents of a computer screen with a special Liquid Crystal Display (LCD) device.

- It's useful for lecture notes. For example, this list contains eleven advantages of the OHP. I find it difficult to remember them all in lectures, so I put them on a transparency. My students think this is for their benefit, but it's really notes for me!

Some objects can be placed directly on the projector e.g. X-rays, protractors

Using the overhead projector

There is nothing more flustering than to wrestle with an unfamiliar piece of equipment in the presence of a class! Practise with it first, preferably with the same (or an *exactly* similar) piece of equipment. Just before the lesson, check the projector hasn't been borrowed, and that it works. Direct sunlight on the screen makes it hard to read, so for preference the screen should not be facing the windows.

For the basic procedure in using an OHP, see the diagram at the top of the opposite page.

Alter the image size to one that is suitable. This can be done by altering lenses, but is usually achieved by moving the OHP towards the screen to decrease image size, or away from it for a larger image. Choose a suitable level of illumination; many machines have a 'bright' and a 'dim' setting. If you move the projector when it is switched on, you risk blowing the bulb. (For a similar reason, it is best to wait a little while *after* switching off, before moving it.)

The keystone effect

Ideally the top of the screen should lean towards the projector. This prevents the 'keystone' effect, which otherwise makes the image on the screen wider at the top than at the bottom (see the diagram at the bottom of the next page).

Tilt the lens/mirror system to position the image on the screen.

Focus the image by rotating the knob which moves the lens/mirror system up and down. [Don't forget your spectacles!]

Some machines are focussed by rotating the lens in the lens/mirror system.

Some machines have a large (unlabelled) bar on the screen side which acts as an 'on' switch.

Make sure the mains cable is safely routed e.g. not across a main thoroughfare.

Do not obstruct ventilation slits — and papers placed near them will blow away!

Look at the transparency itself rather than the screen, and point on the transparency with the shadow of a pen.

Using the OHP

Note that the top of the image is further from the screen than the bottom...

Screen

Projector

.... so the top of the image is larger than the bottom, distorting the image.

Ideally the top of the screen should lean towards the projector to eliminate this keystone effect.

Projector

The keystone effect

271

As well as distorting the image, a 'keystone' image is impossible to focus: either the wider or the narrower part of the screen is in focus, never both.

The screen

Screens for slide and film projectors and for OHPs are identical, and are considerably more reflective (and therefore brighter) than a white wall or whiteboard. They are best placed in a corner at the front of the class. They should be as high as possible so that students have a clear view over the projector head, and over the heads of other students.

Roller-blind screens are usually fixed to the ceiling, wall, or blackboard frame, and are pulled down when needed. Secure them carefully!

Some permanent screens are fixed to the wall and look very much like whiteboards; others are simply squares of special white paint on the wall. DON'T write on either of these; your writing will not rub off, and will probably permanently damage the screen! Screens can be identified by their reflective surface.

Portable screens are usually of the roller-blind type. At all costs acquaint yourself with such screens before erecting them in front of the class, otherwise you will find your class enjoying something very like an impersonation of Charlie Chaplin putting up a deck chair. There are usually two separate buttons to raise the bottom and the top of the screen, and a facility for overcoming the keystone effect. Raise the screen as high as you can.

If all else fails, you can usually project successfully on a pale-coloured wall, or on a whiteboard.

The pens

Use proper OHP pens; your college or school will supply them. If the pen has a black barrel and/or a black pen-top clip, it is probably 'permanent'. You will need to use alcohol or meths to erase, though special rubbers and erasure pens are available from some suppliers. Pens with light grey barrels and/or pen-top clips have washable ink in them, which can be

This is superfine ——

This is fine ——

This is medium ——

Extra broad chisel: ▬ or ——

Write about this size for normal classroom use; photocopied typing is far too small.

erased with damp tissue paper, or less neatly with a licked finger. Washable ink wears away very easily, so do not use it for OHTs you wish to keep.

Yellow and other very pale colours are not very satisfactory for writing – use black or blue. Thicknesses available are: superfine, fine, medium, broad and extra broad. Chisel-pointed pens allow you to vary the line thickness.

The films

OHT films or sheets come in a range of qualities: cellophane for once-only use, acetate for sheets to be used more than once. An extra-thick grade can be obtained for heavily-used transparencies. For photocopiers, heat-copiers and laser printers, it is important to use films that have been especially designed for the purpose.

Copying

Photocopying: White paper originals, books or newspapers can be photocopied on to film, and the quality is excellent (though the print may be too small unless enlarged.) Worksheets can be photocopied either from the original or from the transparency. (Colour photocopiers can produce full-colour transparencies from colour originals; alternatively, coloured transparencies can be produced photo-graphically. However, both colour processes are expensive.)

Thermocopying (heat-copying): This allows colour images, either 'positives' or 'negatives', to be made from flat and flexible originals (not books). Thermocopies can be marked on the underside with OHP pens.

Making your own transparencies

Educational suppliers offer professionally produced OHTs, but most are home-made. Here are some suggestions (see also the diagrams on the next page):

- Try placing lined or graph paper under the film to guide writing and drawing. Place a piece of paper under the heel of your hand to prevent perspiration getting on to the transparency.

- Sketch out complex illustrations on paper first, and then trace the finished design on to film.

- Use a drawing board for engineering drawings.

- Lettering needs to be larger than normal handwriting, print, or type. When writing by hand, use lower case lettering; block capitals are tiring to read. Print; don't use your usual handwriting.

- Try using lettering guides or stencils (these require a fine pen).

- Beware! Most OHPs will not display a whole A4 sheet all at once. For large diagrams, leave at least a 3 cm gap at the bottom of the transparency.

Draw with pencil and paper first....

..then trace this on to the film.
Or you can trace diagrams from books.

A border helps any transparency

Medium pen for headings
Use a fine pen for text, and use colour for a purpose. Put lined paper under the film to guide your writing.

shaded drawings look more solid and three-dimensional.

- The design of the sheets is, of course, critical. Make sure the design:
  - uses a minimum of words.
  - is uncluttered.
  - is eye-catching.
- Try to present data in a visual manner – for example, with charts. Highlight important words with colour and broader pens.

Kiss:
Keep
It
Short and
Simple.

- Too many colours on a sheet are confusing, unless there is a clear purpose for each colour.

- Don't forget you can photocopy on to a transparency – and off it.

- Erase permanent ink with a cotton bud dipped in meths or alcohol. Or use special rubbers or erasing pens. Don't scratch the ink off; this makes the film opaque.

Presentation techniques

Overlay

This is a very effective method, enabling the teacher to break down a complex diagram and show it in stages. For example, a simple outline can be presented first, with succeeding overlays gradually added to build up the whole picture.

Overlays can also be used to show changes with time, e.g. the cycle of an internal combustion engine.

Combination technique

A master transparency is prepared in advance with permanent pens. This is then added to spontaneously during the presentation. The additions are made in water-soluble ink so that they can be erased later, leaving the master intact for reuse. Alternatively a clear film can be placed over the master, and this can be written on during the lesson.

Another method used is to project on to the whiteboard; then you or your students can write over the image on the board.

The reveal technique

One often does not want to show the whole transparency all at once. Some sections can be covered with paper placed underneath the transparency. This allows the transparency to be revealed one section at a time, and yet enables *you* to view the covered sections.

Alternatively flaps can be fixed to the transparency, or better to a mounting frame. Masking tape is best as this allows adjustment.

All sheets stuck on with MASKING tape, not sellotape.

Use the special card mounting frames, or alternatively tape sheets on to each other.

Master in permanent pen.

Water-based pen used to write on master.

Paper flap

First you see one bit

then you see the next bit

and then you see the last bit.

Alternatively you can put a piece of paper under the sheet

Paper

You can also use those sticky office message pads.

Blah
Blah
Blah
Blah Blah

cylinder

drawn

moveable cut-out piston made of paper.

Self-adhesive message notelets can also be used to cover and reveal the transparency. You can write reminders on these flaps, or number them.

Animation

Cut-outs, either silhouettes or coloured transparencies, can be moved over the OHT to produce a limited animation technique.

The diagrams on the opposite page illustrate some of the presentation techniques I have described.

Using the OHP

- Face the class, and don't obscure their view of the screen by standing in the projector beam, or between your class and the screen.

- Don't address your remarks to the screen; use eye contact with the class. Look at the transparency itself rather than the image on the screen. You can point with the shadow of a pen. *However, look over your shoulder occasionally to check that the image is in the right position on the screen, and is displayed as you wish.*

- Number your transparencies and arrange them in order before the lesson. This is the 'in tray'. After use, place the transparencies elsewhere in an 'out tray'.

- Store OHTs and papers away from the fan outlet, or they will be blown on to the floor.

- Switch off as soon as you've finished displaying an OHT; this avoids distraction, minimises fan noise, and maximises the impact when you display your next OHT.

- Don't cover the projector entirely for long periods, as this can cause over-heating.

Storing your OHTs

Use permanent pens if repeated use is desired. Transparencies are best kept in a ring binder in clear 'document wallets'. Keep them with your teaching notes rather than separately, so they are easily found when

notes

OHT in a plastic document wallet

A4 ring binder

needed. Only if the wallets are made of very clear plastic can transparencies be projected inside the wallet.

Alternatively, transparencies can be mounted and stored on card frames designed for the purpose.

Problems with OHPs

- **I can't focus it!** Check that the projector is not too close to the screen. If this doesn't help, and you have eliminated the keystone effect, ask a technician to check the optical alignment.

- **The image is coloured where it shouldn't be.** This is 'fringe colouration'. The effect is usually reduced or eliminated if the distance between screen and projector is altered; but if not, ask if the projector has been fitted with a 'fringe colouration eliminator'. This will impress the technicians, and may get you another machine!

- **One part of the image is too bright.** This is called a 'hot spot'; ask a technician to check the machine's optical alignment. If this doesn't work, try changing the bulb.

- **The bulb's blown!** This is a very rare occurrence, usually caused by moving the projector while switched on, or with the bulb still hot. There may be a lever to switch in a new bulb, or a spare bulb inside the machine. Beware! Switch off at the mains before opening the machine: also, the old bulb may still be very hot. Handle bulbs with a clean cloth, as finger marks will reduce the bulb's life. Safety regulations in your establishment may require a technician to change bulbs for you.

3. The blackboard and whiteboard

Some use board-work like a huge scrap-pad for jottings and sketches; others see it as a neglected art form. Some use it for putting up notes for the students to copy. Others use it to draw attention to the landmarks in the lesson, displaying only the key ideas as they are covered. Some write a five-point summary of their lesson before the class arrives, and barely touch it during the lesson. Maths and science teachers use board-work to demonstrate how to solve problems, and to give instructions for experiments. Some teachers prefer to do their board-work before a lesson, others during it. Most feel lost without a board of some kind, but some think it should be consigned to the museum.

No teaching aid is more adaptable to the teacher's style, and perhaps this is the real strength of the whiteboard or blackboard. You must decide for yourself how to use it; try the different approaches described above, then choose, combine and adapt to develop your own style.

General advice

- Always start with a clean board.

- Don't use your usual handwriting, or block capitals which are difficult to read if used exclusively; use a print style. Novice users tend to write too big rather than too small; in most cases lettering with capital letters about 3 or 4 cm in height is best. Try it out from the back of the class.

- Until you get used to it, plan what you are going to put on the board before the lesson.

- Don't stand in front of the board, and make sure there is no glare on it.

- Talk to the students, not to the board; you may need to raise your voice a bit.

- Use colours only for a specific purpose; use white or yellow for writing the main information.

- Don't get the board cluttered; erase unwanted material – but not too quickly.

The technique

The main problem is keeping your lines of writing horizontal. To achieve this, shuffle your feet sideways as you write, keeping your hand at the same height relative to your shoulders for the entire line. This is easier with a roller board where most teachers write at about eye height, moving the board up every line or two. It's almost impossible to write below chest height; kneel down if you must, but can they see it?

The 'blackboard shuffle'

Hold the chalk as shown on the left, close to the board end of the stick.

To draw a straight line without a ruler: relax and draw with confidence, keeping your eyes *on where you want the line to end – not on the chalk*. Use a similar technique for drawing a circle, or alternatively use a piece of string with a loop in it, in which you place the chalk. Board compasses, protractors etc. are usually available if you need them.

Most whiteboard dry markers have a chisel end; this allows you to alter the thickness of the line. All colours show up quite well, but write with black or blue. Hold the markers like a pencil.

If you are concerned about discipline, look over your shoulder every few words – or better still, use an OHP.

Some tricks and traps

Some classes have a Pavlovian reaction to anything written on the blackboard – they write it down in their notes. If you intend to use the board as a scrap-pad, you must tell the class beforehand that they should not copy unless you tell them. They may need reminding until they get used to this. (If you have two boards, you can use one as a scrap-pad and the other for notes.)

If the board-rubber has not been cleaned for some time, it tends to smear chalk over the board. Use a cloth, or clean the rubber by scraping it hard against a sharp edge, e.g. the edge of the board or a waste bin. Wash the board occasionally with clean soapless water; if this does not help, the board needs resurfacing or replacing – the best of luck!

If a whiteboard smears, it needs washing with meths/alcohol or cleaning with a proprietary whiteboard cleaner – and so does the board-rubber. Board writing is a messy business; think carefully about the clothes you choose to teach in.

If you have a roller board, you can prepare the board before a lesson and roll it out of view until you need it.

Any board work that you intend the class to copy sets an example for the class. If you work untidily, don't expect them to be neat.

Warning! There is an unwritten rule in most schools and colleges that you should always leave the board clean for the next teacher. If you intend to ignore this rule, you would be well advised to attend self-defence classes.

No blackboard, whiteboard or OHP available?

Not everybody teaches in a classroom. Use a flip chart, a portable whiteboard or a portable OHP. Portable whiteboards can be made by framing painted sheet steel. Magnetic boards can also be useful; these are steel boards to which cut-outs are attached with magnetic strips. Most whiteboards double as a magnetic board. Educational suppliers can provide other display equipment if you have special requirements (and the necessary funding) – for example, high-tech boards which print out multiple copies of the board's contents.

4. Models – and the real thing

If a picture is worth a thousand words, how much is a model worth? And what about the real thing?

Models can be commercially produced or made by the teacher. A language teacher may bring cooking utensils into the classroom; an engineer may gut and adapt an old alternator for classroom use. A biology teacher may show her class the heart and lungs of a pig. Models and real objects bring the world into the classroom. (Real objects are often referred to in teaching literature as *realia* – Latin for 'real things'.)

Objects have far more impact than words or pictures, especially if they can be handled. This idea permeates the whole of science teaching, but should not be forgotten by other teachers.

If you intend making a model yourself, the following factors need to be considered:

■ **Scale**
Is it helpful to scale the size up or down? (It is often useful to scale up, so that students can see without getting out of their seats.)

■ **Dismantling**
Some models can be dismantled and reassembled by the student, and/or by the lecturer. Some models are sectioned – i.e. part of the model is cut away, or made of transparent material so that the inside can be seen.

■ **Simplification**
Models can omit non-essential detail which would otherwise confuse the students. Also, parts of the models can be coloured so that they can be picked out more easily.

■ **Scale speed**
A moving model of the solar system would be useless if it only ran at the real speed! So, for opposite reasons, would a model of a four-stroke petrol engine.

■ **Can you use or adapt the real thing?**
Bringing real objects into the classroom usually excites interest. 'Real things' can be sectioned, labelled, partly dismantled and so on to aid your teaching. For example, bird skeletons can be labelled; a computer disk can be cut up so that it may be taken apart; an old barometer can be sectioned or dismantled and adapted for use in the classroom. You may even be able to use the real thing without adapting it. Your imagination is the only limit.

If a model is too small to display to the whole class, take or pass it round – preferably when you are not talking to the class. Alternatively, let them view it in groups. It is important to tell students the differences between the model and the real thing, otherwise the model may confuse rather than illuminate. A huge range of models can be obtained from educational suppliers, though very effective models can be made at home, or by students. Can you think of a model that would be useful in *your* teaching?

5. Charts and posters

Design is very important for charts and posters; in particular, many are rendered useless by an attempt to display too much information.

They can, of course, simply be pinned up, with students left to read them at their leisure; but students usually have better things to do than read a poster, so it is advisable to use it as a teaching aid. For example, you can gather the class round the poster and use it as a focus for part of a lesson; it can then be left up as a reminder. Posters are particularly useful for teachers of foreign languages.

> How about using one notice board in your classroom for a regularly-changing poster display?

Making your own posters

Aim for simplicity, not complexity or comprehensiveness. Less clutter means more impact. You can of course draw your own, but you can also use a 'cut and paste' combination of colour pictures from magazines; brochures and other advertising material; illustrations from books or computer printouts, increased in size by photocopying; photographs; newspaper cuttings; and so on. Bear copyright in mind. Alternatively, you could set your students the task of making the poster!

Key points to consider:

- Can the whole class read it?
- Is it simple enough for the message to be clear? When in doubt – leave it out!
- Is it attractive?

If you have gone to a great deal of trouble to make a poster that you will use over and over again, you can get it laminated. This covers the card with plastic, both protecting it and enabling you to write on it with a dry marker whiteboard pen.

Write to manufacturers for ready-made posters. For example, if you are teaching typing, write to typewriter manufacturers and ask for any posters they may have.

6. The video

Students consider the television to be a source of entertainment. But don't assume that this means they will automatically watch your video with rapt attention; they may be used to chatting, doing their homework and cuddling their boy-friends while watching TV. You will have to work hard to make your students attend to a video, and learn from it.

There are several video formats. VHS is the commonest, but you may also find S-VHS, Betamax, Video 8 and Hi8. Check that your videotape and machine are compatible. On most machines you can fast-forward to the sections that interest you; pause the machine to talk about what the class has just seen; and rewind the machine to replay a particularly important section. Some machines have a 'freeze frame' feature, enabling the picture to be stopped and a still frame retained on the screen. Practise with these features on any machine you intend to use, before the class begins. (If you happened to want to dim the room lighting, could you still operate the machine in that situation?)

Always preview any video you intend to show, and decide what you hope your students will learn from it. Read the teachers' notes if any are provided. Then ask your students to look for the features you have highlighted as useful. For example, you might say: 'I am going to show you a video about the role of the health visitor. I want you to use it to answer the questions on the board.' The questions might be:

1. How are health visitors trained?
2. Who organises the visits?

- and so on.

Asking students to look out for prescribed information will increase their attention markedly.

Don't feel obliged to show the whole of a video; in many cases it is better just to show selected sections. Avoid the tendency to hand over the teaching to the video.

Before the class:

- Check everything works. Are the plugs in, and have you chosen the correct video channel on the monitor (i.e. on the TV)?
- Ensure the monitor can be seen by everyone in the class, and that the volume is correctly set.
- Use the tape counter to work out the sections you want to show on the tape, and write down the appropriate counter numbers; wind to the first section you wish to show. (**Warning:** counter numbers may vary on different machines; don't assume, for example, that those on your home machine will be the same as on the one at work.)
- Read any notes that come with the video cassette.

During the video:

- You may like to dim the room lighting.
- Look interested even if you've seen it a hundred times; if you look bored or walk off, don't expect your students to find it interesting. (For students up to 18 years old, you are in effect legally obliged to remain in the room.)
- Check students are attending.

- Don't forget to use the pause or rewind features to make teaching points during the video.

Video cameras create instant excitement, and they are now as easy to use as audio cassette recorders. Try videoing student presentations or role-plays.

7. Using the slide projector

Slides can be projected on to any reasonably white surface; but a proper screen is best, especially for large numbers, as it has special reflective properties. Try to dim the room lighting if you can.

Before the class:

- Read any teacher's notes, then preview the slides, editing out any that aren't useful.

- Acquaint yourself with the slide projector; many have a 'zoom' feature allowing the size of the image to be adjusted. (Smaller images are brighter.)

- Set up the screen and test the projector's alignment. If the image is too small, move the projector further back or adjust the zoom.

When showing the slides, you may well want to dim the lights in the room – but can you still read your notes? (A penlight torch might be useful.)

8. Using other teaching aids

Games and simulations were dealt with in Part 2; and the computer will be considered in the next chapter. Quite apart from these, there are also tapes, tape-slide programmes, interactive video materials and endless other teaching aids.

Having read this far, you will have a good idea of how to prepare to use these. Read the notes; find out how things work; acquaint yourself with the material, adapting and editing it to fit your own purposes; try to guess any possible problems, and think of ways to avoid them; and then try things out.

32 Computers as an aid to teaching and learning

If you can push a typewriter key you can use a computer, and no combination of key presses can do a computer any harm. In the early days computers got a justifiable reputation for being difficult and mysterious, but modern systems are so easy to use that even an adult can learn to use them!

Can computers help learning or teaching? Many teachers remain sceptical, though it is often fair to say that the most sceptical are those with the least relevant experience. However, like it or not, computers are here to stay. In the 'real world' computers are used widely and routinely, and whatever your subject your students will be expected to use computers in the same way. This is particularly true in post-school education, where there is open access to college computers, and where vocational courses require their routine use.

Making use of computer applications

The screen, keyboard and the other physical parts of a computer are called the 'hardware'. But a computer needs instructions to tell it what to do. 'Applications' are the very complex programs which give the computer these instructions, and control how they behave. Applications form part of the computer's 'software'.

Changing the application you load on to the computer will make it behave in a very different way, allowing you to do different jobs. The most commonly used computer applications fall into three categories. These are spreadsheets, databases, and word-processing applications.

Word-processing

Word-processing applications allow the user to write text – a letter, for example, or a report; as we saw in the last chapter, they are also valuable for worksheet production. They differ in their sophistication and cost, but all do much the same job – turning the computer into a much improved typewriter. Popular word-processing applications include Wordperfect, Word, Wordstar and Ami Pro.

As with other modern applications, students will soon learn how to use them, and so will you. In recent word-processing programs you don't need to remember any cryptic commands; you just choose what you want the computer to do from a 'menu' of alternatives. (If you get stuck, a student will be delighted to help you.)

Databases

Databases can be used in any number of ways; the only limitation is your imagination! Information is stored on 'records' – each record having the same format. These records can then be sorted or searched for specific data; e.g. records of student sporting activities could be

A database stores a collection of records which all have the same format.

searched to discover how many girls play more than three games, or how many boys play football and rugby. I have seen students use databases in the following ways:

- Chemistry students storing data on dangerous chemicals, such as their names, the hazard they represent, means of disposal, storage and so on.

- Hairdressing students storing data on the various products that they might use in a salon.

- Health studies students storing information collected as part of a survey (of student dietary and teeth-cleaning habits) which they had designed.

- Secretarial students making a database of courses that they could do after their present course.

- Humanities students making a database of recommended library books.

- Electronics students making a database of firms in their area which were likely to offer employment.

- In order to keep computer students up to date, they were asked to extract and store data about magazine articles from a computer magazine, with 'keywords' that would enable a student to search for an article on a particular subject for an essay. (Every vocational subject has its trade magazine.)

Spreadsheets

Spreadsheets allow the user to process numerical information. Professional engineers, architects, mathematicians, statisticians, scientists, economists, stockbrokers and accountants all make full use of spreadsheets, so teachers in these areas and in related areas should use them too. They are particularly useful for performing calculations and recalculations that would otherwise be too laborious to contemplate. Most spreadsheet programs will allow the user to draw graphs, pie charts etc. based on their data.

Some uses of spreadsheets I have seen are shown at the top of the next page.

- A case study exercise on the accounts of a small fictional company.

- Investigating mortgages, and compound interest etc.

- Experimenting with the economics of various livestock feeding strategies.

- Exploration of the factors affecting the heat losses from a building.

- Investigating the resonance effects in electronic circuits.

- Costing a meal from a menu.

- Seeing the effect of changing the dimensions of a body on its volume and mass.

- Plotting graphs to show standard mathematical relationships.

A spreadsheet is a grid of boxes called 'cells'. Each cell can hold text, numbers, or a formula.

On IBM-compatible computers popular database applications include dBASE and Paradox; popular spreadsheets include Lotus 1-2-3, Excel and Supercalc. Some applications combine spreadsheet, database and word-processing functions into one integrated package. Examples of this include Microsoft Works and Ability.

Whatever your personal prejudices, one point is worth bearing in mind: few people who learn how to use computers believe subsequently that this was a waste of their time. And, perhaps most critically, students love using computers. They are also invariably quick on the uptake when it comes to learning how to use unfamiliar software.

Computers as teachers: CBL, CAL and CBT

The jargon phrases are computer-based learning (CBL), computer-assisted learning (CAL) and computer-based training (CBT). Much of the educational software that has been developed so far has been produced for the BBC or Archimedes computers, though there are some impressive programmes for the Apple Macintosh and for IBM-compatible machines such as those produced by Research Machines.

Computers can of course display text and diagrams, but they can also show an animated image which is very useful in many teaching situations – especially if the animated image can be slowed down or speeded up in order to make a teaching point. They can also, of course, ask questions, and check the responses to keep your student's score. As a result, they can help you to explain your subject and/or test your students.

It will not be difficult to find material for your subject area at a reasonable price; mountains of the stuff are available. The problem is assessing whether the material is suitable for your needs. Much of the material is imaginative – but some, I'm afraid, is almost useless.

So far we have considered programs that operate rather like a cross between a video, a textbook, and a question book. But there are many other styles of program, including some that are quite unique, not fitting into any category.

Some programs operate rather like simulations with the student (hopefully) in control: for example, a business game, a lunar landing, or a car race. The students must use subject-specific skills and more general mathematical and problem-solving skills to control the simulation. Such programs are very popular with students, especially if there is any element of competition. Other simulations allow students to carry out experiments for which the apparatus is not available in the average school or college.

PRESTEL and other on-line databases can be used to get up-to-the-minute information down the phone line, and even supply new computer programs.

Choosing published programs

It is not always possible to order programs on approval, because the producers fear illicit copying. The best way to start is to have a look at the material that is available in your college or institution. When choosing material for use with students, bear the following points in mind.

- Have you got the minimum hardware necessary to run the program?
- How many students are able to use the material at the same time? Can one disk be used to load a number of machines (i.e. is the program memory-resident, with no copyright restriction)?
- Is there an adequate manual for [i] you and [ii] the students? (The latter may not be necessary.)
- Is it going to take so long for the students to learn how to use the program that the educational value is not worth their effort?
- Is the program foolproof? Is it *student*proof?
- Can you get a printout if this is necessary?
- Do you know how to load the program / reload it if it 'crashes' (goes wrong)?

Writing your own CAL material

It is not very time-consuming to use or adapt applications such as spreadsheets or databases to teach some topics. However, you can also make your own CAL packages by using an authoring language – or, if you are more ambitious, by using a general purpose language like BASIC. This *can* be very time-consuming.

An authoring language allows you to design your own 'screens' with text and graphics. You can also decide the order in which the screens appear, for how long they appear, etc.

When using an authoring language it is possible, for example, to devise a multi-choice test such that if a student gets an answer wrong, a screen appears to explain the correct answer. If they get it right, they get a 'well done' message, quickly followed by the next question. The program could then give the student their score at the end of the test.

Authoring languages are very flexible; the example above is just one of many. Examples of such authoring languages are: Microtext, Pilot, Private Tutor (IBM only), Storyboard (IBM only) and CommunITel.

Value for effort

A word of warning. In designing your own material for computers you must be careful not to get carried away, especially if you are a computer enthusiast. You can easily spend a great deal of time preparing material that brings very little return in terms of student learning. Ask yourself what is the 'value for effort' in devising your material.

Material should be devised on the basis of the following criteria:

- **Need to know** – that is, it should teach indispensable material.
- **Time stability** – that is, it should be most unlikely that the material will become outdated.
- **Invisible technology** – learning should not be overshadowed by difficult technology. Operation of the program should be more or less intuitive.
- **Interactivity** – the material should be genuinely interactive, not just a page-turning activity.

Other uses of computers for the teacher

Computers can also be used, amongst other things, to

- draw graphs.
- produce other graphics-type output.

- communicate with other computers.
- capture and process data, e.g. in a science experiment.
- design leaflets for your courses.
- control 'robots'.
- keep a database of examination questions.

However, perhaps the most common use of computers by teachers is in the preparation of teaching material. Handouts, assignments, tests and other material can be stored on a computer disk, and printed out when required (or even, where appropriate, used on-screen by the students). The resulting advantages include:

- **Material is very easily updated.** This is a very important advantage, as the rate of change of course content, and indeed of the courses themselves, is so rapid nowadays. But even if the course remains unaltered, using material for the first time nearly always leads you to think of ways of improving it. That is very easily done if the material is held on a computer.

- **Material looks professional.** This is an advantage in its own right, but it also makes teachers feel easier about borrowing each other's material, thus saving preparation time. If a teacher devised material last year, for a course that you are teaching this year, you may be able to alter their material easily to satisfy your own needs. Some departments in colleges are organised so that this is a common practice.

- **Some computers will check your spelling!**

One disadvantage – for most of us it means we need to learn how to type, preferably with more than one finger! Never fear, there is good CBL software for this purpose!

Exercise

How could you use databases, spreadsheets or word-processing programs to devise assignments for students in the following areas:

1. YT students who are likely to find employment in the building trade?
2. BTEC business studies students studying office machinery?
3. Horticultural students studying diseases in vegetable crops?
4. Engineering students studying workshop practice?
5. Science students doing an assignment on Newton's Laws of motion?
6. The area of study of your own students?

Putting it all together

33 Aims and objectives

A large insurance firm in New York was having trouble with its twenty-storey skyscraper. The managing director wrote to engineering firms, telling them of the repeated complaints he had received from his employees. They were complaining about the length of time they had to wait for the lift, so he was asking for quotes for the installation of a new lift shaft.

The managing director received a number of quotes for tens of millions of dollars, along with one from an engineer who said he could solve the problem for $9,000. This quote was rejected out of hand at first, but the director was intrigued. Finally he telephoned and asked: 'How can you fit a lift shaft for $9,000?' The engineer pointed out that the real aim was not to fit a lift shaft, but to reduce employee frustration. His plan was to create comfortable places for employees to wait for the lift, with easy chairs, potted plants, mirrors, fish-tanks, magazines and piped music. This solution still works well to this day. Moral: think very carefully about your aims before starting your plans.

1 **Decide on aims**
What do you want to achieve?

2 **Plan the action**
How best can you achieve your aims?

3 **Action**
Carry out the plan.

4 **Evaluate the action**
Did you achieve your aims? Do you want to change your aims?

Almost any purposeful human activity can be said to fall into the pattern shown in the diagram above – everything from arranging your holidays or cooking fish pie to setting up a business or going shopping.

Teaching falls into the same pattern. Teachers first decide what they hope to achieve (aims and objectives), then plan the lesson, then teach the lesson – i.e. carry the plan out. Then they need to evaluate the lesson, asking themselves whether they did indeed achieve the aims set. This evaluation may lead to a change in the aims for the next lesson, or for the next time this same lesson is taught, so the process is cyclic.

Aims and objectives

'Aims' or 'educational goals' are clear and concise statements that describe what the teacher hopes to achieve. These statements of intent are usually expressed in a rather broad and generalised way – for example:

> 'To improve the students' ability to communicate effectively in formal written English.'

> 'To develop an understanding and appreciation of the world's major religions.'

> 'To create opportunities for students to engage in creative self-expression.'

> 'To develop a knowledge and understanding of scientific investigative procedures.'

Some people advocate expressing aims from the point of view of the teacher or the course, rather than from the students' point of view. For example:

> 'The aim of the course is to consider the basic principles of retailing.'

> 'The training package will introduce the basic elements of computer programming.'

It is usually impossible to achieve aims absolutely. Students could work on achieving most of the above aims for a lifetime, and still have plenty to do! Aims are so general and all-embracing that there can be as few as four or five for a fulltime one-year course.

Aims are like compass directions, indicating the general direction in which the teacher wishes to travel. As such they are vital; but they are not specific enough to help the teacher pick learning activities, or assess whether learning has taken place.

There is no general agreement about how to decide aims and objectives, or precisely how they should be written. But there *is* agreement that aims are vitally important.

> **Where do aims come from?**
>
> Aims may be provided by an examination syllabus, by a programme of study, or by the awarding body for a qualification. Later we will see that they may in some circumstances be provided by a 'needs analysis', by 'task analysis', or by negotiation with the students on the course. However, teachers decide most of their own aims, even if they are not written down formally.
>
> What are you are trying to achieve by your teaching? Do you take an entirely functional view, that education provides students with the means to earn a living and to cope in our society? Or do your aims go beyond this?

Learning outcomes

Aims may point you in the right direction, but they don't tell you how to get there, or when you have arrived. So intentions must be described in a more detailed way with what are variously called 'specific objectives', 'behaviourist objectives', 'competences', and/or 'specific learning outcomes'. In this book, I shall call them 'learning outcomes'. They are *testable* statements describing the abilities to be learned, e.g.:

'The student should be able to use inverted commas correctly.'

'The student should be able to solder electronic components on to a circuit board.'

This is much better than *teacher*-centred aims such as 'to describe how to punctuate correctly' or 'to show students how to solder'. If you examine the latter carefully, you will see that such aims can be satisfactorily met whether or not the student has learned anything! It is important to shift the focus from teaching to learning.

Doing so has a number of advantages. It makes clear what students have to practise, and avoids a lesson dominated by teacher talk, where little real learning takes place. It makes lesson planning easier by suggesting learning activities (e.g. corrected practice of soldering, or dialogue-writing). Also, if you know precisely what students should be able to do, it is much easier to assess whether or not they can do it. This enables you to evaluate how successful your lessons have been.

The crucial point is that the outcomes precisely describe observable learner performance, shifting the focus on to what the students will be able to do as a result of their learning, and away from what the teacher will do. For example:

'The student should be able to:

■ State three advantages of the diesel engine over the petrol engine.

■ List the main methods of pest management in Indonesia.

■ Distinguish between fog, smog, mist and cloud.'

Most people have difficulty in writing objectives at first, tending to think in terms of what the teacher will do rather than what the student will learn. Are these specific learning outcomes?

'To introduce the idea of percentages.'   'The Peasants' Revolt'

The answer is no – they aren't. Could you change them so that they were? Have a try before reading further.

Specific learning outcomes or specific objectives should:

- specify precisely and in concrete terms what the student should be able to do.
- be written in such a way that it is possible to determine whether or not the objective has been achieved.
- usually be short-term.
- be drawn up by the teacher to suit the resources, the teacher, and the students.
- optionally, define the circumstances under which the objective is to be demonstrated and/or what constitutes an achievement. E.g. 'Translate passage 6d in less than five minutes, making less than four minor mistakes.'

Here are some legitimate objectives for the topics mentioned above. Notice they identify skills or abilities, and so suggest 'use', 'check and correct' and the other elements of learning.

'Students should be able to:

    – express one number as a percentage of another;
    – express a fraction as a percentage.'

'Students should be able to:

    – state and explain the main events running up to the Peasants' Revolt;
    – explain three economic consequences of the Peasants' Revolt.'

Ineffective teachers say they will 'cover percentages', or 'talk about the Peasant's Revolt', or 'do fractions'. But effective teachers always design lessons by working from the intended outcome. Writing 'specific learning outcomes' or 'specific objectives' is an intellectually demanding task, and it requires a great deal of time and effort. But outcomes are vital; they are the stepping stones which take the learners in the direction of our aims.

Classification of objectives or outcomes

B.S. Bloom's 'Taxonomy of Educational Objectives' attempts to classify all learning into three domains and, within each domain, into skills or abilities of different types or difficulty. It is written from a learning objectives point of view, and describes 'how the learners are expected to be changed by the educative process'. It was first developed in 1951 and has had an enormous influence.

The three domains and some of their subsections are described briefly below in a simplified version. Typical verbs used to write objectives are given for each section of the taxonomy.

■ **The cognitive domain (intellectual skills and abilities)**

Knowledge: *to be able to:*
state; recall; list; recognise; select; reproduce; draw...
e.g. to recall Newton's Laws of motion.

Comprehension: *to be able to:*
explain; describe reasons for; identify causes of; illustrate...
e.g. to give reasons for seat belts by referring to Newton's Laws of Motion.

Application: *to be able to:*
use; apply; construct; solve; select...
e.g. to use Newton's laws of motion to solve simple problems.

Analysis: *to be able to:*
break down; list component parts of; compare and contrast; differentiate between...

Synthesis (this involves choosing and using and putting together diverse skills, abilities and knowledge to accomplish a particular new task): *to be able to:*
summarise; generalise; argue; organise; design; explain the reason for...

Evaluation: *to be able to:*
judge ; evaluate; give arguments for and against; criticise...

■ **The affective domain**

This domain concerns itself with attention, interest, awareness, aesthetic appreciation, moral aesthetic and other attitudes, opinions, feelings or values.

E.g.   *to listen to ...   to appreciate the importance of...*

to have an awareness of...   to respond with personal feelings...

to have an aesthetic appreciation of ...   to have a commitment towards...

to recognise the moral dilemmas involved in...

■ The psychomotor domain

This includes motor skills or physical skills including sense perception, hand and eye coordination, etc.

E.g.   *to plane; to draw; to throw; to weld; ...*

Note that 'to know...' or 'to understand...' are not acceptable beginnings for specific objectives, which should describe abilities that are directly observable and testable. What does it mean to say that a student 'knows', say, the story of Lazarus? Does it mean that the student is able to recognise the story and name it? Or recall it in outline? Or recall it in detail? Or describe its significance? The objective needs to state *what the student should be able to do* in an easily testable form; it could become, for example:

'To recount in outline the story of Lazarus.'

Unlike 'To know the story of Lazarus.' this is clear, it is testable, and it suggests what the student needs to practise.

Similarly, what does it mean to 'understand' osmosis? Does it mean to be able to describe its significance? To explain how and why it takes place? To be able to use the idea to explain novel occurrences of the phenomenon? Or some combination of these abilities? Often what is required is for the student to be able to answer exam-style questions on the topic; if so, what abilities do such questions demand?

Why do we value knowledge? Suppose I gave you a copy of the *Encyclopaedia Britannica* with no index and all the entries in random order; would you be pleased? Whether in your head or in a book, knowledge is useful only if it can be *recalled*, *used* in making decisions, *reclassified*, *searched* for facts relevant to a specific situation, and so on. The words in italics are abilities which can be expressed in specific objective form, practised, checked and corrected etc. The words 'know' and 'knowledge' are too vague for teachers.

General objectives

Many teachers describe their intentions partly in a form which is somewhere between an aim and a specific learning outcome. Such intentions are variously described as short-term aims, general instructional objectives, or non-behaviourist objectives. Examples might be:

'To introduce students to some aspects of modern telecommunications.'
'To outline modern stock control methods.'

If you choose to describe your intentions in such a way, make sure that you include in each statement both the content itself, and what will be done with such content. Make your statements clear and simple. For example:

'To develop an appreciation of Handel's *Messiah.*'
'To recognise the importance of safety checks on building sites.'

These general objectives are then used to generate specific learning outcomes. For example, the safety objective above could be broken down as follows:

'General objective:
To recognise the importance of frequent safety inspections.

Specific learning outcomes:
To list the main checks made during a safety inspection.
To state the main dangers to health and safety on a building site.
To recognise and correct the improper use of a ladder.
[etc.]'

An aim may encompass many general objectives, and in turn each general objective will generate a number of specific learning outcomes.

Developmental and mastery objectives

General objectives are of two broad types: mastery and developmental. **Mastery objectives** are relatively 'easy'. When in the cognitive domain, they typically involve only knowledge and comprehension. They are designed to be mastered by all students, and form the minimum requirement for passing the course. As a result, their achievement depends more on time spent trying to master them than on innate ability, flair or aptitude – *every* student can master them if he or she tries hard enough for long enough. The specific learning outcomes developed from them usually describe skills or abilities which can be attained in a short time-scale, perhaps a matter of minutes. They can then be assessed easily with a simple test.

E.g. 'Recognise and name the main constituents of a simple cell.'

Far from being trivial, targets such as these which are attainable by all the students in a group have inestimable value. Mastery objectives give rise to straightforward learning tasks which are time- rather than ability-dependent. They offer the teacher an opportunity to give weaker students the success, reinforcement and motivation which is a precondition for their present and future learning (see Chapter 5).

By contrast some general objectives, called **developmental objectives,** may never be fully achieved.

E.g. 'Write a clear, scientifically argued laboratory report...'
'Evaluate the importance of full to high employment in western societies.'

Such objectives are highly dependent on previous learning; require high-order thinking skills; cannot be easily and objectively assessed; and take considerable time and effort on the part of the learner before any noticeable improvement in their execution is shown. Their importance lies in their ability to maximise individual development, and to stretch the more able. Continuous development rather than complete mastery is expected.

No finite list of specific learning outcomes will entirely describe a developmental objective; it is greater than the sum of its parts. However, a representative sample of specific learning outcomes can usually be written, describing *typical* abilities that a learner will have once the developmental objective has been achieved. E.g.

'General objective:
Write a clear, scientifically argued laboratory report...

Specific learning outcomes:
The student should be able to:
- break the report into the usual categories of apparatus, method etc.
- refer directly to the results when writing the conclusions.
[etc.]'

These specific learning outcomes or objectives are not usually taught and tested one by one, as can be the case for mastery objectives. Can all general objectives be broken down? For example, can the objective 'To gain an appreciation of the War Poets' be expressed in specific objective form? Some teachers think not. But what does 'appreciation' mean? If you consider that appreciation involves, at least in part, the learner coming to a personal opinion about the meaning and importance of the poems under study, then it *is* possible. Personal opinion-forming is a high-order skill in the cognitive domain, which is learned by corrected practice (see Chapter 34, where teaching methods are suggested).

'General objective:
To gain an appreciation of Wilfred Owen's poem *Insensibility*.

Specific learning outcomes:
The student should be able to:
- express a personal opinion of the meaning of the poem.
- write a personal evaluation of the poem.
- critically appraise an appreciation of the poem written by another.
[etc.]'

Mixing developmental and mastery objectives

Most teaching should involve a mixture of developmental and mastery objectives; in 'mixed ability' teaching this is vital. If a teacher habitually assesses his or her students by their essay or scientific report-writing skills, some students will continue to score badly even when they try hard. Both mastery and developmental objectives must of course be recognised, reinforced and assessed, or the mix will be in vain. It helps, however, to concentrate reinforcement on the mastery objectives when motivation becomes a problem.

Sources for objectives

For most courses, objectives may be drawn up by reference to one or more of the following: the course aims, the syllabus, the programme of study, attainment targets, or statements of competence. If you are devising your own course from scratch, deciding on aims and objectives is a crucial part of the process; this is dealt with in Chapter 37, on course design.

If you are teaching to the National Curriculum, you may be following a programme of study which describes topics to cover, and attempting to achieve attainment targets such as:

> 'Pupils should investigate variation between individuals in a range of living things. They should have opportunities to measure the differences between individuals.'

Topics described in syllabuses, or in programmes of study, or indeed in attainment targets, are all rather like general objectives. They need to be read very carefully, and then expressed in terms of specific learning outcomes.

The content of National Vocational Qualifications (NVQs) is described in terms of 'competences'– e.g.

> 'Fit a four way junction box.' *(in an electrician's qualification)*
> 'Make recommendations for expenditure.' *(in a manager's qualification)*

Learners are expected to gather evidence to show that they have carried out the tasks described in the competences successfully. NVQs are explained in more detail in Chapter 39, on summative assessment.

Competences nearly always involve a good deal of learning, so it is frequently necessary to break them down into specific learning outcomes. Again, read them very carefully first.

If you have difficulty writing objectives, look at assessments for the course. What do examiners or assessors expect learners to be able to do? These skills and abilities must of course be among your objectives. When planning a course, assessment questions are devised from the objectives, *not* the other way round! But for a new teacher working on an existing course, assessment tasks often clarify what students should be able to do, and so help considerably in clarifying lesson objectives.

Devising objectives is no easy matter, but the process of clarification it encourages is crucial to effective teaching.

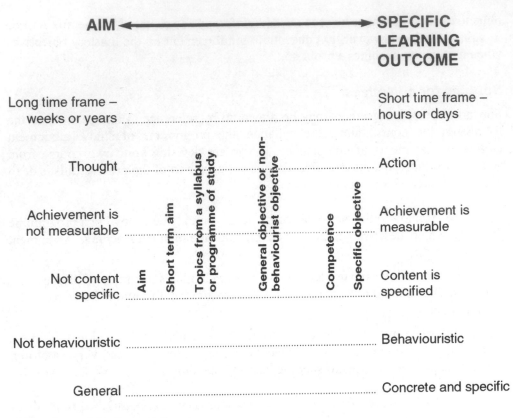

AIM ←——————————————→ SPECIFIC LEARNING OUTCOME

Long time frame – weeks or years	Short time frame – hours or days
Thought	Action
Achievement is not measurable	Achievement is measurable
Not content specific	Content is specified
Not behaviouristic	Behaviouristic
General	Concrete and specific

(intermediate labels, left to right: Aim · Short term aim · Topics from a syllabus or programme of study · General objective or non-behaviourist objective · Competence · Specific objective)

The aim – objective continuum

Embedding aims and objectives

Why do experienced teachers often do without formal lesson plans? As teachers become more experienced, some begin to define objectives less formally but more fully. I no longer formally write objectives for many of my lessons, but I have spent years embodying them in worksheets, assessments and practical activities etc. For example, I do not write down *'Students should be able to use the principle of moments to solve simple problems.'* I find this too vague. Instead, I write question sheets and assessments with examples of such problems, and expect students to achieve a minimum mark on them. The worksheets and assessments, along with other learning activities, are carefully devised to cover what I know from experience students must be able to do. In a sense I have embodied my very detailed objectives in a comprehensive set of learning activities, worksheets and assessments.

I'm not the only one. Many teachers of computing ask their students to work through workbooks specifically designed to teach their students how to use the computer system they are learning. Similarly, engineering teachers design a programme of 'jobs' for their students to make, which introduces them to a carefully considered series of skills and techniques.

If you use a ready-made system like this, don't hand responsibility over to it entirely; to do so is to confuse the learning process with the learning outcome. Completing a learning task, even a student-centred one, does not guarantee learning. Student practice is vital, but it is not the only thing needed, as Chapter 2 made clear.

The limitations of aims and outcomes

What happens if you can't tell in advance what your students will learn? Think, for example, of student nurses writing a journal on their ward experiences, an art class visiting a new exhibition, or a hairdressing student who must provide the styling which her client requests.

At best, only a few objectives can be written in such situations; but if the activity is self-evidently valuable, then write it down as the intention for the lesson. Later we will see how to plan for such sessions; but beware of using such a system exclusively – how will you ensure students do not miss out on vital skills and abilities?

One solution is to define the learning in terms of a series of competences, which you sign off on student record cards as they are mastered. Alternatively students themselves can 'own' and tick off their card; I've seen this work well for courses in adult recreational photography, and for woodwork courses.

Overarching aims

There is a danger in concentrating exclusively on learning outcomes. Important skills relevant to every lesson but not 'on the syllabus' may be ignored – for example, learning how to learn, study or reason; and the development of creative thinking.

And what of developing motivation, appreciation, interest and curiosity? What about ethics, joy, beauty and the human spirit? You may feel you have nothing to offer here, but many people put their teachers amongst those who have been most influential in their human development.

Most learning has as its ultimate aims the satisfaction of material needs: giving students the ability to obtain and keep a job, and the humdrum skills and abilities we all need if we are to cope in our everyday world. But there is more to being human than being fed and watered, and we are in danger of forgetting this if we overindulge in 'short-termism'.

This chapter has included some difficult but influential ideas; I suggest you read it again from time to time during your teaching practice.

Summary

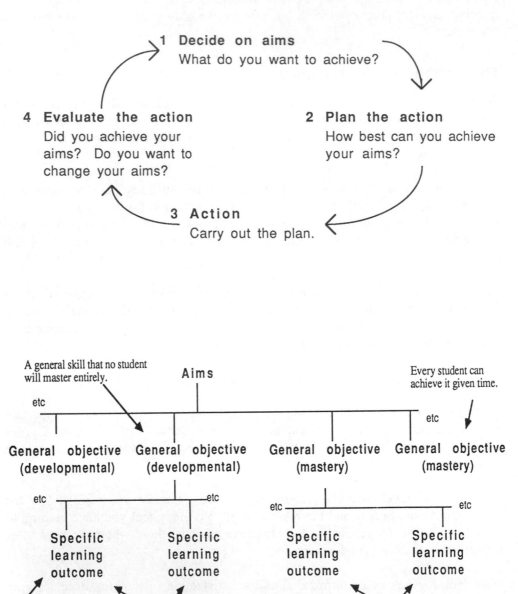

1 **Decide on aims**
What do you want to achieve?

4 **Evaluate the action**
Did you achieve your
aims? Do you want to
change your aims?

2 **Plan the action**
How best can you achieve
your aims?

3 **Action**
Carry out the plan.

A general skill that no student
will master entirely.

Aims

Every student can
achieve it given time.

etc

etc

General objective
(developmental)

General objective
(developmental)

General objective
(mastery)

General objective
(mastery)

etc

etc

etc

etc

Specific
learning
outcome

Specific
learning
outcome

Specific
learning
outcome

Specific
learning
outcome

Example
abilities
only

Usually need to be taught
together, with the general
objective in mind

Can usually be taught and
tested one at a time

☑ **Checklist**

☐ Do you describe your intentions clearly, in the form of aims and of more specific, testable objectives?

☐ Do you have a mix of objectives that **(a)** can be easily mastered, and **(b)** give an opportunity for development?

☐ As well as specific objectives, do you pay attention to overarching aims such as motivation, curiosity, interest, appreciation, reasoning skills, creativity etc.?

34 Choosing activities for the lesson

So, after days of agonising, you have decided on your aims, objectives and specific learning outcomes – the next step is to choose activities to achieve them. This is more of an art than a science, requiring simultaneous consideration of all of the ideas mentioned previously in this book. Remember particularly that learning requires each student to make a personal version of what they are being taught; and that they must improve and expand this incomplete understanding through corrected practice.

Experienced teachers and other educationalists disagree about many things, but there is a rare consensus here: the activities you choose must be related to the objectives you have for the lesson, and they must involve plenty of student activity. The question of which activities best suit which objectives has been considered previously:

Learning physical or intellectual skills: See Chapter 2 on 'Learning practical and intellectual skills'; Chapter 3 on 'The learner's needs'; Chapter 13 on 'The art of showing'; and elsewhere.

Learning facts: See Chapter 21 on 'Learning for remembering'.

Learning concepts: See Chapter 12 on 'The art of explaining'.

Learning to be creative: See Chapter 25 on 'Creativity, design and invention'.

Opinion-forming and **affective learning** are dealt with below and in Chapter 35.

If you find it helpful, you can see all objectives as requiring corrected practice, and therefore requiring the satisfaction of the learner's EDUCARE? needs (Chapter 2). You can use the mnemonic either as a checklist to ensure that learners' needs are met by the activities you have chosen, or as a way of suggesting activities. Try it out for a few lessons, but if you don't find the approach helpful, you are not obliged to use it!

In any case, don't slavishly follow the mnemonic; use your common sense. Sometimes earlier learning will already have satisfied some of these learner's needs. For example, activities designed to achieve one of your objectives may also help to achieve another. But beware of omitting useful activities; most inexperienced teachers overestimate their students. And remember, each learner's need can be satisfied by any number of activities; the mnemonic is *not* a list of teaching methods.

Each learner's needs can be provided in many ways:

Explanation: teacher talk; discovery; questioning; reading; homework; discussion; video; visual aids ...

'Doing-detail' *(being shown or discovering in concrete terms 'what I am expected to do, and how to do it')*: teacher demonstrating the ability; inspecting examples of good work; discussing criteria for success; teacher thinking out loud to demonstrate how to approach a problem; students working out how to do it for themselves; examining a case study; students watching a video of someone doing it ...

Use *(student practice of ability)*: individual work; group work or discussion; practicals; answering questions (written or oral); essays; games ...

Check and correct: teacher marking work; self-check (with or without given criteria); peer-check; questioning; comparing work with an example of good practice; seeing if the device works ...

Aide-mémoire: handouts; personal or teacher's notes; booklets; textbooks; reference books; audio tapes; video; mnemonics ...

Review: questioning; tests; quizes; examinations; practical sessions; homework; games; all the activities mentioned under 'use' ...

Evaluation: examinations, or any other activities where students work alone.

?: teacher and/or peers available and approachable, especially during the 'use' phase.

(Methods such as projects, group work, games and questioning are so adaptable that they can provide any or all the elements for a given objective, if used appropriately.)

Here is a challenge for you. 'Doing-detail' is the most difficult need to identify. See if you can think of at least one 'doing-detail' activity for each of the objectives in the list at the bottom of this page. (Suggested answers are in the box overleaf.)

If the EDUCARE? approach does not suit you, don't lapse into a teacher-centred approach. Take the following very varied list of objectives. Can you see that in each case the student would require corrected practice?

'The student should be able to:

1. Cook an apple tart.
2. Trace faults in a car's ignition system.
3. Calculate the volume of complex regular solids.
4. Lay out a business letter in the accepted modern format.
5. Manage a catering contract for a one-day event.
6. List and evaluate the principal ways in which the coming of the railways affected the lives of people living in Victorian times.
7. Use the French verb *avoir* correctly in simple sentences.
8. Make use of the concept of socialisation to explain everyday observations.'

Answers to the question in the box on the previous page

Here are some possible 'doing-detail' activities for the objectives listed at the bottom of page 305. These are examples only; many other activities would be possible.

1. Watch the teacher make one.

2. Teacher does it, thinking out loud to show the reasoning: 'Well, it can't be the battery, as the headlights are bright. ...'

3. Teacher does one on the board, 'thinking out loud'.

4. Students look at well-laid-out letters, and/or find faults in letters with deliberate mistakes in their layout.

5. Students watch a video which follows a case study of such a catering contract from start to finish. Students draw up criteria for success, or a chronological list of what would need to be done.

6. Students read or discuss, or in some other way discover, what is an adequate 'list' and what it means to 'evaluate' this list – e.g. what evidence is relevant to the evaluation, and what is not. Students criticise inadequate 'lists' and 'evaluations', or examine a model 'list' and 'evaluation'.

7. Students hear and read the verb being used correctly in a variety of ways.

8. Students hear the teacher use the concept of 'socialisation' to explain a varied set of 'everyday observations'.

The rest of this chapter will show you how to choose activities in order to teach objectives involving opinion-forming.

Choosing activities for divergent opinion-forming

Teachers of English literature, history of art, music, social and the other human sciences, philosophy and many other subjects are amongst those who often aim to encourage their students to develop their own informed opinions – e.g.

'Students should be able to:
- give a critical appreciation of Shakespeare's imagery in *Romeo and Juliet*.
- consider the role of the United Nations in peacekeeping since the Gulf War.'

Students are not all expected to develop the *same* opinion, so this is divergent learning. Like all learning, it can be seen as a process of corrected practice, and the usual learner's needs apply. As always, these needs suggest learning activities.

Let's look at some of the EDUCARE? elements:

Explanation: The learner needs the background factual information relevant to the opinion being formed.

'Doing-detail': The student benefits from being shown example opinions on the subject matter – e.g. the opinions of experts, interested parties, peers, former students, yourself as teacher (you can put forward a variety of points of view for discussion), etc. The more varied the opinions, the better.

Use: Students put forward their own opinions, in a form that is at first tentative and exploratory, but becoming progressively more committed and complete.

Check and correct: Students' opinions are criticised by themselves, peers, the tutor etc. As a result of this criticism, the students should modify their opinions towards a progressively more informed, better argued and more defensible position. Corrective feedback should not be overcritical, otherwise the student will develop defensive or withdrawal postures which will prevent constructive modification of their opinion – i.e. prevent learning. The tutor should limit criticism to matters of fact and consistency, and should be tolerant of opinion different from their own.

The other learner's needs – i.e. aide-mémoire, review, evaluation, and query-answering – are self-explanatory. Opinion-forming requires high-order reasoning skills, and attendant issues such as bias etc. should be addressed directly.

The teaching methods suggested by the above needs include reading, question and answer, small-group and larger-group discussions, debate, essay writing, etc. Many activities mentioned in the chapters on groups and games would also be relevant.

Suppose, for example that a social studies teacher has the following objective: *Students should be able to express an informed opinion on the causes of high urban crime rates.*

This objective could be achieved by:

Explanation: Giving the students a lecture on relevant statistics and other relevant background facts.

'Doing-detail': Asking students to read the opinions of police commissioners, politicians, community workers, criminologists, journalists etc.

Use and **Check and correct:** Asking groups to prioritise thirty alleged causes of urban crime, each being printed on its own card (with some fallacious 'causes' included). Groups could play the role of political advisers to the Prime Minister, and make presentations to the class. There could be class discussions, debates, buzz group discussions etc.

Evaluation: These activities could be concluded by students writing an essay.

The skill of opinion-forming

What follows is an attempt to outline how opinions should be formed on difficult or controversial issues; this is itself a controversial issue, and what I am offering is a personal view, intended to help you clarify your own ideas.

Opinions should be developed on the basis of accurate facts, but they arise also from those fundamental values and beliefs which we consider self-evident or uniquely authoritative. These fundamentals fall into the following overlapping categories.

Ethical beliefs

These are our beliefs about the main purposes of life – for example, to bring about the general good by increasing the sum of human happiness and fulfilment, and decreasing suffering. Included, of course, are the beliefs that one should keep promises, should tell the truth, should respect the law, should not steal, and so on. Perhaps the most general ethical belief is 'Do unto others as you would have them do unto you.', as practically all other genuinely ethical beliefs can be derived from this. This 'do as you would be done by' principle is accepted by practically all religious and secular groups, and consequently can be seen as a moral absolute and used to help clarify ethical controversies.

More specific ethical rules are not so absolute, and may indeed conflict: for example, you might break an appointment (a promise) in order to give first aid to a road accident victim. Particular ethical situations, then, can lack clarity; how you decide in such cases will depend partly on matters of fact, such as what you believe will be the consequences of your actions, but may also depend on your value system. It is important to distinguish between relevant matters of fact, and matters of value, when deciding ethical controversies.

Matters of fact can often be impartially decided, perhaps by appealing to expert opinion: for example, 'Does beating up a bully make him more or less likely to bully in the future?' This is a matter for psychology, not personal bias. By contrast, there is no universal court of appeal for matters of value: either classical music has value for you or it does not. The difference between matters of fact and value is all too rarely appreciated.

Persuasion in matters of value is difficult, but not impossible – though there will never be general agreement. However, it can be argued from 'do as you would be done by' that one should always give *some* value to that which others value.

There is little doubt that while ethical reasoning is learned by corrected practice, it is also learned by example, and the teacher has a huge responsibility in this respect.

Some questions on ethical beliefs

What is the constituency included in 'Do as you would be done by.'? Does it include other races, other nationalities (the Third World, for example), animals, foetuses, those not yet born, those who have behaved unethically themselves, etc.? Many ethical controversies are due to disagreement on these matters.

Normative beliefs

These can vary considerably from culture to culture, and from decade to decade. Examples might be attitudes to the role of women, dress, sex, who should have the vote, etiquette, and so on. Normative values and beliefs are very important, because they create social cohesion and stability – though they can also cause dissent, especially if they are not seen for what they are. They are not absolute; for example, there was outrage in the 1960s when a 'mixed race' couple was shown kissing on TV, but this would now be considered unremarkable by most people.

Normative beliefs can be unethical – for example, most of us today would say that the eighteenth century's normative beliefs about slavery were unethical. However, by definition only a minority of people see the immorality of a normative view in their own time. Normative opinions vary from subculture to subculture. They are often regarded as ethical opinions by their defenders.

Some questions on normative beliefs

Should teachers promulgate dominant normative beliefs, loyally to maintain the established traditions which underpin our society?

Or should teachers encourage critical appraisal of normative opinions in the light of ethics, in order to encourage the moral development of individuals and society as a whole?

(Most teachers steer a course somewhere between these two approaches.)

Religious and spiritual beliefs

These of course vary from religion to religion, though there are marked similarities.

It is worth mentioning here that science, once thought to have perfect knowledge, is now considered by all philosophers and historians of science to have only 'today's best guess'. The most cherished scientific beliefs have been usurped.

Hence, even if science had shown belief in God to be false (which it has not) this might be shown later to be an error. The pure scientific view, if it is relevant, is to be agnostic rather than atheist.

Some questions on religious and spiritual beliefs

Should teachers value different religious beliefs equally; or should they give precedence to Christianity, to their own religious/non-religious opinion, or to the majority religious opinion in the school or college?

Should teachers critically question religious belief, or lack of belief?

Psychological and philosophical beliefs

These include such opinions as: 'People are born evil and are civilised by society.', or 'People are born good and corrupted by society.'; 'Society's needs are best served by cooperation.' (or 'by competition.')

Some questions on psychological and philosophical beliefs

Are such beliefs undecided, or even undecidable, matters of fact?

Are they oversimplifications of complex issues best left to behavioural sciences such as sociology, economics, psychology etc.?

Aesthetic beliefs and values

These include taste in art, architecture, music etc. They are partly normative, in that they vary with culture and time; but many argue that they also include an absolute element, because research shows there is more agreement than most suppose, amongst expert opinion from diverse cultures, on the merits of exceptional work.

Helping students with opinion-forming

Our opinions, then, are based on the fundamental values and beliefs outlined above, and on matters of fact. There should be an attempt to discover the *root* cause of any disagreement over controversial issues. Is it due to differences on matters of fact, or value, or belief? Is it due to a disagreement over means and ends, over the likely consequences of certain actions, and so on? Such discussion is best carried out without recrimination; if so, it is very widely enjoyed. From the learning point of view, the *reason* an opinion is held is as at least as important as the opinion itself.

Students should be encouraged towards awareness that:

- Some of their fundamental beliefs are parochial and changeable, whilst others are at least *comparatively* fixed and universal. They should also learn which are which – and why.

- Disagreement over controversial issues may be due to differences in beliefs and values: e.g. 'Should opera be subsidised?' But they may also be due to differences over matters of fact: e.g. 'Which is the best way to prevent criminals re-offending?'

- There is no short cut to certainty, and history shows that science, authority, and the majority have all been wrong at times.

- Opinions which satisfy a strong emotional need have an immense pull: e.g. 'People such as me need a better deal.' When false, such opinions can lead to rationalisation, bias, prejudice, scapegoat-hunting, injustice, and worse.

- Everyone has a right to their own opinion – but also a duty to respect the opinion of others, and a duty to think their own opinions out fully.

Helping students to form coherent opinions is difficult but not impossible. I must state a personal prejudice at this stage. I believe that the skill of opinion-forming is of incalculable importance. Unwarranted certainty can lead to prejudice, injustice and irresponsibility – even to violence and terrorism. Students will only develop opinion-forming skills by corrected practice, and by example. The teacher must foster a willingness to accept doubt where this is necessary, and a critical open-mindedness. If learners are encouraged to accept certain views with blind loyalty, they have no opportunity to practise their opinion-forming skills, and their mental progress is hampered. They may then come to crave certainty where they cannot find it, which is no service to them or to society, and which can have deeply damaging repercussions.

Earlier I was irreverent enough to suggest that the time allowed to teach a skill is in inverse relation to its importance. Sound opinion-forming is necessary both for a stable society, and to enable individuals to steer their own lives. As a consequence of its overwhelming importance, it is usual for *no* time to be allowed for the overt teaching of this skill! Were you taught it? If not, do you wish you had been?

Further reading

R. Thouless, *Straight and Crooked Thinking*. Pan Books
Edward de Bono, *Teaching Thinking*.
R.W. Jepson, *Clear Thinking*.

35

Choosing activities to achieve affective objectives

Every teacher is involved in achieving affective objectives. Bloom's 'Taxonomy' (see Chapter 33) effectively splits the affective domain into two parts. The first of these involves encouraging students to attend and to show interest in their studies – for example, to develop an interest in scientific experimentation.

Developing in students a positive attitude to study has been a major preoccupation throughout this book; relevant factors such as teacher enthusiasm, motivation, reinforcement, human interest, student relevance, relevance to the real world etc. all play their part, and have been dealt with elsewhere.

The other half of Bloom's affective domain addresses itself to raising awareness in learners, and changing or developing their beliefs, attitudes and feelings. Typical objectives might be:

To *develop* a positive attitude to non-smoking.
To *value* a multicultural society.
To *recognise the value of* fibre in a healthy diet.

In the caring professions the affective domain is very evident, and this objective would be typical:

To *empathise* with newly admitted patients, and recognise the therapeutic *value* of making them feel comfortable in their new surroundings.

Such objectives require more than knowledge of facts: they require value or importance to be given to these facts. It is one thing to learn that fibre is important in diet; it is quite another to begin to eat it!

The learning described by such objectives can be seen as opinion-forming. If the learners develop a sufficiently high opinion of the benefits of dietary fibre, they will change their eating habits accordingly. Values, attitudes and beliefs can all be seen as personal opinions, so affective learning can be seen as a high-order cognitive skill: that of personal opinion-forming.

Have you a feeling of unease about changing attitudes and opinions? I hope so. It raises a fundamental ethical question. What topics has a teacher the right to be persuasive about? Perhaps only issues where informed opinion has arrived at a virtual consensus. Opinions associated with matters such as health (e.g. diet) or safety (e.g. use of a lathe) might well fall into this category; but opinions on many political or moral issues (e.g. full employment, or abortion) would not. It is part of the teacher's professional duty to remain neutral in areas of political, religious, moral and commercial controversy. Persuasion in these areas is a gross violation of professional ethics.

For some topics, then, the teacher will be encouraging learners to adopt a particular accepted opinion (persuasion); and for other topics the learners will be expected to make up their own mind on the matter – this is divergent opinion-forming, and has been considered in the previous chapter.

Persuasion (convergent opinion-forming)

So how are learners to develop or change their values, attitudes, or beliefs? This requires them to adapt or change their opinion – and perhaps, as a result, their preferred behaviour. Once again, the skill of opinion-forming is involved.

Research by Reardon (and others) suggests that messages likely to be persuasive may be founded on three factors: Appropriateness, Consistency and Effectiveness (you may not be surprised to hear that she calls this the 'ACE' model!) Imagine, for example, that you are attempting to develop a positive attitude to non-smoking in your students. The students will consider:

Appropriateness: *Is the belief or behaviour appropriate for me in my circumstances? In particular, what will be the opinion of people who are important to me, e.g. family friends and peers, if I adopt this behaviour or belief?* In the case of smoking, questions which students need to address would be:
'Will I lose or gain credibility with friends, acquaintances and family if I do/don't smoke? Do I value the image of being a smoker?'

Consistency: *Is the belief or behaviour consistent with my self-concept, and my other beliefs and behaviours?* Smoking-related questions might be:
'How can I smoke if I believe in keeping fit? Am I happy to think of myself as a nicotine addict?'

Effectiveness: *How does the belief or behaviour affect any of my long- or short-term goals – e.g. does it bring about any desired ends?* Possible questions here:
'If I don't smoke, how much money will I save? Will I find it harder or easier to get a girl/boyfriend? Will I be better at football? Will I get cancer later in life?'

Which of the ACE categories is most influential will depend on the individual and the issue, so teachers should address all three in most cases. It is common but fatal for teachers to ignore 'appropriateness' and 'effectiveness' when dealing for example with social issues such as sexism, racism etc. Thinking in terms of the

ACE model helps to generate questions for group or class discussion. Suppose, for example, you intended to develop a positive attitude towards safety at work on the building site. What questions would the ACE model throw up? Think this through for yourself. (Some suggestions appear in the box at the top of page 318.)

Coping strategies

Some researchers believe that learners need to rehearse mental and verbal responses if they are to feel comfortable with a new opinion or attitude. They need to develop coping strategies to deal with a new belief:

'What would I do if I heard a friend make a racist remark?'
'How could I refuse a cigarette offered by a friend?'

Role-play is often used to good effect here, though it is worth remembering too that devising coping strategies in small-group discussions is an excellent group activity. It is almost always best for the students themselves to be involved as much as possible in the development of these coping strategies. They know best what would be likely to work. It might be useful to add S for Strategies to Reardon's ACE mnemonic, to make 'ACES'.

Activities to develop affective objectives

The activities and teaching methods used to explore values, attitudes and behaviour must involve the emotions as well as reason, and must offer an opportunity for corrected practice in opinion-forming. Commonly-used methods are shown in the following box:

Teaching methods commonly used to achieve affective objectives

Class discussion; small-group discussion; attitude questionnaires (such as that in Chapter 10 of this book); group work; games, simulations and role-play; debates; and surveys of students and others. Active experiential methods are particularly powerful – though sometimes difficult to arrange.

Activities involving learner experiences, human interest stories (be they in video or in written form), and activities which involve empathy and identification with particular characters are also powerful. For example, you could read out a short story in which a schoolgirl, Julie, refuses a cigarette but eventually accepts it when it is offered repeatedly. Then you could ask the students: 'Has something like this ever happened to you?' 'What do you think Julie was thinking?' 'What would **you** have done?'...

All the teaching methods mentioned above were considered in detail in Part 2 of this book.

Changing attitudes takes time and patience, especially when changing ingrained, long-held views. Do not expect overnight success; opinions change a little at a time, usually when the persuader is not present. A dietitian persuading a pensioner to change from white to wholemeal bread, or a social studies teacher confronting a pupil with racist views, cannot expect instant results. During discussions, *listen* rather than talk; watch out for verbal and non-verbal signals of attitudes and feelings, and follow these feelings up. As ever, try to see things from the learner's point of view. How do they think? Why are these perceptions important to them? Why do they think this way?

Strategies for persuasion

(The examples focus on a health worker teaching elderly people modern dietary advice.)

Legitimate

Appeal to authority: If you quote statistics or research, it is usually better to give detail rather than just the bare findings: 'Doctors and dietitians believe wholemeal bread is best. Research shows that...'

Appeal to majority: 'Most people nowadays realise the value of wholemeal bread.'

Moral appeal: 'You owe it to your partner to feed him/her well.'

Request for moderate change: 'Why not buy a little wholemeal bread as well as your usual white?'

Illegitimate?

Confrontation: 'You're not telling me you eat white bread!'

Ridicule: 'White bread! You'll be telling me you live in a cave next!'

Assuming agreement: 'Of course, you all eat wholemeal bread and this provides some of the necessary fibre.'

There are bound to be counter-arguments against the belief you are advocating, though your students may be afraid of voicing them:

'My Grandad smoked for 80 years and it never did him any harm.'
'Heroin isn't addictive unless you use it five or six times.'

These are often best dealt with directly. It is generally recognised that students need to be 'inoculated' against these counter-arguments, or they may be seduced by them later. This should be done with considerable care, especially with less attentive or intelligent students, or you may give the counter-arguments credibility simply by mentioning them.

As persuader you must provide relevant factual material, but this alone is not enough: you must also affect emotions, to provide the motivation for the learners to change their own thinking. They must be given the opportunity to explore the belief or behaviour under consideration *in terms of their own existing values and beliefs*.

Self-persuasion is the only real persuasion. 'You are wrong and I am right: you must change your thinking and adopt my ideas.' is an approach which leads learners to adopt a defensive, face-saving stance. Rather, the teacher must show that the new belief or behaviour is in line with the learner's existing values and 'self-concept'.

'Sensible people don't want to waste money, destroy their health and put off boy- and girl-friends. You are a sensible person. So you don't want to smoke, do you?' is a persuasive strategy. By contrast, 'I believe smoking is bad for the reasons I have given, so you must not smoke.' is unlikely to win converts.

The difference is subtle but crucial. Changing one's attitude because someone else advocates a different one implies loss of face; changing to a new attitude because this is more in line with the 'real me' does not.

> Jesus Christ was an inspired teacher in the affective domain. He used parables perhaps because they examined issues without accusing the listener of wrong-doing; made their point clearly; and offered human interest.

A case study

> Research quoted in the *TES* of November 22, 1991, showed that 25% of 16- to 18-year-olds were prepared to have unprotected sex with a new partner, and that 82% of young people believed that sex education at school bore little or no relation to issues that they faced.

What activities could be used to help achieve the following objective?

'To raise awareness of, and develop positive attitudes towards, safer sex.'

You have two one-hour sessions, one of which will have 40 minutes taken up with basic factual material concerning safe and unsafe sexual practices, the nature of HIV and AIDS, etc.

The group are 17 to 18 years old; they have elected to come to the lessons.

Use the ACE model, and the idea of 'coping strategies', to choose some activities for the session. Then (and only then!) take a look at the suggestions in the box you will find at the bottom of page 317.

Choosing the best activities

Whether one is teaching facts, intellectual abilities or physical skills, or one is attempting to achieve affective objectives, the choice of activity or teaching method is crucial, and depends of course on the aims and objectives you are trying to achieve. Activities must be chosen because they fit your purpose, not out of habit or through fear of trying something new.

Beware of taking too mechanistic an approach in your choice of activities. Expressing learning outcomes in the form of objectives, and then satisfying the learner's needs for each objective as outlined in the EDUCARE? mnemonic, may be necessary – but it is not sufficient. There is more to education and training than drilling students in knowledge and skills. Considerations such as motivation, interest, enthusiasm, and self-expression, not to mention *fun*, should also inform the choice of activities!

Activities which could be used to help achieve the objective: 'To raise awareness of, and develop positive attitudes towards, safer sex.'
(See page 316)

Video of AIDS victim recounting his/her story. *(Human interest)*

An anonymous questionnaire, with % responses made available for discussion in the following session. Questions such as:

How would you feel if your partner insisted on/refused a condom? *(Appropriateness)*

Is it macho not to use a condom? *(Appropriateness)*

What (if anything) do you believe is worth risking death for? *(Consistency)*

Can you list enjoyable safe sexual practices? *(Effectiveness)*

Do you agree with any of the following: 'Young people hardly ever have AIDS.' 'Only homosexuals and drug addicts have AIDS.', etc. *(Dealing directly with counter-arguments)*

(Many more questions would be worth dealing with.)

Small group work: In groups of same sex, students are asked to devise strategies for dealing with a situation where their sexual partner does not want to use a condom. What would they say or do in this situation? *(Coping strategies)*

There are of course many legitimate methods of dealing with this difficult topic; these are only suggestions.

317

Developing a positive attitude towards safety at work on the building site (see page 314). Questions developed by reference to the ACES model.

Appropriateness: 'What would you think of someone who took a few minutes to tie up a ladder properly?' 'Do you think it is macho to ignore safety rules?' 'What would your work mates think of you if you suggested that they changed to a safer practice?'

Consistency: 'Do you think of yourself as a risk taker?' 'Would you take risks if you were alone?' 'Would you use faulty electrical equipment at home?' 'Who gains if you take risks at work, you or your boss?'

Effectiveness: 'What would happen to your wages if you were injured at work and had to take a week off?' 'If you weren't wearing a hard hat, what would happen to you if a brick fell one storey to land on your head?'

Strategies (for coping): 'What would you say to someone who said you were wasting time by tying a ladder up?'

36 Writing the lesson plan

Now you have some idea about the activities that will achieve your objectives, it is time to plan the lesson on paper. You will find this a very time-consuming activity at first. Most teachers plan lessons for the class; some prepare individualised learning programmes. Let us deal with the class lesson plan first.

Lesson planning is an art, not a science; there is no ideal lesson to achieve any given set of objectives. However, the following points always remain important:

- The lesson should be planned to achieve the objectives.

- The purpose of the lesson should be clear to students.

- Final practice of skills and abilities should be as realistic as possible.

- The lesson should be logically structured.

- There should be a variety of student activities and teaching methods.

- On the whole students should be active, not passive.

- Teacher talk should be illustrated with a visual presentation where possible.

- Motivation (remember 'SPERT': success, purpose, enjoyment, reinforcement, target-setting).

- Interest (human interest, student relevance, challenges, puzzles, games...).

- Most activities will take much longer than you expect.

- Have a stretching activity for students who finish an activity early; alternatively, use open-ended activities which always provide something for everyone to do.

- Always prepare too much; there is nothing worse than running out of material!   (Preparation time is rarely wasted; there is always next lesson.)

- Don't forget that activities can go on in series, or in parallel, in different groups.

To fail to plan is to plan to fail.

Lessons often follow a 'beginning – middle – end' structure:

Beginning: Links are made with earlier work, and students are orientated to the lesson's content. The purpose of the lesson is made clear; some teachers advocate reading the objectives out, but most explain them in a less formal way. Consider the starting activity with particular care: do you need to start with a bang, a quiet settling activity, or an activity which accommodates varied arrival times?

Middle: The student activity is introduced; students obtain any necessary explanation and are made aware of the 'doing-detail'. That is, they discover the *what*, *why* and *how* of what they are expected to be able to do. Students then practice with the aim of developing the abilities outlined in the objectives. It may be possible to check and correct their work in some way as they proceed.

End: What has been learned is made clear, summarised and perhaps noted down. A pointer is given to the next lesson.

Of course you may not be able to complete an objective in one lesson, as this pattern assumes. You can also structure your lesson-plan by stating 'content' and 'method', or 'teacher activity' and 'student activity'.

Lesson plan format

Most teachers use a similar format for all their lesson planning; a blank plan is photocopied and filled in for each new lesson.

The format design depends on your individual needs, but should certainly include:

title of lesson; aims and objectives; reference to the paragraphs of the syllabus being covered; teaching aids required; other resources required; evaluation of how the lesson went.

It may also include:

date, day and time of lesson; room; course title; subject; exam board; validating body; course tutor; etc.

Activities and timings are then added to this blank format for each new lesson, and the lesson plan kept in a folder along with relevant worksheets etc. for possible future use.

The lesson plan on the opposite page is for a lesson on a simple topic. Before reading on, look at the construction carefully. Do the activities follow from the objectives?

320

Lesson plan   P. Wright

Class: Office studies Yr 1   **Room:** G 12   **Date:** Tues 4:9:92

Syllabus content: Filing, paragraphs 8.2; 8.3

Objectives: Students should be able to:
- search for relevant information from an alphabetical listing.
- organise information into alphabetical order.

Time	Method	Content
	Intro	State objectives: Tell them how important it is and that it is not as easy as it sounds. Review last week's lesson quickly.
5	Q&A:	Do any of you use alphabetical order for tapes or records etc? Do we all know our alphabet? (Which comes first game): m or l, t or q etc.
10	Discovery:	How are alphabetical listings organised? Class asked to discover the rules from their activity and the telephone directory. Including numbers, Mc/Mac, Saint, St., and initials.
20	Use:	Students look for the following phone numbers in the telephone directory (as a race): 1st Choice Parcels; BCL Builders; St. Clare T.S.; Saint Claire Salon; AVS Video; MacBride P.M.; McKie. S.L.; 1940's Café; de la Siva P.
30	Discuss:	Class give rules.
35	Note:	Rules summarised on the board and taken down.
40	Demo:	I go over sorting exercise on OHT to show use of rules.
45	Use:	Alphabetical filing exercise (3 card sets): Cards given out to pairs of students, played as a race. Bring to me to check the order.
57	Summary:	Summarise rules; tell them about room change.
(If time)		(Filing Worksheet questions 1 3,4,5, plus past-paper questions)

Resources: Telephone directories; filing game cards; filing worksheets

     E ☑   D ☑   U ☑   C ☑   A ☑   R ☑   E ☑   ? ☑

Evaluation: Went well. Discovery phase took much longer than I expected. Some still confused about Mc and Mac, believe it or not. Did I emphasise this well enough in the summary? Races <u>really</u> got them motivated! Must try this again.

Look at the objectives for the lesson again. The lesson plan fits these well, and the activities are motivating. Active methods have been chosen where possible; for example, the discovery method rather than teacher talk was used to find the rules of alphabetical sorting. Most of the learning elements were necessary – and provided.

A variety of student activity is vital to maintain concentration. The diagram below shows the concentration of a student during a one-hour lesson. Note the complete lapses of concentration occasionally, especially during teacher talk. Note also that changes of activity produce an increase in concentration, and that concentration is maintained for longer when the student is active.

In practice, one may need to stray from the lesson plan. If for example students are having difficulty, you may wish to explain further; or if they are bored with an activity, you may want to shorten it. It is very common to run out of time before all the activities are completed. If the lesson does not go to plan, this is not a failure on your part (as long as you have not been induced to chase after a 'red herring'!); if there were genuine immediate needs, the *failure* would be not to respond to them.

> Military strategists' saying: 'Always have a master plan – and if necessary use it.'

It is not advisable to plan more than one or two lessons in advance, in any detail. Decide on objectives, and choose learning activities, but don't arrange timings for them. Lessons often do not finish where you expect, so detailed subsequent plans would need to be revised. Some teachers like to prepare 'topic plans'; a topic might cover two or three lessons, and can be kept from year to year to help in lesson planning – see page 205 for an example.

Lesson evaluation

Each lesson should be evaluated. Chapter 27, on learning from experience, made it clear that experience is not enough to guarantee learning; there must be reflection on this experience in the light of theory. Only people who reflect on, and learn from, past successes and failures are able to improve.

If you are too self-critical you will lose confidence and fail to experiment; if you are too self-confident you will think improvement unnecessary. Either way, you will fail to learn adequately from experience and will not improve.

> 'Only the mediocre are always at their best.' – *Jean Giraudoux*

Don't be depressed if a lesson doesn't go well; it takes a good teacher to recognise a poor lesson, and we all have occasional disasters. Read back over your evaluations occasionally: can you see any patterns? Do you, for example, often make the same mistake?

Your first few lessons

> 'The human brain starts working the moment you are born and never stops until you stand up to speak in public.' – *Sir George Jessel*

Before teaching practice find out about:

Resources: duplicating; the library; resources for general use such as worksheets etc; what rooms you will teach in; whether they have permanent boards and/or OHPs; how one orders specialist equipment e.g. OHPs; coffee arrangements in the staff room.

The people you will teach: their names and previous attainment, along with any special needs. Sit in on some of their classes if you can. Look at their work with an experienced teacher. Can you make a seating plan in advance?

The courses you will teach on: course content; rules and regimes regarding homework, coursework etc.; work experience and exam dates; internal and external assessment procedures; what they have studied before you start teaching them. Agree in detail what you will teach, and write this down.

The college or school: term dates, name and phone number; names of relevant members of staff and their responsibilities; discipline procedures; the general approach and philosophy; provision for special needs.

An unwritten professional code for teachers is:

- Never be late for a class.
- Never criticise other members of staff in front of students.
- Ring in if you are ill and suggest work for your classes; and if possible say when you might be back.
- Leave the room as you found it, and leave a clean board.
- Dress professionally.
- Be prompt and tidy over administrative duties.
- Respect senior colleagues.

– and do whatever you can to help learning teachers!

Don't read from notes. Put up some major headings on the OHP and use these as reminders; this also serves to direct attention away from you. Some people prefer cue cards.

It may help if you introduce yourself, saying what your qualifications and experience are; try not to mention that it is your first lesson or that you are a learning teacher.

Take in a glass of water if you wish.

Check the room, and all equipment, before the lesson.

Try to see the class in session with another teacher before your class; read their work, and talk to experienced teachers about your lesson plans.

Planning for individualised learning programmes

How can I plan and monitor my lessons if the students are working on different projects, or are at different stages in working through a workbook? There are other learning situations where it is impossible to decide in advance what a student will learn – for example, work experience, or simulated work experience where (say) hairdressing students in a training salon are relying on members of the public to be clients. If individual work is the norm, it is usual to abandon the class lesson plan and keep individual records of each student's progress.

The records should be open, so that the student and teacher can consult them together at each lesson on a one-to-one basis. The records can be kept by the teacher, but there is much to be said for students 'owning' them, even if they are kept in the classroom. Another technique is to ask students to write learning journals or learning diaries; these encourage them to take responsibility for their own learning, and reflect on their learning experiences.

Yet another method is to describe what you want your students to learn in the form of competences: for example, students learning word-processing may be given a list of competences such as:

'Can store and handle a computer disk correctly.'
'Can load word-processing software, type text, and save a file.'
'Can retrieve a file and print it out.'
[etc.]

Each student has a personal record of these competences, and works through them at his or her own pace. The students either tick the competences off informally as they are achieved, or produce evidence to prove to the teacher that they have a particular competence. National Vocational Qualifications make use of competences in a very rigorous way, but they can also be used more informally as in the case above.

Whatever method is adopted, it should allow the teacher to check on individual work rates and to set individual targets. The format depends on the teaching situation and the reluctance/enthusiasm of the learner; but it sometimes helps if the work done by the student since the last one-to-one session can be seen at a glance. Here is an example from a record of a 16-year-old dressmaking student:

Maureen Smith

14.2.92   You have cut out and marked beautifully! Don't forget to clip the seams at the waist before you press. See me about easing at the shoulder before you put the sleeve in.

21.2.92   Sleeves very nicely fitted but seams need pressing – ask Pauline to show you hers. Buttonholes look good so far, but do get some more of the right colour thread, and resew the bottom one before you make the incision!

Such a record reminds students of what they are to do, allows targets and tasks to be set and checked, and is motivating if it expresses expectations and officially recognises progress in a positive way. The record would be greatly improved if it recorded student comments as well as the teacher's. Records also act as a reminder of what has been learned, and reading old records through can be a helpful reflective experience for a student.

Exercise

On the following page you will find an unsatisfactory lesson plan. See if you can see what is wrong with it. (A suggested answer is printed upside down at the bottom of this page.)

Answer: There is no corrected practice for students, whether in deciding when repotting is necessary, in choosing pot size and compost for a given plant, or in the actual repotting process itself. Too 'teacher centred'.

What is wrong with this lesson outline?

<u>Learning outcome</u>: Students should be able to repot a house-plant.

	Introduction, aims of session. Question and answer to review last session.
5 min	Why and when repotting is necessary. Show students a pot-bound plant.
20 min	Materials: types and sizes of plant pot, types of potting compost. OHT plus examples of pots and compost to show them. Importance of choosing the right plant pot and compost.
30 min	Demo: removing pot-bound plant from existing pot. Take care!
35 min	Demo: repotting a large, a medium and a small plant.
55 min	Give out handout and recap.

37 Planning courses

If there is a syllabus, a set of competences, or any other material which defines the content of your course, then you can use this to devise a scheme of work. If not, you must decide the course content yourself, a process which we will leave until a little later in this chapter.

The scheme of work

Course content can be defined in terms of a syllabus of topics, a programme of study, attainment targets, or a list of learning outcomes or competences; but this content is rarely set out in a suitable teaching order.

The scheme of work is a plan which organises course content, breaking it up into teaching weeks or lessons, and putting it into a logical teaching order. Sometimes teaching/learning strategies are suggested. Schemes of work guide lesson planning, telling you 'what comes next' and whether you are on target to finish the course in the time available. Schemes should already have been devised for existing courses, though you may want to change them (if so, make sure this is permissible).

A scheme can take many forms, from non-existence to fat folders where elaborate detailed breakdowns of every lesson are provided, along with all teaching materials. Usually, however, it consists of a brief outline of the course, along with references for finding worksheets, assignments etc.

Schemes may (or may not!) include the following information:

- **General information,** e.g. the course title, awarding body, length of course, duration of sessions, venue, previous experience of students, prerequisites for the course, etc.

- **Aims, general objectives, and learning outcomes or specific objectives,** broken down into a teaching order.

- **Content** of the course, organised in sequence, usually with some indication of the time taken for each section of the course. This should include any review sessions, assessments, trips etc.

- **Teaching/learning methods** – though these may be omitted or scant. Activities and teaching methods may be suggested; and worksheets and assignments may be included, or reference given as to where to find them.

- The **student group** may be described in outline – for example, their age, previous knowledge, experience and attainment, etc.

- **Organisational factors** may be described – for example, course structure and methods, work experience, course team meetings and work-based assignments may all be referred to.

- **Assessment methods** may be outlined, along with tests or exams (or references for them). A timetable of deadlines for the completion of assignments may also be included.

- **Evaluation methods** may be described. (Assessment and evaluation are referred to in later chapters.)

Schemes of work may seem very rigid, but this is not usually their intention. It is expected that you will adapt the scheme to respond to your learners' needs.

Extract from a scheme of work

Week 8: Heat Transport - syllabus paragraphs: 6.2 and 7.3

Students should be able to:

- recognise and distinguish between conduction, convection, and radiation.
- state and explain the mechanisms of heat transfer in these three forms of heat transfer.
- recognise and describe examples of each of these forms of heat transfer.

Demonstrations:
Conduction: in a solid and a liquid.
Convection: in a liquid and in air.
Radiation: (e.g. lighting a match from a radiant heater after reflection from concave mirrors).
Factors affecting radiant heat emission and absorption (limited to the effects of shiny and black surfaces).

Experiments: Students design their own experiment to compare the thermal conductivity of aluminium and brass.
Optional experiment: 'The survival blanket' (See sheet in red filing cabinet.)

Discussion of practical applications including house insulation, thermos flask and convector heater. See video 'Heat on the move' (15 mins) (make your own hot air balloon?)

Worksheet: 'Conduction, convection and radiation' (in red filing cabinet).

✶✶✶✶✶✶

Week 10:Latent Heat and Changes of State - syllabus sec. 8.1
[etc.]

Whilst the scheme of work should tackle topics in a logical order, there is a grave danger in isolating topics and then teaching each in turn. You may find that this results in students forgetting topics 1 and 2 while you teach them topic 3; it may also produce a lack of coherence in students' understanding. Try to make use of earlier learning while developing new learning, as explained in Chapter 21 on learning for remembering. When devising a scheme of work, make sure the teaching order is logical, and that allowance is made for revision, exams, work experience, holidays, etc.

Information used during course design

Some teachers – for example, those in recreational adult education, or teachers and trainers in industry, commerce and the public sector – often need to devise their own courses from scratch, without competences, syllabus, or other external requirements. It is impossible to be prescriptive about this essentially creative process, but the following may help to ensure that the course satisfies the demands of the provider and/or the learner:

- a workplace needs analysis
- a topic analysis
- a task analysis
- a learner's needs analysis

These are dealt with below. If you carry out a workplace needs analysis along with others, then the workplace analysis should come first.

Workplace needs analysis

This is sometimes simply called a 'needs analysis', and aims to discover the training needs of the organisation which is initiating the training. (If your course aims to satisfy the personal needs of the learner only, then move on immediately to the next section, on task analysis.)

Trainers can in principle help to remedy deficiencies in job performance, such as low productivity, high wastage rates, high staff turnover, or poor quality. However, one must of course first discover whether such under-performance is due to inadequate training, or to other factors.

It is fatal for training designers to attempt course design *in vacuo*. They must consult widely – with those doing the job for which the training is being devised, and with their supervisors, unions, quality circles, colleagues, clients and customers.

This consultation process may lead to a working party of interested staff, who then determine a first guess at the training needs by stating goals or aims. For example:

'To improve sales staff familiarity with the new computer system.'

Aims or goals should not contain hidden solutions. For example, the following aim is not legitimate:

'To improve staff familiarity with the new computer system by training all staff with the ATS package.'

All aims should of course be achievable by training, and may be suggested by a brainstorming session. These goals or aims can then be circulated for consultation, so that all those concerned can contribute their views on priorities – and possibly suggest additional goals or aims. Questionnaires like the one below may be useful.

Excerpt from a workplace needs analysis survey

	strongly agree				strongly disagree
12. All sales staff are familiar with the new computer system.	1	2	3	4	5
13. All sales staff should be familiar with the new computer system.	1	2	3	4	5
14. All sales staff are familiar with new product development.	1	2	3	4	5
15. All sales staff should be familiar with new product development.	1	2	3	4	5

Please add below any training needs not mentioned above which you feel should be addressed, or any other comments about staff development.

Once any questionnaires have been answered, priority goals are decided. The views obtained on 'where we are now' (e.g. item 12 in the survey above), are compared with those on 'where we ought to be' (item 13) . A large discrepancy in the numerical scores for the two types of question may well indicate an area where there is a training need.

If a sufficient number of *new* goals is suggested in responses to the survey, it may well be necessary to circulate another workplace needs analysis survey before deciding the priority these new goals should have. This new survey should contain both old and new goals, so that a fair comparison can be made between them.

When the training needs have been established, in the form of goals allotted high priority, 'performance indicators' can be devised for each goal. For example, one performance indicator for the goal 'Sales staff should be familiar with the new computer system.' might be a reduction in the number of erroneous computer sales records which sales staff produce, as detected by the accounts department. Performance indicators show whether goals have been met, and can be used later to check on the effectiveness of the training.

> Even if you decide not to carry out a full-blown needs analysis, complete with questionnaires, make sure you still consult widely in the workplace. You will almost certainly find that the comments you receive are helpful, and that people appreciate being consulted. When making a recommendation for training, try to compare the cost of training with the cost of *not* training.

The needs analysis should produce a list of high-priority training goals in the form of *tasks* (e.g. 'Using the new computer system') or *topics* (e.g. 'New product development'). These topics and tasks can be subjected to further analysis in order to produce objectives for the course, as shown below.

Task analysis

This involves a careful study of a task for which training is being devised, in order to break it down into components. The components can then be sequenced and given priorities, with the aim of developing a logically-ordered series of objectives or learning outcomes. If the course is to be of real practical use rather than an academic exercise, this usually requires careful consultation with those who carry out the task in practice.

Suppose for example that one of the tasks thrown up by the needs analysis is that sales staff should be able to 'use the new computer system'. Task analysis may reveal the following:

Task analysis: Sales staff use of the new computer system:

A task analysis may break down to many levels of analysis. Each component of the analysis can be used to develop at least one objective. For example, the components 'Coding by product type' and 'Entering sales data' may suggest the following objectives, along with some others:

'Staff should be able to:
– state the eight major product types, giving the correct code for each.
– enter and cancel a sales record. ... '

Topic analysis

Topic analysis is very much like task analysis, except that it breaks down a *topic* into its component parts. Again, this analysis can be used as a starting point for developing objectives. Like task analysis, it can be displayed in a 'tree' structure like the one on the previous page, or as an indented list of the kind shown below.

Topic analysis: Motivation *   ** Only a part is shown*

success
    setting the level of work to ensure success
      setting individualised targets
        formal targets
        informal targets
    praise and criticism
      praise
        importance of praise
        how and when to praise
        ensuring praise is not devalued
      criticism
        being constructive
        mixing with praise
purpose
    long term purpose
      careers and employment
      development of transferable skills
    short term purpose
      tests and exams
[etc.]

Learners' needs analysis

Courses are often designed, and even implemented, without any reference to the students who take them. This is almost never satisfactory, especially when teaching adults. The knowledge, abilities, skills, experience, attitudes, and expectations of course participants should bear on any course designed for them. No doctor prescribes without consultation and diagnosis! But how can the course designer develop a profile of the learners? This process is usually carried out very early in the course, or if possible before the course begins.

One way of discovering your learners' needs is to ask them to complete a questionnaire designed to discover the extent of their previous knowledge, experience, attitudes and expectations. You may like to include questions in the following areas (example questions are given for students about to start an improvers' French class, and for those beginning a course on the use of a sales computer system):

> **Knowledge** – e.g.:
>> 'Do you know the French for glass, soup, and lorry?'
>> 'Do you know the company's complaints procedure?'
> **Skills and abilities** – e.g.:
>> 'Could you translate the following letter?'
>> 'Are you able to make use of the computer's back-up procedure?'
> **Experience** – e.g.:
>> 'Have you ever read a French novel?'
>> 'Have you ever used a computer before?'
> **Attitudes and expectations** – e.g.:
>> 'How many hours of set reading are you prepared to do per week?'
>> 'What is your main reason for enrolling on this course?'
> **Preferred learning styles** – e.g.:
>> 'Do you enjoy reading round the class?'
>> 'Would you like informal tests?'

Of course, such questions can be asked informally during discussion or during one to one conversation, but the questionnaire is likely to produce the most honest and representative student profile.

It is important for teachers in adult recreational education to appreciate that motives for attending their courses may be very varied. Students may enrol on a French course to improve their holiday French; because they want to do business with a French company; for social contact; for fun; or to get away from the husband for an evening! Unless you are aware of your learners' needs and expectations, you are most unlikely to satisfy them all.

Once student needs have been discovered, you may find that it is necessary to split the class into groups engaged in different activities, in order to meet their disparate needs. You should also (formally or informally) discover whether you are meeting the needs of each individual student; you could use a questionnaire, but a one-to-one conversation after the first few course meetings might be better: 'Is the course as you expected?' 'Is it too difficult or too easy?' 'Is the set book satisfactory?' 'Are the handouts detailed enough?' ...

Some designers of training courses advocate setting a 'pretest', designed to discover the extent of previous learning. This is administered on the first meeting, and learners are informed that their marks do not count towards their course assessment. (However, such pretests have sometimes been criticised as too daunting a start to a course.) Others advocate a 'can do' questionnaire, where potential learners are asked questions designed to obtain detailed information about their knowledge and skills – e.g.:

Could you solve the following equation? $2x + 4x = 3x - 72$

☐ YES ☐ PROBABLY ☐ NO

Affective considerations

Do you want your course to develop in students an appreciation of some matter or other? Are there any attitudes or opinions you want to foster or to change? These should be added to your topic and/or task analysis, and should find their way into your course objectives. Here are some examples of affective requirements for courses.

On a sign language course:
'Learners should develop an appreciation of a deaf person's everyday difficulties.'

On a woodworking course:
'Course participants should value the employment of safe practices when using woodworking machinery.'

On a sales staff course:
'Staff should appreciate the impact of security lapses on company profit.'

Do not undervalue the affective domain. Knowledge and skills may enable learners to do something – but it is often affect which makes them *want* to do it!

Resources

After your consultations and analyses, you will be almost ready to start devising the scheme of work described at the beginning of this chapter. However, other considerations too may affect course design, and chief amongst these will be resource constraints. What equipment, personnel and money will be available to support the course? It is necessary to discover this before even beginning to design it in detail.

Coda

I know what you're thinking. 'This course planning stuff is all very well, but I haven't the time to go through all that palaver.' But I can hear the chorus of your students, complaining as a result of hasty course design:

'From the moment he opened his mouth I didn't understand a single word. I asked the others at coffee, but they didn't understand either.'

Or perhaps:

'It was all very well, but I wanted to know the practical aspects of the subject, not just the theory.'

Or:

'I left the course after the first session. I've kept a horse for three years, and she was telling me which way up to fasten the saddle!'

Or:

'So I arrived at work after the computer course with my briefcase full of handouts, and then to my horror it dawned on me – she never told us how to switch it on !'

Complaints like those above are common; you may well have made similar ones yourself about courses you have attended. Each complaint is important; some of them suggest that the effectiveness of the course was entirely undermined. Each could have been avoided by an analysis described in this chapter. (Which kind of analysis would have avoided the need for each of the above complaints?)

Don't underestimate the importance of course design.

38 Assessment

Assessment measures the breadth and depth of learning. It has been criticised as being inaccurate and unreliable, and for distorting both teaching and the curriculum: it is also true that assessment results are notoriously poor at predicting future performance. And yet society and teachers are unable to manage without it. In the right hands, assessment can inspire, motivate, and provide the feedback which is essential for targeting prompt corrective help. But it can also lead us to ignore what cannot easily be measured.

Purposes of assessment

Assessment serves many different purposes. It can grade the attainment of learners, help to select candidates for jobs or future courses, contribute to evidence on the effectiveness of courses and teachers, and provide a goal for learners. But this applies mainly to the *final* or *'summative'* assessment of a course, which aims to sum up the learners' achievements.

The main use of assessment for teachers is the ongoing or *'formative'* assessment. This is used throughout the course to form judgments on whether, and to what extent, learning has been successful; and to pinpoint learning difficulties so that remedial action can be taken. As summative and formative assessment have very different aims, they are usually carried out in radically different ways. Before we look at assessment in more detail, the difference between norm-referenced and criterion-referenced assessment must be understood.

Norm-referenced and criterion-referenced assessment

Suppose I gave 300 army recruits a test, choosing the best 30% to be trained as engineers, and the next 30% to be trained as technicians. This is *norm-referenced assessment*; it compares candidates with each other, and rewards the best. The marks show how the candidate does compared with the *norm*, or average, for all the candidates. (For statistical reasons, norm-referenced assessment only works effectively for examinations with at least a few hundred candidates.) The percentage of candidates getting each grade remains unchanged, regardless of their marks, unless a conscious decision is made to change those percentages. This has the advantage that variations in the difficulty of exams from year to year do not affect grades, but

is potentially unfair, as students may be better one year than the next. Norm referencing is used, at least in part, for deciding A-level and GCSE grades. It is appropriate for developmental rather than mastery objectives.

By contrast, *criterion-referenced assessment* measures what the candidate can do, awarding a pass if they can do it, and a fail if they cannot. The driving test is a good example. This method of assessment is only reliable if the criteria are well defined – for example, in a checklist, or a list of competences, or a mark scheme. Otherwise different markers will apply different standards, or the same marker may apply different standards on different days or to different candidates. Criterion referencing is appropriate for mastery objectives.

Formative assessment – using assessment to improve learning

Suppose you routinely devised norm-referenced assessments for the students you teach. The weakest 30% to 40% of your students would fail practically every assessment you set, and might well give up. (Look again at Chapters 5 and 6.) Yet many teachers *do* set what are effectively norm-referenced tests – that is, tests which compare students with each other, and which focus on difficult 'developmental objectives' rather than the more accessible 'mastery objectives'. In so doing they often fail and demotivate weak, but sufficiently capable, students. This might partly explain the poor UK participation rate in further and higher education.

Vocational qualifications of workforce
- With degree or higher diploma.
- With an intermediate vocational qualification.
- With no vocational qualification.

Source: 'Every Child in Britain.' Report of the Channel Four Commission on Education

I would argue that most day-to-day assessment should be criterion-referenced. Talent, excellence and flair do need recognising, but this is easily done in other ways which do not demotivate weaker students. There is no need to see assessments as a competitive selection process. Ideally everyone passes! We are so used to the concept of a 30% to 40% failure rate that we are in danger of being blinded to that alternative view of education which sees it as capable of developing *every* individual. This view is not wishful thinking: take the example of the driving test again. It is not easy to learn to drive; many fail first time, and yet more than 95% of those who attempt it pass eventually.

How is this achieved? Principally by:

- allowing learners as much (individualised) instruction as they feel they need.
- allowing them as much practice as they feel they need.
- defining very precisely the skills the learners need in order to pass, so that practice can be focussed accurately.
- making it clear why a learner has failed, so they can correct any errors or gaps in their learning, or develop those skills that don't meet the required standard.
- allowing any number of retakes.

As the driving test shows, we all need instruction, reinforcement, repeated practice and correction, and we all need *time* to learn – but some of us need more of these than others. A teacher who does not take this into account fails in more ways than one. Formative assessment provides the feedback that enables the teacher to maximise the effectiveness of the learning process for every individual student.

Psychologists have shown that when learning even simple tasks, some people take five or six times longer than others. B.S. Bloom, however, claims that if appropriate instruction is provided, learning takes only up to twice as long for slower learners.

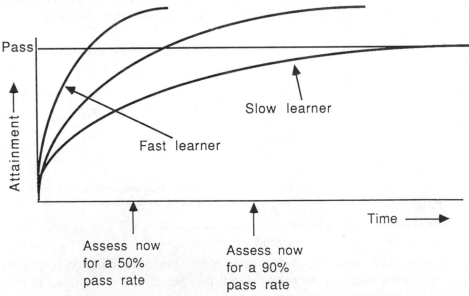

The learning curve

Intelligence, aptitude or ability are measures of how *quickly* students can learn – not, as is often assumed, a measure of *what* they can learn. For mastery objectives at any rate, success requires only that the student tries hard enough for long enough. B.S Bloom suggests that if students are on the right course and the instruction is of reasonable quality, if they are shown the errors and omissions in their

338

learning and given time to put them right, then 90% of the students should pass with a mark of 90%. This is called the '90-90' rule. Incredible? But research bears Bloom out for courses with mastery-style objectives. Let's see how his system called 'mastery learning' worked.

> Recent research compared teaching in the USA with teaching in Japan and elsewhere in Asia. The Asian teachers were much more effective. The researchers concluded that a major reason for this was that the Western teachers emphasised aptitude and ability, while the Asian teachers put emphasis on effort and persistence. Another reason suggested was that Asian teachers were allowed more preparation time out of the classroom. (*Scientific American*, December 1992.)

How is mastery learning organised?

Defining objectives

Mastery objectives should be defined in such a way that they are attainable by all the class after a maximum of a few hours of instruction and corrected practice. Examples might be: 'The student should be able to list the main symptoms of internal bleeding.' or 'The student should be able to solve simple problems using Newton's Laws of Motion.' Developmental objectives such as '... should be able to write a coherently-argued essay.' are inherently longer-term, and would not be appropriate. Mastery learning is hard work for the learner and for the teacher, so limit the technique to essential learning.

Having defined what students are going to master, and having thought carefully about what standard constitutes 'mastery' of each objective, the teacher devises tests to establish whether or not students have attained mastery. *Don't make these tests too hard.* Ideally, summative assessment tests or 'final exams' should also be devised at this stage – though there often isn't time.

Instruction

Instruction for mastery learning is much the same as for conventional teaching. Students are made aware of what they should be able to recall or do, and to what standard, and are given corrected practice, etc. But remember! Whole-class instruction does not allow for individual learning rates. How can teachers accommodate the different times learners take to achieve mastery? This 'differentiation' or 'mixed-ability teaching' involves (among other things) the following points:

- Instruction is individualised, so that students can work at their own pace. This is especially important for the corrected practice phase of learning. Worksheets that take the student through work in a step-by-step manner are very useful, though help must be constantly available. Projects, assignments and open-ended tasks also accommodate self-pacing.

- Mastery only involves competence in the *basic* use of skills or knowledge in a familiar, well-practised context. Students who achieve mastery standards quickly are provided with additional 'stretching' activities which develop them *beyond* the mastery level, or are focussed on developmental objectives.

  Stretching activities should be rewarding. They should not require extra teacher assistance. Again, open-ended tasks are appropriate. These activities need to be devised with care; they should not be mere time-fillers. It is best that students themselves do not see the line between activities designed to achieve basic mastery and those used to stretch. (See pages 49 and 35-38 respectively for the design and sequencing of learning activities.)

- Personalised prescriptions of extra work for students who are experiencing difficulties may help; so will peer-tutoring.

- It is helpful to suggest or have available a range of reading materials at different levels, so that students can choose a text that is suitable for them.

- If necessary, students can be split into groups who learn at similar speeds, or arranged into peer-tutoring pairs.

- Students must be very clear what mastery requires of them. (See Chapter 21, on learning for remembering.)

> 'The essence of mastery-learning strategies is *group instruction* supplemented by frequent *feedback and individualised corrective help* as each student needs it.' – B.S. Bloom, *Evaluation to Improve Learning* (Bloom's italics)

Diagnostic tests

The next stage is that students are given feedback on how their present attainment compares with the course requirements. This is done informally during student practice, but is also achieved by means of 'diagnostic tests'. For younger students, these tests are usually set every eight to ten hours of instruction, and are perhaps 15 minutes long. Older academic students may take 20- to 30-minute tests every four to six weeks.

The tests only require that students demonstrate that they have attained the skills they have been practising. If students have been learning how to do calculations with percentages, then the test will consist of problems almost identical to those on which they have been practising. There is no attempt to set challenging questions to discover flair or ingenuity at this stage. Students sometimes complete a self-marked 'self-test' first, to enable them to discover whether they are ready to take the diagnostic test. It is common for all but a few students to gain a 'mastery mark' of 80%, 85% or even more on their first attempt. The diagnostic test can be marked by the students themselves, though you might like to check the papers.

Diagnostic tests motivate twice: students are motivated to prepare for them; and they are motivated by their success in them. The tests also serve to reduce student (and teacher) anxiety about later summative tests, designed to grade students.

The main purpose and benefit of the tests, however, is that they quickly diagnose errors or omissions in important areas of learning, *so that corrective work can take place to make good these deficiencies*. This prevents 'compound errors' of learning, where one week's poor learning makes next week's learning all the more difficult.

> When learning something useful we rarely get it right first time. Errors and omissions are inevitable. Indeed, they are helpful; learning is a trial and error process, with success achieved by recognising errors and omissions and correcting them to obtain a closer and closer approximation to the goal. Yet many learners are crippled by seeing learning errors as blameworthy. Encourage your students to take responsibility for correction, without blaming themselves for mistakes.

The ideas of mastery learning should of course be explained to the students. They should know the purpose of diagnostic tests; and to keep this purpose clear, test results should never be used for grading or judging, and should be marked on a pass/fail basis only.

Corrective help

You can't fatten pigs by weighing them, so a crucial feature of mastery learning now takes place: students who did not achieve a mastery mark put right their learning errors or omissions, which the test made plain. This makes the mastery learning strategy a self-correcting system.

If the majority of students get a particular question in the diagnostic test wrong (this can be discovered by hand-raising), it is likely that the fault lies in the learning/ materials, in the teacher's instruction, or in the test item. It is up to the teacher to put this right. Then he or she can move class instruction on to the next topic or learning unit.

Students who have not achieved a mastery mark in their diagnostic test are asked to prepare for a similar diagnostic test a few days later (where they are only required to answer questions similar to those they got wrong in the first test).

It will be clear from the first test exactly where corrective help is needed; but there is not usually much time in class to provide this corrective help, if the teacher has moved on to the next topic. For the most part, it is expected that the students will sort out their own difficulties outside class time. However, assistance can be provided by:

- directing the student to appropriate instructional materials.
- 'peer-tutoring' groups (e.g. doing corrections in groups after the test).
- out-of-class meetings of students, or students and teacher, to clear up difficulties.
- encouraging friends, parents and siblings also to help.

> Expect all students to correct their errors in the diagnostic tests, and in their other work. Every student benefits from self-correction.

Corrective learning and retesting continues until the first and subsequent tests, considered together, demonstrate that mastery has been achieved. Students can do their retest in class, while other students continue with individual work – it will only take a few minutes. Mark it straight away with the student present.

Two tests are usually enough. If three or more tests are usually required for some students, then barring any emotional or medical reasons, the instruction or the mastery objective may be inappropriate. Novice teachers usually set mastery objectives which are too demanding.

> 'If a student fails to learn it is the teacher's fault. With appropriate instruction all pupils should get A grades.' – *B.F. Skinner (behaviourist psychologist), 1955*
>
> Discuss!

But will students have the perseverance to continue working until mastery is achieved? For the most part, the time a student is prepared to spend on learning is dependent on evidence of success, and prompt and frequent reinforcement. Because mastery learning sets realistic standards and rewards their achievement, students are highly motivated.

> Mrs Miriam Hargrave (b. 1908) holds the record for achieving success in the face of persistent failure. She failed her thirty-ninth driving test by 'crashing' a set of red traffic lights. But in 1970 she passed at her fortieth attempt.

Research in mastery learning has been done in many countries, and at all levels of education from primary through secondary to schools of medicine, nursing and engineering. At each level, mastery methods have yielded excellent results.

Bloom (1981) found that 'a large proportion of slower learners can learn to the same achievement level as the faster learners. When the slower learners do succeed in attaining the same criterion of achievement as the faster learners, they appear to be able to learn equally complex and abstract ideas, they can apply these ideas to new problems, and they can retain the ideas equally well, in spite of the fact that they learned with more time and help than was given to others.'

> What do the following two people have in common?
>
> Ruth Lawrence of Huddersfield (b. 1971) went to Oxford University aged 12 to study mathematics, and gained the best first class degree of all entrants in 1985, aged 14.
>
> Mrs Fannie Turner (b. 1903) of Arkansas passed her written test for drivers on her 104th attempt in 1978.
>
> *Answer:* they both took the time they needed, and they both passed.

Take Time if you need it

Mastery increases self-image, motivation, attention and perseverance – making future success more likely. Also, students learn how to learn: in particular, they learn to look out for, and put right, errors and gaps in their learning.

> 'When a student does not learn the teacher fails the course.' – *B.R.Bugelski*

Mastery learning has been criticised because it can lead to 'teaching to the test'. But if the mastery objectives are well chosen, 'teaching to the test' means teaching to essential objectives, which after all cannot be bad! Of course, it is true that though such teaching is necessary, it is not sufficient. There *is* a danger of over-reliance on mastery methods; they cannot be used for developmental objectives, and can lead to the neglect of important objectives *not* chosen for mastery.

Also, much of importance cannot be measured by tests at all: self-image, motivation, curiosity, interest, creativity and so on. In education as elsewhere, what is least easily measured is often what is most important. So there is more to learning than mastering key objectives – but it still makes sense to use mastery learning where it *is* appropriate.

Mastery learning seems to promise the moon, but there is a catch. It requires a great deal of preparation: typically eight tests (each with a retest) need to be devised for each year's work. It may of course be possible to share this work out between teachers, or produce the material over some years. Mastery is only really viable for courses that run year after year without substantial change. We are not all blessed with such circumstances.

Mastery learning is not new: indeed, it could be argued that it is simply a statement of established good practice. However the idea that everyone can learn if they want to – given enough effort, corrected practice, and time – is too often forgotten.

Mastery marking

Many teachers use the mastery philosophy in marking course work. If one of my physics students does not show mastery (a mark of 8 out of 10 or better) on a piece of work on mastery objectives, I ask them to correct and resubmit it until they *do* achieve an 8 out of 10 mark. Students who have gained a mastery mark are asked to correct their errors too, but need not show their corrected work to me. Many students who would be depressed and discouraged by red pen comments such as 'This work is not up to standard – $^4/_{10}$' are content to find 'Please do questions 4 and 5 again for a mastery mark.' Most students welcome the opportunity to put their work right; they do not usually resent the time it takes, and they learn a great deal from the process.

This is hard work for my students – but not as hard for *me* as you might expect! Students soon learn to check their work as they do it, comparing it with their peers and clearing up troubles with me before presenting it. They begin to accept responsibility for their learning. It is not in their interests to have to redo work, so few hand in work that is below the '8 out of 10' standard. I check resubmitted work after lessons with the student present – they only have to redo the questions they did badly, so it doesn't take long. Resubmitted work is usually up to standard.

For GCSE students, I have a worksheet (a set of questions) for each topic, and when students have achieved a mastery mark on a worksheet they tick it off on a personal 'mastery-sheet' that they keep in their folder. They also record their mastery test marks on the same sheet. They enjoy having a record of their success, and they don't like gaps in their record! They work hard to tick off all the topics. (See the top of the next page for an example of the kind of thing I have in mind.) An alternative scheme for recording students' mastery would be a large wall poster in the form of a table for the classroom notice-board, with all the worksheets along the top and students' names down the side.

```
+--------------------------------------------------------------+
|              Part of a student's mastery record              |
| Mastering GCSE physics                                       |
| Name: Sarah Austin                                           |
|                                                              |
| WORKSHEETS:              MASTERY MARK        MASTERY TESTS    |
| Measurement                                                  |
| Forces and elasticity                                        |
| Energy transformations                                       |
| Work, energy and power                                       |
| [etc.]                                                       |
+--------------------------------------------------------------+
```

Self-appraisal

Another method of formative assessment is self-assessment, or self-appraisal. This involves learners reflecting on their strengths and weaknesses, setting targets for themselves and evaluating their attempts to improve. Essentially the learner is using the reflective learning cycle described in Chapter 27.

Self-assessment ensures that learners take responsibility for their learning; it can be encouraged by periodic one-to-one teacher-learner discussions, by target-setting, by profiling, and by the learners being asked to write about their learning and personal development in a journal, diary, or record of achievement.

Self-appraisal is particularly well suited to the education of adults. The teacher discusses with each learner what he or she hopes to achieve, and what difficulties are being experienced. Periodic one-to-one discussions are then used to make sure the learner's needs are being met, and to encourage the learner to set personal targets and monitor his or her own progress. Self-appraisal can be formal, with timetabled meetings and learning journals; or very informal, with periodic teacher-learner chats.

Self-assessment has come to the forefront of educational thinking recently. The idea is simple and not hard to implement, yet it is very effective. But it is very demanding of the teacher's time. Profiles and Records of Achievement can be used as a tool for self-appraisal.

Whether you use mastery learning, self-assessment, profiling, checklists of competences or some other method, make sure you develop a 'little and often' technique for formative assessment that gives you frequent feedback on learning. Coursework marks are not sufficient for formative assessment, as they can disguise a weak student who gets help, or copies. Without reliable feedback, your teaching will never be effective.

39 Summative assessment

Summative, or terminal, assessment takes place at the end of a course or academic year. As mentioned at the beginning of the previous chapter, the aim may be to sum up what the candidate can do (criterion referencing). This might be done with the aid of a checklist of skills or competences, and/or by reports or profiles. Alternatively, the aim may be to grade candidates, or place them in a rank order (norm referencing may be used). This is usually done by means of an examination, designed to differentiate between candidates on the basis of the breadth and depth of their learning.

Summative assessment in school and post-school education is in the middle of a turbulent revolution at present. Practice varies from subject to subject, but it also varies from year to year for any given subject. I will only give a brief outline of the basic methods here. It is vital that you discover the detailed requirements of assessment for the courses on which you teach, and any personal responsibility you may have in this respect. Do this as soon as you know what you are teaching, and ask experienced teachers for advice.

Methods used for summative assessment: a brief outline

Profiles

Everyone is familiar with the school or college report. Profiles and records of achievement extend reporting to include a systematic coverage of the learner's achievements, abilities, skills, experiences and qualities. As mentioned in the section on self-appraisal they can be used formatively, as well as summatively, and are commonly used for both. Like any report or reference they are subjective, but they give information which cannot be measured objectively. They typically report only positively, and are written by the learner, but drafts are agreed by the teacher. They give information on the learner's:

- personal and social development, self-awareness, and social skills.
- attainment progress, and motivation.
- career aspirations.
- interests and hobbies, both in and out of school or college.
- achievement in core skills such as problem-solving, communication, information technology, numeracy, manual dexterity etc.

Ideally the students should be involved in their profiling as much as possible, using the profiles as a basis for self-assessment. The documents are the property of the learners, and can be used, if they wish, when seeking employment or educational progression.

Some profiles are in a grid format, listing core skills and achievement in those skills in terms of hierarchically-ordered descriptors. This may mislead readers of the profile into believing assessment was more objective than it really was, and the format is too restrictive to allow adequate description of more subjective criteria. Ticking a box labelled 'Can present a logical argument' is meaningless unless the context is clear, as everyone can present a logical argument at *some* level.

Other profiles are in an open-response format: effectively they are a series of headings under which the student writes appropriately. Combinations of the grid and open formats are common, and profiling design and practice vary markedly from institution to institution.

Profiles have been criticised by teachers for the work they generate; for lacking validity and being unreliable; and for giving unrealistic impressions, in that they report only positively. Some commentators doubt whether employers read the longer grid-style profiles. However, since the learner's academic achievements often make it very clear what the learner *cannot* do, it seems fair to redress the balance with a profile, especially as the self-appraisal involved is so valuable. If you use profiling, make sure the learners do as much of the work as possible!

Competences

Assessment can also be carried out on the basis of checklists, or a set of competences; this is a widely used method where a criterion-referenced assessment is required. The achievement of these competences can be graded as (say) 'excellent', 'good' or 'satisfactory'. Alternatively, a simple 'can do' approach can be adopted, where assessment is on a 'passed' or 'not passed' basis. In either case, re-attempts are encouraged when a pass is not attained.

Competences are the method used to define the content, and organise the assessment, of National Vocational Qualifications (NVQs). Let's take as an example an NVQ in Horticulture, which addresses the 'key purpose' of 'providing ornamental beds and borders'. The units of competence in this NVQ might be:

Produce plants from seed.

Establish ornamental beds and borders.

Maintain ornamental beds and borders.

[etc.]

Each of these 'units of competence' has a number of 'elements of competence'. For example, the unit 'Maintain ornamental beds and borders' might have the following elements:

- Weed a bed and or a border by hand, with or without the aid of tools.
- Maintain the appearance and health of plants.
- Maintain the soil condition and physical appearance of the bed or border. [etc.]

Each of these competences can be assessed separately, or in any combination, at any convenient time by an accredited assessor. The assessment of each competence is then checked by a 'validator'.

Usually a 'range statement' or 'range indicator' is used to define the scope of a competence. For example, a competence such as 'Assist with planting ornamental plants' might be given the following range: 'Container-grown shrubs, herbaceous plants, bedding plants, and bulbs'.

The learner or 'candidate' submits evidence to an assessor in an attempt to demonstrate the attainment of a particular competence or competences. If the assessor agrees that the competence has been achieved, it is 'signed off' by the assessor; if not, any further work required to demonstrate the competence adequately is usually made clear.

Such competence-based schemes have the advantage that they set realistic work-based standards, agreed by experts in the vocational field (the industry's 'lead bodies'). Hence they have the support of the relevant industry. They are accessible to learners in work, in that they encourage (indeed, may even require) work-based evidence, and do not require the candidate to attend a course. Past evidence of skills can be used to meet competences by a process called 'Accreditation of Prior Learning and Experience' (APL/E) – though this can be a time-consuming and costly process.

Criticisms of NVQs include the suggestion that the lack of grading means both that the able are not stretched, and that potential employers have no means of using NVQs to differentiate between candidates with the same qualification. Some say they lower standards, and put too little emphasis on the candidate's understanding of the skills and techniques assessed.

NVQs are overseen and 'kite-marked' by the National Council for Vocational Qualifications (NCVQ). There are five levels:

Level 5: professional   **Level 2:** roughly GCSE standard
Level 4: for people in a supervisory role   **Level 1:** basic level – introductory
Level 3: roughly A-level standard

General National Vocational Qualifications (GNVQs) are assessed on a similar basis.

Continuous assessment

This is the process by which work done during a course is assessed as part of the learner's summative assessment. For example, many BTEC courses are assessed on a basis of 30% tests/exams and 70% course work.

Like most modern developments in education, this 'internal assessment' will involve you in considerably more work than external assessment, but it does have the advantage of increasing student motivation considerably. In many instances the assessment conditions, and therefore its findings, are much more realistic; who, for example, would want to write a poem or complete an engineering design in one time-constrained sitting?

> Don't assess core or 'common' skills such as 'problem-solving' or 'working with others' without *teaching* these skills!

In order to ensure that internal assessment has been carried out in the prescribed manner – and to the same standard – in different schools and colleges, a moderator will usually view all or part of the marked coursework. Again, procedures vary greatly, and it is imperative quickly to ascertain exactly what is expected of you. For example, when must coursework be submitted to the moderator or validator?

The examination board or validating body will provide written guidance on such matters, but some of this material is famously voluminous and opaque. Seek guidance from an experienced teacher in the first instance.

Examinations

Make sure you are aware of the form of the final examination, and ensure students have had some months of practice in answering papers of the appropriate type. Past papers are available from the appropriate board, and are an excellent homework source. Examiners' reports on past papers are published by some examining boards, and these give valuable information on common mistakes and omissions made by candidates.

If students find past paper questions daunting, it is often because they find the language used to frame the questions difficult. So work through some yourself on the board; then do some as worked examples with the class volunteering the answers; then let them loose on a few questions in pairs. They may take some months to gain confidence. If the first time they see a past paper is in their mock or practice examination, their marks will be a big disappointment.

Graded tests

Graded tests use the mastery learning philosophy for summative assessment. A pioneer in this field has been the Graded Objectives in Modern Languages (GOML) movement, with tests similar in principle to the music examinations of the Associated Board of the Royal School of Music. The GOML tests are criterion-referenced, taken when ready, and can be retaken. They have been popular with students, aiming to provide the frequent positive reinforcement of certificated success through the setting of attainable short-term goals.

Psychometric tests

Psychologists have devised special tests to measure intelligence quotients, verbal reasoning, non-verbal reasoning, manual skills, basic skills in reading and arithmetic, etc. Other tests measure aptitude – for example, the candidate's aptitude for learning how to use a computer, or their mechanical aptitude. Yet more tests claim to measure personality, and to indicate whether a candidate would be suitable for management training. Such tests can be expensive, and most require special training in their use.

It is generally recognised that there is a danger in relying too heavily on the results of such tests since, for example, they do not take motivation into account. Also, the results are not as stable as is sometimes claimed; education can raise IQ scores by as much as 30%.

However, such tests find many uses in schools and colleges. For example, pretests can be given early in a course (or even before it starts) to pick up language, communication or mathematical difficulties, so that remedial action can be arranged where necessary.

Question styles

Here is some advice if you are about to write examination questions. Don't if you can possibly help it! Writing exam questions, especially objective test items (multiple choice questions), is very time-consuming. Why reinvent the wheel? Try to obtain a store of past papers, and also to find internal papers used in your school or college in previous years; rifle textbooks or books of questions. Adapting these saves time.

Be clear on the purpose of your examination. Is it to grade and differentiate, or to diagnose learning problems? Are your questions fit for your purpose? All questions should be clear, concise and unambiguous, and written in everyday language. This is harder than it sounds, and if you adapt or write questions it is worth getting them checked by another teacher.

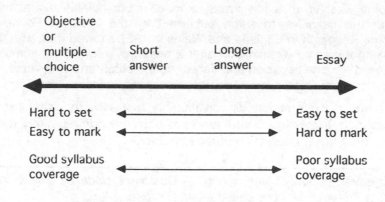

Characteristics of question types

Problems with assessment

Validity

The validity of an assessment depends on whether it actually measures the knowledge or skills it is designed to assess. For example, an objective test cannot measure a candidate's practical skill, or his or her ability to develop a coherent argument. To be valid, an assessment must also sample across a large proportion of the topics on the syllabus, and sample all the appropriate levels in Bloom's taxonomy. The breadth and depth of learning sampled by the assessment must be correctly weighted in the marking.

Validity is also compromised if questions are difficult for the candidates to understand, or are culturally biased. It is common for teachers to confuse learning difficulty with the student's difficulty in understanding the language in which questions are framed.

Reliability

In public examinations different examiners should award the same mark to the same script, and each year's paper should award the same grade to a student of a given standard. Also, the same examiner should give the same mark if they unknowingly mark a script twice on different days. In practice, perfect reliability is impossible to achieve, and in particular essay questions are less reliable than objective test questions.

'During the 1960s schools were regularly putting pupils in for the same subject with different boards and getting totally different results.' - *Peter Newsom in the TES, October 16, 1992*

> The 11-plus was (is, in a few areas) a much more reliable examination than most. Yet the definitive research published by the National Foundation for Educational Research in England and Wales in 1957 showed that, with the same pupils taking the same examination after a period of a few days, something like 10% 'passed' on one occasion and 'failed' on the other, and vice versa.

The reliability of examinations is considerably increased by using carefully designed marking schemes which allot marks on objective criteria, rather than leaving the mark to the general impression of the examiner.

> 'You will never amount to very much.' – *Comment made by a Munich schoolmaster to a ten-year-old pupil called Albert Einstein*

Developing an assessment strategy

Every course needs an assessment strategy. This should be related to the aims and objectives for the course, and should respond to considerations such as:

- What are the purposes of your assessment: to grade, or to diagnose? (You may also assess to motivate, get feedback, acknowledge progress, certificate, select learners, evaluate courses, or some combination of these.)

- What is to be assessed? How is it to be done?

- Who will assess whom, and when? Are marks required for reports or moderators?

- What will happen as a result of the assessment, particularly to those who have done badly or very well?

Once the strategy has been decided, methods appropriate to this strategy and to the aims and objectives of the course need to be devised. For example, a computer training course for adults of varied experience may choose to use a checklist of competences that learners tick off for themselves. A school mathematics teacher may decide on a series of mastery tests, and a grading examination at the end of the year. A course to develop counselling skills may use learning journals, and have periodic one-to-one tutorial sessions where issues in the journal are discussed.

As always in education, the choice is made on the basis of fitness for purpose, and value for effort.

Devise mark schemes along with the tests, and keep them safe for use next year, along with a monitoring copy of the paper on which you can write suggested amendments. This enables you to improve the assessment process, and allows comparison of students from year to year. Saving and amending tests and mark schemes takes organisation, but it saves many precious hours of work.

Mark schemes

- Contrary to fable, it is unusual to give most marks for the more difficult parts of a question or paper, as this strongly biases the test in favour of the most able. It is usual to apportion marks on the basis of the likely time taken by the candidate to complete the answer.

- Candidates should be aware of how marks are allocated.

- Work out solutions to numerical problems in advance, to ensure the questions are possible and valid.

- Mark a very good script first to check the mark scheme!

- If you wish to grade or discriminate, set a large number of moderately difficult questions, rather than a small number of very hard ones.

You will of course need to keep records of your assessments; find out what has been done before. Don't keep more records than you need.

Coda

Because only the measurable can be reliably assessed, much of importance is usually ignored by the assessment process − and therefore, all too often, by the *teaching* process. Both teachers and students tend to the pragmatic view: 'If it's not assessed − ignore it'. And so the assessment tail is rightfully accused of wagging the dog.

At least a third of young people emerge from school branded as failures. The emotional damage inflicted on our children and young people by this process can only be guessed at by people like you and me, who for the most part have succeeded in our learning. Some of these 'failures' go on to reject the norms of the society which has rejected them, and pass into a twilight world of Giros, drugs, petty crime and imprisonment. It is no accident that over 50% of those in prison are functionally illiterate.

Failure also has its economic consequences. Advanced economies like ours cannot compete on the world market with cheap labour, but only with the skills passed on by education and training.

In February 1993 the Audit Commission reported that less than 50% of 17-year-olds were in full-time education. About one third of these either drop out of their courses, or fail them. Most commentators believe too many students are pursuing academic rather than vocational courses.

This social, psychological and economic damage is due in large part to a curriculum which is heavily academic (see pages 97-98); to norm- rather than criterion-referenced assessment, with a consequent bias towards the achievements of the able; and to a tendency not to recognise and reward qualities which are difficult to measure. Try not to mirror these mistakes in your own assessment. However the summative assessment of a course is organised, for *formative* assessment consider using competence-based systems, profiles, graded tests, and other mastery methods. These reward the successes of every learner, and encourage the self-belief on which future learning relies.

☑ Checklist for your assessment system

☐ Is your assessment system related directly to the aims and objectives of the course?

☐ Do you diagnose learning difficulties systematically and frequently?

☐ Are students' efforts to overcome the above difficulties evaluated?

☐ Are students expected to improve and resubmit inadequate work?

☐ Do your methods recognise the efforts to learn which the less able are making?

☐ Do your methods stretch the able, and recognise their achievements?

☐ Do your methods recognise and reward important qualities which are difficult to measure objectively?

☐ If mastery methods are not used in your school or college, is it possible to phase them in over two or three years, and perhaps share the preparation load?

☐ If you use mastery methods, are your tests easy enough?

Exercise

Compile a summary of the advantages, and disadvantages, of the main methods of assessment outlined in this and the previous chapter.

Further reading

Benjamin S.Bloom et al., *Evaluation to Improve Learning*. McGraw-Hill Book Company

Murphy and Torrance, *The Changing Face of Educational Assessment*. Open University Press

40 Evaluating lessons, teachers and courses

Questionnaire

If you have done some teaching already, please answer the following questions; if not, please leave the questionnaire until you have. The purpose of the questionnaire, and how to score it, will be made clear later. Record whether you agree or disagree with the following sentences, by marking each with a tick or a cross.

When I think about my teaching experience: ✓ or ✗

a1. I don't think about past success and failures, I just get on with the job.

a2. I am careful not to jump to conclusions too quickly.

a3. I appreciate being able to talk things over after a lesson.

a4. I teach as well as I can; if students don't learn, it's their fault.

a5. I guard against bias in assessing my effectiveness.

a6. I don't mind admitting failure.

b1. Gut feelings are usually better than resorting to theory.

b2. I like to understand my actions in terms of a general principle.

b3. I enjoy puzzling out why things happened as they did.

b4. On the whole, intuition beats thorough analysis.

b5. I enjoy looking at things from the student's angle.

b6. I find theories about motivation and learning interesting.

c1. On the whole, it is best to find one effective technique and then stick to it.

c2. I like the challenge of trying out new ideas.

c3. I find it difficult to come up with new ideas.

c4. I prefer tried and tested ideas to newfangled ones.

c5. It is best to adopt the accepted way of teaching your subject.

c6. I am grateful for suggestions on new ways of teaching better.

Good teachers are not born, nor are they made by tutors. They make themselves. What's more, anyone can teach well. Research shows that there is no personality type that makes a good teacher. Whether you are a shy introvert or an enthusiastic extrovert you can teach effectively, but only if you know how to learn from your mistakes and your successes.

Practice makes perfect? No. Some teachers have had thirty years of practice and still can't teach. Practice may be necessary, but it is not sufficient. So how exactly should we learn from experience?

In Chapter 27 we saw that the experiential or reflective learning cycle best describes how we learn from experience. This is true whether we are learning how to cook, how to drive, or how to make successful human relationships. *Whether consciously or not*, we will learn how to teach with this same cycle:

1. Concrete experience: This is your experience of teaching. Sadly, it is not possible to learn to teach by lying on a beach in the Bahamas. We need practice. Whatever your problems in learning to teach, lack of practice is unlikely to be one of them.

2. Reflection on experience: Here you evaluate your experience to discover in what areas you were effective, or ineffective.

3. Abstract conceptualisation: Here you ask questions such as 'Why was the last half of that lesson so effective?' or 'Why did I fail to achieve my last objective?' You learn the nature and importance of concepts such as reinforcement, assessment and so on, and find generalised reasons for your successes or failures.

4. Planning active experimentation: Bearing in mind what you have learned from experience, you ask questions such as 'What would I do differently if I taught that lesson again?', 'What shall I do differently next lesson as a result of what I have learned?' and 'What new methods, styles or techniques should I try out in order to improve my teaching?'

Perhaps some people fail to learn how to teach effectively because they are unable or unwilling to cope with the difficult process of learning from experience. For example, if the reflection phase is to be effective the evaluation must be honest and undefensive, however painful it may be. I don't need to remind you of the capacity for self-delusion in others. But what about yourself? The logic of the learning cycle suggests that we should accept knowledge of our weaknesses eagerly and grate-fully, as this will help us to improve. But when we stagger out of our latest Friday afternoon beating in room R101, this is unlikely to be our mind-set. We feel angry and defensive, and anxious to protect our pummelled ego; so we cast around for scapegoats. They are not hard to find. The class, the room, the timetable, the Head of Department, the blackboard... 'And anyway, it wasn't *that* bad, really...'

Only very rarely are learners genuinely to blame for an ineffective lesson, or course of lessons. Learning and teaching strategies should be made to fit the students, not the other way round. After all, tailors don't blame their customers if their suits don't fit. Having said this, there are occasions when a teacher is given an imposs-ible brief. For example, as was mentioned at the end of Chapter 9, the curriculum in schools is in many ways inappropriate for non-academic learners.

> The worst is not, so long as we can say, 'This is the worst.' – *King Lear*

We should not blame our learners for an ineffective lesson, but neither should we blame ourselves. There is nothing wrong with a minor disaster, so long as you can learn from it. Mistakes are not only inevitable, they are a necessary part of your learning process. If you don't have the occasional failure, you are not experiment-ing enough. One must go too far to discover how far one can go.

But if some people fail to face up to their failures, then others do not acknowledge their successes. For them, tiny errors are blown up out of all proportion. If your lessons are evaluated by someone you trust, you will get a more objective view of your teaching skills.

> 'Our business in life is not to succeed, but to continue to fail in good spirits.'
> – *Robert Louis Stevenson*

The reflection phase is difficult to get right. It should be carried out on a no-blame basis, and it should be honest about both successes and failures.

After the reflection phase comes the abstract conceptualisation phase. There are also traps here. Answering questions such as 'Why didn't that activity work?' or

'What went wrong at the end of the lesson?' often requires considerable thought. It is hard sometimes to find the time or the inclination to mull over our lessons, let alone learn something useful from them. The aim here is not just to use experience to find concrete practical advice ('I must change worksheet 2: it is too hard for most of them.'), but to discover *general principles* from our experience ('Worksheet 2 is too hard because it assumes knowledge of algebra which some of them don't have: *I must accommodate the varying prior knowledge of students on my course.*')

Lastly, the active experimentation phase also has its difficulties. Many novice teachers are frightened of experimenting, and stick with a narrow repertoire of tried and tested methods and techniques. They develop strategies for survival, rather than really effective teaching strategies. Don't be afraid to take risks with new ideas, and try them more than once before rejecting them.

Scoring the questionnaire

To learn successfully from experience, your mind-set is crucial. You must be honest in reflection, determined in conceptualisation, and daring in experimentation. This is not easy! The questionnaire at the beginning of this chapter was designed to discover what you will find most difficult about learning how to teach from experience. It is based on the reflective learning cycle.

Score one point for each of the following if you marked it with a **cross**:
a1, a4; b1, b4; c1, c3, c4, c5.

All the others score one point if you marked them with a **tick**.

Work out a separate score out of six for the **a**, **b** and **c** sections of the questionnaire. Section **a** corresponds to the reflection stage, **b** to abstract conceptualisation, and **c** to planning experimentation. The higher your score in each category, the easier you are likely to find that phase of the learning cycle. We all have a weak phase or phases; if you score less than three in any one phase, you may need to work on yourself in this area.

Managing self-evaluation

Self-evaluation is the means by which we manage our learning from experience. We may evaluate a lesson, a course, or a specific aspect of our teaching, such as our ability to use question and answer, or our ability to foster motivation. Evaluation is a continuous cyclic process, though it may be 'summative' – e.g. a summing-up evaluation of a completed course.

In order to evaluate teaching, one must first define what one is striving to achieve. Lesson evaluation should be based on the lesson plan's clearly stated aims and objectives. You may also like to state your personal teaching aims. These are general aims for all your lessons, which should ideally be listed in order of priority, as they can sometimes conflict. Your list might start:

1. To value and reinforce each student's attempts to learn.
2. To cover the objectives for the course.
3. To stimulate an interest in my subject.
4. To recognise the relevance of my subject in the real world.
5. To foster amongst pupils an atmosphere of mutual support while learning.
   [etc.]

Others feel uneasy about having a formal list of such aims, and prefer to leave them unstated.

Evaluation may be done by a checklist, by filling in a proforma, or by writing freely about the lesson. Most teachers use a combination of these methods. Similar methods are usually used when your lesson is evaluated by a tutor, a colleague, or a fellow student. I suggest you design your own self-evaluation form, but leave space for generalised comments; there is a danger of over-categorising.

On the next page, you will find an example of a detailed evaluation proforma which could be photocopied on the back of your lesson plan proforma. The example overleaf has been filled in. (For your own form you might want to adjust the space for some sections, especially if you plan to hand-write the entries – the form overleaf was set out so that, for convenience, it would fit on a single book page.)

Alternative headings for a self-evaluation sheet might include: communication skills; introduction; teaching methods; teaching aids; student involvement; direction and control; timing; strengths and weaknesses; appearance of teacher; voice and mannerisms; teacher confidence; discipline; student interest in content; appropriateness of objectives; appropriateness of methods; worksheets and other resources – and so on.

As you become more experienced, you will find this or similar proformas too detailed for general use, and will usually rely on 'general comments' only. However, you may still want to concentrate on one feature of your teaching – for example, your use of a specific teaching method, or your ability to produce motivation in your students. You could evaluate this feature of your teaching over a period of time, perhaps for only one group of students. This is a great way of problem-solving. The checklists at the end of each chapter in the Teacher's Toolkit section (Part 2 of this book) can be used to provide criteria for evaluating your use of a specific teaching method.

> Murphy's Law ('If anything *can* go wrong, it probably will.') has recently been criticised by engineers as being too optimistic. It is soon to be changed to: 'If anything can go wrong, it already has.'

LESSON EVALUATION

LESSON PLAN: aims and objectives, choice and variety of activities (EDUCARE?, ICDIP, ACES), timing, pace, etc.

Seemed OK. Plenty of student activity – shame it didn't work! Review of last lesson worked well; they really enjoyed answering my questions. Not enough doing-detail, see note later.

ENVIRONMENT: seating, temperature, ventilation, lighting, safety, etc.

OK. Trailed OHP lead under desk – found my red pen in the process!

LEARNING AIDS: choice, design, and use.

Using blackboard and OHP at the same time worked well. Forgot to go to the back to check on clarity of OHT, but pretty sure it was OK.

IMPLEMENTATION OF PLAN: class management, use of teaching methods, start and close of lesson.

Didn't really define the task clearly enough (again). They needed more doing-detail – I should have done one for them on board. They all got off on the wrong track at a blistering pace. Should have checked and corrected early in the lesson, instead sorted out Sam's and Anthony's homework queries. This could have been done later, after lesson if necessary.

COMMUNICATION: language, voice, body language, jargon, feedback, Q&A, explaining skills, summary.

All right; more question and answer would have helped when I was explaining what they were supposed to do - might have picked up on misunderstandings.

TEACHER-STUDENT RELATIONSHIPS: empathy, rapport, discipline, humour, acknowledging student feelings.

All right really - nice bunch. Sometimes hard to settle them when they have the Friday afternoon jitters. Spent some time talking to their regular teacher about this.

MOTIVATION: success, point, enjoyment, reinforcement, target-setting

Good, but must make sure they are mostly successful next lesson.

WERE OBJECTIVES ACHIEVED?: test, homework.

No, but should be next lesson. Must make students do more, me less.

GENERAL COMMENTS:

Try a settling activity to start their next Friday lesson.

Effectiveness of lesson (on a scale of 1-5): 5

Two successful things about the lesson were:

Good rapport is being developed. They worked quite hard eventually.

One suggestion for improvement:

Tell jokes at the end of a lesson, not the beginning.

One teaching principle demonstrated by this lesson was:

Showing is better than telling - exemplars help define doing-detail.

Other methods to facilitate learning from experience include discussion with other teachers (novice or experienced), and a diary or learning journal. A mentor (a critical friend with some experience of teaching, who is prepared to view your lessons and give you advice) is also an enormous help. Your diary or journal may be a public or a private document, where you write your thoughts concerning your teaching and learning; if you wish, you can consciously make use of the reflective learning cycle in your writing.

> Try videoing or taping one of your lessons; or swap lesson observations with a fellow novice teacher. You could also ask your students to fill in an anonymous questionnaire, like that described below under 'Evaluation, monitoring and review of courses'.

Keep your evaluations. They make interesting reading, and you will continue to learn a lot from them for some time. But most important, make sure you *do* learn from them, and change your teaching as a result.

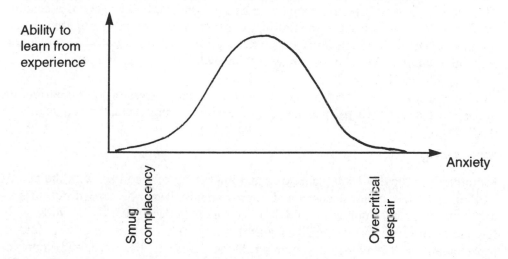

If you find that you have a persistent problem, then ask for advice. There are always experienced teachers ready to help; they know that learning to teach is difficult. Asking for advice is not an admission of failure, but evidence of your desire to succeed. You may find it helpful to observe a lesson where an experienced teacher is dealing with a problem which is the same as, or similar to, the one that troubles you. Lonely anxiety is counterproductive and unnecessary, and experienced advice is priceless and free – seek it out!

The aim of evaluation is to make you into a 'reflective practitioner' – that is, someone who reflects on his or her teaching with the constant aim of improving it. The process is continuous throughout the career of the teacher. I'm still self-critical about my teaching, and still trying out new ideas.

Monitoring, evaluation and review of courses

Like your teaching, the courses you teach should be subjected to self-corrective feedback; it is the only way they will improve. I have seen even well-established, successful courses substantially improved by this process. In post-school education, validating bodies often make monitoring, evaluation and review a requirement for running one of their courses. For most school courses, there is no *requirement* that evaluation takes place – though it may still be taken very seriously.

You should, of course, monitor and evaluate the effectiveness of your contribution to the courses on which you teach, even if the course is not evaluated as a whole.

Monitoring

Monitoring is the day-to-day checking and improving of a course, with the aim of making relatively minor changes and improvements. It can be carried out inform-ally, but in post-school education it is common to have weekly or fortnightly 'course team meetings', attended by all the tutors on the course and a few student representatives. The day-to-day running of the course is discussed, and improve-ments agreed. For example, business at my last meeting included two requests by student representatives: one for more co-ordination of assignments, so that they were more evenly spread over the course; and the other for more copies of a certain course book to be placed in the library. Arrangements were made by tutors for a chemistry assignment to be 'written up' on computer to give the students more IT experience, and there was plenty of routine administrative business.

If the course is run or 'validated' by an external agency such as BTEC, RSA or City and Guilds, the course will also be monitored by an external 'moderator' or 'validator'. The moderator/validator visits the college up to three times a year; he or she is responsible for ensuring that the course meets certain minimum requirements, and that assessment is carried out to the required standard. Advice may also be passed on concerning good practice in other schools and colleges. GCSE and A-level courses may also have moderators, but they are only responsible for validating the marking of coursework, and do not usually visit the school or college.

> Some teachers advocate having an open course diary, or an open suggestion folder for assignments, worksheet activities etc. Students are invited or requested to write comments and suggestions for the improvement of the course or course materials, as the course progresses.

Less formally, knowledge of students' work and learning rate, and of the ideas and irritations of students and tutors, all helps in monitoring a course. Monitoring is a natural improvement process that any professional would undertake without thinking, but the most substantial changes result from an evaluation and review.

Flow diagram to show evaluation and review, and monitoring of courses

Evaluation and review

An evaluation and review is carried out at the end of a course; the aim is to arrive at an informed decision about the course's effectiveness, or some aspect of it, and to use this to make suggestions for improvement. (A short course may be evaluated by asking students to write down one positive aspect of the course, and one way in which they felt it could have been improved.) The following topics are amongst those commonly considered (though clearly *any* aspect of the course may be evaluated).

- Aims and objectives.
- Teaching strategies.
- Assignments, worksheets, textbooks etc.
- Course organisation.

363

- Course documentation (e.g. student coursebook or handbook).
- Assessment.
- Resources.
- Learning outcomes, including a comparison of students' entry qualifications etc. with their subsequent performance on the course, dropout rate etc.

It would take too long to consider all these points in detail in any one year, so an evaluation may briefly overview the entire course, or focus only on its troublesome aspects. A more systematic approach is to draw up a timetable, so that every aspect of the course is evaluated over, say, four years.

Evidence for the evaluation can come from:

- students' performance on assessment tasks and coursework.
- the moderator's report.
- the opinion of teachers, support staff (e.g. technicians) and students on the course – including those who dropped out of the course.
- minutes of course team meetings, and other monitoring information.
- consultation with industry or commerce if it is a vocational course (especially if it involves work experience).
- consultation with those initiating the training, if the course has been commercially commissioned.
- consultation with other members of staff who do not actually teach on the course – for example, the appropriate Head of Department, and possibly also library staff and those responsible for quality control or equal opportunity policy.

Opinions may be collected by discussion, memo, questionnaires, or structured interview.

Questionnaires and structured interviews

A student questionnaire is a popular 'evaluation instrument'. It is usually completed anonymously, and ideally includes students who have left the course, if there are any.

There are three commonly-used methods for collecting the students' responses. A space may be left under the question in which the student is invited to write; alternatively one of the following methods may be adopted – both have the advantage that the responses can be easily quantified:

- The question may invite a yes/no or a tick/cross response, e.g.:
  Did you find the section on computer programming useful? YES/NO

- The student is asked to agree or disagree with a statement on a given scale, e.g.:

	strongly agree				strongly disagree
The computer programming section was useful.	1	2	3	4	5

Often questionnaires mix response styles. The questions asked should, of course, be related to the main aims of your course, so you must devise the questions yourself.

Your questionnaire should aim to discover whether you are meeting the aims and objectives of the course, and any other priorities that you set for it (e.g. cost, enjoyment, student progression). Also, you should try to uncover any problems with the course. Typical topics and questions are shown below.

- **Admission**
  Were you given sufficient guidance in choosing this course? Was it the right course for you? Did the course differ in any way from what you expected?

- **Resources**
  Were the classrooms adequate? Did you have adequate access to library, computers, refectory, lavatories, sports facilities...?

- **Course content**
  Can you give an example of an activity you thought particularly interesting/ useful? Was there enough student activity? Were activities sufficiently varied? Did you enjoy the assignments/practical work? Were they sufficiently work-related? Were you clear what was expected? Was adequate time given? Was adequate work set? Was content sufficiently challenging, or was it too easy or too hard? Were you actively involved in your own learning? Did you enjoy the teaching methods chosen? Would you have preferred others?

- **Learning**
  Questions on the students' feelings about their learning are sometimes useful, e.g.   Do you now feel confident enough to book a hotel room in French?

- **Assessment**
  Was work fairly marked? Do you feel you were kept aware of how you were doing on the course?

- **Course management**
  Did you feel the course was reasonably well organised? Was the course literature adequate? Was the induction useful/satisfactory?

- **General**
  Do you feel the teachers on the course were effective? Have you enjoyed the course? State two things that were particularly good about the course. State two things about the course that could be improved. Please give the course an overall mark out of ten.

It is important to choose your questions to suit the learners – for example, younger learners may need simple direct questions. Mature learners can themselves suggest questions for the questionnaire, and contribute valuable ideas for improvement. Whatever you do, make sure you include the last four 'general' topics from the list on the previous page, and leave some space for unstructured responses (e.g. inviting 'Any general comments?' under each heading in the questionnaire).

An alternative to the questionnaire is the **structured interview**, a one-to-one interview based on prepared questions. This may be a useful method for obtaining the opinion of former students, employers etc. Don't always take the student responses too literally; their opinion needs to be interpreted – but not ignored!

> 'Success is overrated. Everyone craves it despite daily proof that man's real genius lies in quite the opposite direction. Incompetence is what we are good at: it is the quality that marks us off from animals and we should learn to revere it.'
> – *Stephen Pile*, **Heroic Failures**

Action plan

Once the course has been evaluated, suggestions are drawn up for its improvement. This is called the action plan; without it the evaluation would have been a waste of time. Ideally, someone should be made responsible for carrying out or overseeing each improvement, and a deadline should be set for the implementation of the improvement.

Then, in your next evaluation you will find you have a *different* set of problems!

☑ Checklist for evaluating lessons ...

☐ Have you designed a comprehensive lesson evaluation form?

☐ Do you fill in an evaluation for every lesson?

☐ Do you make conscious use of the reflective learning cycle in improving your teaching?

☐ Have you taken concrete steps to improve your effectiveness in whichever phase of the reflective learning cycle you find most difficult?

... and courses

☐ Is there a system in place for evaluating the courses you teach on?

☐ Are you going to evaluate your contribution to the courses you teach on?

41

How to teach and remain sane

Most novice teachers expect teaching to be difficult – and then find it is impossible! It is impossible to give your best to every student all the time; impossible to avoid ever making mistakes; and impossible always to understand why students behave as they do. It is impossible to teach every student everything, and impossible to remain calm, reasonable and professional at all times.

There have been times during the writing of this book when I have found myself feeling guilty. It describes best practice, as a book of this sort should, but it is a counsel of perfection. Don't assume that you will be able to meet its every suggestion at all times. You will be fortunate indeed if you are given the preparation time and the other resources required to do the job as well as you would like.

Try to use your time as efficiently as possible. Save and improve your worksheets, games, and lesson plans from year to year. Organisation saves a great deal of time, but it might take you two or three years to get what you need even roughly sorted out. Can you share some of this work with a colleague? For at least some of your needs, is suitable material already available in the department?

Efficient use of time

The ideal Teacher Organiser is a set of folders which contains:

- a timetable.
- seating plans for all your classes.
- schemes of work.
- a set of topic plans, or an 'idea bank' of teaching strategies for each topic you teach – e.g., games, activities and experiments to try, interesting things to mention, etc.
- lesson plans.
- monitoring copies of worksheets, tests and assignments etc., on which you can write improvements for next year.
- assessment strategies and mark schemes.
- a folder of resources such as notes, handouts and OHTs, etc.
- a year planner with dates for submission of coursework, term dates, dates for reports, and so on.

Your first year of full-time teaching is very likely to be the hardest year's work you ever do. Don't do more than you need in the classroom; remember the students should be doing the work – not you! Teaching is acknowledged to be a very stressful job, so make sure you get plenty of exercise, and don't rely on temporary solutions like smoking or drinking to unwind. Allow yourself time to relax without feeling guilty about it; put tasks into an order of priority; and learn to say 'no' when you know you already have too much on your plate. And don't forget to talk about your problems with others.

All that can be expected of you is that you do your best in the circumstances – especially when you are not responsible for the circumstances!

Index

References in bold define the term concerned.

Laziness, 104, 213 (*see also*
   Motivation)
Learners taking responsibility, 19, 44
Learners' needs, **12, 15-25**
  analysis, 332-4
  cognitive, 13
  emotional, 7
Learning
  activities, 2, 4-5
  cycle, 356-8
  difficulties, 2
  engine, 36, 49
  experiences, 11, 13
  facts, 22
  intellectual skills, 10-14, 23
  journal, 361
  nature of, 27
  outcomes, 293-301
  practical skills, 10-14
  time, 49
  untaught, 8
Lesson evaluation, 355-62
Lesson plan, 319-26
Libraries, 171, 244-245
Lifeskills, 186

M

McGregor, Douglas, 104
Madsen, Becker and Thomas, 81
Maladjustment, 7
Mark schemes, 352-3
Marking, 55, 61, 64, 218-9
Marland, Michael, 53
Maslow's hierarchy of needs, 43-4
Mastery learning, 339-344
Mastery marking, 344
Mastery objectives, 30, 297-303
Memory, 3, 200-7, 266
  long-term, 1-4
  short-term, 1-2, 110
Mentor, 361
'Mind map', 99, 203
'Mind sets', 233

Mirror image, 128
Mixed ability, 30
  teaching, 340
Mnemonic, 12, 204
Modelling, 8, 68, 130, 133
Models, 280
Moderation/validation, 362-3
Monitoring copy, 212, 367
Monitoring courses, 362-3
Motivation, 32-47, 44, 75, 138, 149
  check list, 45
  long term, 33
  short term, 33
  'SPERT', 45-6
Multiculturalism, 66
Mutual respect, 70

N

NVQ, vii, 347-9
Names, 73
National Curriculum, vii, 299
National Vocational Qualifications, vii,
   347-9
Navigation, 10
Needs analysis, 329
Negotiation, 44, 77, 332-4
Noise, 78
Non-sexist writing, 65
Non-verbal communication, 71, 153,
   164
Norm referencing, 336-7, 346, 353-4
Normative beliefs, 309
Notes, 2, 260

O

Objectives, 291-303, 319
Overlay, 275-276
'One-to-one', 21, 138, 156, 324-5 (*see
   also* Talking to students)
Open learning, 21
Open questions, 152-3, 161
Open tasks, 30, 145